DATE DUE

NOV 1 8 2009			
GAYLORD			PRINTED IN U.S.A.

2005

The book represents a major attempt to place music in wider perspectives offered by numerous music-traditions which deal with theoretical frameworks of music. It is music theory, pitched at an ambitious high.

In twenty-seven closely argued essays, the author touches diverse music-centred studies such as religion, philosophy, linguistics, poetics, theatre-arts, folklore, aesthetics, musicology as grammar, history, intercultural inquiries, area-studies, oral traditions, inter-art relationships and Indology.

He insists on keeping performance at the centre of his investigations and hence succeeds in avoiding dangers of dry pedantry—which may excessively depend on the written material and methodologies developing with it.

Further, all essays are permeated with an intense Indianness, intent on voicing the Indian viewpoint. However, the writing steers clear of scholastic chauvinism because of the authors genuine and unwavering regard for the world of fundamental concepts and ideas, whether indigenous or foreign, that have governed Indian musical behaviour. The effort is an invaluable guide to students of Indian music and culture—presented as mutually dependent entities.

Ashok D. Ranade, vocalist (Hindustani) composer, voice-culturist, ethno-musicologist, learnt from Gajananrao Joshi, Pt. Ganu, Pt. Bodas and Prof. Deodher for twenty years. Studied and taught English and Marathi literature. He has written in Marathi, Hindi and English on music, theatre and culture, audio, multimedia albums and numerous well-received television presentations to his credit.

Essays in Indian Ethnomusicology

Essays in
Indian Ethnomusicology

Ashok D. Ranade

Munshiram Manoharlal
Publishers Pvt. Ltd.

ISBN 81-215-0807-X
First published 1998

Typeset, printed and published by
Munshiram Manoharlal Publishers Pvt. Ltd.,
Post Box 5715, 54 Rani Jhansi Road, New Delhi 110 055.

Contents

Preface

I took over as the founder-director of the Music Centre University of Bombay, now Mumbai, in 1969 and soon realized the need to begin a long-term self-learning programme. It required attending to new approaches to music-studies prospering in many other parts of the world. Ethnomusicology, musical acoustics, voice-culture, musical psychology, music-aesthetics, folk-music-researches, investigations into popular music—appealed as new tracks leading to a fuller interpretation of the Indian musical reality—in its unmatched glory and significance. The necessity of getting better acquainted with contributions of various Indian regions also dawned on me.

I began immersing myself in these disciplines and other related branches, holding fast to one principle: to keep the Indian performing tradition at the centre of all scholastic perusals. In view of the inherent performing core of music as a phenomenon, I could hardly have done otherwise.

The twenty-seven essays in this volume are sincere steps towards developing a better grasp of the nature of Indian musico-cultural richness—despite personal limitations of mind, matter and milieu. I hope the aim is well-reflected in the pages to follow.

All the essays have been re-written. A few have been published, in their earlier versions, chiefly in *Sangeet Natak*, the journal of the Sangeet Natak Akademi, New Delhi, and the NCPA Journal, brought out from Bombay till the 1980s. I record with pleasure and gratitude association with these publications and the interest shown by late Dr. B.C. Deva and the late Dr. Kumud Mehta, as also Mr. Abhijit Chatterjee, the present editor of the *Sangeet Natak*. I thank Mrs. Shubhashree Dasgupta for preparing the index.

ASHOK D. RANADE

Bombay
1 May 1998

1

Categories of Music

INTRODUCTION

Music-categories are fundamental classes in which the totality of musical material of any society can be naturally organized. The categorization, because of its naturalness, reflects corresponding genera of kinds of experience received from different musics. Insight into musical categorization makes one cautious in claiming universal validity for musical theories or asserting 'infallibility' of musical judgements. Each category poses a variety of questions and necessitates formulation of conceptual frameworks of disparate philosophical import. All music categories need to be identified and examined if musical reality is to be comprehended in its fullness. Against this background five categories can be identified and discussed. They are: primitive, folk, devotional, art and popular. The pentad does not and need not exist in all societies—at least not concurrently, and certainly not in equal proportions. However, their presence or absence may, in itself, constitute a feature of the cultural profile demanding interpretation. In general, the more the number of music categories in existence, the greater the degree of socio-cultural complexity in society.

What are the criteria used to differentiate the categories?

It is obvious that criteria employed cannot be identical because the terms and inherent, conceptual content of the categories display differing basic orientations. For example, the terms 'primitive' or 'tribal' exhibit an ethnological bias while the term 'folk' owes its origin to folklore, a new discipline traceable to the nineteenth century and its sociological churnings. Two terms, 'art' and 'classical' (used in India, rather incorrectly, as interchangeable) are clear products of philosophizing about a particular kind of value-experience. The much-maligned term 'popular' is linked to cybernetic processes and cumulative operations of mass media. Finally, 'devotional' takes us both to theology and metaphysics. In the present context, our main concern expectably, would be the experiential content of the terms irrespective of their terminological origins etc.

PRIMITIVE OR TRIBAL MUSIC

In perspective-studies of music, the two adjectival terms 'primitive' and 'tribal', are, somewhat regrettably, used as near-synonyms. Even if the terms are taken indicate broadly similar cultural content, the term 'primitive' certainly appears to be more accommodative, both in etymology and usage. Besides, it also carries a more qualitative (albeit a more general) connotation. On the other hand, the term 'tribal' suggests a narrower range as also a more direct linkage with the core-thrusts in anthropology. Primitive, in its root-meaning suggests 'the most ancient phase', while 'tribal' signifies 'that which pertains to a group of clans under a recognized chief and usually claiming a common ancestry'. The Indian equivalents to 'primitive' and 'tribal' are *adivasi, vanya, aranyavasi, girijan* and *adima*. While the first and the last draw attention to the aspect of antiquity, the rest refer to habitat which, obviously, is an anthropological criterion. In contemporary understanding 'primitive' and 'tribal' allude to a type of musical expression related generally and genetically to a particular body or group of people. People described as 'primitive' are, in addition, assumed to be in developmental stages identified as food-gathering, hunting, pastoral and agricultural. However, these and other, non-musical and ethnographically formulated, explanations can hardly answer the question most relevant in the present discussion: What is primitive in music and why? Admittedly, it is difficult to avoid equating primitivity in music with music of those conventionally classified as primitive because most of the data on primitive music has come to us as a result of ethnographic and ethnological investigations, and yet, it is essential to focus on the experiential content of primitivity if we want to fruitfully analyze, understand and evaluate primitive music.

Perhaps it may help to dwell a little more on dictionary sources to develop an awareness of diverse shades of meaning the terms have acquired. Such a scrutiny would reveal chronological, aesthetic and sociological weightages the terms have come to enjoy. It would then be easier to appreciate why the term primitive is preferable to tribal in the present context.

Primitive:
1. (a) not derived, primary; (b) assumed as a basis
2. (a) of or relating to the earliest age or period; (b) closely approximating an early ancestral type; (c) belonging to or characteristic of an early stage of development; (d) relating to, or constituting the assumed parent speech of related languages
3. (a) elemental, natural; (b) relating to or produced by a relatively simple people or culture; (c) naïve; (d) self-taught, untutored

A further set of meanings refers more directly to the qualitative aspect:
1. (a) something primitive; (b) a root-word
2. (a) an artist of an early period of a culture or artistic movement; a later imitator or follower of such an artist; (b) a self-taught artist; an artist whose work is marked by directness and naïvete; (c) a work of art produced by a primitive artist
3. (a) a member of a primitive people; (b) an unsophisticated person[1]

It is symptomatic that the same source does not dwell much on explaining the word tribal. It merely notes 'of, relating to, or characteristic of a tribe'.

On this background it seems safe to conclude that the term 'primitive' enjoys a wider cultural connotation while the term 'tribal' has been employed chiefly to denote members of certain cultural strata defined in specific ethnographic contexts. Semantic fields created by the terms indicate that, at one point of time, it would not have been acceptable to say 'tribal art', nor would it have been tautologous to use the term 'primitive tribe'. During its semantic development the word 'tribe' appears to suggest a context and project a content with minimum cultural overtones. This has also happened in India. In addition, the term 'tribe' has acquired a specific Indian connotation. It is therefore not surprising that Nadeem Hasnain refers to a more than dozen definitions of the word tribe but ends by listing four major characteristics (noted by D.N. Majumdar) as more relevant to Indian conditions.[2]

The main features of Indian tribes, according to Majumdar could be summarized as below:
1. In India a tribe is a territorial group.
2. All members of an Indian tribe are not linked by ties of kin-

ship. But, within every tribe, kinship appears as a strong, associative, integrating principle.

3. Members of an Indian tribe speak one common language, their own or/and of their neighbours.

4. Other distinguishing features of Indian tribes are (for instance) dormitory institutions, absence of institutional schooling, a moral code different from that of Hindus or Muslims, etc.

However, even after considering the Indian definitional deviations, a basic question remains: Is it unavoidable that a category of music carry a definition which is producer-oriented and not directly product-related? Are there no product-qualities in music describable as primitive? If this question is not faced squarely it would be impossible to detect presence or absence of primitive qualities in music produced by non-tribal societies, groups or individuals. It is imperative that music categories are defined with a focus on the experiential content of music. To succumb, instead, to a submerged Darwinism and regard primitive music as original music of the less evolved humans—is to deny musical primitivity, though it is a legitimate channelisation of a genuine human impulse and sensibility. In other words, what is primitive in music must be determined by musical criteria. Therefore it follows that no music should be identified as primitive *because* it is made by people conventionally identified as primitive. Primitivity is directly linked to human experience and not to socio-economic status and allied factors. The primitive category of music produces recurrent, pervasive, and legitimate moulds relevant to a particular kind of musical expression as well as experience. Music cannot and should not be confined to a body of sugary sweet sounds legitimized by anemic aestheticism. It is essential and beneficial that all musical categories are treated with equal seriousness. This is of course not to lessen the importance of ethnographic evidence and data on tribal music. The suggestion is that the data is to be treated as a material useful to reach more basic and sound conceptual conclusions for discussing categories of music and related experiences. To put it differently, features of tribal music are to be examined in order to facilitate detection of primitivity in urban music, literature, etc.

PRIMITIVE MUSIC: CHARACTERISTICS

- Dance, instrumental music and vocal expression are closely woven together. Hardly any scope is allowed to describe items separately as of dance, music, etc.
- In general, the performing impulse, whether in dance, music or drama, acts in response to three cycles, namely, birth-death, day-night and the seasonal. To that extent this music is nearer to processes governing human existence. For example, the Madia-Gond-s from Bastar have the following dance-music rituals in direct relationship with the cycles mentioned: *bhimul-pandum* (praying for rains), *irupu pandum* (harvesting *mahua*), *marka pandum* (pounding corn), *nukanarendana pandum* (new corn), *kara pandum* (cutting bamboo).

Music is for everyone, everything and almost for every occasion. Consequently, all critical phases and events in human life find musical expression. Almost everything appears to *cause* music. Music is all-pervasive. As perceptive researcher-artist Swaminathan has pointed out, primitive art is an example of an eternal process of give and take. Whenever something remarkable takes place, human beings receive and therefore they must 'return' as a response.

Primitivity could be said to set a high premium on song than on music. In other words, composer and not necessarily poet, is regarded important. Song, in this context is a particular kind of formulation resulting from a distinctive processing of musical material. It is symptomatic that a number of tribes have a word to denote song but none to indicate music. The primitive connotation of song is however markedly different. Comparatively speaking, non-primitive life-patterns are less song-dominated and, to that extent, there is less music-permeation, at least it is not as complete as of the primitive. A noteworthy feature of primitive songs are their seemingly unending structures and renditions. Performers would easily add to songs extempore. They may also continue to perform the same song for hours. A peculiar kind of formlessness characterizes the renditions.

What may not easily occur to us is that the primitive song/music is ritualistic even when it does *not* form part of a ritual. One senses a saturating ritualistic charge in every performance. This kind of rituality is felt as an atmosphere. Participants create it through their intensity, preoccupation with minute details, assumption of a certain elevated stance as also through a feeling of internal compulsion they communicate so successfully. Therefore it is not surprising that 'arranging' performances of primitive music without, or outside the ritualistically defined framework, is inevitably confined to a small number of items—further, this kind of presentation would hardly represent the spirit of primitive music. Ao Naga-s for example, wait for the Motsu festival to cover their drums with new leather—thus making it nearly impossible to have the related performance on any other occasion.

Audience, as it is normally understood, plays an unusual role in primitive music, chiefly, because the place of passive listeners is taken by participants, who join in the proceedings—though in varying degrees. Norms of audience-participation are laid down in the culture concerned. It must be added that verbalization of these norms is *not* a precondition for their existence and acceptance.

A related important fact needs to be mentioned. Even if the audience is an integral component, the performers appear to direct their music to an entity external both to themselves and audiences. Music is not made for its own sake nor for the silent, passive viewers/listeners—and yet it has to reach out to complete the act. This peculiar self-sufficiency of primitivity is also ascribable to its closeness to nature. (This is in contrast to conditions in some other categories, for example, popular music is directed outwards on account of market-forces etc.)

Examined in its entirety, primitive element in music relies more on rhythm than on melody. Rhythms are embodied through instruments, movements, percussive speech or similar other modes of vocalizing. Rhythm (as contrasted with melody), controls primitive music to such an extent that instruments conventionally employed for carrying out melodic tasks are also used to generate rhythms. Rhythm in primitive music, apart from its overall preponderance, additionally displays distinctive structural and substantive qualities which obviously require a separate and more technical treatment.

Melody in primitive music is chiefly marked by a noticeable indifference the quality normally described as 'sweetness'. So much of the non-primitive and non-folk music is made with the avowed aim of creating sweet/melodious sounds, that these qualities are unfortunately considered as musically obligatory. It is to be noted that performers themselves, while critically rating performances seldom apply the criterion of sweetness as the *sine qua non* of music. In the same context it is also to be marked that utility, goodness, beauty and such other 'value-aspects' are not identified separately and considered in primitive music.

Roles of language and literature in primitive music demand attention. Language, for all apparent purposes is not regarded indispensable. For example, meaningless sounds and syllables are used abundantly. Phonetic and non-linguistic or literacy patterns enjoy more scope. Half-formed sentences, proverbs, slogans, and similar other formulations gain both legitimacy and currency in primitive music-making. A general anonymity prevails, which is, rather uncharitably often associated with lack of literary quality.

Primitive approach to music rarely distinguishes between writers of songs and composers of tunes. More importantly, 'collective composing' is allowed a definite foothold. Alternatively, it has been often pointed out that even though a sole individual may consolidate or crystallize a particular tune by himself, the tune is likely to partake of many existing tunes. To that extent, the tune could be said to be hovering in the air. Very frequently, to create a new song it suffices to connect the available body of tonal and rhythmic moulds to new phrase and occasions. One may put it that though primitive creation is not collective, primitive creativity is invariably so. This way of looking at the concept of creation or originality is unlikely to gain acceptance in many other music-categories.

It is easy to guess that music, so tightly fastened to human existence, can hardly be expected to have direct, one to one relationships with all its referents. Consequently, symbolism becomes an important feature of primitivity in music. Performance, as well as its peripherals are permeated with symbolism. The generous use of non-musical resources in primitivity actually proves conducive to symbolistic operations as they are multi-levelled and varied in intensity and prominence.

Special mention must be made of the diverse uses of musical instruments. Very often they are also allowed to play role of non-musical objects and their simultaneous existence on two levels normally adds to their evocative power. It is possible to trace primitivity of shapes, sizes and playing techniques to other non-musical contexts of instruments. However, in spite of their overall multi-purpose character, instruments have precise musical functions. They are therefore associated firmly with affective states of minds and definite events of music-making. Equations struck between emotional states and instruments contribute to the general potency of the latter as agents of communication in larger cultural contexts.

In order to get an idea of the nature of cultural orientation of any cultural phenomenon, it helps to learn about the authority enjoyed by different sensations and sensibilities. Primitivity, with its accent on collectivity, often depends on harnessing the tactile. Body-touching, holding of hands, close formations, hand-clapping and foot-stamping, body-thumping, etc. are to be acknowledged in this context. The olfactory is also allowed greater scope. A generous distribution of sensory experiences, combined with a purposeful, definite and organized exploration—is achieved noticeably well through ritualism.

CHARACTERISTICS: FOLK MUSIC

A striking feature of folk music is the relative paucity of instrumental music. The main reason is the dominant position the song enjoys as a genre in the category. Instruments are generously employed in folk music, but mostly to accompany the sung component. In fact, instruments are often content to imitate vocal expression. Understandably, many folk-instruments reveal a notable lack of capacity of prolonged, solo performances. Even when solo renderings are made, they are in short spurts and usually repetitive. It must be recognized that a majority of folk instruments display limited 'vocabulary' of musical sounds of their own. As a consequence, the resulting musical idiom is not rich. In fact instruments are so closely identified with songs that instrumental solos are after described as songs. *Prima facie* instruments make heavy demands on acquisition of individual, technical skills—largely a specialist phenomenon. Folk music has a very limited room for 'professionalism' which specialization asks for. Finally, the restricted role allotted to instrumental music is directly linked to the categorial accent on collectivity. The top priority given to community-expression and the element of individualism permeating instrumental music obviously exercise near-opposite pulls. It is possible that entertainment, a prominent drive behind instrumental music, is a weaker component in the hierarchy of the categorial merits and this too contributes to its low placement.

Collectivity emerges as one of the most important characteristic of folk music. It is symptomatic that only two of the five categorial names, i.e., folk and popular—strongly reflect collectivity. In folk music, collectivity has far-reaching consequences. It is the controlling agent in conception, performance, propagation and communication of the emotional content as well.

Creation of folk song is seldom attributed to a single individual. For some time, it was even averred that folk songs are created collectively. A more viable position is that songs are communally recreated. It is thus posited that a cultural group is motivated from time to time by a common desire to move to a certain kind or manner of reorganizing the available musical material as a cumulative consequence of socio-cultural events. Thus, a song begins to acquire shape, partially and in phases. It is as if the entire atmosphere is charged with it, even though the final form, a musicological crystallization, may await more energetic actions by one of the involved individuals. On this background, the general anonymity of folk songs is meaningful. It indicates recognition of the collective contribution to emergence of songs. However, describing the emergence as recreation gives the individual his due (at least theoretically.).

And yet, the collective-creation theory is not to be summarily brushed aside because many times a 'new' folk song merely presents an edited, modified or an altered version of song/s already in existence—if not in wide circulation. Folk songs continue to be in societal repertoire only after they are processed by the group according to its felt needs. Stanzas are therefore added to or dropped from prevailing songs. This shows how folk song, as an entity, enjoys a continuous creation.

Collectivity is also emphasized by the fact that a majority of folk songs engage groups as singers and/or listeners. Obviously all song-types are not performed collectively to the same extent. Further, collectivity is more related to effectiveness of songs than their actual mode of performance. Songs require a group in order to achieve an impact. (Like a dramatic performance, as it might occur.)

The most significant aspect of collectivity under discussion is, however, their emotional content. Personal ordeals or love-hates seldom figure in them. Content is so generalized as to ensure a wide appeal. This same concern for a wider appeal is also reflected in the song-tunes. This is borne out by structural analysis of folk songs. Also noteworthy is the recurrence of themes related to three human cycles (birth-death, day-night and seasons), which, in essence, affect collectively.

It is clear that the remarkable durability of folk songs is, in a large measure, due to the all-embracing role played by collectivity. Folk songs outlive generations because they address themselves to the societal mind and not to individual spirits. They voice eternal human issues though, touching something topical, is not a taboo. Folk-songs could well be described as articulations of the collective psyche.

Too often, folk music has been defined as manifestations of illiterate people resorting to oral tradition in performance, propagation as well as preservation. The view could only be valid in cultures which elect to reduce their respective art-musics to writing in a major way. In Indian, and in many other contexts, oral traditions cannot be, and need not be, understood as choices made due to various inabilities or incapacities (for example, illiteracy). I have discussed elsewhere major characteristics of oral tradition. In the present context it is sufficient to note that oral tradition *cannot* be defined merely in terms of the presence or otherwise of certain modes of transmission. This is the reason why Rajashekhar's oft-quoted statement that 'poetry of children, women and low castes travels from mouth to mouth' cannot be taken to connote folk music. It merely confirms prominence of oral transmission in folk, as well as, sophisticated expression. And yet, oral tradition appears to influence folk music in some specific ways. They call for some explanation:

    (i) Folk songs can enjoy a state of continuous creation (as clarified earlier) because of the oral tradition. Writing down of compositions is not altogether avoided but a low premium is placed on written versions. The fact, *not* having definitive editions, in a way, encourages changes as well as distortions.

    (ii) Oral tradition is distinguished by its capacity to produce and carry forward a body of folk songs from generation to generation. Songs and song-sets, transmitted from person to person and generation to generation, exemplify the process of slow accretion as well as existence of a flexible core.

    (iii) Oral tradition evolves and uses demonstrable techniques of composition and preservation. It thus supports agents of consolidation and the tendencies towards change.

Folk music obviously enjoys a multiple motivation. Individual, societal as well as artistic motives bring it into being. However, of specific significance is the societal motivation because it is logically connected with the collectivity discussed earlier. It should not be overlooked that societal motivation unambiguously accepts non-musicality as a legitimate component of folk music. Folk music could therefore be expected to respond to societal needs of a didactic hue as opposed to aesthetic demands related to art music or recreational claims made on popular music. In other words, non-art functions have a great role to play in folk music.

The strength of the societal motivation becomes clear, the moment we observe connections of folk music with religion, language, rituals, sacraments and such other cultural components. To a great extent, folk music is what it is because of non-musical contexts operative in its conception, performance, propagation, reception and preservation. It is logical and inevitable that folk music is defined as expression of a specific culture.

Regional, religious and the linguistic orientations of folk music stress its culture-bound character. Functionality also offers another proof of its societal motivation. This is not to suggest that the category is devoid of artistic appeal. What is reiterated is that in its priorities, the aesthetic ranks low and the artistic in it is always detected in combination with many other motives.

Functionality of folk music can be appreciated at a more psychological level. Thematic insistence of folk songs on cultural myths, repeated allusions to societal dreams or past heritage constitute instances of a subtler functionality. Through it, folk music strives to represent a great number of non-musical yet cultural realities. This explains the significant rise in song-sets of a society during periods of stress and strain. Even if no actual rise in the number of songs is detected, a high degree of stimulation of the societal mind can hardly be missed.

For all practical purposes folk music does not have a chronological beginning and end. It is of course obvious that theoretically every composition or a song-type must crystallize into a stable form at some particular point of time. Hence, to maintain that folk music defies chronological placement is merely to repeat its ageless appeal and sideline its actual, chronological beginning/end etc. It may be added that the general anonymity of folk music is also a result of the non-importance of the mundane time-dimension. If there is too close and definite a link between music and specific events, personages, periods, etc.—the related music is likely to drop out of circulation. Like culture, folk music is 'undatable'. It is rather absurd to describe it as old or new—and in that sense it is always contemporary.

Finally, folk music is both changeable and non-changeable. It enjoys a special kind of flexibility, directly and causally connected with its identity. Its proneness as well as reluctance to change may need a little reasoning. To incarnate both conservatism and adaptation is not an easy feat.

Conservatism

Folk music is conservative because it is an expression of the collective mind. Society, taken as a whole, is less keen to accept the new or reject the old than an individual. Societal mind is more than a sum-total of individual minds operating in it. That is to say, society is motivated differently, at different levels and hence a change at any single level is bound to take place only after a slow and complex process.

The way of folk music is paved with too many intentions. Expectably, a simultaneous satisfaction of numerous desires and fulfilment of all or many of intentions would largely remain a theoretical possibility. Motives or intentions of utmost variety would have to be satisfied, partially or completely, to arrive at an optimum level of overall satisfaction before change in music is accepted. In short, a very difficult task indeed.

Examined thematically, folk music reveals a preference for themes with universal appeal. Themes appear to be subjected to innumerable eliminations or filters before they find a place in folk music. This is also a reason for the slow change folk music accepts or opts for. Changes in folk music would have to be culturally inevitable.

Functionality of folk music acts as an added impediment to change as it indicates a linked existence. If the related functional partners do not prove amenable to change they cannot take place—at least not easily. Musical changes in isolation are not conceivable in case of folk music.

However, it should be noted that the reluctance to change is not equally severe in all kinds of folk music. In this respect some general observations could be made:

(i) Music associated with religious ceremonies, marriages and other sacraments or rituals displays extreme conservatism.

(ii) Relatively speaking, music connected with common human experiences such as love, separation or reunion is more likely to change.

(iii) Folk expressions bound with entertainment—activity such as games, dances, etc. are prone to change.

(iv) There are instances of changes introduced because performers themselves felt inclined to change. Obviously, contingencies of performance itself would be causally related with such changes. Needless to say, in this context the term 'performers' indicates performing groups in the culture concerned.

Adaptability

Folk music exhibits noticeable adaptability. To adapt is to change, but with a difference and hence some general observations are in order.

(a) In case performers are involved in a competitive situation and spirit, pressure to adapt mounts and proves effective.

(b) The largely unwritten tradition of folk music is certainly responsible for some of the changes. For example, folk music accommodates changes in language, articulation, composition-technique and size of the body of songs in circulation etc. while transmitting the corpus from person to person, generation to generation and place to place. A near-total reliance on memory is causally connected with many of the changes. On a majority of occasions debates about originality, authenticity, etc. are consequences of unintentional changes which find their way in the corpus.

(c) Folk music of people who migrate expectably evinces adaptability—mostly traceable to the changed environment. It must also be noted that, upsetting many theoretical apple-carts, melodies may migrate independently of cultural groups to which they originally belong. One may come across near-identical melodies irrespective of distances, dissimilar texts and performing traditions. Such melodies have been aptly called 'wandering melodies'.

(d) When a body of professional castes, singers or groups takes up certain songs, qualitative changes are bound to be introduced because performers themselves feel the need to improve the appeal and enhance their power to elicit patronage. Better techniques, discernible skills, etc. come into play. Performing models, thus created, tend to affect their original inspirations. The concerned folk music moves nearer to art music if such mutations are strong and frequent.

(e) Folk expression also changes on account of exposure to education. Significant changes in style, presentation and idiom are inevitably ushered in, even though the corpus, as a whole, may retain its identity. This particular kind of change may be described as indirect as it is consequent to a gradual and almost imperceptible educational influence.

ART MUSIC AND FOLK MUSIC

Perhaps, the most important single factor to bring about changes in folk music in various ways is its proximity to art music, in certain places and during at certain periods. Effects of this cultural and musical neighbourhood are qualitative enough to need a separate discussion.

It needs to be stressed that a major feature to distinguish between folk and primitive musics is the proximity of the former to other musical categories. To a great extent primitive music functions in musical isolation. In contrast, folk music is positioned to easily exchange influences with primitive as well as art music. Obviously, existence of multiple musical streams speaks of a cultural complexity. Some of the features responsible for a culturally complex milieu can be enumerated. They are: use of multiple language-layers, a large scale reliance on the written, modernity of the economy, pace of industrialization and proportion of mechanization in the general life-pattern. In some measure, the cultural complexity also hints at a corresponding multi-stream musicality of a people. Art music, necessarily linked to cultural complexity, reveals many controls in operation and some of them spill over to folk music. Their presence is detected when folk music is musically analyzed.

Folk music is closely tied with a particular group of people and their culture. It is therefore often held up as an instance of a national expression. In other words, groups culturally too diverse, can hardly be expected to have the same or very similar folk music. In this context countries such as India pose a problem. Such countries, in spite of their general and cultural oneness has many regions with their own folk music. If we are ready to forego political definitions of the term 'nation', we may describe these nation-linked music-s as national expressions. A notable feature is the relative homogeneity of vocal music of a nation as compared to its instrumental music.

A nuance of the situation can be identified. More than one nation can have the same art music. Therefore art music cannot be strictly regarded a national expression. This is not so in case of folk music. Once again the Indian situation needs a special consideration with its single culture, more than three systems of art—musics, and several folk musics. The point is that folk music, more than any other category, closely and inherently represents a specific culture.

Being a national expression, folk music proclaims immediate ties with specific geographical areas. Folk music logically responds to natural surroundings as 'folk's' are intimately affiliated to particular locale. More significantly, folk music is 'geographically' oriented *because* it responds to nature as a vital force. The category is unique in that it keeps pace with the three cycles governing human life. The three cycles are: birth and death, day and night and the seasons. However, it is not to be assumed that folk music realistically reflects the nature around. In fact, on occasions it is possible to detect natural descriptions or depictions which are to be interpreted as collective wishes for something a community yearns for. (One exceptional case is of course of Israel—in its context, folk music preceded the nation becoming a reality.)

It may appear that the principles of one region, one culture and one group operates in the category and consequently migration would be difficult in its case. However, it does not turn out to be so. Migrations of groups and the largely unwritten tradition of the category bestows on folk music a remarkable mobility. Between vocal and instrumental expressions, the latter crosses boundaries easily— even though the people to whom it originally belongs may not have migrated.

Folk Song

Folk song is always regarded as the most dominant component of folk music and its multiple roles have been widely recognized. It is useful to discuss the concept at some length.

Folklorists and ethnomusicologists are often told that the term folk song gained the importance it did because of its serious and influential discussion by the German literary personality Johann Gotfied Herder (1744–1803). Interested deeply in philosophy, theology, arts and literature, Herder worked at Weimar in 1770s and came in close contact with Goethe. During his twelve-year stay in a conducive atmosphere, Herder earned fame for his collection of folk songs (volksleider) brought out in two volumes (1778–79). The collection is better known under the title *Stimmer der Volker in Liedern*, due to the second edition edited under that name by J. Von Mueller. Examined in perspective, the work in fact marks the end of Herder's association with that unique German movement—'Strum and Drang'. The movement (which barely lasted for a decade from 1770s) exalted freedom, nature, folk poetry, lyric view of writing and reaction against rationalism as a carry forward from J.J. Roussou (1712–78). In Germany, while it lasted, the movement heavily relied on Herder's 'Von Deutscher Artund Kunst' (1773) as its manifesto. Herder's contribution to the movement chiefly consisted of two ideas: the idea of perception through total personality (thus cutting through the unshared belief in the primacy of reason) and the high estimation of poets and literary ventures coming closer to nature (notably as in the Bible, Shakespeare, Ossain and Folk songs).

It must be admitted that identification of musical category may pose problems especially when dealing with uncodified categories such as folk and primitive. The concept and the term 'folk' has the dubious distinction of generating diametrically opposite views. On the one hand, there are those who hold that folk music is the origin, the root of all music while others argue that it is, in reality, a non-existing phantom category which owes its prosperity to the simplistic and romantic outlook of writers active during the last two centuries. In particular, J.G. Herder, credited to have brought the term 'folk song' into circulation, has been criticized for some flabby thinking on a subject of Musicological importance. Walter Wiora[3] defends Herder vigorously. More importantly, he breaks a new conceptual ground while concluding that Herder's concept of folk song is richer and far more significant than older notions such as natural/artificial or elite/non-elite music. In my opinion, the case could be stated slightly differently and facts from Indian musical traditions could be employed to clarify a complex musico-cultural situation. The point to be debated is not whether Herder was the first to introduce the term. The real issue is whether musical categories could be assumed to enjoy matching term-clusters in all historical periods. In other words, is it possible to suggest that Herder provided a term for something which had existed all along or something which existed under a different name? Interestingly, Wiora makes four major observations suggesting existence of a pre-Herder phenomena sharing features with Herder's notion of folk song:

1. Since antiquity, there have been reference to songs sung by the lower social classes and which were not considered worthy by the upper classes.
2. The names of rural folk songs such as *carmen pastorale* indicate a wide vogue as also a rough musical quality. It is important to note that such coupled terms signified people's songs widespread in the country.
3. Expressions such as *carmen patrium* demonstrate elements of native speech as well as indigenous traditions. Around 1300 Guido of St. Denis spoke of people's songs and their styles.
4. Early in history, songs have frequently been brought under one heading because they had certain common characteristics. (Herder was to do the same later.) Adjectives such as wild, rough, and unsophisticated were employed in this context. For example see the terms: *carmen inclutum, inconditum, incomptum, rude, robustum, inclutum et hirtum, cantus plebisonus* etc.

Herder alluded to Montaigne's distinction between art and nature as the origin of his own idea. However, Wiora argues that Montaigne was merely echoing the medieval dialectic between art and nature which abounded in poetry and rhetorics since ancient times.

Wiora proceeds to note that, coming as it did at the end of the Strum and Drang period, Herder became less enthusiastic about the term 'folk song' by 1779, chiefly because he was disappointed by the material from Germany. It could hardly answer the description he has put down. Yet, it would be useful to note features of folk song according to Herder and noted by Wiora:

1. Herder did not have an exaggerated opinion about the ranking of folk songs as art. He, in fact, held these songs were to be collected as raw material of poetic art.
2. Herder repeatedly mentioned the regional as opposed to the universal popularity of folk song and he also makes a blunt statement that 'beautiful is seldom everywhere at all times.
3. Contrary to the general expectations, Herder did not dwell on the timelessness of folk songs. In this respect two of his statements are instructive. In the first he suggests that songs

collected by Charlemagne, if found, would be objects of antiquarian study. Secondly, he exhorted contemporary poets to sing 'naturally and briefly' as in the old songs. It is not surprising that, due to his qualitative definition of folk songs, he could include Goethe's poems among folk songs.

4. Prior to coining the term 'folk song' Herder spoke of 'nature's—poetry so different from poems made for paper' because of variation and oral transmission. He was specially fascinated by the fact that 'folk songs' were not written or read but sung.

5. Herder, in line with the linguisticians research-angle of the times, wanted to throw light on the origin of songs by comparing existing primitive tribes.

6. Herder maintained that folk songs are sung by rural and lower classes of people who also possess a cultivated art.

7. For Herder, educated persons (like Goethe's) writings could be described as folk songs if endowed with certain qualities.

8. Herder described folk songs as 'a lively voice of the people; of mankind, in the sense of ethnically varied nature of man'— once again a feature accentuating the aspect of diversity.

9. In his opinion, folk songs provide germ and substance of great art. Herder's literary bias becomes obvious as he gave examples from Greek literature and Shakespeare as 'growing' from this source i.e., folk songs.

This brings us to a discussion of the category of popular music.

POPULAR MUSIC: CHARACTERISTICS

Popular music is a feature of a sub-culture known as popular. It is helpful to define popular culture and prepare the necessary conceptual background to discuss the category. 'Popular culture is a surfacial manifestation of cultural forces operating in a society partially responsive to aesthetic motives. The said responses are only partially aesthetic because of three factors: impact of mass-media, repercussions of changing patronage and commercial and religious pressures that function intermittently'.

It is essential to remember that the term popular does not stand for an aesthetic concept. With some other concepts such as amateur, professional and modern, the term popular has socio-economic, cultural and chronological dimensions. As a consequence, it becomes inevitable and proper to bring in extra-musical values and criteria to discuss it. The category deserves special attention because a large segment of the total music in modern societies is made in this category.

(i) Universality: Universality has two aspects—chronological and territorial/geographical. Popular music is universal for all practical purposes.

Perhaps an explanation would help.

It would be incorrect to argue and assume that popular music is a creation of the twentieth century. An intensive American study of the category, phenomenal growth of the modern mass-media (which constitute a prominent shaping influence of the category) during the century has created an impression that emergence and operation of the category are limited to present times. This cannot be valid, primarily because the category owes its emergence to a simultaneous existence and independent operations of various sub-cultures in a society. A homogeneous society is, realistically speaking, a mere theoretical possibility. Societies have subcultures operating at various levels with differing intensities. Social homogeneity and functioning equality of subcultures may have to be described as ideals or *ramarajya*-possibilities. A cumulative effect is that most subcultures are attracted to folk or popular categories of music. Societies, characterized by inevitable socio-cultural distinctions lead to musical differentials. This leads to circulation of musical forces, creating in the process, the ever-changing category of popular music.

(ii) The category prominently displays 'middle-class' influences and effects of urbanizing processes. Urbanization and existence of multiple societal layers are casually related. If industrialization is not interpreted too technically, any recourse to new production modes and employment of new means for that purpose should be identified as industrialization in its essence. It is known that migration of people from rural areas to cities in search of livelihood and emergence of a comparatively new technology are features that have recurred so frequently, that they demand to be described as historical features inherent to growing cultures.

(iii) Many factors contribute to create situations in which more and more people come to enjoy leisure hours. This too has been a familiar feature of human civilizations. Thus people tend to pursue more hobbies and appear keener to spend more time on development/enrichment of personality. Consequently, a number of new disciplines, arts, crafts are cultivated with semi-aesthetic and semi-commercial motives. Popular music is one of the products of such circumstances. Entertainment, education, a desire for commercial gain and other diverse drives operate at the same time to create popular expression.

(iv) Mass-media have a special role to play in the category. The media deeply influence conception, propagation and reception of popular music.

(v) It has often been pointed out that popular music strikes roots in a culture at a time when a perceptible rise in population is noted. In most cases it may not be an absolute rise but a large-scale demographic redistribution due to migration etc. Smaller groups are likely to be more homogeneous. Population growth would bring about heterogeneity and stratification leading to the rise of popular music.

(vi) Patronage-changes consequent to different socio-economic and cultural developments are often qualitative—depending on the discerning powers of the new patrons. A wealthier but less knowledgeable patronage compels artists to seek a notionally lowest common denominator in their presentations. Popular music often ranges around this point, taken as a reference.

(vii) Popular music is affected by changes in patronage almost immediately, unlike in other categories. Audience-responses to producers and propagators of popular music allow a very short time-lag. In other words, the category exhibits the maximum synchronization between forces of supply and demand.

(viii) The remarkable near-correspondence between stimulus-response becomes possible because popular music is a product of the entertainment industry. Supply-demand, production-costs, distribution and sale, market-research, survey etc. build up a formidable mechanism related to production rather than creation. Art, aesthetics and similar value-oriented approaches are, if necessary, relegated to background in the related 'transactions'. If its business-compulsions are not taken into account, popular music can hardly be understood for what it is and does.

(ix) The most important moving force behind popular music is the desire to satisfy the most obvious musical needs of the masses. Art music tries to manipulate time-dimension and thereby win ascendancy over it, folk music goes around it while popular music intentionally attempts to keep pace with it. The general import of popular music, its specific expression and style, titles, blurbs, write-ups and all related matters are finalized only after the ruling fashion of the day has been ascertained. Popular music can truly be described as the journalistic treatment of musical material.

(x) In a sense popular music is functional. It is linked to specific modes of fashions society happens to prefer at a particular point of time. Fashions have a useful task to perform: to create easily manipulatable devices of image-building or image-reinforcement. Fashions naturally change with great frequency. To create popular music is to create musical fashions.

(xi) On account of the great number of non-musical forces shaping it, popular music may appear to proclaim musical inferiority. However, this is not so. A heartening feature of popular music is a kind spiral rise in quality it usually registers. Examination of popular musical material over a period makes a case for applying the concept of 'progress' in music. Because of its alert stances and readiness to change, popular music tends to move from lesser to better levels of musicality over a period of time. Popular music has an assimilative power which ensures that, after a reasonable lapse of time, it settles on music of recognizable quality.

CHARACTERISTICS OF ART MUSIC

1. The most significant feature of art music (sometimes inappropriately described as 'classical' music) is the patently aesthetic intention of performers. 'Art' performers are set apart from other musicians because of this primary orientation. Of course the product does not enjoy aesthetic quality *because* of the motivation. And yet, one cannot overlook the

qualitative differences between promptings of primitive, folk, devotional, art and popular musicians. Briefly stated, a performer in primitive music is engaged in playing a role, a folk-musician entertains or participates in a collective, duty-filled task; a devotional musician performs ritualistically, directionally and mediately while in popular music performers take seriously to catering to mass needs at a point of time. On this background, art-musicians are distinguished by their conscious efforts to establish themselves as 'artists' according to their own perception of what is aesthetic/artistic. Art-musicians aesthetic/artistic perceptions and criteria born thereof, may/may not be explicitly verbalized, but their existence and application is beyond doubt.

2. In art music, concurrent operations of two music-related traditions, namely, performing and scholastic, are prominent. The scholastic, of necessity, relies on writing and the written. More importantly, it follows procedures inherent to every form of codification. Pertinent rules, methods and techniques are systematized in accordance with established practices. It is obvious that scholastic tradition takes its raw material from the existing performing tradition, but it inevitably lags behind the performing. Scholastic traditions are required to register only those items which the community has allowed to consolidate. Relationship between grammar and literature (in linguistic continuities) provide a useful conceptual parallel.

3. Art music tends to concentrate on selected performing aspects such as vocalization, instrumentation, movement or *abhinaya* etc. In other words, compared to other categories, art music has less of a package-character. Modes of expression are deliberately isolated, cultivated and exploited; energies are channelized and intensively put to use for achieving perceivable effects.

4. It is art music which offers the maximum scope to soloists. Roles of the main and accompanying performers are well-defined and developed. A highly differentiated sensibility is vital to place the solo element so centrally and to allow it to shape the entire performing activity. Art music formulates aims, methods and techniques to this end. Consequently, various musical ideologies, family traditions etc. emerge with

their respective—and marked emphases.

5. A whole array of musical forms, based on patterning of musical elements (notes, rhythms, tempi, etc.) into specific structures, is available in art music. On the other hand, genres in other categories of music are the combined results of many active, non-musical factors (for example events in human life-cycles, seasonal changes, associated rites and rituals etc. come to mind). Art music genres also display a hierarchy based on the degree of technical competence. As a result, certain forms are regarded more prestigious *because* of the demands they make on performers in terms of the required skill, techniques etc. On examination, it also becomes clear that the hierarchical edifice is dependent on a number of criteria which are grammatical in import.

6. A highly structured teaching-learning process essentially features in art music. Emergence of *gharana*-s or *sampradaya*-s; guru-s with their exclusive followings, pedagogical reputations built over years, importance attached to initiations, tracing of musical pedigrees are some of the notable components of the process. Methodical curricula are inevitably followed even though they may not be written down. Anthologies of skeletal compositions, notations, codifications etc. are prepared, preserved and often maintained with utmost secrecy and reverence.

7. Audiences of art music are a class apart on account of their non-participatory contribution. Compared to other musics, art music depends for its effectiveness on presence of a more organized audience expected to have a taste for the sophisticated impact of art music. Perhaps, no other category finds it essential to educate its receivers as does the art music. In addition, the audience is also expected to contribute to music-making by expressing its approval/disapproval in accordance with the established norms forming a part of the cultural pattern. Acquisition of taste for art music or its appreciation constitutes a learned behaviour and it is symptomatic that in art music, attempts at conducting appreciation-courses are well-received.

8. Art music is also characterized by its all-round efforts to combine with other arts and art forms. This leads to creation of composite arts and art forms. The process appears to be para-

doxical because art music initially moves to delink itself from other arts for establishing an independent aesthetic/artistic control. However, the paradox disappears when it is perceived that on both occasions differing motivations come into play. The initial delinking is prompted by a keen desire to demarcate a kind of autonomous area of operation in order to shape an identity of its own and to evolve a set of criteria etc. On the other hand, the later efforts to effect union with painting or drama or dance etc. are directed at enrichment of the total aesthetic experience. Emergence of ballet, opera, *ragamala* paintings etc. would come to mind.

9. Art music employs abstraction at every possible level. For example, it diminishes the scope allowed to language and literary manifestations, reduces importance of the topical and functional relationships with ritual and routine life-patterns, unfolds an impressive array of instrumental forms of music, tries to stabilize skeletal compositions as definitive. As a cumulative effect of these and such other measures, art music creates its own universe of reference and proposes to adhere to a contextual framework built of musical elements alone. This is the reason why non-representational and noticeably arabesque quality of art music attracts attention. Abstraction necessarily means total dependence on musical parameters operating in musical perception. To an extent this should explain the comparatively limited appeal of art music.

This brings to conclusion a brief mapping of four of the five categories of music that make the complete musical reality in India. The fifth category, namely devotional music, is discussed separately because it is rarely accepted as an independent musical mould. Musical categories are not water-tight compartments and allow exchange of musical influences. Items, genres, styles, presentation-formats and the like may move from one to the other category. In this movement they undergo alterations or modifications. A special type of categorial transfer needs to be noted before proceeding to the fifth category.

Collectors of folk music in the European tradition virtually pushed oral versions of songs to rural areas and consequently created a written tradition because the collected versions were systematized, notated and analyzed to some extent. As a number of collectors were also composers, these folk-songs became art-songs with folk origin and flavour. Bela Bartok (1881–1945), or Kumar Gandharva (1924–92) would be notable examples.

A very important corollary is the soloist's freedom to emphasize an expressive individuality. Freedom to interpret, innovate and finally claim originality can hardly be conceived in any other category than the art. And yet, Indian music is unique, in the final analysis, because it is enriched by five categories of music—even today, when globalization is blurring all distinctions.

REFERENCES

1. *Webster's New Collegiate Dictionary*, Springfield, Mass., 1981, p. 907.
2. Nadeem Hasnain, *Tribal India Today*, p. 17.
3. "Reflections on the Problem: How Old is the Concept of Folk Song?", *International Folk Music Council Yearbook*, 1972–3, pp. 23–33.

2
Devotional Music in India

The present attempt to examine the category of devotional music is, in fact, a part of larger inquiry. Three qualities from the spiritual aspects of personality, namely, religiosity, mysticism and devotion relate to music. They indicate overlapping but progressively narrower areas of musico-spiritual relationship. India proves a happy ground for investigation of the three relationships as the country enjoys multiplicity of both religions and musics. In addition, both have extended traditions. Further, the linguistic plurality only adds to the fascination.

It might be helpful to distinguish between religion, mysticism and devotion, even at the risk of appearing somewhat elementary. A widely reported definition of religion would be, for example, "A belief binding the spiritual nature of man to a supernatural being, as involving a feeling of dependence and responsibility, together with the feelings and practices which flow from such a belief."[1] Mysticism, according to the same source, is "The belief that the knowledge of the divine truth or the soul's union with the divine is attainable by spiritual insight or ecstatic contemplation without the medium of senses of reason. . . . Any theory of advancing intense meditative and intuitive methods of thought or conduct."

As far as the term of our immediate interest, devotion, is concerned, the following lexicographic aid is noteworthy:

Devotional : 1. of or relating to devotion
           2. used in worship
Devote   : from *de* (intensive) + *vovere* (vow)
           1. to give or apply (one's time, attention or self) entirely to a particular activity or cause
           2. to set apart for a specific purpose or use
           3. to set apart by, or as if by, a vow or solemn act

The core meaning of the term 'devote' is, 'to give over by or as if by a vow to a higher purpose'.[2] 'Devotion' is from Middle Latin *devovere,* 'to vow firmly or without reservation, hence to concentrate'.[3]

It would be thus clear that the three concepts are adequately dissimilar from each other to justify an equally different trinity of associated musics despite existing interconnections. For example, the religious, being the most inclusive, may rely on heavy observance of external forms. The two others essentially refer to states of mind featuring specific kinds of intensities. In accordance with these distinctions the degree of musicality permissible in each case expectably varies and hence the situation does not allow a blanket generalization.

Indian music is repeatedly described as devotional. This description, though intended as complementary, causes discomfort to practising musicians and perceptive musicologists who follow the performing tradition alertly. The truth of the matter is that no music becomes devotional because its maker was/is in a devotional frame of mind while making it. Categories become real when performer's intent, musical content and formats of presenting music firmly unite to produce a sizeable musical corpus. The norm applies to devotional music.

The Indian equivalent to the term devotion is *bhakti* from Sanskrit *bhaj* to honour, adore, to worship. It finds the first unambiguous mention in the *Shvetashvatara Upanishad* (*c.* 1200–600 BC) though the content related with the doctrine could be traced to the Vedas (*c.* 1000–800 BC). The *Gita,* of course, lays great store by it. The doctrine becomes a cultural force much later in the history.

Unlike any abstract philosophical idea, a cultural force encompasses diverse areas of life and creates/controls wide-ranging patterns of social behaviour. Initially emerging as an idea, *bhakti* flowered into a philosophical thought-stream (Bhakti-marga) with numerous *pantha*-s as its offshoots by *c.* AD 400. The cults succeeded in making the idea more concrete and manifold in expression due to their numerous and varied prescriptions and prohibitions. *Bhakti-sangeet,* devotional music, as it is known today, is a musical response to an essentially religio-cultural circumstances.

It is not difficult to surmise why the Bhakti-marga has proved attractive over a period of two thousand years. Of the time-honoured ways of achieving the state of final release (*moksha*), the path of knowledge (*dhyanayoga*) proved difficult for men of ordinary intellect. Hathayoga proved perplexing and arduous on account of the extraordinary demands it made on an individual's capacity to subjecting mind and body to strict observances and austerities as also on will-power. Tantra, on the other hand required an uncommon elevation and/or sublimation or sensuality which made the path of salvation somewhat more perilous, and sometimes socially dangerous. The path of devotion brought together feelings and forms easily recognizable, generally acceptable and nearly pleasurable. Further, at least ostensibly, it did not tax the devotee's innate qualities and strengths inordinately.

Of equal significance is the inevitable connection Bhakti-marga enjoys with the doctrine of *avatara*. The periodic divine incarnations, aimed at helping the common humanity in distress, made God substantial as well as more fruitfully imaginable. But more importantly, the *avatara*-s provided comprehensive basis for development of an intimate relationship between worshipper and the worshipped. Many channels were explored to bring into being and keep alive this interrelationship—music being inevitably one of them. The concept of *avatara* was well crystallized by AD 1000. The number of *avatara*-s was gradually stabilized around ten. It has been perceptively pointed out that the first five of the ten (namely, *Matsya,* Fish; *Kurma,* Tortoise; *Varaha,* Boar; *Narasimha,* Man-lion; and *Vamana,* Dwarf) are mythological, the next three (Parashurama, Rama and Krishna) represent the human heroic element, the ninth (Buddha) and the still to come Kalki accentuate the religious. Vishnu, the preserver, has remained the mainstay of the concept even if Shiva and Ganapati etc. also had reincarnations. From the ten *avatara*-s, those of Rama and Krishna remain the most popular and the Bhakti-marga would hardly be the force it has been without these personalities at its core. It must be noted that the *avatara* doctrine was further elaborated to appear at three levels— metaphysical (*purushavatara*), philosophical (*gunavatara*), and finally, anthropocentric (*leelavatara*).

The Bhakti-movement, which finally came to have the content described so far, had its first impact in the Tamil-speaking regions of India. Saint-poets known as Alvars went from temple to temple singing praises of Lord Vishnu. By AD 800, they had succeeded in reaching all strata of society. The traditions record that the south-born *bhakti* moved on to prosper in Karnataka, flower for a while in Maharashtra, before finally turning to Gujarat. To put it more factually, Vaishnava *bhakti* spread all over the country through saint-poets and philosopher-devotees. While the latter took care of the philosophical and theological perspectives, the former went to the field, reaching masses in the process, composing thousands of songs and creating abundant musical forms. However, neither mysticism nor the doctrine of *avatara* could be said to be exclusively Vaishnava. If so, why did Vaishnava approaches prove specifically musical?

An important clue is available in the very nature of the Vaishnava kind of *bhakti*. *Bhagavatapurana*, a basic work, laid down nine modes of devotion. They are listed as, "To listen to his name, to do his *keertana*, to touch his feet, to worship him, to offer respects to him, to accept his servitude, to be intimate with him and to open ones heart to him" (*Bhagavatapurana*, 7.5.23). What is worth-noting is that three of the nine mode stress the role of sound and prescribe ways of processing it into more meaningful manifestations.

This preoccupation with the element of sound ensured emphasis on music and language—two entities evolving from the fundamental element of sound. The fact is obviously related to the Vaishnava crystallization of numerous musical and poetic forms. Even in matter of *mantra*-s, the Vaishnava-s leaned towards meaningful language rather than nonsensical sound-clusters which were usually regarded more auspicious. Though it is true that both Yoga and Tantra emphasized use and importance of sound, the sound-types/kinds they pressed into service would hardly be expected allow prominence to sensuous or pleasurable qualities of sound. Notably, the *beejamantra*-s in Tantra relied on sounds of short duration and phonetic hardness while the *anahata* (the unstruck and therefore the unheard) sound associated with the yogins remained outside the pale of normal human perception.

The Vaishnavas were able to catch imagination of the people and establish easy relationship with them because the cult accommodated within itself three figures/images identifiable with three phases of human life. Thus, Balakrishna, Radha-Krishna and Yadavaveer Krishna create close parallels with innocent childhood, amorous youth and heroic/warrior—the three images/phases recurring in human career. As folk music continuities all over the country deal with these same phases, a tri-directional correspondence appears to have developed. The *avatara*-s allowed a free anthropomorphic treatment of all themes to the Vaishnava-s and a parallel existence of similar themes in folk music afforded them, i.e., the *avatara*-s a firm base in the people's psyche. It is therefore instructive to remember that Devotional music is characterized by its close links with folk music on one hand and art music on the other. It is to be expected that finally, musical categories constitute a qualitative continuum of musical perceptions and actualizations and yet, some categories are nearer to one another.

The Vaishnava philosophical accent on *dvaita-bhava* (the initial separate existence of devotee and deity) offered limitless possibilities to create roles and character-situations. This in-built provision for the emergence and actualization of the audience-performer-performance trinity, opens ideal avenues for dance, drama and music—the three chief performing expressions.

From the essential duality-principle mentioned earlier, a corollary follows. The reference is to the elaborate array of cravings (*asaktis*) classified in the authoritative *bhakti*-text, *Naradabhaktisutra* (Narada's Aphorisms on Devotion). Briefly stated, the eleven types of cravings and mythological personalities exemplifying them are:

1. Craving to know and narrate greatness of God, exemplified by Narada, Vyasa, Shuka, Saunaka, Yajnyavalkya, Shandilya, Bhishma and Arjuna.

2. Craving for the beauty of God, exemplified by people of Mithila in love with Rama, as also by the people of Braja in love with Krishna.

3. Craving to worship God, exemplified by Lakshmi, Prithu, Ambarisha and Bharata.

4. Craving for constant remembrance and contemplation of God and his name, exemplified by Dhruva, Prahlada and Janaka.

5. Craving to serve God, exemplified by Hanuman, Akrura and Vidur.

6. Craving to form fellowship with God, exemplified by Arjuna, Uddhava, Sanjaya and Sudama.

7. Craving for God as husband (and oneself as consort), exemplified by Rukmini and Satyabhama.

8. Craving for God as son, the devotee being a parent, exemplified by Kashyapa-Aditi, Dasharatha-Kaushalya, Nanda-Yashoda and Vasudeva-Devaki.

9. Craving to confess everything to God, exemplified by Ambarisha, Bali, Vibhishana and Shibi.

10. Craving to become one with God, exemplified by Uddhava.

11. The intense craving for God caused by separation from him, exemplified by Uddhava, cowherds and maidens from Braja.

It thus becomes obvious that every conceivable human relationship has been attributed to the god-devotee bond. The listed cravings provide intense and varied basis for the role-creation earlier referred to. These different dualistic relationships between God and devotees have unfailingly created places, atmosphere and occasions to express and channelize devotion. The process was more prominent in case of Vaishnavas and hence the scope offered to performing arts was abundant.

Vaishnava cults were fortunate to have some outstanding poets among their fold. Though it is true that their poetic products enjoyed authority they did because of the 'felt' devotion of the concerned writers, it must be recognized that these devotees were also excellent craftsmen. Despite turning out compositions in great numbers, they have usually maintained a remarkably even quality, which is a sure tribute to their writing prowess. They chiefly wrote in regional languages and the regular employment of non-Sanskrit prosodic moulds helped secure them an easy acceptance as well as circulation. Their works have been critically acclaimed in literary aspects such as imagery, vocabulary, etc. It is significant to know that writers of devotional poetry are traditionally known as *sant-kavi*-s, i.e., saint-poets. The Vaishnavas were so thorough in their approach to *bhakti*-oriented poetry, that a new and comprehensive statement of poetics was deemed necessary.

Perusal of history confirms that in many cases, musicians of proven merit and established stature have subsequently become followers of the *pantha*-s. They were naturally encouraged to utilize their musical talents in service of God. With experts in operation, the common man's natural attraction for music could be better exploited. The ranks of devotees swelled and collective devotion became a major mode of expression.

It is easy to imagine that accomplished and practising musician-devotees would tend to introduce added sophistication, intricacy of design and technical virtuosity in conception and performance of music. The highly codified traditions of Haveli Sangeet and Manipuri Sankeertana exemplify the trend. However, as devotional cults aimed at collectivity and large audiences of inclusive constitution, the devotional impulse gradually preferred to opt for two contemporaneous systems or streams of cult-related musics—contingent of course on the overall multiplicity of music current in regions concerned. Thus, normally, one of the streams featured heavily codified, art-oriented music while the other remained simpler in structure and technique-generating a more user-friendly music, to use modern term. While the latter exhibits affinity to folk music, the former moves closer to art music. No wonder that the folk music-oriented devotional music has proved to be more durable of the two. In fact, during the successive ages, institutional supports to art-oriented devotional music weakened as wealthy patrons, royalty, etc. had their authority curtailed on account of socio-political changes. There is also a room to believe that art music and its professional practitioners, for whom the art-oriented devotional music was generally a prohibited area, were keen to absorb its attractive features and in the process make the original superfluous. Professional art musicians, being more versatile and audience-responsive, could effect meaningful deviations from the conventional, art-oriented, devotional music. This is the reason for backsliding of the rich Haveli Sangeet tradition. Its attractive features were incorporated in Hindustani Khayal-music, though not always with better results. The *dhrupad*-rigidity or the ritual-based quality of Haveli Sangeet was ignored by Khayal-singers while borrowing extensively from the devotional tradition.

The second sub-tradition, nearer to folk, is represented by Dhaula-geet which runs parallel to Haveli Sangeet or the Varkari-music of Maharashtra. Musical examination of both these traditions reveals similarities and distinctions of significance. While they certainly cut grooves similar to art-tradition in matters of theme, ritualistic slant, seasonality etc., they also deviate to stress collectivity of expression and simplicity of structure; the overall thrust of these sub-traditions has been to move nearer to the common man's life.

It is against this background that some musical features of the devotional category deserve attention. Nearly all of them can safely be treated as defining characteristics.

1. Devotional compositions invariably include name of the saint-poet-composer in the last line. *Mudra,* as the feature is known, can and does carry out various other indicative functions. Art music also displays this feature.

2. Compositions from the category are in regional languages described collectively as Prakrits (in contrast to Sanskrit). Prakrit languages are often regarded innately sweeter and musical.

3. Metrical moulds employed by the saint-poets were also of

the Prakrit origin. These are held to be more conducive to music-making because of their structural flexibility. These meters allow stretching of individual words, line-endings, or mid-line positions—a detail helpful in creating melodic continuity, so essential to Indian music.

4. Devotional music chooses to favour rhythms of three or four beats or their multiples. What is marked is a general reliance on medium tempo and a preference for less expansive time-frames, i.e., *tala*-s. Those employed by the category are often, and aptly described as *ardha-tala*-s (half-*tala*-s). Rhythmic cycles thus realized are remarkably similar to those used in folk music. It is not accidental that rhythmic manifestations in these two categories prove appealing or 'catchy', though considerably repetitive. Musical categories intent on reaching masses usually depend on rhythmic frameworks less difficult to grasp (this is so in film-music too.).

5. The slogan, 'music for masses' also applies in case of the melodic contours of devotional music, especially in the stream moving away from art music. Indian devotional music resorts to a very limited number of *raga*-s or melodic skeletons similar to *raga*-s. Further, these *raga*-s are characterized by a certain elasticity of grammatical structure. Such *raga*-s are often and properly called *dhun-raga*-s, i.e., *raga*-s identifiable with mere tunes or elementary melodies. Such *raga*-s bear similarity to folk tunes circulating regionally. Names such as Pahadi (of mountain-regions), Kafi (from Sind), Mand (from Marwar), make the point. These loosely structured tunes allow easy shift to other *raga*-s. On account of the manner in which they are ushered in devotional category, the *raga*-s also suggest or allude to other, similar *raga*-s. Lastly, devotional music also uses *raga*-s conventionally classified as seasonal, again a feature the category shares with folk music.

6. Devotional music displays a judicious mixing of choral and solo renderings. During its performance, the audience is expected to participate according to norms prescribed in the tradition. In-built provisions exist for participation. Points of participation are frequent and predictable—iteration of God's name in chorus being prominent. Involvement thus becomes more intense and the repetition carries a hypnotic charge.

7. Most instruments engaged in the category are designed to promote rhythmic pulses. Sonorous and hardly built, they are conducive to production of wooden and metallic timbers. Autophones or *ghana* and membranophones or *avanaddha* instruments are dominant. Expectably, these instruments are atonal and they normally project ranges rather than pitches. This is also reflected in the way they are tuned. What is remarkable is that even the blown and the strung instruments, designed to produce melodic contours, bring out rhythmic stresses. Hand-claps have an active role to play. All these instrumental characteristics are noticeably shared by folk and devotional categories. Solo or the virtuoso element is rarely encouraged. The closer the devotional music is to art music, the more the freedom granted to solo element and the technical virtuosity of performers. One ethnomusicological, rather than an organological, feature of instruments pressed into service, is the sacred status they often enjoy. They are worshipped, adorned and revered on specific occasions, in definite contexts as also for certain effects.

8. With its distinctive motivation and emotional contexts, the category develops its own repertoire of musical forms. On account of the narrowed emotional spectrum, absence of musical grammars of complexity and assumed audience responses, the repertoire is narrower (which, however, does not mean that it is musically less rich). *Abhanga, virani, gaulan, pada,* in Maharashtra, and *keertana, pada, bhajan, choupai,* etc. in other traditions form the musical repertoire of devotional music in India. These can hardly be mistaken for forms from other musical categories.

Today, devotional music is rendered from the concert stage and also in a highly 'processed' manner. A similar transformation is taking place in folk music. That should not however deafen us to what the original *avatara*-s of both the categories have been trying to convey. Confusion of musical categories usually leads to incorrect expectations, application of irrelevant criteria and pronouncement of inappropriate aesthetic judgements. Seen in its proper perspective, devotional music would appear to carry out varied cultural and musical functions—a sure indication of its continued validity.

REFERENCES

1. J.G. Ferguson, *Webster Comprehensive Dictionary*, vol. II, p. 1064.
2. Houghton Mifflin, *Webster's II New Riverside Dictionary*, p. 371.
3. Eric Partridge, *A Short Etymological Dictionary of Modern English*, p. 792.

3

Perspective Studies in Music

In its origin, the word perspective meant an intense looking over. Later, the word came to indicate a technique of representing three-dimensional objects and depth-relationships on two-dimensional surfaces. Yet another influence is added to the semantic field of the word as it also means relationship of aspects of a subject to each other and to a whole. It is not figurative to say that perspective-studies I propose to discuss are results of a very intense 'looking over' at music. The marshalling of intellectual forces involved, fields of knowledge drawn upon and the complex methodologies evolved for the studies under consideration exemplify conceptual activity of high degree, strength and effect. Further, the studies certainly amount to depicting depth-relationships in two-dimensional modes as the largely non-representational, non-verbal as well as evanescent musical experience is kept at the core. Finally, the studies constitute concurrent attempts to cultivate music extensively, as well as intensively. The basic article of faith is that music needs to be examined as a part of larger socio-cultural framework, even if it can be pursued in isolation, and for itself. The three encompassing perspective-studies are respectively, comparative musicology, folkloristics and ethnomusicology. (The last can also be aptly and preferably described as cultural musicology.) The trinity obviously displays certain common features—'family-resemblances' as one may call them—though each discipline is today sufficiently crystallized to justify separate and fuller treatments. It is helpful to begin by discussing traits common to them.

COMMON CHARACTERISTICS

1. The triad propels examination of musical material beyond the actual, musical act. Investigations necessarily touch upon non-musical areas in order to bring into action wider and

socio-cultural frameworks.

2. These studies are marked by an in-built provision for undertaking inter-disciplinary approaches. Further, a noticeable tendency permeating them is to make repeated references to thought-structures known as Sciences of Man, i.e., anthropology, ethnography and sociology.

3. The trinity displays a less direct concern for the musical quality of performances under scrutiny.

4. For all practical purposes, the studies are inclined to either of the two poles: musical grammar or cultural formulation touching on non-musical areas and interests. Among the three, comparative musicology displays grammatical orientation to the maximum while the other two lean towards anthropology.

5. Finally, on account of their cultural bias the disciplines allow endogenous as well as exogenous examinations. Investigators belonging to traditions under examination are described as 'insiders' and they are required to temporarily suspend their sense of belonging. This, in fact, becomes a substantive precondition for the undertaking. On the other hand, those not brought up in traditions (and hence described as outsiders) are required to invest themselves with a sense of belonging to the new, or alien tradition. It is obvious that the outsider's as well as insider's views need to be considered together.

Comparative musicology, folkloristics and cultural musicology can be compared as well as contrasted on the backdrop of features they have in common. I propose to do so under five headings: subject-matter, major contributory disciplines, relationship with performing tradition, scope afforded to musical analysis and aims. Positions of the three approaches are to be juxtaposed.

COMPARATIVE MUSICOLOGY

Subject-matter
Music theories of art music of two or more cultures.

Major contributory disciplines
(i) Music theory codified as grammar by cultures under review.

(ii) Scholastic tradition with standardized procedures of textual criticism, lexicography etc.

(iii) Music history.

Relationship with performing arts

(i) Close and moving away in recurring cycles.

(ii) Musicological studies usually follow performing traditions. It is rare for the two to be co-orbital. In fact it is merely a theoretical possibility.

Scope for musical analysis

Musical and Musicological analysis from the core of the inquiry. Items with cultural perspective are peripheral.

Aims

To develop a better technical and structural understanding of music systems under study.

FOLKLORISTICS

Subject-matter

Musical traditions falling within the purview of folkloristic study of one or more cultures.

Major contributory disciplines

(i) Those developed in folkloristic studies

(ii) Musicologies of related cultures

(iii) Value-disciplines in low key-operations

Relationship with performing arts

Close, though in varying degrees depending on the nature of the genre.

Scope for musical analysis

Musical analysis plays an important role while Musicological analysis has a low priority. Cultural factors are allowed an increasing consideration.

Aims

To create an integrated vision of the folk-mind to diminish divisions between different strata in non-homogeneous cultures.

CULTURAL MUSICOLOGY OR ETHNOMUSICOLOGY

Subject-matter
One or more musical continuities within a particular musical culture considered in its entirety.

Major contributory disciplines
  (i) Anthropology and musicology of the culture concerned.
  (ii) Trinity of value-disciplines: philosophy, ethics and aesthetics.

Relationship with performing arts
Performance is central in the initial stages. The discipline moves away from performance in the later stages of the inquiry.

Scope for musical analysis
Cultural items are to the fore. Musical analysis is chiefly employed as an interpretative aid.

Aims
To develop an understanding of man through music and appreciate the *raison d'être* of music through cultural insights.

CLUES TO PERSPECTIVE STUDIES

At this juncture an interesting question demands a response. What clues can lead us to conclude that a particular culture has successfully developed the three perspectives on music? Two of the identified studies deal with material in oral traditions and hence an answer to the question in crucial. Prevalence of oral tradition means that norms ordinarily propounded with regard to collection of evidence, systematization of facts, corroboration of theories, etc., can hardly be enforced without making qualitative and discerning changes. This is the main reason why folkloristics or ethnomusicology, etc. have to prove their flexibility—especially in methodology and conceptualization. Failing to do so has often earned them the doubtful compliment of being 'Western' disciplines and hence inapplicable to other musical cultures. It is necessary to realize the variety of ways in which cultures raise questions, formulate disciplines and forge methods to examine phenomena such as music. Hence a very primary query becomes relevant: What indicates 'study' of music?

Lexicographic hints can be helpfully picked up. For instance, according to Webster, study is 'application of knowledge in a particular field' or 'careful examination or analysis of a phenomenon, development or question'. In Indian contexts one term with a similar semantic thrust is *abhyasa* which means 'to execute repeatedly'. The root-meaning of the term is 'to approach, go near'—an obvious reference to transmission of information, etc. from teacher to the taught. To parallel the term 'study', we have the term *vichara*—derived from *vichar*, 'to think, to reflect or meditate upon' or 'to discuss, to debate, to examine, to investigate'. The point is that the core meaning of all terms noted do *not* suggest a recourse to the process of writing and the phenomenon of written tradition as necessary preconditions for identifying the activity as 'study'. Hence the question: To what extent norms and methods of scholastic traditions, with their customary emphases (on writing and the written) should be considered essential to carry out 'study' of music? Being a performing art, music is permeated with the phenomenon of performance in processes of generation, transmission, reception, preservation and interpretation. Therefore, clues to nature and extent of music-studies would be detected in many cultures in the non-scholastic and performing endeavours.

The position thus advocated contradicts the opinion frequently put forward that perspective studies of music began in the nineteenth century. I submit, that to examine performance-clues closely, is to accept that there are longer histories for perspective studies than is usually granted. It is symptomatic that our successive attempts to 'fix' perspective-studies on the chronological axis usually compel us to place their beginnings further and further back in the past. This should hardly cause a flutter because performing arts are known for their tenacious maintaining of continuities through repeated acts of percolation to or surfacing through unexpected social quarters and cultural strata. Performing perspectives often find their way to new fields of life. Further, urges to perform evince frequent tendency to lie low for long periods only to surface later with an atavistic force. In sum, it is possible to infer existence of perspective studies from a number of unwritten clues. Some of these could be briefly mentioned.

ADAPTATION

In certain periods of cultural history of most of groups with extended traditions, prevailing folk forms are often adapted by practitioners of non-folk media. The process of adaptation logically presupposes close scrutiny of existing array/s of forms to help selecting adaptable features, determining their placement in new setting and employment of finalized combinations to carry across changed content to different audiences. The entire process of adaptation is a proof that a body of people have spent considerable time and energy to analyze, appreciate and assimilate performance-features.

LISTING OF MUSICAL INSTRUMENTS

Non-Musicological works of any given period often provide important evidence of perspective studies. Such works usually draw on a canvass encyclopaedically inclusive and catalogue items, events, procedures as well as suppositions entrenched in minds and day-to-day deeds in the life of the populace. In such works, inventories of musical instruments figure and point to kinds of instrumental sounds accepted by a culture and the music-minded attitude or otherwise of the common man. More notably, these listings serve as a key to our understanding of the prevalent and discernible hierarchy of musical instruments as well as kinds of sounds. Instruments and sounds find place in non-Musicological works by virtue of their success in acquiring cultural circulation independent of their intrinsic musical worth. In addition, it is to be remembered that musical instruments are artifacts as well as objects with symbolic potential. If viewed in a wider perspective, musical instruments certainly function as indicators of societal behavioural patterns not confined to music.

SCHOLASTIC TRADITION AND FOLK FORMS

Folk music exists in a society which enjoys a spectrum of multiple musical categories. The (categorial) musical streams flow simultaneously but one of the streams, namely art music, is necessarily accompanied by a scholastic tradition carefully structured to codify art music as completely as possible. Scholastic traditions are keen on formulating criteria to judge aspects of music which could be examined with recourse to dictionaries, anthologies, manuals, notations, etc. Such Musicological works allude to forms, instruments, regions/areas and groups associated with non-art categories of music. What is deducible is awareness of a larger musical framework as well as values ascribed to musical categories mentioned. Further, because of the inevitable time-lag between performance and its codification in the scholastic tradition, all codified references to performing practices suggest a much earlier vogue of the practices.

Description of Musical Events etc.

Non-Musicological works often carry elaborate, though non-technical, accounts of musical events, performing-objectives, ritualistic commitments, etc. Existence of musical categories could easily be surmised from such descriptions. Non-Musicological narratives also point to prevalent hierarchy of forms, distribution of patronage in a society, etc. A careful perusal of such data usually reveals a highly stratified society struggling to find musico-cultural correlates.

Recognition of Regional Elements

Recognition of musical contributions as 'of/from certain regions' is significant because it stands testimony to a firmly established regional identity. Identification of music after definite areas confirms effective presence of a multi-layered society as also of multiple streams of music. A country like India, combining as it does a subcontinental expanse with linguistic and ethnic diversity, expectably creates a challenging situation when regions are also marked off musically. An acute vision is needed to record diversities existing within a single cultural group—otherwise perceived as one single entity on account of linguistic and geographic affinities.

Advocacy of the Purity-criterion

Finally, existence of perspective studies in music could be assumed if and when advocacy of the criterion of 'purity of music' becomes noticeable. Most of such advocacies are in the form of protests sounded by cultural agencies partial to art music. The cry is—'music is getting distorted, polluted and/or diluted.' Influence of non-art musics on art music and subsequent puritanical objections are to be construed as symptoms of a desire to rank musics, adhere to social stratification and consciously project these and related attitudes. The criteria of purity and authenticity tend to arouse and rally around forces of conservatism. A cry against vulgarization of music can therefore be interpreted as a response to powerful stimuli from non-art musics.

In sum, perspective studies are important because they create conceptual frameworks—both accommodative and elaborate. Without frameworks of such logical rigour, analytical subtlety and extensiveness, it would be well-nigh impossible to make sense of a musically complex situation in its entirety. The names or descriptions under which the studies are carried out should hardly matter. The studies connote attitudes, and all attitudes are observed as well as experienced via musical behaviour of the people concerned. Perspective studies draw attention to the essential multiplicity of music along with its intrinsic relationship with non-musical aspects of culture. They succeed in bringing into focus music and culture as two heterogeneous entities depending on multiple acts of mutual influencing for their respective development. To an extent, cultural musicology so connects culture and musical changes as to postulate a fascinating theory of mutual causation.

4

Researches in Folk Performances

We are all aware that a debate is raging about the Indianness or otherwise of the term 'folk' and yet, certain performances of dance, drama and music in India are almost unhesitatingly and commonly described as 'folk', surely an indication that these certain perform-ances are felt to be qualitatively distinct in their 'impact'. Quite a few individuals, agencies and organizations legitimately hold that expression generally identified as 'folk' is worthy of serious atten-tion and action (including research). This is the reason why a dis-cussion of aims, objectives, relevance, methodology and such other related themes becomes crucial. These concepts and the manner in which folk expression interprets them are 'distinctive' and can-not be assumed to have a universally and easily accepted connota-tion.

Aims are general goals sought to be attained through methodical efforts. Compared to them, *objectives* are less general. They could safely be understood to be the more concrete goals located midway between an initiated activity and attainment of goals identified in its context. *Research* is a diligent and systematic inquiry or investiga-tion into a subject for discovering facts, revising theories or identify-ing applications. The variability of the degree of appropriateness of efforts in relation to needs sought to be satisfied (through the former) is indicated by the crucial concept of *relevance*. Finally, *meth-odology* is the logic of methods directing the entire thinking activity towards clear and coherent intellection. These definitions would of course become more concrete when related to the expression un-der discussion, namely 'folk'. For example, researchers in folk per-forming arts may be expected to carry out complete investigations into a culture with the intention of enumerating, describing, classi-fying, comparing and finally analyzing forms of folk expression. Further, *aims* are also linked to contemporary life, in the sense that they are designed to diminish intensity of the adverse effects of technological and communicational revolutions likely to affect human life through contingent as well as independent operations. These effects could be cumulatively described as disintegration of the societal mind.

Thus stated, aims may appear vague and ambitious. They may even be dubbed as impractical or unrealizable. However, researchers should neither be surprised nor dismayed by the charge. Preambles of all constitutions, the revered Charter of Human Rights, the Ten Commandments and the like also exhibit similar 'vagueness' because it is their function to hold up ideals for the world to see and strive for. In other words, *aims* are universally and purposely set up as eternal challenges. In every case they appear to be almost unattainable ultimates in ideological quests. Even if they appear to be too grand, etc., that is no reason to feel apologetic about them because their being so has a place in the larger scheme of things.

Unlike aims, *research-objectives* are inherently more specific and variable. Objectives therefore change according to the desired results. Care is however taken to ensure that changes are in keeping with the general orientation of the total effort. In other words, no particular orientation governing research-objectives can claim inherent superiority over any other, the sole requirement being agreement of the orientation with objectives in view. Objectives and orientations have to match each other, they should be tuned to each other.

Objectives of researches in folk performances can be twofold. Firstly, they may be directed at collecting data and investigate facts which may not have direct and technical connection with performance-aspect. For example, economic status of performers, their political learnings, housing standards they enjoy, their knowledge of modern banking and their acquaintance with monetary system, etc. can be themes of research of this kind. On the other hand, the second set of objectives is clearly related to performance-aspect. Pre-performance preparations, post-performance procedures of appreciation, etc. would indicate performance-orientation of objectives. It is in this framework that more or less specific and/or variable objectives of research into folk-traditions and the relevance of their orientations can be described as anthropological or grammatical or performing.

An anthropological bias is distinguished by the totality of its viewpoint. This orientation regards folk-expression as one of the strands weaving the fabric of human life.

Grammatical orientation resolves or seeks to resolve into constructional aspects an expression which is already realized or one in the process of being realized. The effort is to deduce answers to questions raised for establishing correctness or otherwise of the expression. Concepts and discussions pertaining to authenticity mostly revolve around grammatical issues with unvarying frequency.

Finally, performing orientation involves study of every expression as an action directed at creating impact on audiences. Though creation of impact is not the sole characteristic of a performance, it is one of its major features.

The three orientations are reasonably, effectively and usefully separable in spite of overlaps inevitable in matters of cultural content. To confuse the three and to adopt an incorrect methodology could only suggest an academic immaturity and scholarly oversight.

At this point it is appropriate to consider the issue of *relevance*. Mutual suitability of objectives and orientations is one instance of relevance. This is a kind of *internal* relevance. Here the appropriateness or otherwise exists *within* the research-field well demarcated by the quartet: researcher, objective, orientation and aims. However, operations of the quartet constitute merely a part of the total community-life. For a research-field demarcated by the quartet mentioned earlier, is it not natural to maintain relationship of relevance with society, which has, in reality, made both the entities possible? This is the *social relevance*, a dimension which has provided much support for a notably agitated view of culture in more recent times.

It is obvious that no blanket statement is possible as the research-quartet weaves a very complex web of relationships. In a kind of phased review of concepts under discussion it however becomes clear that *aims* hold sway in the abstract, rarefied, philosophical atmosphere or level and consequently all research is, by definition, bound to be relevant in its context. As *aims* are highly accommodative, ideological and idealistic, no authentic/serious research can fail to be relevant *vis-à-vis aims*. On account of their ultimate or essential character of *aims*, the entire activity acquires a firmness which steadies, a comprehensiveness which liberalizes and a capacity which engages generations to come. Researchers in folk performance could avoid much anxiety born of the fear of irrelevance if they ensure matching objectives and orientations. On majority of occasions Indian researchers are on target as far aims are concerned but they often overlook to strike balance between objectives and orientations.

Perhaps it would be helpful to restate the argued position on the relevance-issue in terms of two concepts that have engaged modern mind/consciousness—those of social relevance and commitment. It is often suggested that if research is to prove its social relevance, it should be shown to have a capacity for creating better life. In other words, it should form a part of a larger ameliorative programme. However, it must be remembered that betterment of human life or such other 'sloganesque' phrases are, in reality, *aims*. As already explained, *aims* are not be confused with immediate objectives even if the mutual and inherent dependence of the two is not denied. 'Action-oriented research', a phrase which is so fondly and widely employed, is a pleonasm because research is in itself action. In fact, action, by itself is rarely possible, and if possible, too truncated to be useful. Its real and fuller version or *avatara* is the white heat of thought—a result consisting of an intense mental activity firmly concretized. To put it less rhetorically, action-oriented research, so dutifully linked today with social relevance, is in fact, consequent to the objective-orientation correlation already explained. If one is aware of the valid (though often ignored) distinction between pedantic and academic research, it is the latter which attains equilibrium to objectives and orientations. All academic research is relevant and social relevance is one of its unfailing contributions.

The contemporary interest in researching in folk traditions evokes in me a mixed response. It is true that research-programmes in this area are encouraged at all levels—individual, institutional, national as well as international. But it the encouragement given wisely? Perhaps it is time to do some rethinking and allow a realignment of forces. There are indications that this is already happening. For instance, researchers are now equally, if not more, anxious to retrieve as to collect data. The revolutions in communications, varied as well as ongoing, and the leap in harnessing technological resources has enabled us to 'catch and collect' the evanescent in performance. In fact the danger is of facts and information outpacing researchers and their construing, interpreting capacities. Attempts to computerize data or interest in similar processes suggest that the danger has been sensed. However, there is a nagging doubt. Retrieval could only be of something collected and stored systematically. Recourse to advanced technology, etc. can hardly equip researchers to meet the challenge which is of a conceptual nature. Some self-criticism would help in explaining the Indian predicament.

A very striking feature of most Indian research in performing traditions is the tendency to avoid theorization. There is an ease to detect reluctance in raising frameworks on the basis of collected data. This is a serious shortcoming because such frameworks help in determining significance or otherwise of the material. No detail or fact is significant *sui generis*. Facts are in themselves, important, but not significant. Therefore discovering facts cannot automatically be equated with research. It is rather naïve to argue that no theorization is possible unless facts are collected, because fact-finding and conceptualizing are not successive but simultaneous. Further, all concepts are products of at least a minimal theorization. A meaningless collection of facts would be the only possible result unless this is well understood. Conceptual frameworks not only confirm facts but also generate them. No research consists of theory-neutral facts. To overlook this truth is to reduce research to an indiscriminate collection-spree. In their isolation facts may supply information, but they can hardly impart knowledge. Only active theorization can transform a body of facts into knowledge.

I get a feeling that there is a historical reason for the misplaced (and a rather touching) belief in the importance of bare facts. Research in folk-studies in India traces its lineage incorrectly from ethnographic researches. As is known, ethnography is engaged in scientific and detailed descriptions of a particular culture while the task of taking up comparative study of two or more cultures is left to ethnology. It is easy to see that these both approaches adopt a 'total view' model. One of the basic assumptions in this model is that everything is related to everything else and hence to understand any single entity it is essential to collect data on everything. One can guess the reason why the tenet found favour in Indian folk-studies. The pioneers in the first were Germans, the British and a little later, the Americans. They, being sympathetic foreigners, preferred to cast their investigating net very wide out of necessity. Pioneers fare better if they are accommodative than selective and pioneers know this. Hence all details and every fact invited respectful collection for its significance-potential. Facts were avidly collected and diligently explained, i.e. they were paraphrased informatively. Perhaps the tendency to stress facts and the factual may owe its origin to the

event that in 1872 the Census Authority in India initiated anthropological researches. It is also possible that the ethnographical, as distinct from cultural, bias was due to British ruler's motive—to learn
about the country in order to protect the British commercial interests.

However, this is not the whole story. In addition to adopting the
non-selective, total-view model offered by ethno-disciplines, researchers also readily took to the mapping which 'literary' students of folk-
performances were developing. Unfortunately this meant a near-
total lack of awareness of the performing-aspects of the tradition.
Thus literary and/or linguistic explanations/interpretations of place-
names, terms, and symbols dominated the scene. Chronology, etymology, genealogy, imagery-studies, stylistic analysis etc. assumed
an overpowering importance. As a consequence, verbalized expression came to occupy an undeserving centrality—which it continues
to do so even today.

These and such other strategies of research can yield only fringe-
benefits in performing traditions because they miss the core of performance—that qualitative dimension of the co-ordinated, physio-
mental, audience-directed act with non-verbalized, improvisatory and
impact-biased content. The entire content of folklore is customarily
divided into four categories: material culture, oral tradition, performances, customs and superstitions. The first three are actualized
respectively through craftsmanship, verbal performances and non-
verbal enactment. In other words, three-fourth of the total folkloristic content is dependent on non-literary impulses and resources.
Is it not therefore invalid to adopt a literary-linguistic bias?

It is academically unfortunate that the nature of the phenomenon of performance is ignored in the established research—processes in folk performing traditions. Performance needs to be understood as a result of a series of decisions arrived at and carried
out by non-verbalized, action-based, physio-mental events accessible to normal perception. Researches in folk performing expression is likely to remain anemic and bookish, a mere shadow of a
pious intention to research, till adequate attention is paid to performance.

A curious weakness of the total-view-model becomes obvious at
this point. It is as if the model tries to remain value-neutral, presumably because neutrality is essential to maintain scholastic research.
The model therefore remains wary of committing the arch sin of

'imposing our framework on their frameworks'—and thus distorting the vision/experience. In spite of the *prima facie* validity of the position, two questions raise heads. Is the 'just'-looking, observing-stance the cause of a marked indiscriminate collection of data? Secondly, and more importantly, assuming the value-neutral attitude of an outsider (which may be desirable if the researcher, studying an alien culture is himself a representative of a materially superior culture), does the attitude enjoy the same validity and legitimacy for an insider who undertakes to execute a deliberate, temporary and a reversible act of stepping out of his native culture? In other words, do Indians researching into Indian folk expression need to adopt the same conceptual, theoretical and methodological stances as do the non-Indians? Ethno-studies are studies of man through culture and examination of separate/isolated culture-manifestations in the total context of the concerned culture and hence value-neutrality appears to lose ground today as a principle.

In conclusion, it is instructive to note that though more than a score of disciplines are listed as contributory to studies of folk-expression, the three major value-disciplines, namely, aesthetics, ethics and philosophy do not find a place. . . . Time, we recognize lapses and reorganize ourselves.

5

Music and Symbolism

The moment we utter the word music the reference is to the art stage of manifestation. Any discussion of the art-stage is to confront a highly processed reality. This, in itself, removes whole clusters of symbols from the range of the debate. To discuss music is to move away from sound *per se* as also from other sound-related symbols.

In spite of the conceptual priority of articulated sound over its written representation, the former is hardly ever analyzed in terms of musicality. Even seed-symbols such as *aum* have been largely ignored. It seems valid to generalize that oral symbols have not been attended to, aural symbols have been ignored, while auditory symbols are yet awaiting recognition.

Further, discussion of musical symbolism is nearly confined to art music and an added limitation has been to restrict consideration to the feeling-aspect. Where intellectual symbols have received some attention, non-musical fields of perception have been active. In other words, it becomes clear that the total musical reality is in need of a comprehensive statement to determine symbological function in a wider perspective. This position primarily denies us the pleasure of making blanket pronouncements about relationship between music and symbolism. This is because of the existence of five musical categories, namely, primitive, folk, art, devotional and popular—without reference to which it would be unjustifiable to claim validity for any ambitious statements. Each of these categories operates on a separate symbolistic plane and hence poses dissimilar problems. Both music and symbolism are terms needing further differentiation as a precondition to formulation of frameworks so necessary to deliberations in aesthetics, cultural musicology and such other disciplines.

SYMBOLISM AND PERFORMING ARTS

Symbolism operates through symbolic objects, processes and procedures. Two of the numerous etymological connections of the word 'symbolism' throw into relief two of its chief features. In Greek, the related noun and verb respectively mean 'mark' and 'put together'. This, in itself, is sufficient to inspire a somewhat rhetorical question: what is all art but a marking off and a putting together. However, less highly wrought statements on the pervasive significance of symbolism have been axiomatic since long. Art, language, science, religion, history and other specifically human achievements are all stated to be symbolic in their very essence. In other words the pertinence of carrying on the debate of the interrelationship hardly needs to be proved.

As the first step in the debate it is to be noted that music is *one* member of the family of performing arts with dance and drama as the two cognate entities. It is therefore deducible that symbolism manifest in these arts would display some uncommon features *because* of the special characteristics of performing arts as contrasted with other art-families. Against this background some questions can provisionally be put down to ponder over:

From the triumvirate, which art tends to be more symbolic? Why and with that consequences?

What are the functions carried out by symbolism in performing arts?

Is the final significance of performing arts dependent on symbolism? In what measure?

Each of the performing arts merits an independent consideration in view of its separate identity and contribution. However, taking the three as a class, some general remarks can be made.

1. Dance, drama and music enjoy two levels of symbolistic activity: linguistic and non-linguistic.

2. In these arts, symbolistic activity on the two levels takes place alternatively. It is an aesthetic rarity to have symbolistic operations on both levels or planes simultaneously. This is not to suggest that the two symbolizations are mutually exclusive. Employment of symbolism on a single plane at a time merely indicates an optimum utilization of expressive resources that converge on the human aesthetic perceptual faculties.

3. Non-linguistic symbolism, as such, works either through the audio or the video perceptual modes. As is argued later, separation of these channels plays a crucial role in the overall

functioning of symbols.

4. The totality of experiential content of performing arts is further categorized into five, hence, symbological examination also needs to be carried out in all these—if it is to be exhaustive and do justice to music as a phenomenon.

5. Added to the experiential content is the contribution of the fundamental performing dimensions, namely, space and time. Each performance is an instance of dominant temporality or spatiality and this fact influences related symbolization to a very great extent.

6. Symbols are further sub-grouped into personal, cultural and human. This classification emerges as a result of applying the criterion of identifying the source of symbolic potency. However, it should be obvious that other classifications may also prove legitimate and workable depending on the depth and angle of the analysis involved. For instance, emergent/ associational, natural/artificial are other possible classifications. Yet another useful sub-grouping involves expressive/ communicational symbols.

7. A feature common to performing arts is their inherent dependence on audience-contribution. On the other hand symbols and their operations can exist independent of audience-contribution. To that extent symbolistic operations enjoy a fair degree of self-sufficiency.

The septet of general remarks, along with questions raised earlier, prepare background for the proposed symbological examination.

PERFORMANCE: THE PRIME MOVER

At this point one of the questions raised earlier can be partially answered. It was asked whether performing art differ symbolistically because they are performing arts. The answer is in the affirmative and a partial reason is that performance is the prime mover in these arts. As a controlling factor performance consists of a core and its peripherals. In the proposed symbological examination core would naturally get a priority. On this count the pre- and post-performance phases are side-lined. It is the continuous present of performance that should engage our critical attention. The Indian ethos accentuates oral tradition and consequently composing or practising music also partake of the characteristics of performance. Understood in this perspective, music and performance become indivisible partners in most musical ventures.

To come to grips with the problems posed by performance, it is necessary to devote exclusive attention to oral-aural aspects of music. Hence notation, gestures, movements and such other visual and kinesthetic phenomena are to be kept out of consideration. Being an entirely visual symbolization of music, notation can be kept away less guiltily, but that is not the case with gestures etc. They are inherently connected with the act of performance and their exclusion is less excusable. It can only be pleaded that their peripherality alone relegates them to the background but their symbolistic contributions are not thereby denied.

SYMBOLIZATION AND MUSIC-ING

The human urge to symbolize has been variously explained. The most significant explanation traces the urge to the essentially human endeavour of representing rather than presenting. Concepts, relationships and ideational processes—as distinct from objects, events and factualities are found to be basically human concerns and these concerns emerge as symbols while seeking an outlet. To become manifest thus, symbolizing urge must get a suitable medium. Symbolistically suitable medium has four qualities. It is reproducible, divisible it is capable of repeated rearrangements and devoid of fixed, innate meanings of 'dictionary' kind. The element of sound possesses these qualities in abundance and consequently the symbolistic activity has relied on it very heavily. Music-ing, as a predominantly audio, non-linguistic, temporal and acoustic activity is to be examined for its symbolistic achievements against this backdrop, all the while keeping in mind its five-fold categorization.

What are the clues to determine symbolistic operations in music? For want of adequate cross-cultural data no general and universally applicable statement could possibly be made. In addition, is the well-known musical plurality of the country. However, the available ethnological data and musicological positions *do* help in laying down broad guidelines to identify symbolistic operations in music.

(i) Musico-symbolistic activity takes place on three levels—musicological, musico-societal, and musico-psychological. With the usual overlaps and variable operational intensities the triad covers the totality of music.

A very important symbolization of the musicological plane occurs because musical cultures equate given performing practices with definite degrees of excellence. For example, ability to reach very high or low notes, to perform at great speeds, to weave intricate tonal or rhythmic patterns, to produce uncommon vocal/instrumental effects, to synchronize one's own performing moves with unfamiliar musical moulds, to compose or perform within certain numerical formulae, etc. are taken to stand for certain positive, musical qualities. Such equations are not sign-situations because there is no intrinsic connection between these skills and values placed on them. It is also to be remembered that it cannot be assumed that the equations have a universal or cross-cultural validity.

As far as, musico-societal symbolizations are concerned, the operations are displayed through the accepted equivalence between musical objects, practices, processes, etc. on the one hand and non-musical aspects of the material life on the other. For example, the drum-beat languages, the associations between certain events and instruments or between certain occasions and timbres, etc. fall into this category. Once again a clear absence of causal relationship and the uncertainty of cross-cultural existence need to be marked.

Musico-psychological symbolistic activity exhibits a firm acceptance of the relationship existing between musical features and psychological states of performers as well as receivers. The psychological states thus linked to music are not definite, and identifiable emotions but rather diffuse and inclusive mental states. For example, Plato's characterization of modes as valorous, sensuous, etc. or the Indian positions about the *raga-rasa* relationship belong to the third level of musico-psychological activity.

(ii) In addition to operating from three levels, musical symbolism also manifests itself through physical objects, procedures and processes. The manifestations vary in symbolistic intensity and range of affects.

(iii) Existence and operations of musical symbolism expressed through objects, procedures and processes are characterized by three kinds of relationship. Preference or insistence, taboos, and association through coexistence over long periods are the three types.

(iv) It is true that musical symbolism can hardly be deduced through musicological analysis. However, aesthetic preferences, as distinguished from grammatical sanctions, provide an unfailing indication of an already existing musical symbolism. This is so because aesthetic preferences (which are more culture-oriented than is generally granted) are points of maximum vibration of the societal mind. They are the soundings which reveal deeper currents of the collective psychic energy searching for value-supports to hold aloft the entire panoply of human culture. It is symptomatic that traditional aesthetic norms or criteria hardly ever refer to beauty; they refer to psychological states that lie beyond experiences related to sensation. Aesthetic criteria allude to transcendental functions and music is slated to symbolize them under certain conditions.

These four clues are to be used for examining musical categories in order to understand and assess the role of musical symbolism.

PRIMITIVE MUSIC AND SYMBOLISM

Elsewhere, I have argued in favour of making a clear distinction between 'tribal' and 'primitive'. Further, I have suggested that the latter term be restricted to refer to musico-aesthetic criteria and the former to meet ethnological requirements. This specificity of usage would lead to a clearer conceptual mapping which, in turn, would make it possible to detect primitive musical features in music produced by non-tribals. Primitivity, treated as a quality, cuts across extra-musical ethnological categorization of human societies. The possible omnipresence of musical qualities identifiable as primitive underlines the tenuous connections music has with socio-economic and other classifications of human groups. Unfortunately, very little attention has been paid to the presence of primitive musical elements in music made by non-tribal societies and discussion of primitive music has leaned very heavily on ethnographic studies of tribal life. However, this needs to be accepted only as a matter of strategic convenience. There is no conceptual contradiction involved in extending the scope of primitivity and to fall back on descriptions of tribal life and behaviour to explain the nature of primitive in music.

Tribal life is permeated with symbolism and music is no exception. In it, four types of musical symbols are easy to detect: sexual, instrumental, rhythmic and tonal. It is not surprising that almost all symbolistic clues discussed earlier come to notice. Some comments on the quality of symbolism in primitive music are in order:

1. In primitive music literary and linguistic orientation has a minor role to play. In fact, preference for non-linguistic and the non-literary manifestations is so marked that even when pitched at an expressive level, the linguistic and literary moments are deliberately dimmed through employment of other musical means. The reason is that sound *per se* is regarded important and care is taken to keep it to the fore. To that extent linguistic-literary symbolism fails to assume stature and significance.

2. Compared to other musical elements, rhythm and timbre are prominent in their symbolistic use.

3. From the available variety, scraped and struck timbres and percussion as a mode of producing sound are preferred to bring symbolism into action.

4. Primitivity makes music appear uninterrupted and indivisible. A certain formlessness is perceived because there are no firm beginnings or terminations though individual musical units are precisely formed. In other words, the final message is one of circularity and eternity. Straight lines and circles would easily come to mind as the corresponding visual symbols.

5. What does musical primitivity symbolize at the musico-psychological levels? It stands for an undifferentiated state of mind which initiates a process to regain the poise it has lost. The loss of poise in itself indicates disturbance in man's relationship with the external world, inclusive of natural forces. Therefore occasions of joy or sorrow as well as those of natural or supernatural benevolence or hostility inspire symbolistic musical evocation.

FOLK MUSIC AND SYMBOLISM

It is important to remember that folk element in performing arts partakes qualities of primitive as well as art-expression. In fact this is one of the features which endows it with a wider appeal. A related characteristic is the greater role assumed by language and literary quality in folk manifestations. It is deducible that regional character comes into play very strongly. However, examined symbologically, the regional orientation and the linguistic-literary factors impose certain limitations. Consequently, a more restricted symbolism appears in the category.

Folk musical symbolism is mainly melodic, rhythmic-pattern-inclined, instrument-oriented, prosodic and socio-cultural. What does a qualitative examination of the symbolism indicate?

1. Folk musical symbolism is more deliberately employed. Well-defined norms and established social customs developed and preserved by a particular cultural group cumulatively shape it. Compared to it, primitive musical symbolism is more spontaneous. Folk musical symbolism bears marks of intentional construction and persistent cultivation. It follows logically that it is also prone to easier and wider changes in contrast to primitive symbolism which is distinguished by a noticeable constancy.

2. In folk music, structures and presentations exhibit a discernible aesthetic influence. To that extent folk music moves nearer to art music and its symbolism shares features with art musical symbolism discussed earlier. The symbolistic shift towards the aesthetic is detected in the melodic, rhythmic as well as prosodic aspects.

3. Musical symbolism of the musico-societal type operates in folk expression in a very concrete manner. For example, folk performing set and its distribution often reflects the social structure. In this context the important question to raise is: who is allowed to play what and when? Equations between musical and non-musical factors are thus established, investing the former with a capacity to represent the latter. The qualitative shift from the apparently similar correspondence in primitive music is to be noted even though this, by itself, does not mean a movement towards art music.

4. Folk musical symbolism evinces the powerful role of religion and various cults. Rituals, along with language and literature, make their presence felt. A variety of forces ensure that rituals are rigorously carried out, elaborately planned and subtly motivated. This facet comes out very clearly when ritual-con-

trolling functions of melodic and rhythmic frameworks are carefully observed.

5. Folk musical presentations are characterized by a multiplicity of expressive forces which nearly turn them into veritable packages of stimuli. Hence there is a greater need to control and coordinate them. Almost every sense-stimulus is afforded scope and therefore folk musical symbolism becomes apart of a complicated total process of patterning social behaviour in which a number of symbolizing agencies take part. It is perhaps debatable to ascribe symbolistic capacities to all human senses but the multiplicity of senses participating in symbolization cannot be easily questioned. However, what is more problematic is to determine whether all sense-operations are equally perceivable in simultaneous occurrences such as folk presentations. I submit that a firm build-up of associations between musical and non-musical symbolism makes the latter more perceivable and therefore music becomes a controlling agency as well as a symbolistic agent.

6. One feature of folk musical symbolism is particular to it and is not usually associated with art musical symbolism. A fair proportion of its symbolism is likely to be intellectually conceived. The description 'intellectually conceived' means in the present context that the concerned symbolism is deliberately introduced due to philosophical, aesthetic and/or social compulsion. Symbolism of this type is regarded legitimate because its genesis involves symbols which gather more and more strength through association and because they have a wider hinterland. In fact the possibility is that these very symbols might be transformed into emotive symbols with the passage of time. In case the symbols fail to undergo the transformation they continue to operate as symbols of secondary intensity.

At the musico-psychological level what does the folk musical symbolism stands for? The answer is: it symbolizes a differentiated psychological state seeking to channelize the psychic energy of the collective mind. The channelization is deemed necessary because it successfully separates experiential content in more controllable units. This is why folk performances can be received on dimensions normally paired as contrasting—e.g., religious-secular, individual-societal, occasional-cyclical. It is only to be expected that compared to primitive musical symbolism, that of folk musical expression acquires a noticeably demarcated character.

ART MUSIC AND SYMBOLISM

Art music is popularly called 'classical' music. According to established Western usage the term 'classical' refers to identifiable, sophisticated expression traced to definite period in the history of Western art. The nineteenth-century products of English learning took to the term 'classical' instead of the more technical term *shastriya,* i.e., scientific. This may have been the result of the pervasive craving to find and exhibit occidental-oriental correspondence in all walks of life. However, both usages indicate the part of the total musical reality which is more crystallized, firmly segmented and deliberately created than the two musics discussed earlier. Without detracting from its merits it needs to be said that art music is highly artificial. It exemplifies clear motivation, definite aesthetic goals, established music-making processes and a regular dependence on well-formulated grammars. Unless the essentially 'made' character of art music is understood and appreciated, identification of musical symbolism particular to it is hardly possible.

1. It is to be admitted that a large portion of art musical symbolism is indirect. It has come to music via literature and literary theory. Hence it is no surprise that dictionaries of Western music do not accord the status of a full-fledged technical term to 'symbolism'. The term gets a terminological foothold merely on account of some composers and compositions committed to descriptive content of music (e.g., Debussy via Mallarme). In other words art music strongly avers the intrinsic reluctance of music to stand for something else. Music can be made to represent other entities only through the intermediary role of literature. It is in this perspective that positions advocated by Susan Langer and other aestheticians are to be understood. However, their positions fail to distinguish between categories of music. Primitive and folk musics, as has been pointed out, stand for something outside musical expression.

2. It is the induced symbolism of art music which explains the persistent musicological attempts in India to extend the symbolistic connections of art music to other sense-modalities.

In fact the efforts move farther and encompass areas of gemmology, religion, accoutrement etc. The well-known tradition of Ragamala-paintings or that of Raga-dhyana prove the powerful operations of the symbolizing urges to relate music to an extensive array of perception-channels. Of a similar kind is the *raga-ragini* differentiation.

3. Art music is a major instance of total reliance on the oral-aural in order to bring symbolizing processes into action. In this category symbolizing powers are forced into a narrow channel as sound, shorn of non-musical connections, is the focus. This process makes art music eminently non-representational. What is represented by oral or aural tonal symbols is hardly discussed because art music is non-representational. The same feature is however responsible for the variety and density of sound-patterns as opposed to their repetitive and sparse occurrence in primitive and fork music.

4. It stands to reason that art music should (in spite of its largely non-representational character), prove extremely rich in symbolism of the musicological type. This is a dictate of the total framework in which it functions. Due to symbolistic view of physical processes and technical skills involved in music-making, numerous equations are struck between musical qualities and excellences on the one hand and strict adherence to norms, securing definite physical abilities, acquisition of performing repertoire according to accepted procedures, etc. Abundance of musicological symbolism is directly connected with the importance attached to sound-pattern qua sound-pattern. In other words, sound is significant in primitive music because it is sound, while art music holds it in high esteem because it is patterned well. Numerical symbolism in art music is also of musicological import. It is evident in structuring of musical scales, crystallization of musical forms, etc.

5. The patently abstract quality of art music inevitably makes it poorer in musico-societal symbolism. Major channels of symbolization (e.g., rituals) are restricted to the pre- and post-performance-phases in art music. Admittedly, some movements and gestures do occur during performances, but they are peripheral. This same peripherality is noticed in musico-societal symbolism expressed through forehead marks, head gears, positioning and distribution of the performing set.

Popular Music and Symbolism

1. Popular music is a very complex phenomenon and the category owes its existence to musical motivation unanalyzably mixed with the non-musical. The complexity is reflected in music of the category.

2. Popular music, by its very nature, draws on all other categories. The variety of its symbolism is due to these multiple sources, qualitatively so heterogeneous that the derived symbolism is also characterized by a certain incoherence. The symbolism in the category inevitably gives impression of being an assemblage.

3. As a category, popular music is uncommonly bound with contemporary ethos. Hence arises a peculiar feature of its symbolism—it tends to progressively gain in symbolistic power at later periods. The delayed emergence of popular musical items as symbolistic of a particular period from the past is one of its specific qualities logically derived from its intense contemporaneity.

4. On account of its modality and operational agencies involved, popular music throws up items of symbolistic veneer in a short time, though they also become desiccated symbols in an equally short time because the parent music itself gets phased out. However, as explained earlier, possibility of this music enjoying symbolistic ascendancy at a later period cannot be ruled out.

5. At all stages the category depends on the mass media. The symbolism is also conditioned by the state of development of the media. Today, the symbols appear to move towards becoming audio-visual packages—though dominance of the visualizing processes is easily noted.

6

Performance and Peripherals

What is performance? "Performance is a physical manifestation of an intent to make concrete a coordinated, predetermined, psychophysical and action-oriented design. The emerging design directly results from impulses consciously channelling to explore choric, choreographic and histrionic human actions which may or may not be aided by other agencies. The design assumes final shape subsequent to audience-contribution made in accordance with relevant norms established in the concerned cultural group. The original idea of the design frequently undergoes substantial and qualitative changes on account of audience-participation."

What began as an attempt to define nearly ended up as a description. However, it succeeds in highlighting the significance of performance in the Indian context because the descriptions is valid irrespective of the musical category in operation at a given moment of time. And yet, it is not the intention here to discuss the central concept of performance. The movement is eccentric—it directs attention to peripherals of a performance. In the process some crucial questions about the nature of performance as a phenomenon would hopefully be touched upon.

What would constitute a peripheral element *vis-à-vis* performance? What kind of relationship exists between a performance and its peripherals? In what way do the peripherals contribute to the final significance of a performance? To what extent identification of performance-features as 'core' and 'peripheral' is symptomatic of larger, non-artistic and social realities? Having identified peripherals, how can one recognize their role in documentary and archival procedures? These questions need to be considered in some detail.

In general, 'peripheral' means 'surfaced or located in the outer region of vision'. In other words, the peripheral is not entirely unconnected with or unrelated to the core but it is noticeably distanced from it. Peripheral nature thus connotes a relationship of secondary intensity an element enjoys with the core. For example, core of a song is ordinarily provided by voice, tune, text, etc., while the periphery consists of the performer's dress, headgear and such features. If a dance performance is under discussion, dancing spaces and rhythms obviously form the core while colour-combinations or tunes, instruments, etc. constitute peripherals. Though instances can be multiplied, it may be more helpful to identify general principles or criteria of judging peripherality of individual cases.

Major-Minor Bases

Every single performance has one major base of action or activity while other operational bases display either suspended activities or presence in a minor key. However, during the course of any single performance, operational bases may shift with considerable mobility—though at a given time and for a particular segment of a performance-continuum, one single base may remain a major contributor. Non-operational bases continue to be peripheral so long as the performing situation remains unchanged. In general, it is this permanent possibility of potential (and to some extent) unpredictable shifts of operational bases which is the essence of the composite or package character of performances in folk and other categories.

The Tapering Relationships

A very important clue to the core-/peripheral quality of a performance-feature is provided by a kind of tapering exclusiveness of cer-

Diagrams showing pairs of speech, sung sound, dance/movement, dramatic and isolated, etc.

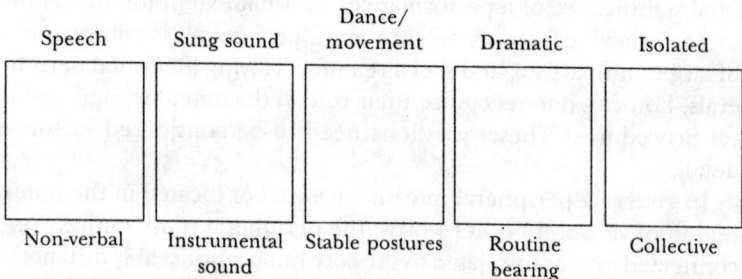

Speech	Sung sound	Dance/ movement	Dramatic	Isolated
Non-verbal	Instrumental sound	Stable postures	Routine bearing	Collective

tain elements. There are five prominent pairs of performance-features which function as bi-polar elements, i.e., if one feature of the pair is in action, the other has a considerably curtailed role. A diagrammatic presentation of the situation would clarify. As would be apparent, twin elements of each pair always remain in notional action though one of each pair would function in so low a key. as to be placed in the experiential field beyond normal perception.

Special Status of the Audio-Video and the Spatial-Temporal

Two entities which belong to a more fundamental strata need to be separately mentioned. The two pairs, space-time and audio-video are present in each performance as chief parameters.

Space-time dimensions and audio-video modalities have a qualitative focus which needs to be independently examined. But they are also characterized by their distinctive way of functioning. They operate in such a way that each 'front', while in action, creates performance-effects normally associated with its polar partner. Thus the entire operation is marked by a process of specific adaptation by polar partners as contrasted with their mutual exclusion. In other words, even if the non-active front is peripheral, it displays a 'virtual' operation (on account of this process of specific adaptation). And yet, there is no mistaking the fact that only one of the fronts carries out the most decisive of the functions. This fascinating capacity of the active base to create performance-effects usually ascribed to its partner is explainable if we follow another trail, chiefly aesthetic in import. In the present context, the virtual quality of experience derived from operations of one of the bases is a clue to its peripheral quality.

Non-aesthetic Orientation

A peripheral performance-feature is generally non-aesthetic in its orientation. In all musical categories identifiable as non-art, decorative, artistic and aesthetic elements are clearly marked by dispensability. The aesthetic, etc. are non-vital components and their absence does not endanger the being, the very existence of the performance. If and when the aesthetic, etc. appears on the scene, it is due to the individual intuition and virtuosity of the performer concerned which are responsible for it. A stylish beginning, a flourish at the end, introduction of attractive mannerisms, deliberate and controlled exaggerations, purposeful but unexpected deviations and such other manifestations are instances of recurring peripherality, especially in the non-art performance.

SUBSTITUTABILITY OF THE PERIPHERAL

Finally, the peripheral quality of a performance feature is also indicated by the degree and ease with which it can be replaced. (This too is more valid in case of non-art performing categories.) Performances in question are found to include sections appended to the main body from time to time and in varying proportions. For example, segments of compositions devoted to salutations to local deities, paeans on the place of performance, praise of the audience, an appeal to patrons are lengthened, shortened, modified or altogether dropped according to the will and requirement of performer. Substitutability or replaceability connotes peripherality.

Under ideal conditions, the general principles enunciated will have to be applied *ab novo* for every performance to identify peripherals with reasonable accuracy. Essentials and peripherals so identified in one context, and on a particular occasion, might exchange their roles on other occasions, and that too at a short notice. The criteria would therefore demand flexible and alert application.

PERIPHERALS AS CONTROLLING AGENTS

To what extent peripherals guide, control or inhibit performance? Making allowances for individual differences some generalizations are possible.

To describe a factor as peripheral obviously excludes its functioning as an inhibiting factor. For example, singer and tight-round-the-neck gown or dancer and obstructive costumes cannot coexist unless other extenuating circumstances such as social norms making it obligatory to wear tight dresses, etc. intervene. In other words, barring non-performing considerations which outweigh performer's preferences, peripherals influence performances by facilitating them as physical act. It has been indicated earlier that non-artistic priorities often govern peripherals, thus adding to the impact of the latter. It would thus be correct to say that the mutual relationship between performance and its peripherals is characterized by a changeable ascendancy.

The manner in which peripherals contribute to the final significance of a performance is to be viewed against this backdrop. The physical facilitation process implemented through peripherals need not engage further attention. This contribution is too concrete to be missed and the principle of changeable ascendancy mentioned earlier recognizes it adequately.

However, a more intangible kind of contribution requires to be explained. More so because, apart from being intangible, it is rarely traceable to a single causal factor or a group of them. All statements about causal relationships between performance-results and peripherals are likely to remain suspect until such times as comprehensive cultural surveys and documentation have made significant advances. On the other hand, no such surveys, etc. can even be thought of unless it is realized that coexistence of performing facts in itself furnishes proof of an hypothesis, if not a theory. Every performance is a non-verbalized hypothesis in action. The intangible contribution of peripherals can generally be described as their 'message'.

A set of major criteria has already been suggested to identify processes, factors or items as peripherals because everything that accompanies a performance cannot be regarded as peripheral. Examined in accordance with these criteria, the non-elite and especially folk performances, exhibit five categories of peripherals. These categories are not only easily perceivable but they also have the capacity to generate messages of their own. Messages of peripherals may add or detract from the overall message conveyed by performance as such. The audiences receive the sum-total of multi-channelled messages from performances.

The five categories of peripherals are to be further sub-grouped into two groups, 'A' and 'B'. Those of group 'A' are discussed here because of their closer ties with performance as a physical reality. The grouping is as shown below:

Group A
1. Positioning and Postures of Performers
2. Headgears and Forehead Marks of Performers
3. Gestures and Movements of Performers

Group B
1. Colour-combinations
2. Decorations and Ornamental Effects

How do the Peripherals Operate?

Prior to a separate discussion of peripherals from Group A, some general remarks about the manner in which peripherals operate would be in order.

It is of extreme importance to note that peripherals usually generate symbolic content of high charge. Symbolism of peripherals is expressed through prescribed and carefully followed rituals. Under normal circumstances, two types of symbolism are simultaneously in action—universal and cultural (i.e., symbolism with the bias of a particular culture). The genesis of symbolism, rationale of its typology and such issues are outside the scope of the present essay. The most relevant symbolic feature to be remembered in the present context is the innate suggestivity of symbols. In fact, the symbolic activity holds power *because* of its ambiguity. To that extent, therefore, peripherals may convey their own message and at the same time, blur the contours of the performance-message, making the latter more potent, in the process.

Working of peripherals also display a discernible independence of affect. The emotive message of peripherals may or may not move in the direction of the overall performance-message. The behaviour of peripherals *vis-à-vis* performance is often governed by the principle of contrast as distinct from that of correspondence. Consequently, peripherals may reinforce or attenuate the performance-message. The simultaneity of non-identical messages conveyed by peripherals and core is bound to compel the auditor-spectator to think and exercise a choice. Further, it is also possible that no single or unambiguous final message is transmitted. The contradictions may remain unresolved—which itself is a state with a disturbing message.

The activated symbolism and operation of the principle of contrasting juxtaposition produce an important side-effect. They combine to create a state of social togetherness because peripherals tend to employ socially binding mores. Societal norms are so formulated that a large number of societal segments are mandatorily involved in a performance via the peripherals. In the process it is ensured that a wider social basis (though non-performing) is secured for the total activity or event. Such an involvement is frequently a pre-performance event, yet implications are unmistakable. The actual performing set may be confined to an occupational caste, etc. but peripherals manage to cast the net wide and wider participation is ensured. Peripherals thus render a service significant in a stratified society such as the Indian.

Contribution of the three peripherals listed in group A is to take place on this background.

Positioning and Postures

During the course of performance, performing set displays a definite pattern in positioning and posturing of performance. In the present context a performing set consists of chief performer/s, accompanist/s and audience. To be a performer, accompanist or an auditor is to assume a definite role with possible extra-musical and cultural implications needing an ethnomusicological explanation. Hence, the first step is to identify roles of the members of the performing set. It is here that the positioning offers major clues.

Position-wise chief performers are identified by their centrality, irrespective of performers linear, curvilinear or circular arrangement. Accompanists are positioned besides and behind chief performers. It is however to be noted that performances relying on drummers as the main controlling agent may be entirely separated from performers. In majority of cases, the 'singing' chief performer occupies the central position in contrast to instrumentalists even when the latter function as chief performers. In this context it is pertinent to note that the Indian musicological hierarchy always accorded a primacy to vocal music over instrumental as well as dance expression.

Positioning of performers in relation to audience is also meaningful. For group expression, the performing line or group faces the audience but often the audience may also be found to surround it. In that event performers trace a circular path—thus two concentric circles are formed.

Postures

In ordinary circumstances three probable and basic body postures are relevant to performance. They are erect, seated and recumbent (which includes both prostrate and supine). These three, or their combinations, can be employed to serve the dual purpose of facilitating performance and conveying additional messages. What is conveyed by the basic postures in themselves? Some general and brief remarks are possible.

The erect posture: At any particular moment of performance the musically relevant performer tends to stand with his feet slightly apart. However, it is to be noted that at the time of climaxes or at the approach of significant communicative moments the performer tends to incline forward. Further, preceding a climatic phase, a crouching movement is also evident. This is specially noted when drummers are in action. Usually, right side and hand are preferred. It is to be surmised that opting for a sinistral usage would indicate symbolic manifestation necessitating an interpretation (unless the performer is left-handed).

Postures are combined with movements during performance and hence it is important to note the way accompanying movements are executed. The more non-elite or non-art the musical category involved, the more the suddenness which characterizes the movement. In some cases, movements border on being jerky though there is no lack of precision. Erect posture, as well as movements that go with it evince remarkably energetic execution and a matching purposefulness. Compared to other possible accompanying movements, the erect posture prefers the walking back and forth movement in the totality of the pattern. Hypothetically, it can be stated that lesser the movement and rigider the maintenance of the erect posture, the narrower is the focus of the communication directed to the recipients.

Sitting posture: Adoption of a sitting posture generally connotes a definite channelling of communication in a performance. A sitting performer faces a deity, patron or an audience. Accompanists face the performer and turn a profile to the audience. The solo element in a performance diminishes in stature to the extent performers and accompanists face each other instead of the audience. Sitting upright is the rule though hunchback posture does not appear to violate propriety.

Recumbent posture: Prostrate or supine postures are hardly conducive to performance. When performers employ these positions, the strongest association is established with the non-human reptilian world. However, if a member of the performing set assumes such a posture during the performance, it indicates a superior, patronizing attitude towards performer/performance. A recumbent auditor also conveys superiority, mostly suggestive of patronage. The only established and dignified recumbent postures are those approximate to the *nirvana* of Buddha and the Sheshashayi posture of Lord Vishnu.

Headgears and Forehead Marks

Between the two, headgears are more peripheral than forehead marks. Peripheral quality of the headgears is easily deducible from the accent on artistry and craftsmanship in their construction. As argued earlier, all artistic qualities are peripheral to the non-elite performing traditions. It has been pertinently pointed out that constructing headgears necessarily involves rising against the force of gravity in order to follow the anatomical body-lines and hence headgears represent a craft. Dr. Ghurye has also stated that unlike in the West, headgears have been considered obligatory in India throughout the course of history.[1]

The manner of wearing headgear forms an important detail. Of the innumerable possible variations of wearing headgears, four need to be mentioned because of their capacity to convey extra-musical messages. Headgears may be worn straight, tilted (sideways), thrust forward or pushed backwards. The four positions carry suggestions broadly of respectful, romantic, combative or insolent attitudes respectively. The basic premise is that a covered head constitutes a norm. The manner, as also the extent of keeping the head uncovered, creates nuance-situations varying in import from culture to culture.

Forehead marks, or *tilak*-s as they are commonly called in India, primarily function as sectarian marks. Headgears and forehead marks together may also indicate performer's caste. It therefore becomes easier to guess the range of social involvement in a particular performance by taking note of the two peripherals.

Gestures and Movements

Perhaps the most complex groups of peripherals comprise of gestures and movements. This is so, firstly, because both have a great deal to contribute to the psycho-physiological aspects of a performance. Secondly, they also have a very significant and considerable role to play in artistic manifestations of mime and acting. Finally, they are a part of the deeper symbolic patterns present in both religious and secular segments of human life. However, alert application of criteria discussed earlier enables one to determine peripherality or otherwise of the gestures and movements in question.

With some simplification it could be stated that movement and gesture are to be distinguished on following counts: (1) Movement may include gesture but not *vice versa*. (2) Movement involves specific limbs while a gesture may not. (3) Movement leads to displacement of specific limbs while a gesture does not. (4) Examined temporally, movements may require longer durations while gestures are normally described as instantaneous. The two however prove problematic in analysis as they occur mostly together.

Before proceeding further with the argument one point needs to be stressed. The gesture-types relevant to the present exposition are not to be confused with those exhaustively described and codified in the Sanskrit texts on dramatics or dance. The vocabulary of gestures systematized in works such as *Abhinayadarpana* by Nandikeshvara cannot be considered while discussing peripheral gestures because the former is unambiguously linked to artistic expression. Gestures employed by artists are a result of a learned, acquired behaviour. Gesture-languages of secret societies, deaf and dumb, tribals or of people who belong to common occupation are instances of gestures that do not remain peripheral.

Against this backdrop what type of gestures are to be considered? Obviously they are not those which facilitate the physical action of performance. Neither are they gestures which are classifiable as demonstrative, emphatic, imitative etc. Even though such gestures find a place in performance, they cannot be characterized as peripheral. There are gestures which are distinct from all these and which play a communicative role in performance, especially of the non-artistic variety. For example, one may mention the oft-encountered hard and abstracted stare, rigidity of facial muscles, jerky body movements, exaggerated throws of hand and feet, grunts, growls, cries, hisses, sighs, exclamations, howls, laughs, or half-laughs etc. interspersed in performance.

Considered in this light, gestures appear to be a psychosomatic manifestation which occur as a part of expressive performance-behaviour. Mainly it alludes to an ecstatic mental state that claims a supra-societal status for the performer. Insofar as it cannot be fitted into accepted classifications, and to the extent it does not refer to any of recognizable emotions of the day-to-day life, such gestures are highly ambiguous. Their ambiguity and the non-verbal claim to supra-societal status is corroborated by the marked preponderance of gestures in non-artistic performances. In fact it is no exaggeration to say that children, women and the socially less privileged classes have a greater recourse to such gestures. Hence, it is not surprising that non-art, especially folk performance, employ these noticeably.

Relatively speaking, art-performances tend to smooth out these. Performances of the popular category on the other hand, take to an accentuated slickness or polish of gestures in presentations, offering in the end a whole battery of artificial gestures. In primitive music alone, there seems to be a overlap with the folk in respect of gestures, but then these are contiguous manifestations and naturally share features.

Do all peripheral categories convey similar messages? At this stage it is difficult to answer the question. However, they appear to be fairly independent of each other in this respect. In fact, as one moves from postures to gestures there is an increase in protest-messages as well as transcendence. The reason seems to lie in the unambiguous and concrete nature of items such as headgear, posture, position, etc. They exemplify firmer connotations and definite applicability in day-to-day life, thus indicating less freedom of expression. In contrast, gestures and nuances and the additional introduction of ambiguity becomes significant. Raptness, rigidity, rapport are pointers to a mentality not encountered in other performing art-categories. The appeal of folk music, both to performer and perceiver, is to be sought in an altered state of consciousness, if one may use the term. From Wundt to Efron and Critchley to Birdwhistle, many authorities have of course dealt with the language of gesture. But analysis of and reference to performing situations are rare. Usually, it is the referential role of movements and gestures which is stressed. On other occasions, performance-facilitating gestures are considered. As indicated earlier, such gestures are not of concern in the present context. Gestures that have engaged us are residual emotive gestures and it is argued that they have a special message of tone and character that distinguishes folk performances from other musical expressions. Compared to messages transmitted by other performance components, those passed on by gestures are ambiguous but more charged. This is a clue to the appeal of folk expression, an appeal which is often disproportionate to its musical worth.

REFERENCE

1. *Indian Costumes*, sec. edn., p. 2.

7
Order in Music

The concept of order is an accommodative concept. It suggests many coherent formulations such as system, organization and design. However, the basic thrust is to indicate a definite, predictable and constructive relationship of components in a particular field of operation or inquiry. Properly understood, the concept can be expected to throw light on both making and receiving of music. At the philosophical level, the concept borders on being an all-embracing thought-mould holding secrets of the entire existence. Nevertheless, to make it more concrete and actually manageable it becomes necessary to bring into play other derived, though, related approaches. For example, in music the two disciplines of musicology and musical aesthetics appear to enhance the workability of the concept. In a wider sense, musicology is equated with any theoretical study of music while the more focused meaning of the term as put to use in musical behaviour defines it as musical grammar of a particular culture. Musical aesthetics represents human attempt operative in musical behaviour of a particular society aimed at systematizing value-concepts pertaining to creation and enjoyment of music. It is proposed to examine the concept of order in the light of these two disciplines.

My observations are confined to Indian music. Firstly, I can hardly claim acquaintance with what is described as world-music. Secondly, contrary to oft-repeated expectations, musics are found to be more culture-specific than imagined. This is so despite the fact that human organism, mechanically speaking, borders on being similar—nearly, identical, world-over. It is no exaggeration to say that there are as many musics as there are cultures. Consequently, the nature of music under discussion would determine the content of the concept of order. Universals in music are not easy to define and the concept of order is no exception.

From the relevant Indian vocabulary some terms appear to cor-

respond well with the import of the term order. They are: *vyavastha,*
parampara, vyuha and *yathakrama*. They are likely to prove good take-
off for discussion with a bias of musicology and musical aesthetics. For
reasons which will become clear as the argument proceeds *yatha-*
krama, vyavastha, parampara and *vyuha* are examined successively.

KRAMA

In reality the term *yathakrama* owes its content to that of *krama* meaning sequence. It is significant to note that as a root, *krama* offers
shades that are different and yet thematically connected. The Sanskrit root means 'to walk, step or to go' as also 'continuity, want of
interruption' 'energy or application' and finally 'development and
increase'.

In other words, the core meaning would be encompassed by 'steps,
gradualism and continuous movement'. Indian music, in preferring
melody to harmony (if not polyphony) as a principle of tonal organization certainly displays the three characteristics. Historical
perspective makes us aware that even in its early, Vedic infancy, the
Indian way of organizing tonal material lay stress on projecting the
minimal melodic units singly (though the musical movement was
characterized by descent).

In addition to the accent on melody, there are other features
making the three meaning-shades more and more concrete. The
enthusiastic allusions to 22 micro-tonal intervals, i.e., *shruti*-s, absence of indigenous keyboard instruments, late arrival of frets on
the scene and use of movable frets would easily occur as instances
of steps, gradualism and continuous movement. The same preferences led to formation of *raga*-s known today as one of the distinctive facets of Indian music. *Raga*-s exhibit principles of *krama* in two
added ways:

Firstly, in the time-*raga* association and the resulting pattern-equa-
tions are established between *raga*-groups and certain diurnal and
nocturnal time-blocks.

A subtler manifestation of the principles is detected in the existence of a certain performing sequence irrespective of whether *raga*-
time norms. Thus *raga*-s which are predominantly elaborated in the
upper half of the octave will not be succeeded by *raga*-s predominantly explored in lower parts of the octave. *Raga*-s, which are essentially slow-moving will be followed by those with faster intrinsic

movement. A similar performing norm is observed in the season-*raga* association. However, this is limited to a very few *raga*-s.

Yet another interesting concept introduces male-female principle in the *raga*-corpus. However, there has been a considerable debate about identifiable and exclusive structural features of *raga-ragini*-s. It is now strongly held that the *raga-ragini* classification, or the extended *raga*-family concept, represents a scholastic move to systematize the ever-growing *raga*-corpus.

There are, of course, other *raga*-classifications and they represent use of varied criteria. The multiplicity of *raga*-s and classificatory systems associated with them provide us with an opportunity to make a smooth transition from *krama* to *vyavastha*, the second aspect of the concept of order under discussion.

Vyavastha is possibly synonymous with system. If *krama* registers an essentially unilinear movement, *vyavastha* includes an additional vertical movement as the principle of classification runs paramount in it. To classify is to group together individual items displaying certain common features. All classifications are matters of convenience. They make complexity and multiplicity more manageable. Groupings and sub-groupings, generative and the generated *raga*-s bring into use the verticality inherent in *vyavastha*.

However, no system is merely a large body of interrelated classifications. A system emerges when classifications, etc. are directed towards and related to larger goals. Indian music sets for itself three goals. They are: development of technical skills, alignment with natural and human cycles of life and attainment of aesthetic significance or excellence, Musicological works, musical instruments, performing and practising procedures, norms of appreciation, etc. have been evolved to meet demands may by the trinity. Even recruitment procedures and the teaching-learning methods reflect these goals. This is how a cohesive system takes shape.

The next concept selected for consideration is *parampara*: a term that can loosely be translated as tradition. It is usual to associate the word with mechanism or process used for transmitting to new entrants the existing musical learning and lore. Indian music is therefore frequently put forward as an illustration of oral tradition. Though this is so, the term can hardly be confined to describe a transmission process alone. In brief it could be stated to have the following features (apart from indicating an uninterrupted succession).

1. Chiefly, it is of two types, scholastic and performing. The former represents grammatical, consolidated, mostly written portions of norms governing musical behaviour while the latter relates to aesthetic, improvised and the performed aspect.

2. It also connotes a way of taking care of forces of change and constancy through the institutions identified as *guru* and *shishya* respectively. Apart from other important features related to actual teaching and learning of music, *parampara* is also causally related to the distinctive musical feature of improvisation.

3. It must be noted that in India the concept of tradition is not confined to music alone and it is also seen to govern other areas of life such as religion, social behaviour, economic transactions, etc. The wide scope of its applications allows patterns of music-making and music-receiving which have a wide spectrum of contributors and listeners.

It is known to ensure strong bonds between certain types of music and classes of music-makers and/or receivers. It is to be remembered that languages, costumes, associated rituals and all such factors find their roles determined by it. Music becomes a major communicator of cultural messages because *parampara* exists to control extra-musical behaviour of music and also to channelize its relationship with other fields of life.

It must be admitted that *vyuha*, the fourth concept has not been mentioned in conventional musicology. However, a near-synonymous concept of *avartana* is of great importance in music.

In particular it brings out a very characteristic features of Indian rhythms generally identified as *tala*-s. As Coomaraswamy and others have pointed out early in the modern era, *tala*-s are not additive. They do not assume their character because of addition of successive units to the existing for improvement in quality. The concept of *avartana* makes Indian rhythms circular. It is to be appreciated that initially *tala*-s come into existence because more and more beats are subjected to arrangements, and stresses are variously distributed. However, the next step is to impose an arbitrary yet an aesthetically determined generative pattern (consisting of smaller, beat-formulated patterns) on the already formulated beat-circle. This generative pattern of *tala* is realized because of the circularity mentioned. If one examines musical performance in detail, the return of *mukhda* etc. would emphasize the importance of reiteration in Indian music and reiteration is but another name of *avartana*. The role of repetition and variation in Indian music is both characteristic and distinguishing.

Conclusion

(a) As in any developed system of music, Indian music borrows or assimilates principles of its order from nature, other arts and non-musical areas of life. In doing so music goes beyond itself and all its definitions prove to be strategies of blurring boundaries.

(b) Musical order in the Indian context would actually mean a hard look at the non-art categories of music, namely, primitive, folk, devotional and popular.

(c) Indian concept of musical order insists on a balance between a collective expression of tradition and individual innovative capabilities.

(d) More importantly, there always is a recognized provision for deviation from standards laid down. Standardization is never confused with regimentation.

(e) One may say that musical order in the Indian context is, in the final analysis *not* an aesthetic order. The ideal is to create an order which is cognate with the supreme cosmic order. To include the unattainable in all discussions of concepts, etc., even at lower levels, is notable.

8

Music and Religion

I must drop a hint at the outset: entities in the title are not placed alphabetically. Their order indicates a bias. I intend to approach the theme from a musician's angle. The final aim is to examine nature and function of music in human society. To study the nature of a phenomenon in reality amounts to study its uses. Society in Indian uses music in relation to religion. In other words the musical bias of the present discussion is due to a musical necessity. In India music and religion converge at so many points that investigation into music invariably means a hard look at religion.

ABUNDANCE OF MUSIC-S AND RELIGIONS

Of the ten recognized world-religions at least seven are well-entrenched in India. Hindu, Buddha, Jain, Islam, Christian, Zoroaster, and Sikh would easily come to mind. Besides some are of the opinion that two modern constructs, namely Marxism and Humanism need also to be added to the list. The number of religions in the country would become astronomical if one adds sects and cults to the major streams. The listed religions have also been with us over a long period.

The impressive chronological placement of individual religions is notably matched by a wide geographical distribution. Each region in the country can either boast of being a birth-place of a religious leader, having a seat of a major propagator located in it, or founding a centre of an intense religious activity within its bounds. The liberal scattering of innumerable sacred places dotting the country can also be appreciated in the same context.

A similar abundance is enjoyed by music on chronological and spatial dimensions. India has at least four traditions of art musics, more than seventeen reasonably identified folk musics, primitive music chiefly associated with 25 million tribals, popular music with cinematic music as its chief component and devotional music in almost each region. The magnificent edifice of music in India is thus created by these five categories, all of which have been highly productive. It is therefore easy to see that music and religion are well-matched in matters of chronological durability, geographical distribution and in their general coverage of life-areas. They are co-extensive as well as co-orbital.

OF MUTUAL LEANINGS

The assumption of music-religion interrelationship is supported by interesting data from an unusual source.

Indian musicians frequently display pronounced religious leanings as revealed in diverse details:

- Musicians repeatedly allude to close connections between *Parabrahma* (the Supreme Being) and *Nadabrahma* (Supreme Being realized through the medium of sound).

- The general repertoire of art musicians, on examination, is reveals a considerable number of compositions in praise of deities.

- There have been numerous instances of *sadhu*-s, *faqir*-s who were musicians as also of musicians who became near-*sadhu*-s. From Swami Haridas to Pt. Vishnu Digambar and from Amir Khusro to Sindhi Khan there is a long line of musicians exemplifying musician-religion bound. It is on record that Ramakrishna Paramahamsa used to sing in an incomparably sweet voice till the time he was known as Gadai. In the very recent past Sant Gulabrao (Gulab Gundoji Mohod, 1881–1914) wrote quite technically on theory of music with some passion. Also to his credit are compositions based on folk tunes. The ratio of musicians taking to renunciation proves specifically instructive because instances of dancers, actors exercising similar options are almost unknown.

This is of course not to claim that musicians are more religious. The suggestion is that they are religiously inclined to a great extent. Religiosity in itself has probably some inner connection with the very nature of music as also with the vocation.

DEVOTIONAL MUSIC AND SANT KAVI-S

In India music-religion relationship is fascinatingly brought out by the category known as Devotional music (i.e., *bhakti-sangeet* which, as the name suggests, is primarily shaped by followers of Bhakti cults. These cults are distinctive manifestation of Indian religious spirit and has brought into being a very rich musical tradition. Bhakti cults, functioning as a major cultural force, reigned supreme—particularly during the period from AD 800 to 1600. They influenced all performing arts and succeeded in putting forth impressive array of genres. The category of music, created and developed by saints, assumes significance because of many factors.

Firstly, devotional music encouraged an extensive use of regional languages and evolved forms in tune with their respective tempers. Secondly, the category helped in identifying and developing centres that offered wide and continued cultural patronage. Consequently, there emerged alternatives to princely courts and court-towns—a situation clearly conducing to artistic growth. Thirdly, the category concentrated on musical as well as thematic content which enjoyed a pan-Indian appeal and comprehension.

Further, it maintained eclectic links with other musical categories. It is to be noted that all saint-poets were constantly on the move and their peregrinations established real and functioning channels of communication all over the country. Finally, saint-poets contributed greatly towards perfecting oral modes of communication already in existence. The category constitutes one massive body of evidence of intrinsic and mutual dependence of music and religion.

MUSICALITY AND RELIGIOSITY: THE PSYCHOLOGICAL ASPECT

However, the strongest evidence of an existing relationship can hardly be accepted in lieu of an explanation. A change in the direction of our inquiry is therefore warranted.

In my opinion, it is useful to go back to religiosity for the explanation sought for. I suggest that we recognize religiosity to be a basic drive. It is *not* an instinct and displays a social content. The drive is responsible for a very special psychological experience often described as religious. Hence, religion is to be defined as an institution brought into being to increase the probability and scope, and enhance the quality, of this experience. On the other side of the posited musico-religious psychological experience is musicality—an equally fundamental human inclination. Musicality is also social and culture-based in content as well as in spread. Specific acoustic experiences, emerging out of this basic musicality need to be nurtured to ensure greater probability, predictability, scope and quality. A totality of this structure is raised in societies and it is subsequently identified as music.

It would be clear that I am suggesting a commonality of psychological experience between two human manifestations, namely religiosity and musicality. I am arguing that the special affinity between them is traceable to a common psychological matrix. The approach would obviously raise types of questions different than those raised, for instance, by historical, philosophical, ethnological inquiries. It is helpful to note some of these questions at this juncture.

The Seven Questions . . .

1. For every religion three main components could be identified: behaviour (*achara*), thought-system (*vichara*) and verbalized expression (*ucchara*), though, during the course of their historical evolution individual religions may have emphasized different components at various time-points. In the totality of such movements, one may ask: how has music fared?
2. In its own way, and for its own reasons, music too undergoes changes. How are such changes reflected in the musico-religious coexistence?
3. World religions naturally have their own respective philosophicological positions on music. To what extent these positions affect the more fundamental music-religion relationship postulated earlier?
4. Even those religions which give music a stern eye seem to have failed in stamping out music from their follower's lives. How to explain the theoretical/theological prohibition and the actual latitude music enjoys?
5. Theologians as well as musicologists have claimed a kind of universality for their respective subject-matters. The former have argued that in religion there is content which transcends barriers raised by place-time-language-circumstances and the like. A similar claim is also made in favour of music. Do these

claims throw any light on the relationship under consideration?

6. Religious and musical abundance in the country adds to the
complexity. Many geographical segments have many religions
with their respective devotional musics. Yet, they subscribe
to the same system of art music. What could be the explanation and the consequences?

7. A valid generalization is possible about conflicts between religions and secular kinds of music because religious authorities often tend to regard certain musical type, etc. as a taboo.
Yet history records instances of how authorities opted to reverse their earlier stand to include the once prohibited music in the accepted corpus. What are the compulsions behind such a strategy? Has the conflict been less intense in
India? Why?

These questions should be borne in mind before we proceed.
Care should also be taken that neither theologist nor musicologist
overwhelms and yet the orientation remains musical.

CHARACTERISTICS OF RELIGIOSITY

Religiosity provides a framework that enables human beings to
receive religious experience. What elements contribute to the setting up of the framework? Elements so identified may also
be described as religious dimensions. Religiosity is thus a cumulative result of characteristics noted. These characteristics are discussed as common to one of the basic tendencies of the human
mind. It is therefore unnecessary to discuss them with reference to
any particular religion. Different religions would possibly give varying weightages to these. Yet, it is difficult to imagine a religion with
out any of them or a religion with one of them entirely absent.

Rituality

Rituality is the first important dimension. It is expressed through
a systematic employment and exploration of movement, utterance
and symbols in the daily, ceremonial or celebratory actions. Rituality
is chiefly aimed at realizing the desired combination, coordination
and use of psycho-physical powers. Usually sanctions offered by divine dispensation, authority of religious texts, dictates of *guru*-s, categorization of certain actions as sins or otherwise are invoked to

place the importance of ritual actions beyond doubt. In this context it is meaningful that even in day-to-day life we tend to evoke authority of protocol, family-customs, civic decorum, laws or administrative rules to legitimize ritualities practised. All rituality has psychological and non-psychological aspects. The two are brought together to formulate prescriptions and prohibitions related to ritual acts in question. It is observed that the non-psychological, i.e., the physical aspect is accentuated by many practitioners—may be because it is easier in application.

Mythology

Individuals or societies are normally inclined to create myths around personalities, incidents or processes perceived to be vital. Further, they try to dovetail the myths with religious as well as secular behaviour-patterns. The Puranic tales or women's stories known as *kahani*-s would easily come to mind in India. These are never confined to gods, goddesses and deities. In reality, they are created even in the ordinary course of life. Musical behaviour is not an exception. Such myths are usually found to generate certain moulds. For example, the following patterns recur:

1. Meeting the *guru* through coincidence, chance or accident, etc.
2. Effectiveness of the guru's blessings or curses.
3. Importance of perseverance in the learning-procedures known as *sadhana.*
4. Sudden improvement in voice-quality or other musical merits (especially as a result of blessings or nostrums given by *sadhu*-s, etc.).
5. A person's success *after* performing for a certain deity, on certain occasions, at certain places, etc.

Myths continue to be created around these and similar motifs and they are widely propagated. In the context of the present discussion, two notable factors emerge:

Firstly, in both the mythologies, similar structures appear and secondly, both have similar purposes. I suggest that this is so because of the psychological affinities between the two.

The Intellectual Aspect

Religiosity has an intellectual aspect expressed chiefly through theology, philosophy and ethics. This part of the religious content, which is comparatively speaking easier to verbalize and therefore to crystallize in scholastic tomes, forms the core of scholastic tradition. Consequently, the intellectual aspect is responsible for the emergence of pedants, priests and such other institutions. To some extent this aspect is distanced from faith and other psychological dispositions. It is also possible to comprehend the aspect irrespective of one's own cultural contexts. A reference was made earlier to the claims of universality of the religious content. In a number of cases, the universality is detected in the intellectual aspect. This aspect is bound to be more obscure if not abstract. Hence grammarians of religion, philosophers and thinkers emphasize three different concerns of the intellectual aspects under discussion namely, theology, philosophy and ethics. One thing seems to be clear. This feature, which is beyond the reach of lay persons creates positions of authority or command. It therefore succeeds in creating a feeling of awe and inevitably leads to stronger claims to universal validity.

Institutionalization

Institutionalization is a feature of great sociological importance. Priests, theologians and others function as authorities to regulate behaviour-patterns associated with their respective offices. Secondly, the gadi-s, temple-seats, math-s, etc., emerge as centres of administration in control of large segments of cultural behaviour. Regulations, rules, procedures come into existence to ensure efficient discharge of religious duties. A hierarchy of offices comes into existence and operates as a mechanism.

It turns out that institutionalization exists in musical behaviour too. The entire oral tradition, in its wider sense, stands testimony to the fact, guru-s, gharana-s; concepts such as huzurg, khalifa are some other instances. Barsi-s and other occasions of music-making are also to be remembered. Of equal importance are the mechanisms which offer patronage to the making, preservation and propagation of music.

THE EMOTIONAL EXPERIENCE

The significance of the emotional component in religious experience can hardly be overstated. It has been very often maintained that ritualism, meditation, recitation, guru's guidance, etc. are collectively and severally aimed at emotional experience. Students of the Indian *sant*-literature would be well acquainted with the repeated and spirited remonstrances against the value attached to ritualism, pedantry, knowledge as contrasted with the emotional experience. It is interesting to note that persons considered to be saintly or recognized for their attainment of an elevated status are rarely questioned in respect of their 'knowledge' of religion, but those recognized for their intellectual grasp of religious matters are invariably asked whether they had revelation or some such emotional experience. In other words, the priority of emotional experience over the intellectual is accepted readily. It must be added that Universality is also claimed about it. Thus a capacity to transcend boundaries of language, region, times (and those set up by religions themselves) is ascribed to both intellectual and emotional aspects.

In musical behaviour, a concept corresponding to religious emotional experience is *dard*—literally meaning pain or affliction. The same concept is also expressed by the word *baat* meaning verbal expressiveness. Musical behaviour also distinguishes between learned, knowledgeable persons, craftsmen, artists, etc. It is to be marked that artists are often distinguished by their ability to evoke an emotional response. Universality of musical experience has been repeatedly posited on the basis of emotional aspect. Whether in case of religion or music—the emotional experience, it is claimed, remains accessible even to a lay, average person provided he has the required faith and a keen desire.

REVELATION

Revelation is a phenomenon closely linked to the emotional aspect. Its main characteristic is the immediacy of experience it refers to. It is argued that there is an omnipotent principle—beyond *guru*, deity, *avatara*, etc. and to communicate or become one with the principle *without* mediation is to have revelation. As an experience, it may be irrespective of one own culture or religion, etc. but it is highly individual. The revelatory mode indicates establishment of direct relationship between the Supreme principle and an individual. In Indian tradition the *ashta satvika bhava*-s are often mentioned as the accompanying or necessary features of the state. Various *siddhi*-s (supernatural powers) attain by a person who had revelations are also mentioned with approval, admiration and awe.

From musical behaviour a parallel concept is *rang*. Once again one comes across a list of familiar features:

1. *Rang* is distinct from experience affordable by learning, or from emotions expressed directly through a piece of music.
2. It is not predictable and one can never be sure of its presence.
3. Symptomatically, it is often said that to create *rang* with any amount of certainty is to attain a *siddhi*.
4. Though category-wise, categorical and theoretical statements are hard to come by, the oft-repeated description of *rang* avers that it is created when music, and the artist making music, become one.
5. Finally, it is argued that if *rang* is present, nothing else matters. In the sense, grammatical irregularities, aesthetic incapacities or presentational deficiencies, etc. are all pushed aside to make way for an overwhelming, all-embracing impact which *rang* connotes.

Rang as an experience does not seem to be confined to any culture or musical system and its claim to universality can be easily understood.

REVELATION AND *RANG*

Perhaps the most important feature common to both revelation and *rang* is that they can hardly be verbalized. The inadequacy of the conventional linguistic resources is felt so intensely that an abundant use of paradox, mystic imagery, synesthetic references become a rule. Not only that the linguistic communication is used unconventionally, but a recourse is made to the non-linguistic, with or without the linguistic encoding. Gestures of hands, eyes, *mudra*-s, symbolic objects, touch-procedures, etc. play an important role. In other words all these constitute an evidence that revelation/*rang* cannot be verbalized. It needs to be noted that in spite of their nonverbalization, gestures, etc. have a content. Their respective messages are conveyed unerringly. It is as if an unwritten science is in existence. The mode is pressed into service *not* because non-verbalization *cannot* do something but because non-verbalization *can* achieve something otherwise deemed impossible.

RELIGION: FOUR PHASES

Different religions acquire their respective structures through gradual development of various characteristics of religiosity noted so far. One may classify religions according to weightages enjoyed by these features. Some of the characteristics may have their sub-divisions and consequently an elaborate system of classification may emerge. Further, some characteristics may be regarded as more evolved, progressive or developed and a kind of developmental sequence of religions may be put forward, an application of the evolutionary principle being implicit. However, the fascinating exercise may not be relevant to the present undertaking. In India four phases or stages of religiosity have been identified as *yatu* (magic), *yajna* (sacrifice), *moortipooja* (idol-worship) and *bhakti-marga* (devotional cults). In these four phases different features of religiosity expectably exist in diverse combinations. How can music, associated with the four phases could be the same? The potency or input expected from music in each case would be different and this would be reflected in the kind of music used. These correlations can be noted briefly.

When religiosity is in the magic-state an undefined and undefinable supernatural power provides bases for beliefs of the members of the group or society. The said power manifests itself as good/evil, benevolent/malevolent etc. During this phase similarity, coexistence and analogy are the functioning foundation of the interrelationship posited between human and non-human components. The sacrifice-phase feature elemental Nature as benevolent/malevolent powers. It is held that propitiation of natural elements ensures unobstructed functioning of agents which generate, support and multiply forces of life. A stage is soon reached when the pantheon increases in size and variety. Deities emerge and they are expected to fulfil wishes and desires of the collective. The next step is taken with the deities leading to establishment of iconic traditions. Once an idol has occupied a cultural niche, its being treated as a human being is hardly surprising. Thus deities become personalities with physical and psychological details falling into their places. Idol-worship however seems to be optional during the devotional phase. The main feature is the associated psychological attitude. The devotee and the support of his devotion enter into an individual/personal relationship. However, in the final analysis, the chief factor is that a comprehensive emotion of love replaces the awe of the untamed, unnamed and the unknown of the magic-state, the ambivalence felt for the power exerted by supernatural forces in the sacrifice-state and the proprietary mechanical regard felt for the deity in the idol-worship state.

This, in brief, is the background for examining music-religiosity relationship.

MUSIC AND THE FOUR PHASES

The next logical step of examining relationship of music with each individual phase is not easy because on both sides there are a great number of variables. For example, religiosity would demand attention to the intellectual aspect, aims of the followers, the power/force of the propitiated deity and the object/target of the devotion. Equally important would be the contemporaneous literary or musical circumstances. In every respect the legendary Indian abundance and variety merely adds to the complexity of the situation.

Both religion and music are communicative processes. A very special feature of all communicative processes is the mutual influencing of the multiple active agents—and these active agents can hardly be studied separately even if analytically it is deemed convenient.

The supreme power, recognized to be so in the magic-state of religiosity is, to a great extent, a generalized power broadly perceived as either good or bad. Further discrimination or analysis is nearly impossible. At this stage musicality emerges as a conglomeration of sounds. This musically has certain characteristic features:

- (i) A very restricted linguistic field surrounds the sounds included.
- (ii) The sounds lack resonance which, however, is not to be confused with loudness.
- (iii) They are inclined towards monotony.
- (iv) The musicality under discussion encourages repetition.
- (v) Extremely low and high pitches find favour.
- (vi) A-tonal, membranophonic and idiophonic are the major sources, in case musical instruments are employed.

Manifestations with these features are bound to be considered musically inferior.

Compared to the magic-state, religiosity in the sacrifice-state is obviously better directed because natural elements are venerated as the 'supreme forces'. Not only is it possible to describe them in great detail, but they are able to arouse a sense of awe and inspire a poetic response as well. For want of a better word, one may say that a feeling for 'beauty' comes into play more openly and consciously. In addition, the act of sacrifice itself becomes a complex procedure. Participants are numerous, language-use is better ordered, symbolism is employed in a major way. Finally, considerable physical movement takes place and it is to be conducted. How does this situation affect music?

(a) A larger number of sounds are employed and they exhibit it more variety than in the phase discussed earlier.

(b) The linguistic material is organized more consciously and with more deliberation.

(c) Musical embellishment and rhythmic expressiveness are in greater proportion.

(d) Recitation comes to the forefront. This is of great significance because recitation is unique in giving scope to both solo and the choral modalities.

(e) In general, artistry as well as craftsmanship have roles to play.

(f) Chordophones, aerophones and chiefly tonal instruments become major music-makers. Music carves out a place for itself as a cumulative effect.

(g) Finally, specialist performers emerge as dominant groups or even castes.

Idol-worship and Music

This phase provides a comprehensive support for all kinds of abstract notions. Icons facilitate human efforts to move beyond verbal descriptions. Vivid recording of events, and in fact narration of stories, acquires prominence. Festivities, celebrations, theatric-dramatic presentations, worship and other ritualistic acts—carried out singly or collectively—find a place. To say the least, conditions are created which are generally performance-conducive. Consequently, following musical features are marked:

- Music is to put a variety of uses and hence it throws up a greater collection of forms and genres.

- Instruments with richer tonal colours come into a greater circulation.

- Diverse poetic meters are employed—accentuating in the process, a natural evolution of different rhythms born of a varied grouping of linguistic units.

- Poetic quality is held in high esteem as an expressive avenue explored with or without the accompanying music.
- It is no exaggeration to say that in this phase rhythms become *real* patterns because, in addition to being mere temporal patterns they tend to become *tala-s* which function as generative frameworks.
- Introduction of dance ceases to surprise.
- Finally, music is made to achieve an *impact* as distinct from treating it to be a mere accessory, atmospheric agent, etc.

DEVOTIONAL AND IDOL-WORSHIP PHASES

It may appear that there is a certain overlap of beliefs, between devotional and idol-worship phases. A subtle difference is however to be noted.

In devotional cults the deity-devotee relationship is one of love and hence it is prone to accommodate more secular themes, items and procedures. Devotional music is able to maintain close ties with the ordinary life of the people because it accepts the secular as a legitimate component of life. On close examination it occurs that worship, idol-worship and devotion are behaviours that cannot be treated as identical. To worship, with an idol as a support for attainment of a specific mental state would merely indicate an onset of the devotional phase. The more accommodative stance of the devotional can be easily understood if its components and the associated, physical supports are taken into consideration. And yet, it is to be admitted that the dividing line between worship-based belief and the one usually described as 'devotional' is thin. Occasions for performance, instrumentation, use of meters, roles allotted to individuals and groups, scope allowed to dance and such other items lead to an inference that (apart from dance-orientation), music-s for the idol-worship and devotional phases similar in their *rang*.

Some reasons can be noted. Firstly, the distinction being chiefly logical and philosophical, can hardly be reflected in music. Secondly, it must be realized that after a point, music would develop and follow its own logic and dynamics. This invariably entails formation of certain conventions which, in turn, are perceived as rules. The moment one talks of rules and the criteria derived thereof, a bridge is built to the category of art music. The reason why this should happen at all is to be explored later. At this juncture is enough to note that there is a great similarity between worship-music and devotional music.

We began by referring to the characteristics of religiosity and followed up with a brief discussion of its phases. These phases were associated with matching kinds of musicality. Before proceeding further it would be helpful to mention specific forms related to each of the phases in the Indian context. Thus during the magic-phase *mantra*-s constitute the chief musical expression. In the sacrificial phase, *richa* (hymn) provide the musical channel. The worship-phase features composition-types known as *stotra, arati*-s while devotional phase produced *keertana, bhajan*, etc. A scrutiny of these forms reveals that:

   (a) Devotional music, as a category is richer in musical values.
   (b) In the Indian context, devotional music also impresses by its affinity to art music. The reasons for this special affinity is a subject of a separate discussion. However, the fundamental questions about music-religion relationship can now be posed.

WHY MUSIC?

It is unmistakable that irrespective of the operative phase and the dominant characteristics—'religious music' (also known as sacred music) appears inevitably on the scene. Why?

In my opinion it does so because of an urge to move away from: prose, intellectualism, consciousness of the mundane and an enveloping egoism. Music facilitates this pervasive movement away. All religions, and those bound by them, state that their final aim is to obtain a 'release'. It is clear that devotional category of music manages to balance musicality and religiosity and yet one has to remember that the category represents only a part of the total religious music in India. Therefore it is necessary that features common to religious music in a wider sense be noted before proceeding further.

It is valid to say that an average human being seeks help of religion so that:

   (a) He is able to remain in the society and yet retains some freedom from societal obligations.
   (b) He succeeds partially or entirely in reaching the core of human personality.
   (c) Nearer home, he liberates himself from his own ego to find

the real 'I'—at least occasionally. In other words the quest is
for the *alaukika,* i.e., that which is not of this world.

SACRED DEMANDS, MUSICAL RESPONSES AND THE RELIGIO-MUSICAL CONSEQUENCES

Religiosity, in general, makes four demands on account of this fundamental call of the 'other world' and as a consequence, four musical features become relevant. The combined operation produces
four musico-religious characteristics conducive to both music and
religion. The causal linkage would become from the following:
    (1) Sacred Demands, (2) Musical Response, (3) The religio-mu-
sical consequences
1. ● To move away from prose.
   ● To move away from intellection.
   ● To seek release from obcessive involvement with the mun-
     dane.
   ● To cut across egocentricity.
2. ● Explorations of tempo and rhythms.
   ● Use of mood-oriented sound-production.
   ● Exploitation of pitch-variations.
   ● Coordination of levels of providing accompaniment to mu-
     sic.
3. ● Evolution of musico-poetic forms.
   ● Evocation of emotional experience.
   ● Reliance on abundant and varied rituality.
   ● Enjoyment of a felicitous anonymity derived from col-
     lectivity.
    It is obvious that some explanations would prove useful.

MOVEMENT AWAY FROM PROSE

In order to comprehend and realize the 'other world' it is essential
to diminish the drag of the mundane. As is normally experienced,
the daily behaviour and especially its communicational segments,
function through language. Further, this language-use relies on the
prose mode to the maximum for this purpose. It is therefore natural, inevitable and legitimate for those in search of the 'other world'
to try to loosen the hold of the prose-modality. However, release
from the prose-mode can hardly be achieved merely by demolish-

ing prose-structures. Release from prose has to result in establishment of a new order and that is verse. To achieve the transformation it becomes necessary to process prose. A very firm step in this direction is to *disturb* the routine prose—deliberately, moderately and in measured manner (to ensure keeping the new mode under control). In this context some special characteristics of the quotidian prose can be remembered usefully:

- On most occasions the daily prose falls short in definite pitch-patterns. In fact, it can be described as intentionally atonal.
- It also keeps away from strict periodicity. Further, the temporal patterns it uses are the least predictable.
- Routine prose is wanting in aural/auditory appeal. The criterion of sweetness of sound is hardly brought into play.

It is clear that moving away from any one of these features in isolation will not suffice to create verse. To deviate from all the three is therefore essential if verse is to emerge. Periodicity leads to *laya*, cyclical and controlled processing of *laya* leads to *tala* and hence religious music depends on mediation of music to escape from the prose-grip. The search for the transcendent (on the periphery of which verse moves) is aided through a deliberate deviation. Music is so inherently temporal that it is natural to turn to it if we seek to alter the texture of the 'prosaic' temporality.

THE *ARDHA-TALA-S*

Before taking up the next theme a minor point needs to be noted. Sacred music, compared to art or popular category of musics, has the limited aim of reaching the stage of versification and hence the elaborate temporal manipulation displayed in art music etc. is not attempted. For example, evolution of variety of *tala*-s as well as composition-types, and strategies of spelling out rhythmic ideas are not deemed necessary to construct verse-patterns and their exploitation is not attempted in sacred music. In comparison with the *tala*-s used in art music, those circulating in sacred music can aptly be described as *ardha-tala*-s. To an extent the category of devotional music is an exception to this observation, but that would need a separate discussion. *Ardha-tala*-s can easily be defined as those *tala*-like, temporal arrangements or frameworks with comprehensible, short cycles and simple rhythmic patterns. The *ardha-tala*-s employ tempi which even a musical layman would catch easily. The tempi are such that it would be difficult to miss the rhythm in spite of one's attempts. Even if one manages to do so, it is possible to catch up with it almost immediately—such is the pace. Perhaps these features of the *ardha-tala*-s have a direct relationship with the human biological rhythms. May be, rhythms maintaining a certain kind of relationship with the pulse-rate/heart-beats/breathing, etc. prove *naturally* comprehensible irrespective of musical training or exposure of listeners. It is imperative that rhythms employed remain accessible in view of the collectivity of sacred music. These rhythms, tonal moulds, etc. will prove obstructive if and when they demand special training or learning. There is no place for a high degree of musical specialization in sacred music and the accent is on an easy follow-up, collectivity and boldness of structures.

CHECKMATE TO INTELLECTION

A progressively diminishing stature of intellection as a strategy of comprehending the ultimate reality, is the next important feature. It becomes clear that sooner or later religiosity is inclined to accept the supreme role of intuition. In fact, a number of religious thinkers regard it to be a sign of progress if an individualized (as contrasted with an institutionalized) philosophy of religion finds preference. However, a subtle distinction needs to be made. Even an individualized religion can follow its course while adhering to intellection. In contrast, the kind of religiosity, which works through sacred music, seek to cut across intellection. The anti-intellection stance is expressed through the primacy accorded to concepts such as self-surrender, faith and *guru*. What is implied is an evocation of non-rational human powers. The state is aptly described by the term *bhava*. If *vicara*, i.e., intellection connotes analysis, *bhava* directs us to an undoubting, unhesitant and all-pervasive spirit of acceptance. I submit that intellection prefers prose because of its inherent analytical quality and unilinearity. Consequently, the utterance replete with *bhava* becomes possible only if, and when, prose is left behind. The intrinsic connection between the non-rational and religiosity checks actions allowed to intellection—this being a by-product of preferences shown to verse-modality over prose. The question to be tackled now is to see why and how emotionality makes music inevitable or mandatory.

MUSIC FOR MOOD

It will not be an exaggeration to say that we are engaged in giving unceasing responses to the environment. Physical as well as psychological responses are registered in many ways. Religious experience, or its cognates, pose problems because they do not consist of specific emotional responses with identifiable meanings. They indicate a kind of mood marked by an inclusiveness. A noteworthy ambiguity characterizes them. Any ambiguity or (for that matter) any simultaneity of multiple messages questions the very validity and unilinearity of definite messages. It is therefore argued that just as significance is less precise and therefore more suggestive as well as evocative than meaning, mood is more ambiguous, accommodative and evocative than feeling. This is where musicality and religiosity bring to notice their mutual and intrinsic relationship. There are occasions in human life when ambiguity does not deserve to be censured. To make such situations concrete it is imperative to identify means of expression (from among the available modes of communication) with the required strengths. Hence, the mutual dependence of religiosity and musicality. The precision, unilinearity and the limited experiential range of intellection can be countered adequately by the multiple-meaning, multi-centered and immensely suggestive moods. Music and religion therefore hold one another to be cognates.

WHY RITUALITY?

Rituality is another vital precondition for the desired movement away from the mundane. Varied and abundant rituals are pressed into service to facilitate disengagement from the mundane. Paradoxical as it may sound; a great number of religions and cults emerged with banishment of rituality on their agenda and yet ritualism has successfully held its sway over the centuries—even in religions which scoffed at it. This is inevitable because rituals, though rightly criticized for many reasons, need to be understood a little differently in order to appreciate their important role. For this purpose rituals can be defined as a ceremonious, regulated, sequential adherence to psycho-physiological actions and procedures formulated and laid down by authorities (individual, as well as institutional). Rituals are conceived and developed because of the urge to

reach the otherwise inaccessible levels of the human (and sometimes non-human) 'minds' and to seek to direct them. Appearance,
continuation, preponderance and dominance of rituals can be understood if they are assessed as positive aspects of an action-plan.
Once firmly established rituals are often thrown away spiritedly but
merely to replace them by a new or a modified set because the human psychological make-up needs rituals as a precondition for a
balanced development. If, and when, we feel that references to and
contexts of, the quotidian life are infrustuous—we long for a special atmosphere or an ambience, a psycho-physical adjustment and
evolution of a suitable mechanism to achieve the release—which
rituality often does.

During execution of rituals the chief musical features which
match the intricate processes are the controlled, definite and perceivable tonal rises and falls. A literal monotone can hardly coexist
with emotional expression and experience—a fact borne out even
by our day-to-day behaviour. However, the changing tonal levels of
the daily life lack in variety, control and definiteness. A deliberate,
controlled use of tone levels carries intimations of the art world.
For example, their presence makes dialogues and speeches dramatic as well as effective. Further, the tonal variations, appearing in
company of rhythms and tala-s without linguistic meaning, are
bound to lead to music. Instruments are therefore employed to
ensure patterning and positive relationship with rhythms/tala-s
when tonal levels are explored in sacred music. Melodic and rhythmic aspects of music are thus brought into guarantee a well-directed exploration of the psycho-physical activities in rituals. It can
easily be seen that as the dimension of sound, human voice and
language permeate our day-to-day life it may not be possible to cut
loose from them unless their usage is radically altered.

MASKING SENSIBILITIES

In my opinion a small detail related to manifestation of sacred music and execution of rituals merits a mention.

The two major motives of ritualistic behaviour are:
1. Release of personality from its adherence to the mundane
   world.
2. Creation of a psycho-physical framework essential to receive
   a kind of ethereal experience.

The premise is this: If sensory and outward movements are controlled, it becomes possible to direct the inward movement. It would therefore be seen that rituals are employed to mask the windows to the world (i.e., sensory organs operating in the daily life). They are, as if, tuned to receive different kind of inputs. This is the reason why formulation of rituals is keen on symbolistic use of colours, shapes, tastes, smells and sounds. The underlying intention is to ensure channellization of the otherwise unceasing wanderings of the mind. It is therefore interesting to note that sounds of conches and bells, tala-s, mridang, fragrances of sandalwood, dhoop, the use of reds, yellows and the blues, closure of eyes and the insistence of loud recitation, etc. occur as very common ritualistic features. These ritual-components have a propensity to mask if not obliterate other related stimuli. The main aim is obviously to intensify a particular emotional state which is culturally, and perhaps biologically, linked with specific items and processes affecting sensory experience. Rituals act as mechanisms to boost or mask experience—though selectively.

COLLECTIVITY AND EGO-CENTRICISM

It is time to examine how collectivity cuts across egocentricity, and what role music plays in this deliberate dissociation.

Our ego-centered attitude and behaviour in the day-to-day life hardly needs any proof. Occasions when we do *not* consider ourselves to be centre of the universe are extremely rare. Culture is expected to replace this narrow 'I' with a comprehensive 'self'. Artists also have similar aims—whatever their area of specialization may be. One may say that, if a person reaches beyond the self but restricts his work to specific fields of knowledge, he is likely to become a thinker while those reaching still further can aspire to be philosophers.

Whatever that be, if one is to succeed in traversing the distance from Ego to the Self, the first requirement is to accept that, in the final analysis, it is the communality and not personality which is paramount. Irrespective of their stated philosophies, majority of religions operate on the premise that societies and not their individual components are the matter. Whether in utterance, thinking or behaviour, the premise rules supreme. It is very often pointed out that the use of compulsion (if not coercion) to regulate/correct individual inclinations/habit-structures is debatable. However the argument can merely be taken as a statement of an ideal. The existing realities point the other way. Pressures exerted by the community seem to bear fruit and the fact is recognized by sacred music.

THE MUSICAL COMMUNALITY

Any occasion of natural music-making, i.e., music which does not fall in the category of art music, sports a special feature: its nature is such that a minimum, predetermined and perceivable impact is achieved even when music-makers are not methodically trained and specifically skilled. In addition, this music-making can be undertaken individually as well as collectively. In a collective manifestation there are obvious limits on individual. The individual is, in other words, brought under discipline. Communality in music-making lays great store by principles of balance and coordination. Both these are impossible to realize if each person does not think of 'others'. To think of a performing set in which soloists, accompanists, etc. are differentiated is to install communality in place of individuality. Communality in sacred music allows a role to every component though roles may vary in duration, strength of projection and such other items. Performing arts obviously facilitate movement out of, and away from, the Ego, the *aham*.

The discussion so far would have made it clear that music-religion relationship is intricate because of the commonality of certain characteristics. The relationship is qualitatively different and ranges much beyond territorial coexistence, temporal association and preferences of the followers. The special interrelationship emerges because human nature needs it—irrespective of religion, cult, language and related music-systems. This is the reason why no religious system could effectively outlaw music and perhaps never intended to do so. Was it the personal disposition of the chief protagonists of respective religions that had something to do with the taboos? Buddha's speaking voice is reported to have been remarkable but there are no matching references to his singing prowess. (Veer Savarkar's remarks, that the course of history would have been different if Buddha was a musician—are interesting though anecdotal.) However, the Buddhist universities were famed for music-education they imparted. Probably the Mahayana Buddhism proved more accommodative. The story of Islam is not different. In India, the Muslim participation in the entire musical life is of unparalleled complexity and richness. However, this is not as relevant in the present context as the Sufi love for music.

It is on this background that I put forward the following conclusions in brief:

1. All religions aim at the supranatural. In fact, the core of religious content is supranatural. Its existence is hardly denied even though it is often described as indefinable and undescribable.

2. Unmediated experience of the religious supranatural is described as revelation. It is admitted to be obtainable by and comprehensible to a select few even though it is mentioned as the ultimate desirable for all human beings.

3. The select few who have attained the stage of revelation seem to single out two agents helpful for the non-selected majority to receive experiences kindred to the revelatory. The agents are: medicinal drugs and music. With the aid of these two the *sadhaka*-s are to loosen ties and tensions of the quotidian world to enter the Path. It need not be stressed that drugs and their use is not to be treated as recourse to narcotic addiction. The experiences created by them are not necessarily easy to attain nor are they entirely and unexceptionally pleasurable. By all accounts to feel disintegration of one's own 'normal' personality can hardly be owned as pleasant.

4. The sacred use of music is to use music as a means. As a consequence, musically inferior efforts can be accommodated. On the other hand, there is the equally cool use of religion by musicians. Musicians crave for *rang* which corresponds to the supranatural and hence they press into service religiosity in its varied manifestations along with addictions.

5. Ambiguity and such other features of revelation, as well as *rang* are detected in the sentiment of love. Thus takes place the logical apotheosis of love in music and religion. Madhura-bhakti, Tantra, Sufi-ways, etc. can be remembered in this context. They all harp on love as a special kind of relationship between man and woman.

9

Myth and Music in India

I must begin with a question or questions which, I admit, have been tackled by better minds. I must raise and answer these questions because they function as assumptions for my handling of the problem: the interrelationship of myth and music in India. The questions are: what is the nature and function of myth and language as also of their interrelationship? I have in fact an uneasy feeling that examination of myth-music interrelationship actually involves *inter alia*, references to religion, ritual, symbol, magic, performance, dreams, memory, thinking, and logic. Music-myth relationship is poised *between* positions on a number of issues—not amenable to discursive thought with equal facility.

WHY LANGUAGE?

Creative human minds 'feel' elements pregnant with possibilities of excellence. In a manner of speaking, they are felt as if 'floating' in the chaos. Overcoming many intervening obstacles the human mind finally arrives at a point when it feels the necessity of 'naming' these felt elements. The mind, in other words, subjects them to the processes of language. The exercise has two main aims: to separate the excellent elements from the rest and to gain control over them. This initial separation is also a primary attempt in creation and the naming is destined to usher in magic and science—the two basic ways of controlling and shaping universes, within and without. Because of the identifiable cores of the elements, 'nouns' come into existence. Nouns refer us to the permanent content of the named entities. However, the fact of change, dynamism, impermanency of entities is soon noticed and 'verbs', are brought into being. They never fail to draw our attention to mutable and developing aspects of the named. However, nouns and verbs i.e., the identified phenomena and their characteristic flux-condition—are also blessed with a qualitative dimension. Consequently, nouns and verbs invoke into existence, adjectives and adverbs respectively. It is easy to understand that, because of these linguistic operations, the original Reality or State gets analyzed into units—thereby diminishing the degree of their inherent mutual bondage. At this point enters the literary sensibility with metaphor as its chief allay. The two combine to reestablish lost interrelationships—though on a higher plane. Thus begins the career of the linguistic-literary spiral.

WHY MYTH?

Alongside with the pre-language struggle described earlier, carried on to identify and separate Reality, in order to understand and control—there is yet another activity which is trying to grapple with the integrated experience as a whole. This is where the invariably multi-sensory imagery, in its abundance and richness, engages the Creative mind. The imagery has a world of its own—intense, organized on non-logical principles and distinguished by a marked capacity to generate more and more patterns of diverse experiences. Of special interest is the fact that these patterns may or may not bear a clear impress of their genesis. Their original source may be camouflaged—consciously or unconsciously, individually or collectively, in one historical period or the other. This is the mythic world, a cognate of the world created by language. The language-world, made of nouns, verbs, adjectives and adverbs, etc., is intended to isolate, analyze and regroup perceived units in order to expand and systematize the field or range of human perception. On the other hand, the mythic world is intended to help in combining, or holding together the intrinsically related diverse phenomena and thus to bring into being unusual perceptual fields as also to activate some of them. The mythic mind has synesthesia, the non-verbals and a continuous dialectic relationship with language as main strategies to help it achieve its rather nebulous but real tasks. Rituals are known to acquire a special place in the mythic operations. The intensity of mental operations, the intricate as well as the delicate sensory coordination necessary and finally, the fundamental nature of the issues at stake—makes advent of religiosity (quality of being permeated with the spirit of religion) inevitable at this phase. Yet, the same psychological set may turn out secular rituals at certain stages of human cultural development, a fact that can hardly be overstressed.

WHY MUSIC?

On the backdrop of the observations it is easy to anticipate the next question: Why music?

Firstly, music is and was destined to complete the story which began with the origin of Speech. It is common knowledge that Speech has been the first celebrated communicative act—of God and Man alike. What does speech achieve? On the one hand it distinguishes Man from other living beings—a setting apart essential to create Ego in Man as contrasted with the Self. Secondly, it is through the agency of Speech that Man expresses and conveys individual emotions instead of generally pro or contra moods/attitudes. Existence, awareness and communication of individual emotions are essential to create and enrich the life of mind. Unless individual emotions are formulated and brought out—life would remain at the level of biologically induced behaviour alone.

And yet, it must be realized that Speech also segments the emotional life of the humans into classified and artificially stabilized emotive states—an act that runs against the inherent continuity of the human psychological life. This is where music steps in—to ensure continuity of emotional life, expression of non-classifiable emotions and to carve out an independent niche for human beings on the biological continuum of sentient beings. Where speech breaks off, music takes off. Sound, circumscribed in Speech, finds its liberation in music.

More importantly, music lifts up the entire world of artistic expression on a plane where it becomes a metaphor of metaphors. Metaphor is a perception of similarities which heightens the related behaviour. Music is a further abstraction of the metaphorical perception designed to liberate perceptual clusters into a wider range of experiences or their memories. Music cuts-off representational bases, and hence, becomes disturbingly suggestive. Ambiguity is its power. Therefore it is not surprising that music has closer connections with the mythic world than with the linguistic-literary. There are of course kinds of music and all of them are not equally distant from language. But such deviations change the quality of experience, demanding a different perspective.

MY APPROACH

I am a performer-academician and hence it would be natural if my approach keeps performance at the centre. Creation-reception-teaching-learning, performance and other phases of musical behaviour should therefore be kept in mind while examining music-myth interrelationship in India. In other words, my approach is likely to be more aesthetico-cultural than historical-textual. Musicology, music-history, philosophy, religion-studies, meta-physics, anthropology and such other disciplines may come on the scene but to contribute to a kind of performance-study of music. It is necessary to make this point because the usual academic approach seems to move from the scholastic to the performing tradition.

There is, I feel, a strong reason for advocating this, rather unacademic, approach. Myths widely evoke basic responses diametrically opposed: they are either regarded to be 'true' or 'false'—to use the common, bald way of putting it. In other words, validity and relevance of myths are always questioned. Other approaches described broadly as rationalistic, romantic, comparative, folkloristic, functional, structuralist, etc. may explain the musical mythos but will they justify its continued existence and relevance? After all, a performing art such as music lives in a present continuous tense, and arguments claiming relevance of non-musical factors would have to establish a link with performance both as phenomenon and tradition. The performance-orientation of my approach is expected to prove conducive in establishing linkage between myth and music.

Towards this end I have kept my ears glued to the current and/or reported music-behaviour in the Indian society. Music-literature is of course noticed but, considering the comprehensive oral tradition in India, weightage is given to performance-practice-even in its non-verbalized forms. I have followed this procedure because of my belief that it is difficult to continue a lie, a falsehood in any performing tradition. In the final analysis performances are shaped by beliefs successfully translated into action and *not* so much by notions intellectually held or conceived. From amongst the performing trinity, namely dance, drama and music, music seems to be more directly indicative of internalized beliefs—perhaps because of its chiefly non-representational character.

The linking of the criterion of continued relevance in the performing tradition should, ideally speaking, result into a perspective which bestows additional cultural validity on musical practices and structures. Nothing strengthens performing arts more than their essential continuity. It is their continuity which consolidates past, validates present and ensures future for performing arts. No amount of documentation, preservation or (a passive) dissemination of cultural values is likely to help unless accompanied by an active, circulating presence of things and truths we believe in. If we hold myths valuable they need to be circulating realities. Only then they can be expected to contribute to the quality of our life.

MYTHS AND THE MUSICAL CATEGORIES

One of the major grounds for claiming legitimacy for myths and the mythical mode of apprehending reality (for that is what it is)—is their inherent comprehensiveness. Universality attributed to myth enables it to transcend boundaries set by time as well as place. In relation to music in India, it then becomes imperative that five categories of musical expression and experience are taken into consideration. A kind of academic narrowness of vision unfortunately seems to confine music-related thinking and theorizing to art music alone. This is hardly justifiable. Musical reality in India is a totality of five categories of music namely, primitive, folk, devotional, art and popular. Myths and mythology related to Indian music would have to ensure reference to the categorial pentad. It is obviously not an easy task and yet any laxity in this respect is bound to sabotage the soundness of theoretical structures propounded, as well as the action-plans associated, with them. As the musical categories are qualitative, the associated myths and mythology are also expected to give a matching response. It would be instructive to mark, for example, how and to what extent primitive and art-myths and music-s differ. It would also be revealing to examine how the mythic and musical contents correspond or contrast. Myths are, to an extent, regarded active shapers of national destinies and people's psyches. Myths would therefore be rightfully expected to control the quality and content of music. An understanding of myth-music relationship, in sum, would function as an agent of creativity—a role too important to be ignored.

There is another socio-cultural dimension to the situation. Cultural thinkers as early as Plato argued about effects of music on society, i.e., human mind, and sounded an alert, to have the right kind of music to ensure proper mentality of denizens. Under the circumstances, music-myth combination could be taken as a potent tool of social engineering.

To anticipate a little, examination of a mythic categorial pentad may reject assumptions of cultural equality. It may bring out developmental distinctions between societies, or sub-cultures within them, and mirror realities uglier than imagined. They may prove too medicinal for our collective comfort (and hence may prove helpful in the final analysis).

MYTH-TYPES AND MUSICAL MYTHS

With the declared intent of performance-orientation and the priority of reference accorded to current traditions of performance, the easiest thing to do would be to put forward the generally accepted myth-types and indicate myths in circulation and subsumed by them. The following myth-types, it is agreed, can be regarded basic:

1. Myths of Origin and Creation
2. Myths of Eschatology and Destruction
3. Myths of Culture-heroes and Soteriological Myths
4. Messianic and Millenarian Myths
5. Myths of Time and Eternity
6. Myths of Providence and Destiny
7. Myths of Rebirth and Renewal
8. Myths of Memory and Forgetting
9. Myths of High Beings and Celestial Gods
10. Myths Concerning Founders
11. Myths of Kings and Ascetics
12. Myths of Transformation

The plan should therefore be to select one myth each for the myth-types and discuss it.

THE ORIGIN AND CREATION

In the making of music, importance of the Element or Principle of Sound can hardly be overemphasized. The group of myths pertaining to origin and creation of *nada* (a term which can be roughly translated as sound for the time being) become relevant.

However, it is essential to distinguish between origin and creation. Origin is primordial and creation is subsequent to it. Yet, Creation does not follow automatically from the origin. Believers attribute Origin to God. Others will have to assume some supra-human agency functioning as the originator. Creation on the other hand is attributable to human beings. Thus two separate mythic structures need to be considered in the present context, respectively about the origin and creation of *nada*.

It can be safely stated that, by the twelfth century, Yoga, Tantra, Ayurveda, musicology, philosophy, religious thought, grammar, etc. had succeeded in formulating their respective contributions towards answering the two issues noted.

Yoga, Tantra, etc. regard the human body to be a micro-universe directly reflecting the macro-universe outside. These disciplines advocate working over the body in such a way as to achieve the final unity of the individual self with the Supreme Being. To facilitate processing of the body, a system of creating psychic centres in it, at definite place, etc. is laid down. Each of these centres is called *chakra* (wheel), with spokes, etc. or *padma* (lotus) with definite number of petals, colour, etc. Each *chakra* is given, as associated, a geometrical pattern, sound vibration, element, colour, presiding deity or animal symbol. The point is that a complete mythos of symbols, sensory roles, assigned gods, procedures for developing/controlling the centres is evolved. This is the psycho-physical, universal-individual, outer-inner background on which we have to understand the *nada*-myths in India.

According to Indian musical mythos, *nada*, the primordial sound, is called *anahata*, i.e., 'unstruck'. The term almost serves us a warning against attempting an acoustical, antiological explanation of the myth. The *anahata nada* owes its origin to awakening of the slumbering psychic energy located at the *adharachakra* in the human body. This 'foundational wheel' is situated between the anus and the genitals. The location is also alternatively described as sacrococeygeal plexus. The energy thus aroused, moves swiftly towards the topmost psychic wheel called *sahasrara* or *sahasrapatra chakra* (the thousand-petal/spoke lotus/wheel) i.e., the point identified as *brahmarandhra* (lit. aperture of the upper cerebrum). In its upward movement, the energy touches on wheels located at the intervening positions such as: *svadhishthana* (at the root of the genitals), *manipur* (at the navel), *anahata* (at the heart), *vishuddhi* (at the throat-larynx junction), *lalana* (back of the neck), *ajna* (between the two eye-brows), *manas* (higher than the eye-brows), *soma* (higher than the *manas*-position). Technical literature on the subject makes it clear that *lalana, manas* and *soma* are not regarded very important and thus the number of *chakra*-s to be considered in our examination comes to seven—a fact musically significant.

Anahata nada, we are told, becomes manifest or expressed on account of two actions of the dormant energy now aroused: upward movement directed at the *brahmarandhra,* and the enroute touching of six important psychic centres or wheels (in addition to some minor ones). It is important to note that the *kundalini* power is to return to its base after having reached the top-point. In fact the entire practice of Kundalini yoga (as the *anahata nada* practice is known) is directed towards involution of psychic energies to the primal source. It consists of reverting an outward flow of energies through introversion. The stress is on an 'unnatural' going back to subtler elements from their grosser manifestations. The movement up is also held to be unnatural. The procedures and techniques of body-control in yoga, etc. reflect the view. Many of them are aptly called *ulti sadhana* (reverse practice). The *anahata* is so fundamental that it pervades the entire universe. Its existence and operations, being on the first mythic plane of Origin, are primordial and pre-language. Perception of this *nada* is a privilege or yogin-s. For all practical purposes, *anahata nada,* in spite of the detailed exposition in the scholastic tradition, would have possibly remained outside the musical mythos if the tradition had not taken the step of linking it to the other variety of *nada* namely, the *ahata* (the struck sound), which is directly involved in music-making. To anticipate a little, the seven psychic centres regarded important for the production of *anahata nada* were also linked to the seven musical notes of the *ahata* kind. The yogic tradition of the *anahata nada* which dealt with the Origin of sound on the first mythic plane, was thus directly related to the *ahata nada* dealing with the creation of sound on the second mythic plane.

AHATA NADA—CREATION OF SOUND

How is sound produced in the human body? The process is described thus:

'Desirous of speech, the differentiated (and therefore differentiating) Self (*Atman*) impels the mind which activates the element of bodily fire. This fire, in its turn, stimulates the vital force of breath stationed around the root of the navel. Gradually rising upwards, it manifests *nada* (successively) in the navel, the heart, the throat, the cerebrum and the cavity of the mouth as it passes through them.'

The tradition then goes on to elaborate on the kinds of *ahata nada* produced from each of the five locations indicated. Thus navel, heart, throat, cerebrum and mouth-cavity are respectively described as agents producing extremely subtle, subtle, loud, not-so-loud, and artificial sounds.

The term *nada* is semantically explained as follows, 'they know that the syllable *na* represents the vital breath and *da* represents fire; thus being produced by interaction of the vital breath and fire, it is called *nada*.' As has been already pointed out, mythic processes are subjected to language which is bound to analyze the phenomenon to its minimal units. The use of semantic and grammatical etymologies is symptomatic.

Finally, a technical feature of the *ahata nada* related to actual performance of music, is its basic threefold division into *mandra* (low), *madhya* (medium) and *tara* (high) combined with their respective placements in the heart, throat and head. We are also told that each variety is in a pitch doubly high than the previous.

ANAHATA, AHATA AND THE PRAYUKTA NADA

Anahata and the *ahata nada* mythos were the first two levels of the Indian mythopoeic (i.e., myth-making) mind, engaged musically. The third and final level is logically the actual practices/procedures followed by music-makers. At this level the two preceding levels find themselves enjoying a kind of translated or a transformed existence. As has already been explained, music-making, being man-made, is to be described as creation and not origin. Corollary to the earlier discussion brings us to focus on the act of 'beginning' the intended music. How can we describe it and what does the act signify? In this context, the following observations, confined to the beginning of the act of music-making, would be instructive:

1. Relativity of pitch being one of the foundations of Indian music-making today, a performer is at liberty to choose any pitch-level as his or her fundamental. Having decided on it, however, automatically determines the fifth and the octave intervals. Moreover, these two are regarded immovable, i.e., they can neither be flattened or augmented.

2. Determination of one's own fundamental becomes doubly important because of the principle of tonality, adopted by a large body of Indian music, at least from the fourteenth cen-

tury onwards. The principle replaced the *murchhana*-system prevalent earlier. The adoption of tonality had two important consequences:

(a) It made possible, the derivation of all the desired intervals—from within the range of one octave.

(b) Modulation of keys became an exotic practice, while returning to the fundamental after every musical excursion, became a distinguishing feature.

3. A performer's chosen fundamental—the veritable foundation of his music-making—is established by a continuous intonation of a supportive tonal cluster usually called drone. It is provided through instruments specially designed for the purpose or by specific applications of other relatively multipurpose instruments.

4. Drone normally constitutes fundamental, fifth and octave (higher or lower) notes employed in different combinations. Usually, drone is produced by chordophonic or aerophonic instruments. The drone unmistakably produces an unforgettable effect of successive and effective pulses of concentration and diffusion of tonal energy. (Finally, it leads to an experience of circularity as well as merger.)

5. Performer's music-making can usefully be described as an act of repeated establishment of relationships with the drone. His alternation between identity and contrariety with the drone creates a larger, atmospheric rhythm of tension-resolution.

6. The drone steps in by breaking a pre-existing silence—and the Creation of music begins. The end of music is also effected by re-entering into the drone and a silence, which being post-music, is however qualitatively different.

7. Finally, what is the stated purpose of the *prayukta* (performed) *nada* as also its parents? A succinct answer is provided in the tradition. The *anahata* is for liberation of the soul, *ahata* is for enjoyment and the *prayukta* for entertainment. And yet, they are linked efforts in an endeavour directed at a common end.

I submit that the way an Indian performer *begins* his performance is an act in need of interpretation. His 'beginning' means at least two things:

1. A metaphor-aided shift is effected in the operational levels

or channels of the three *nada*-s. The action is an ideational adaptation of the *nada*-producing psycho-physical apparatus that has been brought to a critical state in the *anahata*-plane. The adaptation is necessary as the apparatus is to be made suitable for operations at the secondary mythic plane of the *ahata nada*. It has been pointed out earlier how carefully the tradition has constructed correspondences between the two levels—these correspondences as set up—certainly prove conducive to creation. From the *anahata*-systematization only four *chakra*-s are singled out to favour music. Of these four (namely, *anahata, vishuddhi, lalana,* and *sahasrara*), only two are regarded major—thereby the lower level of the *ahata*-operations is indicated. It is through metaphorical insight that musicians are able to exploit similarities existing between the *anahata* and *ahata nada*-s. Equating part with the whole (on the basis of existing similarities) for gaining control over it, through accesses to the part, is a known and major magical strategy. Its use in music-making should not come as a surprise.

2. Much of the non-verbal behaviour of musicians who are about to begin operations, suggests a mental state full of ritualistic signals. For example, he tries to keep the body rigidly still, closes/half-closes eyes or stares in vacant spaces, executes repetitive but arresting patterns of hand-movements, employs expressive finger-movements and generally uses noticeable gestures of eye-brows, facial muscles, etc. What is most remarkable is, of course, the overall charged behaviour of the performer about to launch himself off into performance. The intensity of his total demeanour, his more or less successful concentration of energies, the air of authority he carries, etc. communicate an essentially ritualistic fervour. It would not be incorrect to say that such acts bear out the truth of the proposition that myth is essentially an enactment of a ritual. The act of beginning, i.e., the *ahata nada*, to make music is an act of creation. Creation-myth is an enactment of rituals inherently bound with the *anahata nada,* i.e., the origin of sound.

I think sufficient ground has been covered to establish links between two mythic planes and the actual contemporary musical behaviour related to a very critical phase—the phase which marks off

musicians and creative acts from non-musicians and ordinary events.
I may venture to add that some of the points made during the discussions may prove valid in music-making situations initiated by non-
Indians. To that extent, universality of myths and their trans-cul-
tural relevance would be emphasized.

CREATION-MYTHS: INSTRUMENTS

It is desirable, and (fortunately) easy, to provide an additional dimension to the discussion of creation-myths *because* there are many
myths about creating musical instruments which form an inevitable
as well as important component of human music-making. Some
myths are briefly recorded here.

1. *Pataha*-s
Sage Swati went to a pond to fetch water on a very cloudy day.
During heavy rains, the rain drops, striking on the big, medium and
small-sized lotus-leaves, produced different and pleasing sounds. Re-
taining memory of these sounds, and contemplating about them,
Swati sought help from Vishvakarma (the cosmic engineer) and
made different drums to successfully reproduce the sounds.

2. *Ravanahattha*
Ravana, the king of demons was doing penance to please Lord
Shiva. He went so far as to cut off and offer nine of his ten heads,
one by one, in fire, to please Shankara—but in vain. Noting the
sweetness of the sounds emanating from bamboos rustled by winds,
Ravana decided to employ music as a propitiating device. He produced music (as on a string of a lute), by tearing out flesh from the
part of his arm above wrist and by stretching the sinews as required.

Thus was created *ravanahattha*, a chordophone current in many
parts of India, as an instrument in the folk category.

3. *Dhondro Banam*
An old couple had seven sons and a daughter, the daughter being the youngest. The sons used to hunt and the daughter would
cook at home. After the death of the couple, the family shifted to
the forest. Once, while cutting vegetable to cook, the girl had a cut
in a finger. Blood came out and got mixed with the vegetable, which
her brothers found very tasty. On inquiries they learnt what had

taken place. The eldest brother wondered, "If her blood could make the food so tasty—how tasty would her flesh be." Along with his other brothers, he planned to kill her.

One day, while she had climbed up a tall tree, they spread thorns on the ground around the tree to prevent her escape. The eldest shot her with an arrow. . . . All . . . even the youngest (who did so reluctantly) shot her. . . . They killed her, cut her body in seven pieces. . . . All except the youngest ate their share. The youngest went to the river-bank and wept bitterly. He narrated the story to fish, crab, etc. who came up to listen to him sympathetically. On their suggestion he put the sister's flesh in an anthill.

After some time, there grew a *guloic* tree with beautiful flowers. It also gave out a melodious sound. A *jogi* picking flowers from the tree heard it, cut a branch from the tree and made an instrument— *dhondro banam* (a chordophone with a carved resonator etc.).

(A similar myth is current about *huka banam*.)

4. *Tirio*-s

Pilchu Budhi was buried by her sons in the vicinity of the village. After some time there grew a beautiful bamboo tree. Budhi's voice was heard from the tree. One son thought of making an instrument from the tree with a sound resembling human voice. When he went to cut the bamboo a voice came from below the ground, "Cut the middle portion from which you could construct two flutes, one of 'weal' and another of 'woe'. When you play the flute of weal, I would know that the villagers are living happily, but when you play the flute of woe, I would understand that the villagers are suffering."

REMARKS

A suggestion was made earlier, that valid generalizations about music-myth relationship can be made in India, only if adequate consideration is given to the categorial pentad. The four creation-myths noted make a move in that direction—as the myths draw attention to three of the five categories. The myths about *pataha, ravanahattha, dhondro banam* and *tirio* lead us to art, folk and primitive categories of music. They also afford us the benefit of referring to three of the four major classes of instruments namely membranophones, chordophones and aerophones. This obviously cannot be regarded a sufficient sampler. However, it should suffice to illustrate the point of view adopted.

1. Art music-myth tends to emphasize importance of either the aesthetic or the acoustic principle involved in creating a particular instrument or a class.

2. Compared to folk or primitive music-myths, those associated with art music are more focused. They, i.e., art music-myths try to select and stress a motif or a group of motif to highlight the desired fact, moral, deduction, etc.

3. In art music-myth, 'artistic quality', or 'effect' or 'excellence of music' appears to be a result of special insights, acts of contemplation or observation, etc. On the other hand, in music-myths of other categories, ordinary, gruesome or even morally culpable acts are associated with musical excellence, etc.

4. In music-myths of the non-elite categories, music/musical events appear to involve a greater number and different kinds of persons from the society. Very often, music is portrayed as a collective expression. On the other hand art music-myths draw attention to individuals as effective music-makers.

5. The non-elite categories reveal musical instruments as carrying out multiple expressive roles—going much beyond music and music-making. Paradoxically, they are also seen to stand for very particular musico-cultural functions. A greater degree of instrumental symbolism pervades the non-elite categories and the mythos associated with them.

10

Performing Music: An Instructional Model

To have discussed five categories of music, is only to prepare basis for more detailed examination of each of the processes connected with music. It is normally accepted that apart from performance, a host of other processes such as composing, teaching, learning, reception, analysis, communication, criticism are associated with music. In view of their importance, each requires a detailed examination and, as categories are the fundamental moulds of musical experience in its entirety, the processes would benefit if viewed in the wide perspective of the categories. It is also equally true that categories would become more comprehensible when the processes are explained. I propose to discuss the title-theme, admittedly with three serious shortcomings. Of the five categories I am concentrating only on art music, and that too of the Hindustani variety. The other four categories do have instructional activities. Further, there are at least three more systems of art musics in India claiming attention. Finally, my concern is only with the traditional process of music-instructions. At least in some parts of the country, more music is learnt via the media than we usually care to admit.

It would be fairly accurate to say that traditional model of music instruction pays attention to teaching, learning and practising. Aptitude-testing and periodic assessment, often mentioned separately today, would form part of teaching while evolution and use of self-study procedures would be included in practising.

TEACHING

A very important fact is the primacy accorded to public-performance. All teaching is directed at making the pupil a concert-performer. This does not mean that all music-learners are assumed to have concert-aptitude and capability. What is assumed is that the musical material remains identical for prospective teachers and performers. The emphasis on performance and performing ability seems logical in view of the innate nature of the art with its marked emphasis on orality. The *guru* carefully watches trainees and repeatedly assesses their individual potential to become teachers or performers. Once the *guru* arrives at a decision, the orientation of the teaching undergoes considerable changes. Explanation of grammatical nuances, suggestions for practising, hints about grading the received material find place. Strategies for making music effective, techniques to ensure audience-approval, etc. acquire importance and sometimes specific recommendations are made.

MEMORY AND ITS HIGH PRESTIGE

I have discussed elsewhere, the overall nature of oral tradition and the specific forms it assumes in Hindustani music. One of the features dealt with is the logical and actual importance memory is accorded in the tradition. However, it needs to be emphasized that there is a subtle gradualism in memorization. A trainee is not asked to memorize items in isolation and at his first encounter with them. The item is usually presented to him in various contexts as also on numerous occasion before he is actually asked to memorize it as a part of his learning. For example, if he is to learn a *raga*, or a composition, he is initially exposed to it (prior to his actual learning of it) in a concert situation, or while it is being taught to somebody else or while the *guru* is practising it. Only after a number of such occasions and exposures in various degrees, a trainee is taught the item. It is obvious that the item enters the trainees performing repertoire in a very gradual manner.

A fallout of this gradual memorization is the gestalt character of the entire endeavour. As the item appears in a manifold setting, a majority of its contextual connections are revealed to the trainee prior to the actual learning of it. The actual learning of the item is comparatively a bare affair, a mere passing on of a structure, or a formulation—as the background has been already transmitted. The item consequently becomes an enriched entity with multiple facets.

It would be pertinent to refer to some of the common memorization techniques practiced by performing musicians.

1. Repetition in a definite sequence is an age-old technique. Sequences are changed, but they are so deliberate that, in my opinion, these are preferably described as permutation-

combinations and should be treated as a part of improvisatory techniques. What needs to be clearly brought out is, the serious import it is assumed to have, comparable to a religious charge. For example, a weekday regarded auspicious is chosen for the grand exercise, which therefore is invested with a special aura and sanction. This particular exercise, called *avritti*, is devoted to skeletal performances of complete compositions known as *bandish*-s. This exercise has the advantage of bringing in view to the performer, his own entire repertoire, a fact helpful in a judicious and creative exploitation and exploration of his own resource. A perspective thus offered, is sure to make him aware of his shortcomings and strengths. Secondly, individual items are thus subjected to analysis and improvisation is greatly facilitated.

2. Repetition of isolated, individual and more technical features, though a routine affair, is not ignored. In this connection, changes of contexts rung deliberately and reassembling of structural wholes are worth noting features. For instance, a text of songs is dissociated from its melodic framework to be recited as prose before rejoining it to the melody. Or, rhythm-compositions are first recited without playing, then played and recited, and finally rendered on instruments alone.

Grammatical rules are codified in poetic meters of minimal musical quality such as *doha* and *arya*. Sometimes, minor musical compositions are employed to codify *raga* or *tala* rules. *Lakshanageet*-s and *saragamgeet*-s are two obvious examples. It is clear that couched in this manner, repetitions are much more than mechanical acts.

FORMULAE FOR IMPROVISATION

It may appear paradoxical to talk of formulae and teaching in connection with improvisation. However, it must be admitted that the role of improvisation in Indian music has been both misinterpreted and exaggerated, chiefly because improvisation has been unnecessarily—and rather prematurely—equated with creativity. Another historical reason for the overemphasis on its role has been the operations of nineteenth-century nationalism which followed the apparently contradictory strategies of glorifying the non-occidental and also trying to emulate the occidental. The century busily extolled improvisation but repeatedly tried to evolve comprehensive notation-systems, etc. to create the definitive and the written *alap* following the Western the vogue.

Broadly, improvisation would be employed either to create a new idea or to elaborate or develop an existing idea in a novel manner.

For the first use, it is usual to follow the strategy of aspect-orientation of music. A brief explanation would be in order. Melody, rhythm and language are the three mutually influencing matrices recognized for the purpose. Improvisation could be initiated in either of the three. The deviation thus introduced would naturally mean a change in the total tenor of the presentation. This particular strategy is employed by all forms of music.

Yet another way of improvising in the melodic dimension is known as *murchhana*. It involves adherence to the regular inter-tonal distances even as the fundamental is being shifted for a while to be re-established a little later.

Yet another improvisatory undertaking in *raga*-music is, embodied by procedures known as *tirobhava-avirbhava*. Separate *raga*-s have often common clusters and hence it is possible to create 'shadows' of *raga*-s adjacent to the one actually undertaken for development on a particular occasion. This part of the action is known as *tirobhava*. A little later one is expected to come back to the original *raga*, and this is known as *avirbhava*.

The most important developmental or elaborational strategies is obviously to permutate and combine units.

In this respect, the pitch-aspect is explored through *varnalankara*-s, i.e., methodical employment of four ways of using musical notes to embellish. The four ways identified in the tradition are:

1. Repeating a note
2. Ascending the interval-steps
3. Descending the interval-steps
4. Mixing the three

These formulae have been evolved, documented and named by subjecting the seven *shuddha* notes to the concerned processes. The only precondition is that notes should be in sequence and hence the formulae enjoy a pervasive utility.

The other related device, namely *svaraprastara* is of a more mechanical nature as it chiefly depends on the number of notes included. Beginning with one note and adopting the permutation-combination strategy, it yields 5,040 varieties of phrases of *shuddha* notes. The inherent logic is of course valid also in case of scales formed with *komal* and *tivra* notes. For those interested, the break-up of permutation-combination of the mighty seven is given below:

1. 1 variety
2. 2 varieties
3. 6 varieties
4. 24 varieties
5. 120 varieties
6. 720 varieties
7. 5,040 varieties

Among improvisatory devices *gamak*-s or the special vibratory effects in producing sound in tonal/melodic music occupy a distinctive place. It is unfortunate that all the fifteen varieties of the traditionally listed *gamak*-s are not unambiguously identifiable. However, it is clear that a number of them have a direct bearing on important acoustic attributes of timbre and volume.

With *gamak*-s are *kaku*-s or tonal modulations of various types. These represent a major attempt to introduce tonal colour in music-presentations.

There are also instances in which the miracle of improvisation has been realized through turning to cognate arts, especially to dance and *abhinaya* for generating forms or genres essentially indicative of combined expression of sensibilities active in exploring two or more arts in action.

LEARNING

1. The tradition believes that a trainee's training commences even before the actual training is undertaken. This is achieved through what is often described as *sahavasa* (lit. living together). The process can suitably be explained as musical acculturation. According to it, a disciple moves in society with his *guru*—to concerts and functions, etc. He watches the *guru* engaged in teaching others or listening to others. Further, he assists the *guru* in practice or self-study. In other words, the disciple virtually tries to reach to and understand *guru*-s wider world-view because only that would make gurus music-view comprehensible.

2. A lot of premium is placed on faith, an unquestioning following of *guru*'s instructions in the minutest possible detail. It is not that no questions are asked. But care is taken *not* to

raise questions the moment they crop up. The basic premise is that no answer would be understood unless the questioner is ripe to receive it. It is suggested that unless a certain mental readiness is achieved, prompt and perky acts of asking 'intelligent' questions would merely mean unnecessary and avoidable loss of poise and equilibrium. It is common experience that too often questions are asked to show off, to impress on others one's own cleverness. This is positively discouraged. On the other hand, many have experienced that a question uppermost in one's mind, one that is agitating to the core—is often answered by the *guru* at his own initiative. In fact, questions are often answered without resorting to verbalization. They are answered through performance.

3. It would appear that a number of 'lessons' are learned in presence of a 'public'. A disciple accompanies *guru* in concerts and the *guru* often praises or criticizes him in full view of the audience, a procedure perhaps unthinkable according to modern educational psychology. It is also not rare to find *guru*-s asking disciples to rectify mistakes and present desired versions—all while the concert is in progress. A charitable interpretation is that the public nature of praise or chastisement functions as reward and punishment or carrot and stick respectively. Relevant lessons are learnt, never to be forgotten.

4. A very important place is given to imitation in music learning. However, there is an accompanying, injunction—to understand that which is to be imitated. Often, disciples carry matters to the extreme and ape mannerisms, accoutrement as well as vices of the *guru*, but then that is a case of misusing the tradition. . . .

   Taken in its true spirit, imitation is aimed at formation of habit-structures designed to eliminate loss of energy and time-resources. Certain performing and thinking habits are presented as the well-tried out solutions to myriad musical problems. By adopting these solutions, a disciple can hope to conserve energies—to release them when the unexpected and idiosyncratic difficulties rear their heads. It must be stressed that imitation is not a mechanical procedure and it is also not pursued as an all-time strategy. *Guru*-s are known to urge disciples not to imitate but to create—though the instruction is reserved for advanced students. Many biographical accounts reveal how disciples learn from many *guru*-s at various points of career. This fact is indicative of the inadequacy of imitation, at least of one single model.

5. It is at this stage that argument of the relevance of the concept of *gharana* or *sampradaya* attracts attention. *Gharana* is a comprehensive, performance-oriented, musical ideology emerging from performing tradition and it is usually and suitably accompanied by scholastic formulations designed to interpret the entire musical universe peopled by concepts, forms, styles, practices and procedures pertaining to musical behaviour of well-defined cultural groups. While movement from one *guru* to the other within the same *gharana* is allowed and accepted as 'natural', going out of one's original *gharana* and shift loyalties to another is fraught with risks, social as well as aesthetic. A *gharana* represents a total point of view structured to construe prevailing musical situation in its totality and therefore *guru*-s normally warn against simultaneous instruction in more than one *gharana*. A disciple is however at liberty to decide to learn from *guru*-s of other *gharana* after assimilating one ideology. The risk and the choice are his to take.

At another, and more technical level, the discussion of practice-procedures can also be included with the examination of *gharana*. However, adequate ground has been covered to allow some general observations about the instructional model emerging from the performing tradition.

The traditional model has certainly more accomplishments to its credit than is generally admitted.

(a) It sets quality above quantity. The emphasis is evident in all the three aspects of the instructional model.

(b) A high degree of sophistication is revealed in the overall approach to teaching. While the movement is from simple, limited and easy to complex, expansive and difficult in actual lessons, the overall teaching involves gradual shifts from general to particular.

(c) The primacy of music-making and performance ensures avoiding the over-reliance on dry, bookish inundation of consciousness through verbalization.

(d) Concept of performance as enshrined in the tradition assumes active role of audience. Music-makers are taught the value of their limited autonomy. They are also made aware of the overlapping influences of tradition and its receivers.

(e) Trainees are repeatedly made aware of the need to balance individual talent and prevailing traditions. A seemingly paradoxical situation is the result. Knowledge of the tradition sanctifies performer's deviations prompted by the individual talent in action. Built-in provisions for deviation, as well as conformity, provide fascinating insights, cultural in implications.

11

Music and its Non-musical Users

The title opens up many possibilities of interpreting the subject. It is indeed a tribute to the multi-faceted reality of music that it can be discussed in a variety of contexts. I propose to deal with two of the non-musical uses of music, namely industrial and therapeutic music. For the sake of convenience as well as clarity, I would restrict my comments to India and Indian musicological contexts.

The endeavour is to establish a positive and conceptual relationship between Indian musical scene in its totality, and the selected non-musical areas of life. In my opinion, industrial and therapeutic functions represent the capacity of music to extend its power beyond itself. Therefore, it would only be fair to hope that the present ground-clearing operation may lead to easier exploration of other non-musical applications of Indian music. The Indian view of life seems conducive to affirm such wide-ranging interconnections.

Firstly, because the principle of *nada*, i.e., sound is itself described as an all-embracing phenomenon. Indian grammar, musicology, philosophy and Ayurveda (the science of longevity) feature origin, classification and function of *nada* in a way that leaves very few areas untouched by *nada*. Secondly, both refined versions of *nada*, i.e., music and language, have been traditionally credited with powers reaching far beyond their own respective functions. Thirdly, art music, a very important category of Indian music, ascribes affective capacities to individual notes, as also to *raga*-s, resulting from their combinations and operations. The elaborately formulated *rasa*-theory could be seen to be a persuasive effort to postulate intrinsic relationship between mind and music. Finally, it is of great significance that standard musicological texts define a number of musical matters in terms of fundamental Ayurvedic concepts—suggesting thereby, a close and active interrelationship with a long tradition.

And yet, it is to be admitted that the branch of applied music has not developed to any notable extent in contemporary India. The chief reason has been the failure of the Indian psyche to digest new learning emerging in the British era and assimilate the same with the traditional, integrated view of life. However, this is not the place to delve deeper into that question. The scene is changing fast and it is imperative to attend to the conceptual framework relevant for a healthy growth of a much-neglected field. Otherwise, all attempts to create applied music are likely to be reduced to mere fashions, gimmicks and/or imitative acts. A clear conceptual framework would necessarily consider the contemporary scene as well as evidence of the existing streams of applied music.

At this juncture some observations are in order to differentiate between the two non-musical uses referred to. These observations are a prelude to drawing attention to specific, Indian and musicological contexts.

1. It may be argued that Industrial music is expected to play a chiefly recreational role while the therapeutic variety carries out alleviative functions. Recreation is aptly understood to be an act of 'refreshment in body or mind, as after work, by some form of play, amusement or relaxation'. In the present context the scope of the term extends to include relaxing effects of music even while work is in progress. To alleviate is to make less hard to bear; lighten or relieve pain, suffering, etc.

2. Bodies and minds under strain are subjects of the former, while the latter is directed at cases describable in a given society as psycho-physical deviations.

3. The modern version of industrial music attracts attention essentially as an urban phenomenon while therapeutic music can claim to have a wider area of operations.

4. Today, industrial music may be found to have a generic connection with some forms from the category of folk music. Work-songs would easily come to mind. On the other hand, therapeutic music would find parallel/precursors in devotional, folk and primitive musics.

5. Finally, industrial music is directed to more heterogeneous and collective audiences, or at least to a purposefully grouped audience. In contrast, therapeutic music focuses on deliberately isolated individuals—even if they are physically speaking, members of a group.

What is the process in which music operates in applied situations?

An in-depth consideration of the process will require an elaborate statement on a fundamental issue: The Concept of Medical Man. This will necessitate discussion of philosophical assumptions of cure, known to differ from culture to culture. Such assumptions underlie systems of medicine which evolve and gain acceptance in cultures. It is contended that a changed concept of medical man will necessarily require a corresponding change in the cultural alignment of various components, applications of music being one of them.

Which system of medicine has been *accepted* in India? Can allopathy be stated to be that system? What cultural role is played by indigenous systems such as Ayurveda, Unanai and the Siddha? What do the repeated attempts to bring these back into the medical mainstream suggest? Is it not true that these attempts indicate a reassertion of a cultural preference?

All medical systems are concerned with cure—a phenomenon occupying the gray area between life and death. Cure is therefore a culturally contested concept. Consequently, applied music and the mode of its operation raise questions of philosophical implications. The following remarks are to be read on this background.

Industrial music could be said to achieve its goal in two ways.

Firstly, it creates a conducive working environment by shutting out unpleasant and jarring acoustic stimuli. In the process, it contributes to better concentration of mental faculties of workers exposed to it.

Secondly, musical stimuli are so designed as to reinforce related muscular activities to ensure a greater coordination.

It is to be noted that industrial music cannot operate efficiently if it has an outstanding aesthetic/artistic character. Highly aesthetic music would tend to divert the listeners attention to itself. Industrial music cannot afford to be intensely emotive or intellectual, as that would amount to setting up separate and competing demand-structures. It would not be an exaggeration to say that industrial music needs to be 'pleasantly inconsequential'. The strategy followed is of musical self-effacement and cushioning. Industrial music blanks out or diminishes unwanted aural stimuli and softens impact of rigid and mechanical movements.

In case of sedentary occupations, industrial music appears to rely on applying the principle of contrast. However, to meet situations in which repeated and regular body movements feature predominantly, it operates on the principle of similarity or correspondence.

At this juncture, an important difference between industrial and therapeutic musics needs to be noted. The annoyance or irritation, boredom, etc. of those subjected to industrial music is not expressed through music. On the other hand, there are occasions when those exposed to or engaged in therapeutic music will give vent to their sufferings, etc. *through* music *while* music is operating on them.

Industrial music appears to iron out surfacial and temporary difficulties of people working in specific, short-lived and organized situations. No permanent or long-standing changes in the mindsets of those exposed to music, are attempted or expected. No fundamental alterations in personality-profiles of subjects are aimed at. In the ultimate analysis industrial music works on factors external to human beings involved.

What are the principles on which music-therapy works?

Broadly it works on two levels—physiological and psychological.

At the physiological level, blood-circulation, respiration, etc. are reported to be affected. However, at this level it may be the controlled sound rather than music which actually works.

On the other hand, the well-known *rasa*-theory or the *raga*-season association come into play at the second level. Even though the authority of these correspondence is more profound in art music, they are known to exert influences in other categories. It is submitted that music can work at the psychological level *because* it throws up musical symbols and/arouses imagery. All building-blocks used in music-making, namely music, language, movements, gestures, etc. combine to achieve the task.

The qualifying clause is that musical symbols operate with an overwhelming cultural bias. Different musical categories are characterized by differing symbological potentialities. The therapeutic powers become less and less universal as the cultural factors assume greater roles.

This is the backdrop for considering some Indian orientations:

1. Prior to selecting music for application the categorical pentad of Indian music is to be borne in mind.

     All categories have distinctive socio-cultural and musical features. Music from different categories can hardly be used interchangeably. A decision as to the relevance of a specific category of music in a particular situation would have to made.

2. Diversity of Indian culture also complicates the situation be-

cause music therapy is essentially a bio-cultural phenomenon.

Matters are not easy in respect of industrial music because even today Indian urban life is poised between urban and rural loyalties.

Both musical applications would therefore need sophisticated formulations. Musical receptivities will have to be carefully examined. Mechanical reactions would have to be distinguished from genuine perceptual responses.

3. Very often it is persuasively argued that a large segment of medical behaviour has, today, lost its culture-specific quality. In other words (because of the overall situation of mankind), the bio-aspect has become more standardized, though cultural variations have not disappeared. It can therefore be maintained that effective music-applications, independent of cultural affiliations, orientations, etc. are possible—provided fundamental (and therefore universal) musical features are relied upon. This would naturally mean dependence on sound *as* sound—i.e., as a physical, physiological and universal entity. From this angle, pitch, volume and timbre are understood to be chiefly physical forces which can be objectively measured, employed and manipulated. Human organism is (correspondingly) to be treated as a physiological entity reacting to acoustic stimuli. Reactions of human organism are to be measured and subjected to the required analyzes, etc. Correlations between stimulus-response are to be established to determine the nature of music application.

4. Primacy of sound on account of its universal efficacy is easily recognized in contrast to the cultural, and therefore narrower, applications of sound as music. It thus becomes logical to prefer instrumental sound to human voice as a useful agent. Human voice is richer in culturally specific associations. Instrumental sound, on the other hand, is content neutral and consequently more ambiguous. Instrumental sound lays claim to more effective application in a wider perspective as it allows simultaneous and multiple interpretations of non-musical variety.

The same logic tells us that voice will have more potency in particular cases of application if the diagnosis is definite—though the range of application would be narrow.

Another force, namely language can make the situation more complex. On the one hand, depending on the diagnostic correctness, the language-variable may make applications more effective but it may also confine it to ranges— narrower, in terms of culture as well as kinds of persons involved.

A corollary may be stated. It is customary to associate the term instrument with musical instruments. However, it is hardly justifiable to do so. In the larger context of applied music, an instrument should be understood to be any device or agency capable of producing reproducible sounds. From the receiving end, the conventional definition of sound will also need some broadening. Sounds that generally remain outside human auditory province cannot be excluded from applied considerations of music. One wonders whether the ancient Indian category of *anahata nada* could be relevant in this context.

5. Today it has become essential to point to the neglect that timbre, the third dimension of sound has suffered in our thinking. It is in timbre that there is much more than meets the ear. It perhaps has the most significant contribution to make in applied music. In this dimension, qualitative as opposed to the quantitative aspect comes into operation. It has already been pointed out that applied music generally seeks to effect changes in mental states. I would like to suggest that sound-quality, i.e., timbre be regarded to be the direct correlate of mental, as distinguished from the physical component of human personality. (In fact I am prepared to extend the validity of the observation to the non-human living world.) Correlation indicates states of mutual dependency providing guidelines for future action.

6. In music, all acoustic explorations are either tonal or rhythmic. Indian music is known to be chiefly melodic though polyphonic contributions are not negligible. For the present discussion it is useful to remember that notes prove persuasive and rhythms compulsive on being examined as to their respective affective capacities. This is important for both recreational and therapeutic musics.

7. Finally, I submit that three music-related areas need to be identified for their direct bearing on applied musics. They

are musicology, musical aesthetics and music-lore respectively. They have a number of stated and unstated correlations between features of musical behaviour and definite non-musical uses of music. Musicology and musical aesthetics do not accept relationship of music with the physical aspects of non-musical areas of life. However, these two performance-oriented disciplines have taken definite positions on psychological effects of music on the listeners minds. On the other hand, music-lore claims music to have a direct authority on the physical world around, partially or entirely. This is specially so in folk and primitive categories of music. It is not a coincidence that these two categories allow more scope to human capacity to mythify—as these are the categories in which applied music exists today.

To conclude, it would be valid and important to explore music as a reinforcing rather than an initiating agent in applied situations. Further, for all practical purposes, music should be regarded to have a special intrinsic relationship with human mind—the development of which is sadly lagging behind our concern for our bodies.

12

Music, Growth and Aging

India is one of the major ancient cultures of the world. It is not far-fetched to assume an intrinsic connection between ancientness of cultures and importance accorded to longevity-aging as a phenomenon. It is logical that cultures would value, tolerate or discourage aging in accordance with the larger aims they have set for themselves.

The relationship subsisting between music and aging would, in its turn, be affected by these deeper cultural preferences. Nature, purpose as well as efficacy of music *per se* would inevitably as influenced. As a consequence, significance attached to processes of music-making, performing, preserving and receiving would also be shaped by perspective cultures may adopt on aging.

Thus stated, the case may appear to place music-aging relationship on a conceptual map of daunting proportions. However, the following discussion would hopefully bring out the possibility, necessity and adequacy of considering the theme in a field tightly defined by parameters of vocabulary, mythology, religion, Ayurveda, Yoga and Indian musicology. Music, being a performing art, its performing tradition could expectably be allowed to have the final say—performance being an entity characterized by special adherence to a kind of perpetual present tense.

THE LANGUAGE-PERSPECTIVE

A distinction is required to be made between perspectives offered by terminology developed in different specialized disciplines, and the overall estimation of aging expressed in the day-to-day vocabulary and usage. After all, the mundane world, and its day-to-day activities reflect and refract our most commonly held images/views.

The strategy followed is to form clusters of words related to the phenomenon under examination. When taken together, these clusters demarcate semantic fields relevant to the theme, namely music and aging. The Indian abundance of languages would obviously render a thorough examination difficult. Therefore, the material discussed here is taken from Sanskrit and Marathi traditions and it is to be considered illustrative of a more detailed investigation. Words which mean/suggest old age, growth, longevity, life-span, life-phases, deathlessness, as also proverbs recording comments on these are scrutinized to obtain a perceptive (even though a slightly generalized) picture of the Indian collective thinking about aging.

Firstly, age, it is suggested, is determined by the number of years human body manages to pass through. This, the chronological aspect, seems to be the most objective perspective on aging. The methodology and mechanisms perfected for measuring the element or phenomenon of time are logically pressed into service.

Secondly, aging is described in terms of loss or diminution of bodily powers. Diminishing physiological efficacy is linked, in most cases, to deteriorated state of specific faculties and organs.

Thirdly and notably, the notion which runs through word-clusters holds aging to be a phase leading to intangible and psychological gains in aptitudes, attitudes as also in certain abilities. Maturity, wisdom, growth, enrichment and the like are some of the benefits mentioned directly.

Fourthly, even though there are words connoting immortality, it is clearly signalled that immortality is to be entertained as a mythical state.

Finally, it is deducible that the four foregoing insights are not assumed to coexist, i.e., their correlation is not taken for granted. All states, apart from aging as a chronological phenomenon, and death-birth as termination/beginning respectively of life-processes, are considered 'manageable'. It would be seen later that other disciplines also corroborate the view, though in various degrees. Religion as systematization of faiths, philosophy as science of first principles, mythology as coherent evolution of legends pertaining to creation, Ayurveda as statement of indigenous interpretation of the concept of medical man and Yoga and coordinated and complete view of human existence—would come to mind in this respect. (Perhaps folklore may also be considered to subscribe in a similar manner.) When plurality of musics is added—the complex problem under discussion assumes challenging, though fascinating dimensions.

Ayurveda

An appropriate opening move in discussing aging *vis-à-vis* Ayurveda—would be to narrate apposite legend.

According to the received lore, one tradition of Ayurveda began with Indra, the king of Gods. Sage Maricha Kashyapa was its chief protagonist. Later, Jeevaka, the son of sage Richika was responsible for consolidating the tradition, which however, was not adequately recognized *because* Jeevaka was very young. Finally, in utter desperation (or with a rare insight into human nature.) Jeevaka thought of a shrewd ploy. He managed to gather many of the respected preceptors at Kankhal, a place on the banks of the sacred river Ganga. In their presence Jeevaka then dived deep—only to surface as a venerable—looking old man. Since then he became known as Vriddha Jeevaka, and what is more important, his school (as represented in the *Kashyapasamhita*) gained wide acceptance. The linkage, which the narrative establishes between old age and recognition-respectability-legitimacy is unmistakable. It is of equal importance to note that *Kashyapasamhita* focuses on Kumara-bhritya (paediatrics including obstetrics and gynaecology). The tradition, lost in India, is reportedly supported by a lone manuscript located in Tibet. Further, the Samhita is not included in the *vriddha trayi*, i.e., the trinity of texts regarded basic in Ayurveda.[1]

Ayurveda (the science of life) presumably has its origins in *Atharvaveda*. Often pithily described as *ayushah vedah* (science of life), it collects data from a wide array of sciences because life itself is linked to numerous sciences. During the course of history, it was also called Aryavaidyaka, indicating thereby the Aryan contribution to its crystallization and systematization. However, the non-Aryan contribution to the making of the system is considerable and the fact is rarely contested. For example, the Buddhists were chiefly responsible for developing methods and technology of using metals in certain medical preparations. The assimilative genius of Ayurveda needs to be underscored to establish its representative character, especially to understand the Indian concept of the 'medical man'.

Pade made a stimulating observation that Aryavaidyaka is known as Ayurveda because it aims at extending duration of life of all individual constituents of the human organism.[2] This idea has obvious and direct connections with the phenomenon of aging. It also makes an important suggestion that the rate of aging of individual components is likely to vary. In this context that the matter of life-expect-ancy (*ayurmaryada*) becomes a relevant consideration.

Vidyalankar reports that the tradition was to hold human life-expectancy to be one hundred and twenty years and five days.[3] It is symbolic that all major Ayurvedic texts (namely *Charaka*, *Sushruta*, *Asthanga* and *Kashyapa*) consist of 120 chapters. (It is interesting that maturity is placed at 60 years—the halfway mark to the final exist, though proverbs, etc. contradict by opening that at that age 'intelligence is lost. (e.g., *satha so patha* or *sathi buddhi nathi*). Many well-known *mantra*-s, however, mention hundred years as the ex-pected/desired life-span e.g., *jeevema sharadh shatam*. *Charakasamhita* seems to assume one hundred years as the normal life-span though shorter or longer life-spans are not ruled out (*Vimanasansthanam*, VIII.122).

By the time of *Mahabharata*, Ayurveda is credited to have crystal-lized all of its eight major concerns. From the eight, the last two Ayurvedic departments respectively deal with *jara* (old age), and *vrishyachikitsa* (potency-augmentation). *Rasayana* (promotive therapy) and *vajikarana* (pertaining to aphrodisiacs) are synony-mous concerns. *Charakasamhita*, a masterly text on Ayurveda, sig-nificantly examines the two sections germane to the present discus-sion. We are told that the present text of the Samhita is the original *Agniveshatantra* refined later by Charaka and further redacted by Dridhabala. As a consequence, it is difficult to decide on the date of the Samhita. However, it helps to remember that Atreya Agnivesha can be placed before Panini (700 BC and after *Atharvaveda* 1500 BC); Charaka near-about 200 BC and Dridhabala in AD 400.

Following items reveal an interesting facet of the Ayurveda-story:

(a) Some scholars hold that Charaka is the name of people who belonged to a branch of *Krishna Yajurveda*.

(b) A branch of *Atharvaveda* was known as Vaidya Charana—a term signifying roving medicine-men (Interestingly, the Samhita itself stresses the theme of shifting movements of elements in the body.)

(c) C. Kunhan Raja interpreted Charaka to be a Pehlavi word (*careka*) which later came to denote 'inferior' people. It might be linked with the fact that Charaka had strong Saka associa-tions.

Prof. Sharma has rightly pointed out that the *Samhita* was popu-lar even in non-medical circles as is seen from *Naishadhyacharitam*

(4.116) and *Laghumanjusha* (the latter work was translated into Persian and Arabic during the tenth century). He also notes a curious fact that a Charaka club was established in New York in the year 1898. On this backdrop some notable features on the *Charakasamhita* could be listed:

One of its minor structural feature is that, unlike other texts, it carries subject-index, chapter-headings, etc. at the end. The last two chapters are appropriately called Samgrahadhyaya.

Charaka chiefly refers to the north-western parts of India. Other areas, which find some definite mention include Bahlik (Balakistan), Pahlev (Persia), Cheen (China), and Shalik (Central Asia). The regions probably indicate spheres of influence, as well as cultures, the text drew upon.

Even though Charaka mentions Brahmins and cows respectfully, they do not seem to be elevated to a sacred status. Notably, the word *pashand* (impious, heretical) does not occur in the text—voicing thereby a kind of a religious, accommodative and scientific attitude.

In general, the *Samhita* represents continuation of medical concepts originally propounded during the Vedic period. However, it constitutes a step forward because it forges a rigorous relationship between pathological and physiological matters on the one hand, and philosophical assumptions, physiological functions as well as therapeutic measures on the other. For example, the philosophical concept of *panchamahabhuta* (five elements), the theory of *tridosha* (three bodily elements) and Uniformity of Nature (i.e., the inherent correspondence between physical and biological worlds)—all form part of a cohesive thought-frame in the *Samhita*.

Charaka displays remarkable rationality. The *Samhita* is consistently advocates *yukti*. In an age, when *daiva-vyapashraya* (super natural therapy) was in vogue, it stresses the role of *yukti* as a *pranamana* (i.e., a means of valid knowledge). Sharma has rightly drawn attention to the repeated use of the word *pariksha* (investigation) in the *Samhita*. It is not a coincidence that Charaka devotes considerable space to explain nature and methodology of investigation through discourse. (Vimanasansthanam, VII.3–67).

Charaka's accent on the concept of *purusha* leads him to a *dehamanasa* (physico-psychological) point of view. To allocate a special place to *satvavajaya* (psychotherapy) is a worthy contribution.

Charaka's sound view of the mind-body relationship is closely related to his perception that every individual presents a different proposition which may deviate from the generalized, universally accepted model. In Charaka's exposition each person's having his own *prakriti* (individuality) and *satmya* (suitability) for treatment are highlighted.

According to Charaka, the function of Ayurveda is to assist nature (*svabhavoparama,* i.e., 'recession by nature' is the term used). His emphasis on promotion of Life is therefore logical. *Rasayana,* the branch dealing with this aspect, is the first chapter in the section on therapeutics—a fact indicative of the priority. With the same logic, he stresses good conduct as a factor leading to healthy and long life (i.e., life of the normal span of hundred years).

Charaka does not refer to castes by birth and yet the wide variety of occupations mentioned includes: musicians, story-tellers, reciters, masseurs, etc. These are listed as persons whose services should be made available to patients in hospitals (Sutradhyaya, 15.7).

Charaka expresses belief in rebirth. The chief Vedic gods, namely, Mahadeo, Vishnu and Brahma are mentioned. Even though worship is advocated as a cure, Charaka emphasizes the role of good conduct as the mainstay of fruitful life.

Charaka's early appearance and his representative statement of the Ayurvedic position merited discussion in some detail. Some later addition to the tradition would complete the story.

Rasayana-chikitsa, the branch dealing with old age and related matters continued to evolve. The cumulative perception of the Ayurvedic tradition on old age could therefore be obtained when contributions of this branch are taken into consideration. Hence the following observations can be made:

1. Old age is finally placed between 70–100 years by Sushruta.
2. Old age is considered natural and therefore inevitable along with hunger, thirst, sleep and death.
3. Old age is, quite logically, considered to be of two types: *yathakala* (in accordance with years) and *akal* (out of time).
4. Old age is linked to unavoidable diminishing of all powers. (In fact, a later Ayurvedic text sets a clear time-table for a hundred year span with each decade characterized by an appearance/disappearance of definite psycho-physical disabilities.)
5. Effects of old age are further analyzed occupation wise in keeping with the overall scientific temper. For example, peo-

ple leading a sedentary life (enjoying *assyasukha* as the texts put it) are, we are told, prone to particular types of maladies.

6. Following its own theoretical premise, Ayurveda concludes that it is the *vata* element which becomes the main source of all trouble in old age.

7. The tradition differentiates between two kinds of strengths: *kalabala* (strength according to age) and *yuktibala* (strength acquired by following certain rational applications).

8. *Rasayana-chikitsa*, the branch focusing on old age lays down that its proper application results in the following: long life, good memory, comprehension, freedom from disease (youth like) enthusiasm, hair *not* going white, skin *not* developing wrinkles, lustrous body and voice, generosity of mind, strong sensory and action organs and finally, development of a good-natured attitude.

9. The said *chikitsa*, it is advised should be taken up during middle age, or even during the early years.

10. No special reference is made to music and musicians, though maladies of the upper bodily portion, are mentioned as specific to old age—voice being one of the main sufferers.

MYTHOLOGY AND AGING

Mythological perspective on aging significantly moves in directions different than those followed by Ayurveda. In the final analysis, it is appropriate to hold that mythological insights, combined with the Ayurvedic, offer a complete idea of old age as it is understood/received by the Indian mind. This is the reason why, for example, agelessness and deathlessness become two of the major mythological motifs. Some of the observations based on perusal of Puranic mythology are noted:

1. Gods are described as *ajara* and *amara*, i.e., ageless and deathless respectively.

2. There are 'non-godly' personalities who become *chiranjeeva*, i.e., immortal, on account of operations of different boons/curses, penances, observance of vows, etc.

3. One particular substance, *amrit*, is credited with the property of making its consumers immortal. Nectar was the seventh item to come out of the ocean as result of the well-known churning of by gods and demons.

4. A capacity to hoodwink or avoid death is ascribed to a *mantra* called Mrityunjaya (victory over death).

5. An interesting variation on the theme of avoidability of death is made through the myth of Sanjeevani *vidya*, i.e., a branch of learning which enabled practitioners to revive the dead. Shukracharya, preceptor to demons was its main repository. *Sanjeevani* is a kind of elixir which restored life to the dead. It is also spoken of as a plant which revives, and restores.

6. Another identifiable motif is reversal or transfer of the aging process. In the first case, a person advanced in age succeeds in reversing the process of aging in order to become young again. In the second case, he transfers his own old age to a younger person—thus youth and boons are exchanged. For example Yayati, cursed by Shukracharya to suffer a premature old age, was able to exchange it for his son's youth. Sage Vriddhaharita propitiated sun-god and requested restoration of youth to enable him to practise penance. Yet another age-reversal story is that of sage Chyavana who took a dip in the river at the instance of Ashvinikumaras (physicians to God) to emerge young. In exchange, the Ashvinikumaras received the privilege to drink *soma*, a divine substance. A tributary to river Gautami is called Vriddha. The story goes that the river is, in reality, the water sprinkled by sage Gautama's son on his aged wife.

7. A successful maintaining of an unimpaired youthful state is also mentioned to be consequent to administration of certain drugs or to taking bath as ordained in certain rituals.

RELIGION AND AGING

Dharma (a term, of which religion is a very unsatisfactory translation.) has an in-built provision for aging and the aged through the concept of *ashrama*-s (i.e., stages of life). Of the four stages sequenced as Brahmacharya, Grihastha, Vanaprastha and Sannyasa respectively, the last two cover old age in normal circumstances.

A Vanaprasthin, i.e., person who accepts Vanaprasthashrama, leads life of extreme simplicity and austerity (with or without his wife)—by leaving home to take up an abode in forest. He is not expected to sever contacts with the world, but he is also expected *not* to get involved in mundane affairs. Reduction of wants, proximity to nature and a deliberate delinking from different life-stimuli are the most characteristic features of Vanaprasthashrama.

Kautilya's *Arthashastra* (Bk. 1, chap. III) lays down duties and privileges of the four classes/stages in great detail. Of the four, Vanaprastha, unlike the Sannyasins maintained ties with administration of the polity, a fact signifying the diminishing but real role allotted to the aged in society. In case, a Vanaprasthin was to be fined for any wrongdoing, etc., he enjoyed the alternative to perform a ritual called Mahakacchavardhana in atonement.[1] This clearly brings out that what was intended was a tapering off of roles played by the old in worldly affairs. Sannyasa, with utmost renunciation as its chief characteristics, would probably remain outside the purview of the present discussion.

MUSIC AND AGING

This is the general background on which relationship of music, growth and aging is to be examined.

Some qualifications need to be noted for the discussion to follow.

Firstly, in India no music-related inquiry can claim a general validity unless sufficient attention is paid to the categorial pentad of music consisting of primitive, folk, devotional, art and popular musics.

Secondly, even within the narrow area of the usually discussed art musics, one tends to overlook that India has at least *four* identifiable systems of art music in Hindustani, Carnatic, Sopanam and the one practised in north-eastern parts of the country. It is no exaggeration to say that the world eagerly awaits a person well-acquainted with all the four systems.

HINDUSTANI ART MUSIC, GROWTH AND AGING

As far as Hindustani art music is concerned, the following observations can hopefully claim wide interest as well as validity.

1. From the total corpus of *raga*-s, *tala*-s and *bandish*-s (the terms can be loosely translated as melodic frameworks, rhythmic skeletons and text-tune compositions respectively)—none are specifically marked for aged or aging musicians.
2. In actual performing procedure or practice, musicians are

advised to concentrate on medium ranges in pitch, tempi
and other, generally technical aspects to ensure 'effective/
competent performing accessibility' of their own, learnt
musical corpus—even in old age.

3. Musical maturity, performing sophistication/subtlety and
cultural wisdom are all indicated by an inclusive term *buzurg*.
The term, originating from Persian means 'advanced in age;
ancestor; father; grandfather, etc.' Another derived term,
buzurgi, denotes an abstract quality associated with this state.
However, the term *buzurg* enjoys accretions of meaning and
it connotes a person of rank as well as of a saintly disposition.[5] There is reason to believe that the term gathered the
other-worldly overtones from Sufism which has greatly influenced Hindustani art music.

Those accepted as *buzurg* are accorded certain privileges
on music-making occasions. If they are participating artists,
they perform at later time-slots as the juniors are expected
to perform in the earlier slots. If they attend as listeners, a
place is offered to them—near and facing the performer in
traditional performing situations. Usually, performers do not
commence proceedings without seeking permission of
buzurg-s, who, in their turn, bless the performer and wish
him well.

4. Each *buzurg* is not expected to display high performing ability. He is, however, well-versed in musical lore and often
knowledgeable on account of close association with, or rigorous training from, master musicians of the recent past. In
other words, depth of learning (as contrasted with technical
brilliance), quality of musical wisdom and worldly maturity
compensate for his shortcomings. At this end of the spectrum of the concept of *buzurgi*,—the connotation impercep-
tibly shades off into that of the *guru*.

5. Almost as a corollary to the earlier feature, all *guru*'s are
treated to be on par with *buzurg*-s irrespective of their age,
though the converse is not strictly true.

6. Musicians are not known to retire formally, though they are
known to decide *not* to perform in public or not to accept
engagements when they judge their performing ability to be
below standards, they themselves have set in the past. Yet,
musicians have often staged a kind of come-back, much after

they are past their prime (age-wise). Under such circumstances, they are evaluated and assessed differently.

CORROBORATION

So far the discussion has hovered between conceptual-historical on the one hand, and scholastic-theoretical on the other. At this juncture, performing evidence of three kinds could be introduced to corroborate insights gained.

Firstly, there are accounts of old/aged musicians performance. The accounts throw considerable light on musicians, listeners as well as the music rendered.

Secondly, there are audio recordings of senior musicians offering data on the repertoire, rendering as also on the music-makers attitude to music.

Finally, there are *bandish*-s i.e., compositions which deal with the theme of old age.

It is obvious that the triad could offer different, though complementary views.

PERFORMANCE-ACCOUNTS

One may begin with a tabulation made on the basis of performance-accounts of eight major vocalists active during the nineteenth-twentieth century. The data could obviously be augmented by more accounts. More variety is possible, especially by quoting from instrumentalists and female musicians experiences. Finally, different coverage of the same performances could be used to diminish a likely bias.

TABULATION

The illustrative tabulation and other known instances give rise to certain observations:

   (a) On most occasions, the artist is singled out for praise because he defies the expected deterioration of powers of musical execution, generally associated with advancing years.

   (b) Initial appearance, as well as later diminution/disappearance of vocal tremor, is invariably mentioned.

   (c) Loss of speed in *tan*-s (i.e., faster passages in vocalization) is

List of Audio-illustrations

Sr. no.	Artist	Performing Age	Pitch	Genre	Raga
1.	Abdul Wahid Khan (1895-?)	70	White Four	Khayal	Darbari
2.	Mushtaq Hussain Khan (1894-1964)	?	White One	Tappa	Mishra Kafi
3.	Rajab Ali Khan (1875-1959)	Bet. 80-84	Black Two	Khayal	Bageshri
4.	Gajananrao Joshi (1911-87)	74	White One	Khayal	Gauda-malhar
5.	Ramakrishnabuwa Vaze (1871-1945)	82	Black Four	Drut Khayal	Bhairava Bhatiyar
6.	Krishnarao Pandit (1893-1989)	80		Drut Ekatal Chaturang	Miya ki Todi

noticed. However, those reputed as *tan*-specialists seem to have retained the requisite efficiency and skill even in old age.

(d) Memory-lapses are commented upon. However, deeper concentration in music-making processes it suggested as a possible cause for memory-lapses.

(e) Taken as a category, aged artists seem to create a charged pre-performance atmosphere—a factor which changes the entire character of the performing situation. In all probability, aesthetic criterion of suggestivity and ambiguity become pronounced in the profile. As a consequence, artists could be expected to take greater risks in making subtler as well as more deviant statements.

(f) Older performers seem to set less premium on the impact their music may or may not create on listeners. I hold that, on account of an increasing introversion, the flow of their music is directed either towards themselves or to an abstracted aesthetico-philosophical entity, namely Tradition. They belong to a tradition and their particular performance is oriented accordingly—irrespective of audience and its responses.

(g) Aging performer's music is frequently more allusive, in the sense, that these musicians acknowledge and illustrate, tacit and overt influences on their music exerted by earlier music-makers. Tributes to musical benefactors are actually paid during presentations by using words such as *unki yaad ati hai* (I remember them). The final musical structures and their textures are therefore replete with ideas which are clear indications of exciting possibilities—though in actuality, they might be inadequately developed.

(h) The type of artists discussed are also distinguished by a kind of 'period quality' in their manifestations. In matters of idiom, gestures, presentation-format, protocol, phrasing, imagery and the like—they appear to evoke a not-so-contemporary ambience. Past and present mingle tantalizingly in their outpourings. Listeners, depending on their backgrounds, may be nostalgically disturbed or may experience an unsettling incongruity in the senior's music.

(i) Finally, the veterans generally exhibit lack of inhibitions in presentations. For example, their rendering of amorous song-texts could be more explicit, though bounds of propriety are not transgressed. Similarly, their use of 'sad' music would be darker—in which shedding tears could have an unabashed existence. What enables them to enjoy this artistic freedom? Firstly, they are free from the fear of failure in execution of musical intentions *because* they have already accepted the possibility. Secondly, their explicit expression is not likely to be misunderstood. Perhaps one may also allow one more aesthetic possibility: their artistic involvement in music could be more intense and unhindered because they are not entangled in it 'personally'.

THE AUDIO-EVIDENCE

With the usual proviso that the sampler could be usefully supplemented, variety could be increased and more factual details can be gathered—the audio-recordings considered throw-up some important and plausible conclusions:

On the whole the recordings sound an optimistic note. Irrespective of a definite diminution of powers to carry musical ideas to their logical conclusions, the veterans make music which holds attention—indeed a very primary factor in any performing art, and by no means a mean feat to achieve.

On occasions' performers seem to be conscious of the great number of monsoons they have weathered. Pt. Ramakrishnabuwa Vaze's records bear labels which clearly mention his advanced age. During the performance Pt. Gajananrao Joshi ruefully voices his inability to do justice to musical ideas. A number of vocalists are heard to clear their throat repeatedly—an obvious indication of vocal difficulties encountered. At least in some cases, this cannot be ascribed to artists ignorance of recording conventions.

Very rarely, musicians have gone for softer options in selecting forms, tempi, *tala*-s or *raga*-s etc. For example, Pt. Krishnarao Pandit has sung *chaturang*, a genre of music which has in-built switchover from one musical element to the other within the same composition—making demands on memory and alertness.

Pt. Ramakrishnabuwa Vaze has selected a tempo which, in itself, is demanding. Further, he executes small but tricky passages requiring quick vocal movement. On the other hand, Mushtaq Husain Khan sings *tappa*, a genre studded with complex vocal patterns. Also needed is the ability to traverse wider pitch-ranges. At the most, some vocalists have lowered their tonics.

Most performers appear to have retained verve in music-making, though vigour of execution is on the decline. Aggressive musical designs are evident in Ustad Rajabali's or Pt. Vaze's renderings. Their attempts to execute speedy, attacking tonal progressions, or energetic launchings of intricate rhythmic motifs are worth listening to.

The tendency to dominate musical proceedings is also observable. The soloists allow little or only an interrupted scope to their younger accompanists—often cutting into the latter's elaborations. Sometimes they also appear to be musicians in a hurry. The element of silence, the principle of allowing music to sink in, through a judicious employment of pauses is frequently ignored. Pt. Vaze or Ustad Rajabali's music are good instances.

One suspects that there is no vigilant attempt to build up a musical structure, neither is there a careful husbanding of musical resources. There is repetition, bypassing of normal sequence and an erratic quality in progressions. Ustad Rajabali and Pt. Ganjananrao Joshi are examples.

Sometimes the musicians appear to be obsessed with certain musical phrases or passages, in which they have probably espied opportunities to introduce meaningful variations. Instances are detected in almost all musicians.

Among vocalists there is greater reliance on consonants and closed vowel-sounds. Obviously, open vowels pose problems of maintaining continued air-pressure as well as resonance. However, it does not follow that word-content or literary centres in the compositions are treated with more respect. In other words, performers habitual musical strategies are not changed—though marginal changes are introduced in techniques they employ.

FROM THE CORPUS

The third kind of performing evidence is the *raga*-compositions existing and in circulation. A neat verbalization of this kind of evidence is difficult chiefly because musical experience as such, depends on arousal of an ambiguous aural imagery in a major way. The maximum that one can do is, to put down observations, and yet believe in the possibility of alternative interpretations.

The musical corpus accepts aging as reality and equates it with obvious signs of physical deterioration. Many song-texts consist of word-pictures depicting well-known effects of old sage.

However, it is noteworthy that the deep-rooted theory of *rasa*—in Indian aesthetics notwithstanding, *raga*-s in which song-texts on old age appear are not invariably sad. In other words, descriptions of old age often coexist with cheerful melodic contours and energetic rhythmic frameworks. This could be interpreted to mean that music *as* music treats old age as an excuse for musical exploration of an extended gamut of human emotions.

Perhaps the message is to regard old age as an experience capable of inducing and shaping paradoxical emotions. In the process, what is firmly ruled out is the monochromatically mournful depiction of aging as an unbearable human condition. It could be maintained that music gazes at old age with philosophical equanimity and aesthetic curiosity.

Thematically speaking, old age and death are touched in music with less frequency than other life-experiences such as birth, initiation, marriage, separation, union, communion, coronation, and festivities, etc. But this may be ascribed to the euphemistic tendencies of Indian musical cultures—especially, its art category.

CONCLUSION

The Indian mind has woven a complex web to deal with aging and growth. To an extent, disciplines such as medicine, mythology, religion, language and musicology appear to send out signals of musical opposition (if not of contradiction or cancellation). And yet, in the final analysis, the spirit is of acceptance of old age as a human condition or a phase capable of granting an experience of a positive import. Indian recognition of aging is not a case of making virtue out of necessity. The phase is treated with grace—because of its 'felt' capacity to bestow Grace on us.

REFERENCES

1. Shankar Daji Pade, *Ayurveda Rahasya athava Vagbhat Vistara*, p. 2.
2. S.V. Vadodkar, *Aurvedacha Itihasa*, preface, p. 2.
3. Atrideva Vidyalankara, *Ayurveda ka Brihad Itihasa*, p. 174.
4. B.A.S. Saletore, *Encyclopaedia of Indian Culture*, vol. I, sec. edn., pp. 126-7.
5. Thomas Patrick Hughes, *Dictionary of Islam*, p. 48.

13

Performing Arts and Narrative

Common sense definitions of narrative and of related terms point to acts of telling of a story, providing an account or describing an event as the core-concept. Other associated terms refer to the act of narrating, the art or technique of narration, a person (or indirectly a work) carrying out the task of a narrator. Established etymological connections lead to the process of knowing, especially the particulars, of an event or an act. It has been noted that as an artistic literary strategy, narrative was not unambiguously recognized till the late eighteenth century in the English lexical tradition.

Generally speaking, the Indian terminological response offers a varied picture. For example, *varna* (to describe), *katha* (to tell), *akhya* (to relate), etc. are in circulation. Narrations have developed into forms or formats known as *kirtana, kathana, varnana, akhyana, upakhyana, akhyayika, vrittanta, charitra, katha prabandha, itihasa*, etc. Each of these has its own respective specialized performing agency. In this connection, *kathaka, kirtankara*, etc. would come to mind.

However, it is necessary to admit that the moment narrative takes a step in the aesthetic direction, it moves away from its core meaning, as also from its concern with sequence, factuality and particularity. Aesthetic benefits accrue when narrative borrows/assimilates time-manipulation and ambiguity from music, character-creation and role-depiction from theatre (or drama, to be precise). Because of the initial movement away from 'pure' language-use, statements turns into narration, narration into dialogues, felt and specific emotions into evocative mood. In other words, combination of narrative and performing arts inevitably shifts and lifts the problem of their interrelationship to an aesthetic plane where two *arts* and *not* two activities engage in competition—if not get locked in a combat. Interrelationship of arts involves problems of their classification which, finally, leads to the most fundamental parallelogram of forces governing creation, communication and reception of all aesthetic endeavours. The forces in operation occur and operate in two pairs: verbal/non-verbal and audio-visual. Sensibilities of artists, potencies of communicative systems and sensitivities of receivers are fully tested in multi-art manifestations.

The role of performing arts *vis-à-vis* narrative, which unfolds its wide spectrum (well brought out by the terminological cluster and performing agencies associated with it), is to be examined against this background. Instances of dramatized, choreographed and musicalized narratives may be analyzed to determine nature and outcome of the interrelationship between narrative—an intrinsically literary phenomenon—and its appearance in combination with one or many of the performing arts. To facilitate the discussion, I prefer to concentrate on three narrative forms from Maharashtra which are music, drama and dance-oriented respectively. The strategy is to abstract from performance, identifiable, operative, structuring principles and to combine, with perceptions thus obtained, other insights gathered from musicological terminology. To rely on performing—as distinct from scholastic—tradition is not to question the relevance of the latter. However, it is helpful to note the inevitable time-lag subsisting between performance and the accompanying/associated scholastic model. Items such as distribution of the performing set, instrumentation and vocalization and details, melodic contours and rhythmic patterns, scope allowed to character creation, range of improvisation and quality of audience-participation need to be closely examined.

POWADA—A MUSIC-ORIENTED NARRATIVE

Themes of *powada* are usually conducive to:
1. Description of heroic deeds
2. Eulogy to hero-figures
3. Description of cataclysmic events
4. Description of memorable events
5. Imparting didactic messages through a story

Themes are obviously amenable to the narrative mode. Descriptions, as well as dialogues, have a place in the scheme of things. Both highly Sanskritized and less Sanskritized compositions are heard. Narratives in *powada* pick up pace quite early, a point which assumes importance in the analysis of its construction. It has also been pointed out that seven, out of the three hundred-odd extant compositions, belong to the period 1680–1749; about 150 are from the period 1713–1819, and the rest from later years. *Powada*-s have been composed in modern times—in fact they are composed even today—but there has been no major deviation from the format crystallized in the traditional corpus.

STRUCTURE AND RENDERING

The first noticeable feature is the 'proseness' of versification. Further, recourse to end-rhymes, reliance on assonance and alliteration, use of fairly lengthy stanzas with regularly recurring sections—along with a metre-change, are also prominent. Insertion of a musical refrain consisting of meaningless syllables—*ji, ji, ji,* is functionally important. The meters employed are conducive to a fast-paced presentation.

In rendering, the form impresses as a solo expression. Vocal accompaniment in mainly restricted to a high-pitched signing of the refrain and to repetition of lines, if and when the soloist so desires. *Naman* (invocation), verse, prose narration, musical refrain (*jheel*), changed meter (normally known as *chal*), the connecting stanza (*milavani*) and identification of the poet (*mudra*) are the main structural features, clearly reflected in compositions.

Narration is usually in the third person and performers rarely assume roles. However, according to V.K. Rajwade, the well-known researcher in Maratha history and culture, in the earlier vogue, performers used to assume roles. He therefore categorized *powada* as a *shravya* as well as *drishya* kind of poetry, thus moving it closer to dramatization.

Other notable facets are:
(a) Intended open-air performance
(b) Heterogeneity of audience
(c) Standing posture of performers
(d) Soloist's role as a poet-composer

MELODIC AND RHYTHMIC SETTINGS

- Melodic frameworks are simple and repetitive. Mostly, they explore middle and higher ranges of octaves.
- There is no elaboration of musical ideas, which in themselves, are closely constructed and forcefully articulated. Empha-

ses, and *not* subtle effects, are the prime avenues of music-making.

- There are musical flourishes but embellishments are far and few.
- Rhythms-wise, *ardha-tala*-s, rather than *tala*-s are noticed. Melodic frameworks do not even suggest *raga*-s.
- Tempi range from fast to faster. All tempi serve the purpose of providing firm time-frames to the text. These time-frames do not in any way try to create spaces for display of rhythmic virtuosity, etc. On most of the occasions, rhythms and tempi provide a musical underlining to textual messages.

The Utterances

In view of the nature of its content, the aim to create attitudes rather than to relate facts, and this does not surprise. Forceful utterance is favoured in order to exhort listeners. An unrestricted mixing in utterance of the voiceless fricative 'h' is therefore easily explained. The outdoor performing conditions also necessitate noticeable projection of voice. Due to fast tempi and the typical instrumentation, utterance in *powada* is highly stressful. Words are nearly pounded into listener's ears. The cumulative impact is of great vigour, verve and valour. The reasons, of the customary male dominance in the performing tradition of *powada*, are clearly and closely bound with the performing conditions, utterance being one of them.

The Instrumentation

The main instruments are *tuntune* and *daph*. *Tuntune* has one string which is tuned considerably high. More importantly, it is rhythmically plucked and thus ends up accentuating rhythmic pulse than providing melodic support. *Daph* is not precisely tuned, but it has to sound high-pitched enough to satisfy the player. Consequently, a notably pronounced rhythmic pattern finally emerges to help organizing the verse as also shape utterance. Both instruments do not leave behind tonal shadows and rhythmic units are boldly defined. Instruments create a pulsating and discontinuous, though well-controlled, progression.

The Performing Set

The all-male performing set consists of one soloist (who is also likely to be the poet-composer), two vocal and one rhythm accompanists. The soloist sets the tone and leads. The group stands and performs with audience in the front. The soloist often, and aggressively, moves forwards/backwards. He may also introduce a crouching movement to enhance the effect. Facial and eye-gestures are not pronounced or important in the total communication. In fact, accompanists are frequently noted for their passive faces, merely displaying facial distortions traceable to strains and stresses of singing in high-pitch.

The Improvisatory Element

Significantly (and in view of the musical format also logically), improvisation is more or less confined to the textual aspect. It is useful to note items which remain constant and those which allow change:

- In the best traditions of epic poetry, descriptions of battles, deaths, coronation ceremonies and the like tend to be stereotyped and hence interchangeable. To an extent these constitute the changeable items.
- Eulogistic descriptions enjoy a similar mobility.
- *Mudra*, the poet-composers' name, as well as *naman* (invocation) i.e., the portion consisting of names of deities, *guru*-s, etc. obviously remain constant.
- Patron's name is a changeable feature.
- Description in prose, being less tightly structured, are prone to change. However, the ways in which prose passages are composed remain the same because of their obvious and immediate relationship with the total performance format.

It is fair to conclude that *powada* is one of the most literature-oriented of the musicalized narratives. On the one hand, it represents a stream away from undiluted prose and yet, it just manages to be somewhat more than a verse in tune. *Powada*-music is of a monochrome variety. The narrative, i.e., literary restraints, do not allow bodily movements which can claim dance-potential. In the prevailing form, *powada* also lacks capacity to create characters. To use T.S. Eliot's formulation, it does not have a built-in provision for a 'third voice' in poetry. What then is the contribution of music, as a performing art, to its narrative duties? Art this stage I would like to mention two concepts to be discussed later. They are: parallel structure and ambiguity.

DRAMA-ORIENTED NARRATIVE

In this category, the form which should engage our attention is Naradiya Kirtana. It is one of the seven types of *kirtana*-traditions existing in Maharashtra. The present performing format is the result of a long evolution owing a great deal to Bhakti cults and their fascinating interplay with other religious doctrines. Key terms to be adequately understood for analyzing Naradiya Kirtana are: *gadi, yajaman, bidagi, poorvarang, mulapada, uttararang, akhyana, rang* and *arati*. Some of the terms are more immediately connected with performance, while others shed light on the cultural setting of this musico-dramatic form.

The entire performance is divided in two halves, namely *poorvarang* (first half) and *uttararang* (the latter half). The first is devoted to musico-philosophical discourse. The *kirtankara* (as the performer of *kirtana* is known) selects a theme of religio-philosophical import to suit his intellectual equipment and temperament, as well as to meet demands of the patron or occasion—if so required. The theme is suitably and repeatedly introduced with a 'text'. The text is elaborated with the help of references, and quotations from supporting authorities or works. Music is kept to the minimum, even though no strategy is spared to make the presentation interesting. This needs a special mention because the totality of oral tradition in India seems to have taken care to allocate specialized forms and agencies the task of communicating content of required depth and intensity by following a principle of division of labour. *Kirtana* testifies to the fact. There is some corroborative evidence in the tradition bearing out the fact. For example, *pravachana*, as a form, is also devoted to exposition of religio-philosophical themes, but it eschews music or other performing arts. *Pravachana* is designed and expected to be informative, thought-provoking and philosophically dense, while the *kirtana* is to assume the role of a didactic, entertaining and appealing communication. The *kirtana* artiste, having elaborated the text to the required measure, rounds off the first half with a musical interlude in which he takes the liberty of *singing*, i.e., dwelling on and elaborating *musical* ideas with the help of suitable musical forms. The brief, but qualitatively distinctive section, stands out on account of its intended and undiluted musicality.

It is in the *uttararanga* that the dramatic aspect of the narrative comes to forefront. The artiste now selects a legend/myth, etc. for narration (which is called *akhyana*) preferably from mythology or legendary history as an exemplar of the text elaborated in the first half. Use of music is more abundant and, in some traditions, even dance is offered some scope. Gestures, facial expression, body-movements (to an extent), speech and tone variations—and such other channels are extensively employed. In fact, it can be safely said that except the *aharya*, all types of *abhinaya*-s discussed by Bharata are well utilized. Of essence is the fact, that the artiste creates and assumes roles—with the third person narrative being used as a jumping board to effect changes from one role to the other. Improvisation has therefore adequate scope. The live contact and interaction with the heterogeneous but receptive audience also plays a role. Occasionally, the performance may appear directed at the patron— the *yajamana*,—but generally speaking, his presence merely provides an excuse for the artiste to fly into higher reaches of eloquence, wit, imaginative narration and evocative utterance to win over the audience. In spite of all twists and turns of a well told story, the artiste never overlooks to remind the audience of the 'message' he has repeatedly propounded in the first half—the original statement (*mula pada*). This statement is skilfully interwoven, interspersed and contextually emphasized as would be a theme in a well-constructed dramatic or fictional plot. At the end of the performance, prayer is offered to the artiste's *guru*, family deity, and patron's god, etc. Members of the audience take part in the *arati*, bow down to the artiste (obviously taken to represent sage Narada) and his seat (*gadi*). It also puts money in the plate taken around. The patron pays *bidagi* (remuneration), usually afterwards—but that too is described as an offering. A successful *kirtana* is remembered and spoken about, as if it were a music concert or a dramtic performance. As I have stated elsewhere, it is the *rang* theory and *not* the *rasa* theory which is intrinsically relevant to Indian performing arts, of which *kirtana*, as a one-man show, is a fair representative.

It is interesting to note that a similar kind of story-telling (without music, movement, gesture, etc.), has a specialized form allotted to it. It is known as *purana-kathana*.

Against this backdrop a question crops up once more: Why is the story-telling combined with the musico-dramatic, didactic, indoor and semi-ritualistic presentation? No form can originate, evolve in multiple aspects and develop a complex format unless it has the capacity to meet definite aesthetic and socio-cultural demands. Is it because the strategy and art of narrative, operating in a setting provided by a comprehensive oral tradition, intrinsically needs performing arts to realize its own aim? In case of *powada* it was noted that the raising of parallel structures, and generation of a creative kind of ambiguity was the essential contribution of the performing arts to narrative. What about *kirtana*?

One may single out the creation of characters as the special contribution of the form. As Indian theoreticians have often maintained, one basic human need is to become *many* in spite of being *one*. If a well-mounted dramatic presentation is a complete realization of that urge, *kirtana* appears to be its partial concretization. It is not surprising that the modern Marathi drama of the late nineteenth century, or even its earlier versions, drew so heavily on *kirtana* tradition. The semi-ritualistic, and a rather secular thrust is also to be mentioned. The *kirtana* tradition is accommodative enough to allow a liberalized, as also a more 'earthy' view of gods. In it gods and goddesses vie with each other to be more human than humans. They are full of human frailties and aspirations. Till the last turn of the 'plot', the members of the pantheon continue their 'humanized divine' functions, and only the final intervention of the supernatural element distinguishes them from ordinary human beings. The point is that this totality of circumstances is ideally suited to create characters and roles which, in organically constituted plots, soon acquire a life and will of their own,—thus taking the highway to a dramatic dreamland. It is interesting to note that performing arts, and especially drama (with its variations and sub-genres), thrives wherever the *avatara* concept is explored as the concept is an open invitation to a fascinating exercise of crystallizing ideas into concrete and dynamic agents of action.

DANCE-ORIENTED NARRATIVES

The best specimen of dance-oriented narrative is perhaps the form known as *jagaran*.

In a ritualistic presentation for Khandoba (a sublimated folk deity), a group of three-four performers sing songs of Khandoba and dance to the accompaniment of *dimdi* (a small rim-drum), *tuntune* (a one-stringed, plucked, drone-cum-rhythm instrument), and tinkling bells held by the female dancer-devotee called Murali. The male accompanists are known as Vaghya.

The main feature, among others of ritualistic nature, is the verse-cum-prose narrative of a story which includes the usual mythological attractions such as descriptions of miracles, passages bridging gaps between sacred and profane, moving references to the plight of downtrodden and underprivileged, humour bordering on horse-play and finally, the curious mixture of didacticism, amoral realism, symbolism and metaphysics. An added attraction is, the customarily well-draped Murali. Her dance clearly moves closer to art, though the patterns, movements and gestures are extremely limited in variety and scope. However, the singing, though fast-paced and high-pitched as in *powada*, is interrupted to make way for dance-oriented movements—often at the least expected movements and places. Further, the dance-movements, when introduced, do not maintain relationship of correspondence with the 'message' of the song. On most occasions, dance-movements take place when the chorus sings refrain in a high pitch and consequently they stand out in relief-attracting attention. This juxtaposition with a redundant component (as no information is likely to be conveyed through the repetitive chorus) is meaningful. The strategy is—as it is in art music: there is an international blurring of the selected aesthetic surfaces.

It must have been noticed in the foregoing analysis, that the discussed forms belong to the non-elite, 'folk' category. At least in India, it is preposterous to come to aesthetic or cultural conclusions unless the categorial pentad of Indian expression is taken into consideration. Primitive folk, devotional, art and popular categories deserve attention because they are *not* producer-oriented and represent fundamental moulds of experience which come naturally to the Indian mind. Narrative, as a mode of expression obviously spans over all the five categories. Under the circumstances, what are the criteria/norms which can be identified as effective in the marriage of narrative and performance? The ideal answer would entail separate and detailed discussion of each of the categories. This has not been attempted because folk forms themselves are 'packages'—inevitably bringing together, diverse performing expressions to prove a good sampler demanding considerable sharpening of conceptual tools. For all purposes, the situation is less complicated in other categories, on account of aesthetic as well as socio-cultural factors. For example, in art music, the declared and operative impulse is artistic by intention, the receiver is also inclined to concentrate on audio and non-verbal channels. Moreover, the attitude (—of all concerned) towards temporality, undergoes a radical change in art music. The cumulative result is to deny value to chronology and sequence, and appreciate the non-rational (sometimes even the 'irrational') and simultaneous. This can obviously be a hindrance to narrative, unless it is composed to meet the special situation. In other words, narrative may begin its career in art music with so many handicaps that the race becomes meaningless.

It is significant that art music can have a recognizable narrative only when drama becomes its partner in a joint venture. Art music combined with drama (opera, as the combination is loosely called), handles narrative but the principles of parallel structure and creative ambiguity play a dominant role again.

The story is not different with other categories. For example, the devotional category has all types of *lila*-s (*Ramalila, Rasalila* etc.)— that are veritable packages of narrative and performance. Presentations based on the *dashavatara* (ten reincarnations) also demand similar consideration. Primitive funerals and related rituals are other instances of narratives being a necessary component. Even the popular category is full of forms combining narrative and performing arts. In accordance with the nature and dictates of the category, popular presentations may respond to the temporary and fashionable. However, very often their 'mixes' are better organized or produced with polish. This includes narratives which are more catchy. In other words, a category-wise examination would prove a very challenging proposition.

14

Notation: A Wider Perspective

To consider notation in a wider perspective may lead to different kinds of studies, depending on the chosen context. For example, discussion in a historical context would mean dealing with the chronological account of a particular notation-system such as Hindustani or Carnatic. Another way of contextualizing it is to bring together a number of notation systems in order to compare and contrast them. Yet another possibility is to step beyond the field of music, and discuss notation with reference to the entire family of performing arts. Finally, one may take a view that use of the concept in other sciences and disciplines such as mathematics, chemistry, geography is also to be included in this connection.

It may be deduced that expanding ripples raised by the concept are a natural consequence of fundamental process/es common to areas mentioned. This is to suggest that an important wider perspective on notation is provided by the underlying symbolizing process. With some anticipation, I would put it that quite a few of the controversies, generally raging around notation in India, are in fact, traceable to the reluctance to face issues raised by symbolization in music.

In this widest sense, symbol is anything chosen to stand for, or represent something else. Ordinarily speaking, every notation system could be said to rely on systematized groups of symbols represented graphically to stand for structural and progressional musical elements. For instance, musical aspects such as rhythm, pitch, scales, distribution of textual matter, etc. appear in notation systems because such aspects are structural. On the other hand, most of those items pertaining to tonal quality of progression of music, during a certain span of time refer to elements related to music-making or musical development of ongoing processes. In this way, notation tries to keep in view both aspects of musical events, static as well as dynamic.

However, the most significant feature of any notating situation appears at a deeper level. To notate is to devise and establish visual structures to represent events which essentially take place in the realm of a non-visual sense modality. Hence, to notate is to 'translate', or try to 'translate', manifestations of a non-visual sense modality. In musical notation, it is the aural mode which undergoes this 'translation' process. In dance-notation, a similar approach is taken to deal with patterned physical movements.

At this point, an interesting side-issue deserves to be mentioned. It would appear that written language also carries out a similar translation process. Language, in its written forms, consists of visual symbols devised and systematized in response to the original audio stimuli. I have intentionally brought to notice the similarity between the two basic processes. How is it that the linguistic act of translation of audio into video mode has not attracted adverse comments? The origin of language and script are considerably distanced in time from each other (as are music and notation) and the latter has certainly followed the former. Scripts have of course been criticized for their phonetic inadequacy, but the essential utility of scripting as such, has not been questioned. On the other hand, musicians in India have reacted strongly to the idea and phenomenon of notation. Perhaps, something more than a mere change of modality is involved. However, keeping the matter aside for future consideration, it would be helpful to note some objections to notation before proceeding further:

1. Indian music lays special emphasis on improvisation. Consequently, there is an ever-present theoretical possibility that no music can ever be performed twice. Improvisation means that music changes and that too without warning. In view of this situation, notation would merely become a record of what has already taken place and been relegated to the past. Presentations of Indian music are true instances of the Heraclitan flux and also of aleatory principle (i.e., the principle of chance) in operation. To notate Indian music may therefore amount to denying it a trait unique to its personality.

2. Advocates of notating systems have often argued that notation is merely to be employed in order to preserve authentic framework-compositions. Both in intention and actuality, notation is expected to be skeletal. However, the argument is of deceptive validity because very little scope is afforded to the

skeletal-compositions in Indian music. It is the elaboration of musical ideas implicit in compositions which forms the essence of Indian music. Under the circumstances, the entire exercise of notating Indian music seems to have only a marginal utility.

3. It must be remembered that performance of Indian music depends a great deal on a live exchange of influences between artiste and audience. In fact, through its responses to the artist, the audience encourages him to strive for better musicianship—even at the cost of deviating from the original plan of what to present and how. A written score, and a vogue depending on it is sure to cut off live interrelationship between audience and performer at the source. To say the least, this strikes at the roots of the Indian way of allowing music to flower into significant form.

4. One more likely consequence of notating is certainly of dubious value. Notation is bound to lead people to think that notated versions are 'the' interpretations or 'the' versions. Such versions would then be stated to be definitive editions of works in question. Standardization brought about in such a manner is sure to sound the death knell of Indian musical creativity.

5. Finally, to rely on notation for preservation of music is an act of anachronism when we have more and more high-fidelity devices of sound-recording, etc. at our disposal.

The stage is thus set to discuss the process of symbolization which, as has been suggested earlier, is basic to notation and notational symbols. In all probability, a better comprehension of this fundamental process would make it necessary to review the entire situation. The procedure adopted is to briefly state the essential characteristics of the symbolization process and link them to notation.

To symbolize is essentially human. In fact, to be human is to symbolize. Whatever human beings do, think and feel—is covered by symbolism. Being so human an activity, it is inevitable that music is also subject to symbolization processes. Notation is therefore a by-product of a deeper symbolizing activity which music itself is.

However, musical symbolism is not confined to notation. I have argued elsewhere that musical symbolism is mainly to be perceived as musicological, musico-societal and finally musico-psychological. Even though these symbolistic expressions are not mutually exclusive, a majority of symbolistic operations belong to either of the three varieties. Notational symbolism clearly belongs to the musicological category. Musicology, largely being a grammar of music in India, comes into existence as a post-event formulation. It is logical that one of its product, i.e., the notational system, should follow a similar dynamics. This is the reason why all notational systems have a natal relationship with art music, even though musical symbolism is not in itself confined to art music alone. When applied to other categories of music notation gains an extended scope for operation, but it does not undergo a conceptual change. Notation is a created symbolism and hence its intrinsic connections are with an equally deliberate entity namely, art music. It is therefore to be expected that both qualitative and quantitative shortcomings of notation are found mostly in context of non-art musics.

Symbolization takes place at various levels and consequently symbolistic typology comes into being. Broadly classified, symbols are universal, cultural and personal. This typology refers to origin of symbols a well as to their range of application or validity. Further, symbols can be expressive or communicative. Depending on their mode of origin, symbols are also classified as natural or created. It is clear that all such classifications put together bring home the many-sided operations of symbols.

Turning to notation, how can we characterize notational symbols? Are they universal, cultural or personal? *Prima facie*, it seems that generally notational symbols include all types. In this respect it helps to remember controversies about universality of certain musical elements. Expectably, the considered opinion has been to be wary of claims to universality and to stress the need to accept infinite diversity of musical expression. However, our concern is restricted to symbolistic typology with reference to the notational aspect and therefore some generalizations seem to be in order:

(i) Symbols to represent basic characteristics of sound are universal. For example, highness or lowness, proximity or separateness of individual sound-units have symbols with near universal validity.

(ii) Demarcation of internal musical divisions, subtler pitch-variations or such other musical particularities induces symbols of exclusive cultural validity.

(iii) Composers are known to have resorted to personalized symbol-systems to indicate qualitative features of their mu-

sics more clearly and directly. Timbre, the least standardized of the three acoustic dimensions, is also prone to attract
personal symbols.

It is understandable that personal symbols are more expressive
than communicative while universal and cultural symbols are more
communicative.

The third classification also continues the trend in following
selected interconnections. Consequently, universal notational symbols could be described as natural and the personal as 'created'. The
most important feature of symbols is their infinite generative force.
The primary motive for symbolization, as an activity, can be best
expressed by one of the typically pithy sayings in Indian philosophic
thought. It explains the birth and expansion of universe as caused by
the will of the Supreme Being which says "I am one and will be many".
In other words, individual sensibility feels cribbed, cabined and
confined on account of limitations imposed by one's own person,
society, medium of expression, or mode of exploring a particular
medium. A keenly felt urge to go beyond oneself, and get enriched
by experience otherwise not available, swings into action as it were.
The ambitious task is accomplished by symbolic objects, procedures,
and processes with varying frequency and intensity. It is against this
background that symbols are described as entities which tend to
represent rather than present. Symbols thus enlarge the area of
influence and expand range of experience at the same time.

In this context the following notational features invite attention:

- To notate is to move away from individual performance and
  to treat the musical material for potential performing and
  non-performing musical or music-related events. It is also to
  dissociate music from a particular performer and to make it
  accessible to many.
- Notational systems seem to make an in-built provision for
  interpretation. Portions, passages, and movements are loosely
  notated to give performers a choice.

Symbolization has two other features allied closely with symbological motivation. They are mentioned separately because of their
far-reaching consequences.

Symbolization operates through reversal of the fundamental
experiential dimensions of time and space as also through compulsive, mutual and supportive functions of the audio and video sense
modalities.

Symbolization is inclined to create a perceptual, dimensional mirror. If the actual experiential act is on the temporal plane, symbolization takes place on the spatial plane, and *vice versa.* Similarly, if the primary experience is in the audio mode, symbolization occurs in the video mode, though the reverse is not true. The matter of identifying the modality best suited to the primary and actual act of experiencing is a question of choice, but once the choice is made, the sense modality in which symbolization takes place is very nearly predetermined. It is very inefficient and hence rare, to have the primary activity as well as the symbolization in the same mode.

To turn to notation is to immediately sense the conversion of musical temporality into a deliberate, notional spatiality. All time-values in music become space-values in notation. All audio experience is turned into video representation. By virtue of its being spatial and visual, notation responds to the basic human desire to perceive bi-dimensionally. We are disposed to isolate dimensions and modalities for the sake of artistic activity, but nature or life compels to allocate at least a minimal role to the ignored dimensions and modalities. It is significant that of the five the musical categories, it is the art music, the most non-visual of them all, which concerns itself with notation the most. A corroborative evidence is that non-art musics suffer more if presented exclusively through the audio while art music thrives in such situations.

A number of symbolistic operations would appear less mysterious if the very real human quality of synesthesia is remembered. The phenomenon of transferred sensation has a significant part to play in symbolizing. In the present context is necessary to know that synesthesia does not enjoy an unlimited sensory mobility. There are synesthetic pairs of senses for the transfer of sensations involved. The sense of sound and sight constitute one of the major pairs.

I would venture to put forward a hypothesis in connection with notation: The shapes and figurations of notational symbols indicate that they result from the synesthetic relationship between sound and movement translated graphically. Sounds, when produced and heard, give rise to body movements and gestures. The latter are subsequently translated into visual presentations on which notation systems rely for their basic itemization.

Symbolization brings forth relationships between two or more entities otherwise enjoying independent existence. Thus understood, one of the two referents in musical symbolism can be identified to be extra-musical. Therefore the instances of musical symbolism in which music stands for social hierarchy, seasonal cycles, various phases of human life, etc.

The extra-art connections of musical symbolism play an important part in bestowing significance on music. It is easily seen that art music, by its deliberate concentration on the temporal and audio, etc. allows very limited scope for extra-musical symbolism and significance derived therefrom. Consequently the symbolizing proclivities are forced to operate in a narrow channel—namely, of notation. Through notation musical symbolism tries to gain advantages other musical categories get from extra-musical symbolism. Finally, symbolization relies on a medium possessing following qualities:

- Divisibility—the capacity of the medium to allow subdivisions according to symbolistic requirements.
- Ambiguity—an innate capacity to suggest a variety of meanings. To put it negatively, the medium must reject firm lexicographic pinning down.

A look at various notational systems shows that visual symbols are easy to alter, modify, or cancel. Further, the notational components lack strong lexical content in themselves.

Notation has a technical aspect which has been frequently discussed with both favour and fervor. However, I submit that the deeper issue of connections between symbolizing propensities on the one hand, and of the special correlation between audio and video modes need more attention.

15

Limits, Borders and Boundaries: Performance

Let us begin with some definitions to help coping with the innumerable available choices. The definitions are based on terminological usage commonly recorded in standard dictionaries.

Limits are agents employed to mark off one unit from the other tangible as well as intangible life areas. The Indian equivalent would be *maryada*. *Borders* are physical, external and perceivable divisions naturally operating in the tangible world. The Indian equivalent would be *seema*. Finally, *boundaries* are notional (and not national) admissions, by individuals or cultural groups, that they have exhausted possibilities and potentialities of selected life-areas. Expectably, the notional mark-off, i.e., boundary, is too varied to fit in any single term. Different life-areas normally enjoy their own distinctive conceptual structures and requisite terminological clusters, developed gradually but inevitably.

Without exaggeration 'boundary' could be identified as the most accommodative of the three terms. Being notional, boundaries are stable, as well dynamic at the same time. They operate collectively because they exist as a web. Never disappearing completely, they register constant shifts. In the ultimate sense, boundaries are initiators of action as well as interaction because they compel an active relationship between ever-felt extremes. In their presence, bi polarities, imagined as well as imaginable, disappear. We generally recognize bi-polarities because they invariably simplify the world around. Hence, boundaries need to be appreciated as powers—constantly engaged in creating (in us) a spectral awareness, a function which necessarily rejects validity of bi-polar views of reality. Shifting boundaries people the world in which we place dichotomies such as activity and art, sensation and emotion, sense and thought, subject and object and ultimately, seer and seen. The story of human culture is a tale being told by boundaries. To understand a culture is to study how it sets up, transcends and resets boundaries. A similar strategy of focusing attention on boundaries also helps in understanding human nature. I may as well note, with some anticipation, that one of the chief tools available to human genius, in its ongoing efforts to deal with boundaries as a phenomenon, is performance. Against this backdrop, I intend to discuss data drawn chiefly from Hindustani music, drama and dance. However, the inherent qualities, experiences and cultural placement of the performing arts in India would mean occasional sorties in other areas of life.

TIME, PLACE AND CIRCUMSTANCE

There is some truth in the common view that all boundaries are finally felt as boundaries of time, place and circumstance (i.e., *desha, kala* and *paristhiti*). All actions, including those conventionally described as inactions, are subject to these real restrictions and they, it is argued, can hardly be called notional. However, it is easy to see that these limitations and their functions are necessarily nullified by a special human possession: mind. Further, mind has three inter-linked and mutually influencing powers—in memory, imagination and interpretation. Through operations of the trinity, human beings ceaselessly try and occasionally succeed in shifting boundaries of time, place and circumstance. It should be obvious that the conceptual map, thus put forward, holds true even in non-art areas of life. The map is however to be processed and refined according to the special requirements of each area of life. Additional and derived concepts are required to be identified and systematically placed, methodologies are to be hammered out, techniques perfected, experiences received and evaluated, conventions created and those judged to have adequate potential are finally to be consolidated to build a tradition. In this way, cultures and subcultures emerge to move inexorably and spirally, towards—who knows what?

THE ART TRANSFORMATION

To manipulate basic boundaries through using memory, imagination and interpretation is however not sufficient to bring in quality—the one distinguishing aspect of all art-experience. The three powers must bring into being entities endowed with an aesthetic potential to ensure presence of quality. Over centuries, and on account of contributions from numerous cultures, this transformation of experience into art becomes a reality. In the specific context of performing arts, the process of transformation had succeeded in extracting rhythm from time, space from place, and situation from circumstance—these being fundamental to music, dance and drama respectively. This is not to suggest that, rhythm, space and situation are *essences*. They are, however, original pulses or impulses of the respective arts. With some simplification, they are comparable to the first cry of a new-born. The cry marks the beginning of a life— but not that of a deliberately drawn pattern. In other words, the three concepts require to be elaborated, added to and modified. More interestingly, they are also explored in combination with concepts inherent to other arts or life-areas. The analogical transfer, and the subsequent use of the resulting non-art concepts never fail to generate fascinating creative activity as also a critical response. In a manner of speaking, what takes place is a conceptual *transposition* intended to create a melody which, though different, yet retains identifying marks of its original self. Significant chapters are added to this story when genres, mediums and techniques play their respective roles.

Whether at the level of identifying the basic concepts of place, time and circumstance, or while discussing the derived trinity of space, rhythm and situation through operations of memory, imagination and interpretation—the effort is directed at shifting boundaries to different planes and for various purposes. These measures result in enrichment, refinement, and valuableness of experience. Performance, the distinguishing feature of dance, drama and music—creates and shifts boundaries. In the process, it finds opportunities to utilize and extend possibilities of the human mind. This makes us work towards the ideal of establishing meaningful and durable mind-body relationship.

It is against this backdrop that some instances of creating, transcending and resetting boundaries (through powers of memory, imagination and interpretation by exploring channels of rhythm, space and situation), with performance as the agent—are to be examined. This is, to say the least, ambitious. However, there fortunately exists one genre in history of Indian performing arts which displays the protean capacity to adapt to jealous demands of music, dance as well as drama—and that too simultaneously. I refer to *song*. The Greek god Proteus possessed two special powers: he could prophesy and could also assume different shapes and features. However, there was a snag. To succeed in eliciting a prophecy from him one was obliged to bind him down securely to one shape. Song may be said to exhibit similar despairing volatile tendencies. A song is a song and yet differently so in musical, dramatic and dance contexts.

This is the reason why the thesis usually put forward: song is a test of crossed boundaries and an indicator of the depth of cultural changes. When a song changes, everything can be assumed to have undergone a transformation. I wonder whether the proposition can be stated from the other side. Can a song be consciously and deliberately changed in order to bring about deeper cultural changes? Is it possible to posit a reverse causation? Further, is permissible to maintain that the case actually indicates a more complex phenomenon—namely, that of mutual causation? Perhaps these are questions for the better minds to tackle. I seek an easy way out—of raising questions, but only to back away from them. It is also possible to hold that causation is merely *one* of the principles governing and explaining life as a mode of existence. Causation constitutes an important, but by no means an exclusive relationship, making sense of otherwise puzzling diversities of life. The urge to enjoy a harmonious coexistence of disparate components, and the inborn human compulsion to acquire non-representational (or least minimally representational) centre in order to reflect (and thus put forth all human concerns with considerable abstraction)—these are the two factors which make the song genre so pre-eminent. A song, though generally interpreted as a musical entity, is, in reality, a package of life experience. To carry out a contextual study of song is, therefore, a major strategy of cultural investigation (and perhaps of cultural rejuvenation).

For illustrative consideration of the changing character and effects of song in India, it is necessary to present data from various periods and regions. This quest for comprehensive data-collection is also to be combined with a alert concern to maintain direct linkage with music-making and music-makers. The idea should be to devote attention to song-related features which provide cultural frameworks conducive to song-changes. For the sake of convenience the following features may be listed:

    1. Linguistic and musical competence of the music-maker.

2. Character of cultural centres with which the music-maker is in contact.
3. Song-maker's exposure to alien musical systems.
4. Song-maker's attitude towards non-indigenous cultures.
5. Song-maker's approach to religion.
6. Inherent musicality and the general status of prevalent verse-forms.
7. Latitude allowed to the song-genre for appearing in diverse and/or free settings.
8. Recognition of the Hindu-Muslim complementarity.

It is possible that some other aspects can be added to the list, or that the situations analyzed and personalities discussed may fail to establish linkages with each of the identified aspects. However, it is believed that in most cases, the mutual correlationship of song-conducive features and the song-creator's work would become evident.

AMIR KHUSRO (1253–1325)

Born in village Patiyali, district Etah in Uttar Pradesh, to a Turk father and Brajabasi mother, Khusro had the benefit of exposure to linguistic and cultural diversity in his impressionable years and, that too at close quarters. When Khusro was barely eleven—he lost his father, a fact which encouraged closer relationship with his mother. Women have been known to be repositories and carriers of folk-songs. It is symptomatic that Khusro began writing poetry at the tender age of eight and by the time he was twelve, he had gained a considerable facility in composing verses. I want to suggest that closer ties with his mother and inclination to write verses helped to create, in his mind, a pro-attitude towards imaginative and musical moulding of language. In a way, it was therefore a foregone conclusion that he became known for mastery over Persian, Turkish, Arabian and Hindi. It is also significant that he expressed high regard for Sanskrit, though he never came to learn it. Obviously, he stored in his memory, the fascinating rhythms of different languages, as they were written and/or spoken—in a period known for a predominantly oral tradition.

According to some accounts, Khusro's mother was a Hindu. He was, we are told, looked after by his mother's father. In other words, circumstances were culturally variegated and Khusro's sensitive mind (which must have become more alert due to father's absence), grew up in a situation full of nuances.

In an event-filled life of 70-odd years, Khusro reportedly travelled to and stayed in, the following places: Patiyali, Delhi, Lucknow(ti), South Multan (1276), Herat and Balakh (1284–5), Avadh and Bengal (1324).

Also on record are his numerous court-tenures, of varying durations, under (no less than.) ten different rulers: Kishli Khan (1265–7), Bugra Khan, Shahjada Muhammad (from 1276), Giasuddin Balban (1285 onwards), Amir Ali Jamdar, Kaikubad (1287–9), Jalaluddin Khilji (1290–5), Alauddin Khilji (1295–1316), Qutbuddin Khilji (1316–20), and Ghiasuddin Tughlaq (1320–5).

It is important to note that all places he stayed in were centres—culturally active and noticeably different from each other. In addition, his patrons also displayed varied cultural orientations. For example, Khusro's stay at Multan brought him in contact with Sheikh Kadawa, son of Sheikh Bahauddin Zakaria, proficient in Persian music. His visit to Bengal obviously exposed him to the Vaishnavite tradition, musically so potent.

Under Kaikubad's patronage, Khusro received special favours, firstly, because Kaikubad's mother (like Khusro's) was a Hindu, and secondly, because Kaikubad was a lover of Indian languages, especially, those described as dialects. A lover of music, Kaikubad made an important deviation by expressly cultivating secular, as distinct from the sacred stream of music—flowing so abundantly in India. It is from his times that Avadh-based music and musicians secured a firm footing in Delhi.

The next period in Khusro's career is specially meaningful in the present context. Three Khilji monarchs successively became his patrons, and each one signalled a musico-cultural change. It is during the Khilji reign that more than seven hundred Sufi-s dispersed all over India though, it is to be noted that the first Khilji—the 70-year-old Jalaluddin—persecuted Sufi-s for their political ambitions. Jalaluddin was enthusiastic about secular music.

Alauddin Khilji, on the other hand, worked with Sufi saints—through Khusro. From his successive and successful campaigns, [Gujarat (1297), Ranthambor (1299), Chittoor (1303), Devagiri (1306–7), Dwarasamudra (1310), Madura (1311), interior Maharashtra (1312)], Alauddin was instrumental in introducing diverse musical elements in Delhi. For example, from Gujarat he brought Paramaras—a caste of musicians known for their musical expertise as well as physical beauty. During the celebrations of his son's (Khizr Khan) marriage with a Hindu princess, Devalrani, he brought to Delhi performing troupes from the south. These groups settled in Delhi. Qutbuddin Khilji was himself a noted performer, as was the later Khusro Khan, who assumed the name, Nasiruddin on ascending the throne. Ghiasuddin Tughlaq, the last of Khusro's patrons, loved music to the extent that he convened an assembly to decide on the vexed issue of legitimacy of music according to Islam.

In sum, Khusro's patrons and the places he worked at, ensured exposure to and assimilation of, diverse musical influences. Musical forms, melodic frameworks, instrumental timbers, larger systems employed to organize, as well as to exploit, the varied and usable material—all made a deep impact on him. Not only had he a ringside seat to watch the fascinating spectacle of cultural confrontations at rulers courts and the Sufi *khanqah*-s, but he could play a major part in most of them.

Khusro's attitude to religion is an important component of his musicianship. It is known that he became a favourite disciple of Sheikh Nizamuddin Chishti at a very early age.

The cultural role of Sufi-s in India has a long history. Some facts relevant to the present discussion are:

1. Sufi sects, which were welcome and found firm footing in India, were those who were well disposed towards music.
2. Sufi saint's insistence on using common people's language, along with ritualistic use of music helped in making music a part of everyday life as also for every individual.
3. The ecstatic role allotted to music by Sufi-s clearly proved conducive to propagation of song-form, as a package of dance, language and music.
4. Sufi adoption of the Basant festival and the *rang* ceremony is a pointer to their Indianization.
5. Sufi *qawawal*-s could be described as popularizers of the Perso-Arabic system of music.
6. The Sufi institution of *sama,* with its accent on collective devotion, combined with the prolific and wide-based poetic achievement of Amir Khusro, became a major musical force.
7. Amir Khusro's Sufi attachment allowed him an easy access to the common Indian because the latter found the Sufi-s exciting and yet familiar. This was so mainly on account of the basic devotional inclinations.

8. Sufi-s and Hindu saints, along with their respective kinds of music, form a parallelogram of forces which Khusro could easily explore and exploit on account of his overall religious stance.

Khusro reportedly authored over 99 books. In the third volume of his poems, he also refers to his having composed many works in Hindawi. Unfortunately, these have not been so far unearthed. However, Sufi-s and Hindu saints in devotional movements all over India, are known to have stressed the role of Prakrit languages. It is safe to conclude that Khusro strengthened the trend—in opposition to the Perso-Arabic dominance by writing songs, if not poetry in Hindawi. It was song which helped in fighting off the pressures of languages backed by the establishment, as also the insistence on the written tradition. Both Hindu saints and Sufi-s prove the fact.

What Khusro contributed to the Hindi poetic tradition is not our concern at the present moment. However, it is necessary to note that he is credited with having added new forms, prosodic moulds, imagery as well as a new content or tone to the prevailing poetic literature in Hindi.

Islam was well established as an Indian religion by the time Khusro was active on the cultural and political scene. Generations of Muslims were born and nurtured in India, since the first Islamic Arabs entrenched themselves in the subcontinent. To many Muslims, India was motherland and traditions developed in India were for them worthy of admiration and preservation. To such Nationalist or Indophile Muslims, the constant 'looking for guidance', to the land of birth of Islam—was hardly acceptable. Amir Khusro was one of them. Hence, his assertive praise of Indians, Indian climate, flora and fauna, languages, customs, and manners. He went so far that his loyalty to Islam was itself suspected by Maulavi-s and their ilk. Amir Khusro's love of the land is amply brought out in his work *Nuh Cipher*, completed in 1318. It has nine *(nuh)* chapters (*ciphers*, i.e., spheres) consisting of 4,506 poetic lines. The chapters respectively deal with:

1. Praise of Qutbuddin Khilji and description of his campaign to Devagiri.
2. Buildings commissioned by Qutbuddin Khilji.
3. India and features of Indian culture.
4. Instructions/suggestions to the emperor and his servants.
5. Indian winter and hunting.

6. Birth celebrations of Shahzada Muhammad.
7. Description of Nauroz and Basant festivities.
8. Outdoor games.
9. His own poetry.

Against this background, Khusro's high regard for the Brahmins (he compared them with Aristotle), or his exalted praise for the unique, pacifying qualities of Indian music appear natural and sincere.

It is true that nothing from his available output deals directly and technically with music. One of the possibilities is that, some of his writings or treatises on music are yet waiting for a dramatic discovery. Or perhaps, he chose to develop an intuitive and performing approach to musics he was aware of. In other words, he chose to order his musical knowledge and perception by composing songs of a new type rather than adopting a full-scale technical-theoretical approach.

However, it must be recorded that Khusro is credited to have formulated a new musicological systematization (*mata*) described as Indraprastha Mata or Chaturdandi Sampradaya. Experts point out that it established a twelve-note scale and described and classified *raga*-s on that basis. In the complete process, a radical departure was registered—from the traditional approach of constructing *grama* for the basic tonal organization and composing *murchhana* for musical elaboration. He is also reported to have brought into circulation *tarana* and *kaul*, two specific genres which were additions to the prevailing array of musical forms. It is rightly pointed out that neither the singing of God's praises (which was a feature of *kaul*), nor the use of meaningless syllables as auspicious in music (as was practised in *tarana*), were novelties on the Indian musical scene. This merely proves the cultural and musical complementarity of the Hindu tradition and Khusro's Indianization of the alien (as contrasted with the Indian), Islamic musical tradition, namely, the Perso-Arabic.

TAPPA IN BENGAL

The second case study I propose to take up is separated by centuries from Khusro and songs he created.

Ramanidhi Gupta, popularly known as Nidhubabu, was born in a relative's house in Chanpta village (district Hoogley), in 1741. The

family had moved from Calcutta, shortly before his birth, to escape
the troubled conditions arising out of the Maratha campaigns. However, at the age of six, he was taken back to Calcutta to ensure sound
education. By this time, the English had built a fort in Calcutta and
the place had become safer. Ramanidhi's father, Harinarayan Gupta,
soon arranged for his son's learning Persian and Sanskrit. Ten years
before the battle of Plassey, which was to change the destiny of Bengal entirely,—to learn English could not have been an easy task,
nor would everyone have imagined that learning the *firangi* tongue
would prove important. However, Harinarayana arranged for
Ramanidhi's private tuition from a missionary. It is difficult to over-
estimate the significance of the act. Ramanidhi's first marriage took
place in 1761 and his first son was born in 1768. However, unfortunately he lost both wife and son—very early, and was remarried in
1771. In 1775, Nidhubabu entered government service by securing
employment in the British collectorate at Chapra where, he spent
all 'extra' time with musicians specializing in Hindustani *khayal, tappa*
and *ghazal.* He stayed in Chapra till he was 55, when he retired and
came back to Calcutta (to get married for the third time in 1794).
He lived a long and fruitful life in his parental house, attracted a
large following and notable fame. He had begun composing Bengali
tappa-s from his Chapra days. At the age of 97, i.e., in 1937–8, he
published a book of his own compositions under the title *Geetaratna*
and earned an apt sobriquet—the Shouri Miyan of Bengal. He died
on April 15, 1839. Certain song-conducive features of the situation
in Bengal, prevailing at the time of Nidhubabu's successful evolution of the new song genre could be identified:

1. Nidhubabu was not enticed by the prevalent non-elite forms
    of music such as Panchali and Kavigan, but took intensely to
    Hindustani music as propagated by Muslim musicians in the
    areas west of Bengal. It is to be noted, that in spite of his love
    for Hindustani musical expression, he never attempted a visit
    to Gwalior, the known Kashi for *tappa*-singing etc. Even
    Lucknow did not figure in his music education. It is instruc-
    tive to remember that Shouri Miyan, acknowledged to have
    created a prototype of *tappa* during the reign of Shuja-ud-
    daula III (1753–75) of Lucknow, could not have become a
    household name in a place like Chapra where Nidhubabu
    stayed from 1776–94. The point is that, Nidhubabu appears
    to have created a new prototype by deviating from three ma-

jor musical sources of his times, namely Bengali folk music, Hindustani art music and the prevailing *tappa*-music. His *tappa* was a deviant song.

2. Nidhubabu's one major, conscious and premeditated contribution was the use of Bengali language. He explicitly says:

> *Nanan desher nanan bhasha*
> *Bina shodeshiyo bhasha pure ki asha*
> *Koto nodi sarobor, kiba phol chatokir*
> *Dhara jol bine kobhu ghuche ki trisha.*

> Kamod-Khamaj, Teental

3. Another notable facet of his compositions was a secular content. He clearly deviated from the Indian devotional model of singing about love indirectly, and preferably through mythological pairs (usually) Radha and Krishna. In this context, it is interesting to note that Nidhubabu was unambiguously charged for obscenity of his songs. Bankimchandra (1838–94), the famous novelist and Haraprasad Shastri, the well-known writer on Indological subjects, were among those who preferred the charge. Experts have pointed out that the anthology of his compositions, which Nidhubabu himself published towards the end of his life, does not contain a single line to deserve the charge. It is therefore rightfully suggested that, in all probability, many obscene compositions were being passed off under his name—as happens to any creator of widely appreciated songs. I would like to add that, to some extent, the charge was thrown up because of the demytholization of love—which his songs celebrate so eloquently.

4. A minor, but notable particular is Nidhubabu's status as a musician. He could be described as a near-amateur. Till he retired, he divided his energies between official duties and music. However, even in his post-retirement phase, when he was offered patronage chiefly by Rasikchand Goswami of Baghbazar, Nidhubabu never went to anybody's house to give a concert. Students of the cultural history of Bengal have marked well that Hindu musicians (in contrast with Muslim), do not find a clear mention in court-records because they functioned on non-professional basis. Nidhubabu's patrons had to make a pilgrimage to his house to listen to him.

5. In *Geetaratna*, only 95 compositions are included. The anthology, however, produces two interesting bits of musicological and performing information. Firstly, the author makes a specific recommendation of the performing time-span of *raga*-s used. Secondly, *tappa* compositions are composed in *raga*-s such as Alaiya-bilawal, Yaman, Adana and Yaman-puriya, Yaman-jhinjoti, etc. This is contrary to the generally held view that the genre was to focus on *kshudra*, i.e., light or minor *raga*-s. Two other features are: the slow tempo Nidhubabu adopted for singing *tappa*-s, and composing of specific *tala*-s for rendering. Obviously, a very major change is brought about by manipulation of tempi. The compositions would appear to a contemporary listener, more like Hindustani *thumri* than *tappa*.

6. Even though *tappa* is legitimately held up as Nidhubabu's chief contribution, it is instructive to note that his innovation covered a wider area. I submit that his non-*tappa*-innovations were destined to finally crystallize in *tappa* as the most a complete or representative expression of Nidhubabu's musical genius. As far as Nidhubabu was concerned, *tappa* was the musical summation. His contributions to two other genres, namely *akhadi gaan* and half-*akhadi* have been talked about. On examination, they do not indicate any distinctive musical features *not* displayed by his *tappa*-s. According to available descriptions, both forms were presentation-wise more dramatic. They involved presence, arrangement and performance characterized by a competitive spirit, often degenerating into expression of unabashed and unfair hostility. They also relied heavily on a controlled use of a number of instruments. Obviously, greater funding and conspicuous patronage were the prerequisites. Nidhubabu's introvert, secular and highly individual musical vision must have been ill at ease when he toyed with these forms.

The musician in him gradually came to rest in *tappa* in which he proved to be a *vaggeyakara* at his best.

THE *LAVANI* IN MAHARASHTRA

One leap across limits of time and borders of geography and we get another notable instance of song-change. I refer to the crystallization of the form known as *lavani*, and especially the type called Baithakichi *lavani* based noticeably on *raga* and *tala*. Honaji Bala (1754–1844) is regarded creator of this form which drew on the Hindustani system of art music.

Honaji Sayaji Shilarkhane was a Nandagavali by caste. The profession of *shahiri* was a family tradition, as Honaji's grandfather Satappa Gavali and uncles, Kushaba and Bala (Bahiru) were known practitioners of *tamasha*, a presentation-framework of which *lavani* was an important component. Honaji probably lost his father early.

Honaji tended cattle and *tamasha* was, ostensibly, his hobby. His performances were a result of musical partnership. Honaji composed and, reportedly another artist, Bala Karanjkar sang them—hence the paired name Honaji Bala. It is, however possible Honaji, who lost his father early, was looked after by his uncle Bala Bahiru (who was perhaps Honaji's *guru*), and hence the name. During the reign of Sawai Madhavarao Peshwa (1774–95), Honaji received recognition as well as patronage. His compositions on the *rang* (colour) festivities of the Peshwa, and another on the battle of Kharda against the British were appreciated in the court. Rewarded generously by the Peshwa, Honaji was also well-received at the court of the Gaekwad-s of Baroda. Honaji was brutally murdered around 1844, presumably on account of professional rivalry and extreme hostility.

It was during the reign of Bajirao II (1775–1851),[1] that Honaji effected the revolutionary song-change (if anything can be described as revolutionary in music) associated with him. The change is marked by following features:

1. Honaji stabilized the style and idiom introduced by his uncle—by continuing low pitched singing, as also the slower tempo. It should be obvious that both these factors directly facilitate musical elaboration, and use of music marked by persuasive delicacy than aggressive dazzle.

2. At the second phase, the slower and quieter music of Honaji's *lavani*-s, was merged with the vogue of *baithak*, i.e., the mode of music-presentation in which artists sit down to perform in a drawing room.

3. Thirdly, at the instance of patron Bajirao, Honaji went a step to compose new *lavani*-s, in various *raga*-s and *tala*-s.

4. The courtesans, accustomed to sing *khayal*, *tappa* or *dhrupad* in the *baithak* mode, were coached by Honaji to sing Marathi compositions. Predictably he also thought it necessary and

proper to replaced *dholaki* by *tabla*. It is reported that there was stiff opposition to the newly evolved genre from Bajirao's favourite courtesan, Vyankat Narasi. For sometime Honaji had to leave Pune for Bombay, where he trained a professional singer called Ahilya Kamathin to render his *lavani*-s. Honaji, then came back to Pune and regained his hold by overcoming all opposition. It was then that the Baithakichi *lavani* struck firm roots.

5. The printed body of Honaji's songs is not a great help in reconstructing the tradition. Firstly, because, curiously, it hardly contains compositions short enough to be described as Marathi *thumri*-s. However, there is room to assume existence of such compositions as *Shaligram* (1924, third edition) and *Kelkar* (1963), Honaji's two major anthologists, allude to such songs. Secondly, and rather surprisingly, the songs carry no indication of *raga*-s and *tala*-s in the headings/titles of the printed compositions. On the contrary, there is an invariable mention of other composer's compositions (e.g., Rama Joshi, Saganbhau, etc.) to suggest actual tunes of compositions in question. It is logical to argue that what has been recognized as Honaji's unique contribution should have figured in some way in the printed documentation. In one of my presentations, I have therefore ventured to suggest that Honaji merely began a musical evolution which was to bear fruit soon after his death and the honour of working out musical implications of Honaji's vision may go to the later and Bombay-based artists. However, the significance of Honaji's pioneering achievement is in no way diminished.

Baithakichi *lavani,* as the genre is described, is in need of reappraisal—by performing musicians and practising musicologists alike. In all probability, it suffered an eclipse because other forms, with similar or same strengths, appeared on the musical horizon of Maharashtra. Stage songs and *kathaka thumri* may easily come to mind. However, the matter requires an independent inquiry. Of equal importance is the fact that tastes of two new classes emerging during the British period of Indian history, namely, merchant and middle classes underwent changes. However that too is another story.

CONCLUSION

The three case-studies of *vaggeyakara*-s are obviously to be treated as samplers. Dance-oriented and drama-dominated song would have to be scrutinized to complete the inquiry to give it the promised wide perspective. To that extent, much ground remains to be covered. And yet, sufficient boundaries have been already crossed to allow observations common to cases discussed, and suggest conclusions ranging much beyond the scope of the immediate inquiry.

- In order to cross boundaries, it helps to cross borders. Our heroes achieved the feat, at a pace which allowed them to gather multiple impressions. I suggest that these impressions finally proved useful to the trinity because impressions gathered enriched the repositories of our heroes sensory imageries. It was the sensory imagery which the trinity crystallized into the selected avenue, namely song-making.

- They exemplify the Indian mode of transcending the final boundary—the one in the individual unconscious. In India, Hindu mind seeks Islamic support to come to terms with the robust, the earthy, mind the sensuous of its own unconscious. On its part, and the Muslim seeks to achieve a similar acceptance of reality—by creating a place for the Hindu clarity, charitableness or tolerance and austerity in its own unconscious. Acceptance of each other's ultimate values at the unconscious level is well reflected in Indian art, literature and generally in all things of the mind. To complete their own respective stories, both Hindus and Muslims have to cross psychological boundaries. It is not accidental that valuable results were obtained because Amir Khusro's Muslim faith could include respect for Brahmins, Nidhubabu's creative mind could combine a new musical format of Islamic inspiration with secular Bengali poetry and Honaji's genius could secure a release from the hold of an aggressively set, mythological and narrative form to enter into a world of leisurely moving, sensuous and earthy music-making in the Hindustani mode.

- The three song-makers made repeated deviations, major and minor, from the already established and accepted formats before arriving at the new song.

- The song, as a genre, nearly proclaims a qualitative superiority of the individual mind over the collective and/or social. Notably, the three song-makers clearly opted for structures inherently less rigid and hence more conducive to elaboration of musical ideas as well as to individual interpretation.

- As a corollary to the defiant assertion of individual mind, song-makers seem to prefer paradoxical combinations to safer equations of proven legitimacy. Thus, Amir Khusro moved nearer to Indian languages but combined with them a non-Indian musical idiom. Nidhubabu preferred a new musical idiom but not the language conducive to it, while Honaji opted for new instrumental timbre, stricter and highly coded *raga-tala* frameworks—but only to employ them in a looser form.

- Finally, in a song—are merged the non-representational, abstracted and somewhat mystical urges felt by lyricists among poets, musicians among music-craftsmen and visionaries among those who try to understand reality through intellection. The non-verbal, paradoxical, non-rational and the extremely individual cannot hope to have a better vehicle than a song—to cross all kinds of boundaries.

REFERENCE

1. Bajirao II finally surrendered to the British in 1819, bringing Maratha sovereignty to an end.

16

The 'Felt' Space in Music and Theatre

What does the term 'felt' mean? Whatever may be its correct meaning, my intention is to contrast the term with some other spatial descriptions such as 'actual, measurable and objectively perceived'. Two other terms come to mind because they resonate with the term 'felt'—mythical and virtual. In my opinion the triad draws attention to an important aspect: quality of experience afforded to users by space in action at a particular point of time. By mentioning the triad at the very beginning I am, in a way, setting the tone for what is to follow. It is symptomatic that etymologically, the word 'to feel' means 'to experience by touch', indicating thereby, a kind of immediacy. It is like playing the *tanpura* to fill the performing space before a musician begins his ambitious quest for music that can reach the skies. It is my express wish to concentrate on the nature and quality of space as a component of theatric and musical performances. Not that the relevant scholastic traditions are being passed by. But they will be called on only in dire academic emergencies. This same bias perhaps justifies thinking of music and theatre together, even though the discussion begins with reference to music.

THE SPACE OF OUR INTEREST

It would be well to remember that space and music, as entities, are on entirely different planes. Space is a fundamental dimension while music is a highly processed, artistic and, in fact, an 'artificial' reality. (One is reminded that the Sanskrit word *kritrima* is derived as *kritya nirmitam*, i.e., deliberately created.) I suggest that we should care to distinguish between ether, space and arena—employed, respectively, to connote natural force, physical dimension and finally a highly processed activity, controlled and created by performance. Indian terminological equivalents would be *akasha*,

avakasha and *rangavakasha*—the third being our chief concern.
One may also note at this point temporal parallels helpful to conceptual understanding. They would be Time (*kala*), temporality
(*kalikata*) and rhythm (*laya*). When we note the third formulation
namely, sequence (*krama*), causality (*karan-karya bhava*) and event
(*ghatit*)— the transformation of nature into art (—to borrow from
Ananda Coomaraswamy) is complete.

Thus, the present brief keeps both ether and space, out and away.
Arena (*rangavakasha*), the performing space is further divided into
musical and dramatic spaces. In a matching comedown, the inquiry
descends from metaphysical heights to aesthetic planes. In addition, loyalty is pledged to performing, as contrasted with scholastic
traditions. Obviously, there are enough qualifying clauses to clear
the space for an intelligible discussion. Moving from a fundamental
dimension to performing perspectives, illustrates a progressive narrowing down. Thus we lose in the name of comprehensiveness to
gain in tangibility and specificity-providing the endeavour with a
local habitation and a name.

MUSIC AND SPACE: SOME ISOMORPHISMS

Terms come into being when responses are verbalized, verbalization is codified when experience proves too diverse, and finally,
codification tries to catch up with performance—because performance gives rise to new responses. Therefore, terms in circulation
are windows on performers universe. It is in this context that some
musico-spatial isomorphisms claim attention.

In general musical usage, a number of musicological terms display spatial character. For example, we speak of long and short notes
and phrases, as also of tonal spaces. Spacing of notes is repeatedly
referred to. Further, some musical features are naturally explained
in spatial terms. For instance, a chord is usually recommended for
its capacity to evoke tonal depth. As a musical arrangement, mono-
phony is easily connected with a linear experience while polyphony
is noted for its plane juxtaposition of musical notes. Equally common, is the description of the harmonic way of organizing tonal
material as 'vertical', and of the melodic as 'horizontal'. The question to be posed is: Why are spatial terms considered necessary and
adequate for the task entrusted to them?

It has been argued that putting spatial terms to use in context of essentially temporal experiences is ascribable to analogy—a much favoured tool in the human thinking process. This is why Berlioz was prompted to exclaim 'High and low pitch are only literary ideas'. The suggestion is that spatial descriptions of temporal phenomena are, logically viewed, clear cases of attributing properties of the former to the latter. At this stage of the discussion I would submit that there may be more to it than using analogy as the facilitating, descriptive device. The matter needs to be analyzed, though a little later and also at a deeper level.

AN INTER-ARTS PERSPECTIVE

Yet another way of relating music and space is through embarking in inter-arts comparisons or exchanges. A concept that has proved rather attractive in this connection is 'architectonics', meaning 'structural design in a work of music'. Derived from *architektonikós* (Greek for 'a leading builder'), the term has been persuasively introduced in literary criticism to indicate structural harmony as also to stress organic unity of form and content. As is known, an evolutionary phase of literary criticism in the West accorded the highest place to music in a hierarchical systematization of arts, because music offered an easily perceivable example of the unity of form and content. It has been astutely pointed out that the view (a la Pater—'All arts aspire to the state of music') was symptomatic of ascendency of time-arts over space-arts. To bring in the idea of the architectonic in critical reasoning, perhaps indicates a turning of the tide in favour of space-arts—as the concept leads to application of spatial norms to non-spatial expressions. Such procedures are not unusual, but the question is: What is the rationale governing them? The wide spread existence, and periodic recurrences of inter-art isomorphisms imply something more than mere analogical transfer or reorganization of art-families.

It is not surprising that more ambitious attempts to associate architecture with music are on record. For example, M.A. Dhaky, a well-known researcher in Indian arts and architecture complains that "the correspondence between ancient Indian music and architecture is somewhat hazily drawn, even unsuspected in most quarters." (p. 397.) In fact, he goes on to assert that "The musical system for a given region and period, on the observations so far made, must then reveal parallel principles of creation and creativity as the

contemporaneous architectural system on its part and in its legitimate field would do." (p. 398.) It must be noted that Dhaky writes
about the architectonics of the Indian *shastriya sangeeta* alone. One
may wonder why 'reception or appreciation of music as a building'
should be confined to *shastriya sangeeta,* if mutual dependence of
music and architecture runs so deep. Dhaky states his premise with
clarity. The key passage reads, "The classical music system in the
like manner follows a coherent logic of layout and exposition by
way of pattern-sequences which at its intense moments are mentally
visualized in terms not only of colour, light and line, or ethereal
figures or solid sculptures, but also as a complex organo-geometric
construction that uses sound dots and dashes, lines and angles, curves
and vibrations, lights and shades, voids and masses, and within this
fabric infuses the very essence of the principle of life itself." (p.
398.) Dhaky moves on to identify structural features in Hindustani
and Carnatic musics as parallel to those in Northern and Southern
temple-architecture.

To seek correspondences between music and architecture by
constructing music *as* building, or by explaining construction as
music is tempting, and ventures in this direction represent a tradition. For example, approving statements about correlations between
French Gothic architecture and New Music; Renaissance classical
architecture and Opera; Baroque buildings and highly ornamental
music in vogue—are well-known. These efforts are definite improve-
ments on the earlier statements which were content on referring to
seats of culture as seats of music. For example, Athenian acropolis,
Roman forums, Byzantine basilica and palaces, Romanesque mon-
asteries, Gothic cathedrals have been listed in histories of music as
conducive to the art but architectural contribution was not otherwise explained. The attempted pairing of architectural and musical
forms/styles, as correlates, seeks to achieve this. Dhaky's arguments
fall in this category.

However, in my opinion the thesis of firm and intrinsic correlations between classical musics and architectural manifestations in
India—is more alluring than convincing. The reasons can be briefly
stated:

  (i) There is no valid ground to assume existence of only two
       systems of classical music in the country. How does one apply
       the thesis to north-eastern music, etc.?

 (ii) The confident attempt to establish music-architectural correlationships can hardly succeed if the inquiry is confined to art musics alone. Unless the thesis is satisfactorily extended to primitive, folk, devotional and popular categories of music—deductions are likely to remain sweeping generalizations.

(iii) Similarities or parallels, even though genuinely perceived and clearly stated, are inadequate to function as correlates because correlates must convince as mutual dependencies.

(iv) Even juxtapositions of structural parallels, etc. become suspect, if architectural items antedate musical features specifically related by centuries. The same objections holds true when musical features antedate architectural data put forward.

(v) Difficulties of dating origins of musical features with reasonable certainty can hardly be overestimated. Performing arts are known for their exceptional continuity—a fact denying significance of chronological priority, etc. It is logical to expect correlates to come into existence simultaneously.

(vi) Overemphasis on temple-architecture *vis-à-vis* music is disturbing, because it ignores existence of palaces, drawing rooms, outdoor spaces as formative factors in Indian music-making.

(vii) However, there is a more fundamental reservation. Arguments put forward about musico-architectural correlationship appear to assume that such a relationship, to be culturally meaningful, must be a relationship of correspondence. To say the least, this belief is a gross simplification.

In my opinion a thesis, favouring musico-architectural interrelationship cannot be viable if its basis are sought in stylistic correspondences and such other features. The main reason is that architecture, if not too severely shackled by functional considerations, is keen to create aesthetic spaces which appeal to visual and tactile sensibilities. Performing arts, on the other hand, would be interested in suitable acoustic and kinesthetic modalities, in addition to the visual. It is therefore imperative to concentrate on the *rangavakasha*.

THE FOUR SPACES

The proposed study of *rangavakasha* with reference to music justifies a preliminary four-fold classification of space.

Music, by the sheer fact of its being a physical activity needs space, which, however should not detain us. Space, like Ether, is out of bounds for our discussion. Space required, created and used for music-making as a physical activity, is actually a music-related space. The kind of space, actually and directly contributing/affecting music-performances is what is relevant to us. This is *rangavakasha* or musical-dramatic space. Thirdly, keen music-lovers have insisted on identifying a kind of inner space, the existence of which, music-makers (engaged in the process), feel kinesthetically. Finally, in music itself there are phrases, features, patterns, embellishments and the like, that elicit responses equated with spatial experience. A thorough statement on the musico-spatial interrelationship would mean attending to these four spaces—a formidable task indeed.

ARCHITECTURE AS ACOUSTIC SPACE

On numerous occasions, statements on musico-architectural correspondence amount to claims that architecture reflects music and *vice versa.* Further, it is often hinted that both display the said qualities because of a common underlying factor, such as, motive force, etc. This is conceptually seductive but, more often than, not leads to aesthetic stagnation. Music and buildings are closely related because architecture creates *rangakasha,* i.e., performing space. This performed in space is made vibrant by musicians, dynamic by dancers and electric by actors. In music, *rangakasha* can be equated with the acoustic space.

For our purpose, acoustic space can be defined as space selected to produce, transmit and receive music as aural experience. Music, as a tradition, evolves over a number of centuries. In normal circumstances, its development could therefore be expected to be linked to conduciveness or otherwise of acoustic conditions surrounding music-makers. And yet, this is not invariably so. Acoustic spaces, though extremely varied, are not as varied as the occasions on which music is made. The linkage between music and acoustic space also reflects intriguing cultural choices. In other words, musico-acoustic suitability does *not* seem, to be the only criterion influencing the interrelationship. Hence, it is of no avail to single out salient musical features such as primacy of human voice, circularity of rhythmic designs, preference for solo mode, and look for matching acoustic, architectural features to validate existing musico-spatial relationships.

Musical spaces, which emerge and stabilize in a culture, are not to be treated and interpreted as products of musico-architectural forces alone. Coming together of architecture and music is natural and inevitable, yet, the result is not inevitably 'agreeable' in the normal sense of the word. What is more important is that the said agreeableness does *not* appear to be culturally essential. The disagreeable quality of the union in question does not appear to lead to any value-loss. It is hardly correct to assume that acoustic space is to function for the sole purpose of making music uniformly sweet, efficiently performed and immediately acceptable. As it happens in case of many cultural activities, musico-spatial act may be purposeful and yet unpleasant on many occasions, seemingly wasteful at times and paradoxically motivated at unexpected junctures.

It needs to be admitted that the traditional aesthetic outlook in India was jolted into a new consciousness with the advent of a culture which fostered 'arranged' musical concerts, 'staged' plays and organized art-'exhibitions'. Accent on pleasurable and sweet became discernible. Further, the pleasurable was also reduced to 'pleasant looking' and the sweet to uniform, effortless audibility. To add to the aesthetic woes, the emphases were shifted to the logical, rational and the simple. In general, non-verbalized modes, ambiguous significances and life-like paradoxes came to be derided in artistic evaluations in modern India. Management of performing space also succumbed to adverse effects of these shifts in taste.

THE TRADITIONAL ACOUSTIC SPACE

The backdrop now demands that acoustic spaces traditionally used for music-making in the country be analyzed. An ideal inquiry would require exhaustive discussion of the performing categorial pentad inclusive of genres therein. This task is indeed formidable. However, it is possible to examine kinds of spaces in which music was performed. From this angle, outdoor locations, temples, drawing rooms, palaces and auditoriums suggest themselves as the Indian arenas, i.e., *rangavakasha*-s. It would be presumptuous to describe the examination undertaken as an acoustic analysis. The focus, in fact, would be on culturally examining musico-acoustic relationships thriving in India for varying lengths of time. Awareness of *rangavakasha* in reality, means awareness of musical or dramatic ideas in action. Performing categories and spaces, considered along with their chronological and geographical distribution, should help in selecting items suitable for elaborating the idea.

THE *SAMAGANA*

The ancient, ritualistic, religio-musical *samagayana* could be considered first. The performing space of *samagayana* was characterized by the following features:

1. It formed a part of meticulously organized, well-directed rituals and hence, secured highly motivated audiences, very often well-versed in presentation-procedures and knowledgeable as to the content.

2. The tradition chiefly explored two modes—recitation (*pathana*) and singing (*gayana*). Of the two, *gayana* required rigorous training, rehearsing and skill. It had a perceivable performing potential.

3. The descending *sama*-music exacted a sharper listening and keener sensitivity.

4. Vocalists participating in the performance formed a group with well-distributed vocal resources. Performers identified as *udgata, prastota* and *pratihara* were allotted specific tasks. In some phases, renderings acquired a choral character.

5. The elaborate construction of the *gatravina* suggests: (a) primacy of human voice, (b) importance of solo modality, (c) a concern for the well-uttered word.

6. *Sama*-s audible at close quarters were known as *deva* or *sarvaparoksha samhita,* those rendered in high pitch and audible from afar were described as *asura* or *sarvapratyaksha samhita. Sama*-s exploring the middle ranges were called *rishi* or *paroksha-pratyaksha samhita.* (Mitra, p. 42)

7. One of the *sama*-classifications impresses on account of attention paid to vocal timbre. Singing in bass voice was known as *devahu,* to do so in thin/weak tone was called *vakvashuhu* while that which resembled crying aloud was described as *amitrahu.*

8. *Vina* and *dundubhi* were chief instruments associated with the genre. Selection of the instruments and their purposeful deployment indicate ragness of audibility and intelligibility,

both varied and accepted.

It is a safe guess that, on the whole, softer instrumental sounds outnumbered the sonorous, and the plucked chordophones could boast of more variety than the bowed.

9. The *sama*-performers could be imagined to sing in open/ semi-closed spaces, dotted by vegetation with audience on all the four sides. They were partially shielded from natural forces, seasonal vagaries and spaces were mostly devoid of reflecting surfaces.

It is of course true that *samagayana* was not the only music of the Vedic period and the acoustic portrait was different for other, extant forms.

BHARATA'S *KUTAPA*

From *samagayana* to concerted musical expression in Bharata, is to take a leap from religious sacred to sanctified artistic. In spite of shared elements, *dhruva gayana* in *Natyashastra*, could *not* be similar to *samagayana* consecrated in the *Samaveda*. Bharata was no Bhadradvaja. He was a keen explorer of *rangavakasha,* and his main concern was achieving impact on the spectator. Bharata's management of the acoustic space could not have been entirely governed by the musical considerations *because* Bharata was dealing with dramatic space. By his time, stone architecture had taken roots in India, distinctions between the *nagara* (elite, sophisticated) and *adima* (primitive) had become sharper, entertainment/enjoyment was being accorded more legitimacy and the overall cultural fabric had begun to sport a weave of urban complexity. All this and more is reflected in the *kutapa* of *Natyashastra.*

1. Positioning of the *kutapa* clearly indicated a broad principle: sonorous and powerful instruments were to be located at a distance from the audience, and those with a softer sound were to be placed nearer. The acoustic implications are easy to deduce.

2. *Kutapa*-types reflected the variety of dramatic demands made on instrumentation. Separate instrumental grouping, dominated by chordophones or membranophones—with one group made of theatre-trained persons, indicates definite views on mood-music relationships, instrumental symbolism and sonar output. It is noteworthy that *kutapa* is only *one* of

the acceptable and serviceable musical group-expressions, i.e., *vrinda*-s.

3. *Vrinda*-s were graded as *kanishtha, madhyama* and *uttama,* i.e., inferior, medium and superior—depending on the number of participant artists. It is significant that groups having more participants than recommended for the *uttama* category, were criticized because they created *kolahala* (uproar, noise). This is undoubtedly a case of acoustic criterion applied to control space and sound-source behaviour.

4. Two more musico-acoustic features attract attention. Firstly, the entire musical effort seems to be rhythm—controlled-as is apparent from the central location and deliberate choice of sonorous membranophones. This is also borne out by the dance-dominated concept of Bharata's dramaturgy. Secondly, enlistment of singing-merits of participating groups, is rounded off by a reference to similarity of voices (*shabda-sadrishyam*). It may not be incorrect to say that this specific requirement is about the felt need to have more body to projected sound and a noticeable degree of homogeneity. In other words, no special efforts seem to have been made to introduce and explore additional tonal colour which could have been a logical theatric requirement. The concerns were ostensibly volume-audibility and coordination-homogeneity.

MUSIC AND DEVOTION

Bharata's *kutapa* exemplified a useful, premeditated and impact-oriented management of acoustic spaces constructed to ensure continued, intensified and functional identification of both receivers and performers. In the performing activity, performers retained the initiative. The quality of performance *as* performance, was the prime consideration. Devotional music, on the other hand, presents a different picture and raises some new questions—compared to the artistically motivated space-management in theatre-music. To anticipate a little, devotional musics are of two types, each directing listener-sensibilities *away* from music itself. In the first case, music becomes a bridge to an altered state of consciousness while, in the other, it becomes a partner in a group of rituals designed to bring into being a cohesive cultural pattern.

DEVOTIONAL MUSICS—THE TRANSCENDING VARIETY

In the present context, a form of Sufi-music needs a mention. The Sufi-*sama* music is of two kinds, one functions as a transcending force while the other strives with great success to create music of considerable power and substance, as is exemplified in *qawwali*. Both types enjoy long and fruitful Indian traditions.

It is true that *sama* is, broadly speaking Sufi sacred music. But *sama* literally means 'listening' and this core-meaning has obvious acoustic implications. Despite the Islamic frown on it, music is irrepressibly employed by its Sufi followers to create a particular state of mind. In the kind of ecstatic manifestation under study, music is explored to bring about a state of mind appropriate for performance of the *hadrah*, a sacred dance which, in turn, is intended to lead practitioners to God. Examination of the Sufi method (as distinguished from Sufi doctrine) points to the significance attached to Remembrance of God (*dhikr*-Allah). This Remembrance is to be achieved through Invocation of the Divine Name, i.e., *dhikr*, a procedure depending on purposeful and selective exploration of musical dimensions. In this connection, a pervasive recourse to low and high pitches, rising and falling phrases, repetition of motifs circularity of beat-patterns, the 'masking' potential of scraped/struck timbres, enveloping capacity of incremental volumes, hypnotic patterns generated by discontinuous sounds, etc. are worth noting. More than one description of the *sama*, employ the word 'ecstatic', and undoubtedly with abundant justification. This is particularly so in case of *dhikr*. In the matter of acoustic space the phenomenon allows following deductions:

1. In *sama*, performers are also listeners.
2. *Sama* is chiefly an occasion of collective music-making.
3. In it, performers prefer to arrange themselves into circular or semi-circular formations—a feature notable for creation of direct, though criss-crossing sound-lines.
4. Music-making in *sama* is closely linked to two extra-musical characteristics: participants pass into a psychological state inducing dance-like movements. Secondly, the spatial arrangements indicate and affirm supremacy of a guiding personality.
5. Repeated Islamic controversies about the use of musical instruments notwithstanding, certain chordophones and

membranophones have gained acceptance. A majority of these instruments lack the capacity to produce and hold continuous sounds. All music-making agents in *sama* are predominantly engaged in securing a hypnotic grip through rhythm.

6. The *sama*-space, or rather the utilization of it, is not intended and designed to propagate a clearly defined sound. All factors operate and direct energies to create powerful aural effects. No sharp lines allow a well-registered configuration of sounds, though there is an easily discernible overall pattern to the entire proceedings.

7. It has already been suggested that the basic impulse activating *sama,* and of agents working for it—is to move away from music. It is logical that the inexorable pull of the thwarted music-making or performing instincts therefore compels into existence another musical genre namely, *qawwali,* performed in the same architectural space.

I have argued elsewhere that coming together of religion and music unavoidably generates two powerful streams of religion-related music, respectively inclined towards folk and art music. It is symptomatic that *qawwal*-s (as the singers of the genre are known), *qawwalbacchon ka gharana* (the school of music traced to the sons of the *qawwal*) and the highly sophisticated form of Hindustani art music, namely *khayal,* are identified as links in the developmental chain.

HAVELI SANGEET

I referred to a variety of religio-musical manifestation which keeps closer to the abstract, codified and eminently musical art music. The tradition of the Vaishnava Haveli Sangeet, flourishing in centres such as Mathura, Brindavan, Nathdwara, etc. exemplifies religio-musical development impregnated with art-instinct. Exploration of the associated spaces expectably reflects the performing logic.

Haveli Sangeet has two main varieties and both have their own special characteristics, musical and other. One is known as *nitya-kirtana*. It consists of music, performed daily for Lord Krishna, at different times of the day, along with rituals displaying a high degree of anthropomorphism. The *utsava kirtana,* as the second variety is known, has, on the other hand, closer ties with the seasonal cycle and numerous festivals dotting the Indian calendar meaning-fully. The *nitya kirtana* is music associated with eight ritual-based occasions called *mangala, shringara, gwal, rajabhoga* (all between 6 A.M. to 12 P.M.); *utthapana, bhog, sandhya arati, shayan* (all between 4 P.M. to 7 P.M.). The festival music-cycle moves with the sixty-four cel-ebrations distributed in six seasons (further sub-grouped into three). Haveli Sangeet (also known as Pushti-marga and Ashtachhap for historical reasons), is highly systematized—musicologically as well as ritualistically. Salient features of its space-management are:

1. It is highly space-specific—as it is performed in locations as per the norms laid down. Time-slots are also allotted for spe-cific compositions, etc. Related architecture is predomi-nantly in stone.

2. *Nitya kirtana,* with its primarily solo, vocal and ritualistic character, eschews use of *jhanjh*-s, the powerful autophones similar to cymbals. This same instrument is, however, put to the maximum use in the festival music, which is also distinc-tively choral. Both music-s strictly adhere to musicological rules pertaining to *raga* and *tala* usage—as laid down in the Hindustani system.

3. The general deployment of instruments in the tradition is revealing. It has place for *surbin* (a string drone), *been, sarangi pakhawaj, kinnari* (triangle), *jhanjh, duph, upang* (an hour-glass drum), *khanjari* (rim-drum with metal discs), har-monium (during the last about 60 years or so). A few addi-tions can be made to the list by including conch, *bansuri, khartal,* etc. The enumeration adequately brings out the 'musical' thrust of instruments, namely their capacity to pro-duce a sustained tone. Instrumental inclusions and exclu-sions, the norms they conform to and deviate from, indicate cultural sensitivity to their respective timbres as well as their symbolic importance and standing.

4. Haveli Sangeet prefers medium tempi and moderate *raga*-elaboration. It also restricts the compositional corpus to writings of eight poet-composers-singers accepted as the chief devotees of the fold at certain historical junctures. Ob-viously, these features were helpful in ensuring that the sec-tarian music did not suffer from reverberation in perform-ance, and that it gets the required slow and detailed phras-ing to meet the demands of maximum intelligibility.

5. When Lord Krishna is the presiding deity it is to be expected that, at some point, theatric element would assert itself. Haveli Sangeet has built-in scope for assumption of roles and enactments—so essential for theatre. In *Dadhi-leela* and *Mahadeva-leela* for example, performances move to open squares. Selected devotees impersonate, dance and sing. Compositions, and the manner of presenting them are prescribed. An important feature is the flexible use of space. Shifting, and deliberate changeover to a different kind of space are remarkable instances of quick performing reflexes.

6. Of equal significance is a similar space-shift taking place during festivals in rainy season with *hindola* (swing) assuming an active role. Related performances once again reveal a high degree of purposeful codification in control of musical, as well as non-musical forces. An example of dance-controlled shift and exploration of performing space is offered by the Maharasa festival.

Dhrupad

One would have liked to discuss Haveli Sangeet and Dhrupad simultaneously, if that could have been achieved—so closely linked the forms are. Their historical closeness and musical affinities have inevitably given rise to controversies about chronological priority and related issues. Forays into their respective contexts reveal a fascinating interplay of musical and cultural forces, which, however, is a separate story. The immediate concern is how and why the form displays its particular spatial concerns.

The chief informant in this respect is Nayak Bakshu Dhadi who was Raja Man Singh Tomar's (coronation 1486, died 1519) chief musician. The Raja contributed greatly to the cultural and musical fame of Gwalior. He was instrumental in crystallising the form and for this purpose, relied mainly on Nayak Bakshu. Man Singh's son Vikram Jit, Raja Kirot of Kalinger and Bahadur Shah of Gujarat (1526–37), were Nayak Bakshu's successive patrons. Nayak Bakshu's Dhrupad compositions, or those in his tradition, were so captivating that they gained wide currency among musicians. It is through such singers that Shah Jahan (1628–58) came to know of their value. On his orders an anthology of Bakshu's selected compositions was prepared. On account of the number of compositions included and their aesthetic value, the anthology was aptly called *sahasrasa* (one thousand flavours). A copy of the work is dated 1656 and the copyist is from Ahmedabad. Following points emerge from a close perusal of the work:

1. Contrary to the notions usually held in many quarters, Dhrupad is *not* highly religious. In fact, through its themes it reflects the Goshthi-culture, described in the *Kamasutra*. Anxieties, joys, reliefs and beliefs, concerns of the sophisticated city-dweller, i.e., *nagaraka* are the warp and woof of Dhrupad-content. The fact indicates performing space in which artists and listeners were close to each other. Hence, details of grammatical and musicological import find their way in the compositions. Obviously, such texts cannot function as musical carriers over large acoustic spaces.

2. Compositions are addressed flatteringly to a patron, who is the hero of compositions. This too is a sure sign of performing space which is limited in expense. The hero is not praised for his martial exploits—it is his cultural accomplishments which are eulogized. This sounds reasonable as singing praises of hero as a warrior would take place better in court, and a different form of music was available for the purpose.

3. Bakshu, we are told, stood above all others—including the legendary Tansen, because Bakshu was able to sing alone, i.e., without accompanists, vocal and rhythmic. He could accompany himself on the *pakhawaj* to control his music. It is added, that he could also sing high, clear and sweet to the delight of listeners. Once again, the acoustic space to be covered, audiences to be reached and surrounding sound-levels to be transcended—suggest less crowded, uncluttered and intimate atmosphere in which music was made.

4. Bakshu's compositions, though anthologized nearly hundred and fifty years after his death, refer to performing conditions obtained in the early decades of the sixteenth century. By the time of Akbar (1542–1608), the spectrum of patron-praises sung by Tansen and others in Dhrupad-s had considerably widened. Bravery in battles, victory in wars, seasonal and formal greetings, etc. became common themes. Tansen's performing set of two vocal accompanists and one

pakhawaj-player came into vogue. Larger performing spaces, more pronounced formal character of occasions of music-making, highly stratified court-hierarchy and stone-architecture which resounded to music are the natural deductions. As the decades rolled on, Dhrupad evolved to culminate into a highly dignified, codified and elaborate musical genre restricted to male-singers. In the process, music-making shifted from smaller and intimate spaces to larger, formal and often ceremonial spaces.

Instances of performing spaces and musics associated with them, can of course be multiplied. Acoustic portraits can also be drawn in greater detail. However, certain deductions are possible about the cultural model emerging through the musico-acoustic behaviour-patterns. The deductions can justifiably be accepted as hypothesis in action, reflecting the Indian spatial philosophy. After all, the deductions are based on actual musico-acoustic usage over long periods. Objective, quantified and statistical readings, when combined with these deductions are likely to be the *sthayi* and *antara* of the musico-acoustic studies in India.

1. Traditional performances seem to be less than eager to find for themselves acoustically conducive homes. Performing spaces very often fall short of acoustic ideals as propounded today. Performing spaces, accepted traditionally, can hardly be described as performance-facilitating.

2. Indoor spaces have been generally associated with nuances, subtle expression, masked sound-lines, complex structuring and weightage given to literary inspiration. In contrast, outdoor spaces have choral, rhythmically bold and signal-permeated musics linked with them.

3. The earlier the period of music, the more the dependence on audience as a contributor to music-making. Later the period, the more the proportion of passive listeners who formed the 'audience'.

4. Traditional music-making did not set store by the criteria of maximum intelligibility of speech-signals, unalloyed pleasantness of auditory experience, complete visibility, etc. The totality of musical experience was intended to be a combined product of artists, listeners and the culture shared by both of them.

5. Memory, aesthetic literacy, extra-art considerations and pro-

cedures adopted for heightening receivers sensitivity featured regularly in the traditional situation. The collective action set in motion a compensatory mechanism to integrate experience of all events—aesthetic or otherwise.

6. The concert hall, as it appeared in the twentieth century, created, for the first time, an entirely passive listener. A 'no man's land' came into existence to separate performing area from the auditor's space, both in music and theatre. It is symptomatic that many forms in modern expression struggle to negate influence of this non-doers space.

7. In the evolution of Indian architecture, stone-age followed a wood-age, which had, in its turn succeeded a mud-age. Broadly speaking, later phases continued the architecture of the preceding—in spite of changes in the medium. However, performing spaces created by architectural developments affected more perceptibly and substantially.

8. One point needs to be made, even at the cost of introducing a paradox. *Rangavakasha* is a simultaneous affirmation and negation of space. The initial attempts to 'fill' the space with musical energy, etc. indicate that artists sense the space as volumes inviting to be filled, but they also know that to fill this space is much more than occupying it. When the desire to occupy the space is satisfied, there emerges a realization of an undivided space. Probably, the acoustic energy functions to annihilate distinctions between actually stimulated spaces on the one hand, and those which are sympathetically vibrant.

9. How does a performer in temporal arts 'feel' the *rangavakasha*? The answer is related to the paradoxical affirmation-negation phenomenon mentioned earlier. In the final analysis, a performer tends to measure his own artistic successes by his capacity to magnetize, charge or electrify areas adjacent to that which is directly stimulated. This, the 'influenced' area, is not covered with acoustic energy, etc. and yet, it is affected by performance and performers. In this manner, performers ultimately have to contend with three kinds of spaces:

    (i) Space in which performer initiates activity (performed space).

    (ii) Space which performers cannot reach/cover unless they

convert the initial activity into impact-oriented, creative and coordinated efforts (sympathetic, activated space).

(iii) Spaces adjacent to the two earlier spaces (influenced space).

Performers seem to enjoy a kind of territorial imperative. They are compelled by a sort of inner urge to reach beyond— an eminently spatial longing. How does he realize his objective?

10. It must be recognized that progressively and over centuries, human tendency has been to divide, firmly and somewhat rigidly, the three spaces referred to. The divisions have been effected by creating 'no man's corridors' between the spaces. It is significant that most of the experimental work in performing arts aims at eliminating them. In traditional models spaces shaded off more imperceptible and gradually-making smooth transitions from one to the other. To put it differently, traditional spaces exuded tolerance while their modern management breathes fire of spatial and aesthetic fundamentalism.

11. Modern acoustic sensibility has also legitimized the concept of specialized spaces, i.e., spaces exclusively meant for music, dance and drama. Not that this acoustic ideal is regularly attained. We have been eagerly building multi-purpose halls with discernible frenzy. And yet one gets a feeling that there has been a dissociation of sensibility in two ways. From the beginning of the modern period in Indian history, Indian performing impulse has moved away, rather abruptly, from the traditional composite genres in which dance, drama and music were combined. Secondly, it has also registered a shift away from 'collective ceremonial' to 'public formal'. The shifts would not have led to a dissociation if they had followed natural changes in sensibilities. However, the shifts have been results of hasty socio-cultural engineering by persons working towards modernity in the colonial India.

CONCLUSION

Can there be a conclusion for an ongoing search? Only a mystic suggestion: let us remember that space can be heard and touched—

there lies its immediacy. To this extent there is a universal aspect to the situation. The existing differences between region-based cultural changes are being effected on account of various factors. There are therefore some battles which it should be possible to fight jointly. One such battle is against mutilation of sensory personality. We are losing interest in and consequently sensitivity to (at least) aural, olfactory and tactile. It is time we sit up and take notice.

17

Time, Laya and Tala: Perspectives in Cultural Musicology, Musical Aesthetics and Musicology

To understand time—(if that is at all possible.)—and its manifestations in Indian music, essentially three perspectives are required.

Cultural musicology, also known as ethnomusicology, is the most accommodative of the three views. It posits that no culture can be understood and felt, unless music of that culture is comprehended, and *vice versa*. Obviously, the discipline has, in its outland, extra-musical areas such as religion, mythology, literature and yoga. Musical aesthetics had narrower range as compared to cultural musicology. In the main, it functions as a scheme of concepts and criteria leading to formulation of a judgement of taste. Musicology, the third perspective, expectably indicates tighter focusing as the attention is directed to grammatical frameworks crystallized over a number of centuries. (As its sources, musicology explores both performing and the scholastic traditions.) With a slight simplification, one may also note that musicology places emphasis on *rules* as distinguished from criteria. In spite of the customary overlaps, the three perspectives offer contexts adequately understood and exploited by concerned cultures.

A pertinent question can be raised at this stage: In what way these contexts contribute to our discussion? To state briefly, musicological perspective enhances appreciation of the particular kind of temporality music enjoys as an art, while contexts made available by musical aesthetics enable to understand qualitative uses of Time in music. Cultural musicology safeguards an apposite relationship between music, as a patterned sound, and music as *one* component of a larger spatio-temporal design. For all practical purposes, musicology invariably lags behind performance, and to that extent, perspectives provided by the former need to be repeatedly updated. On the other hand, musical aesthetics would be simultaneous with, if not significantly antecedent to, performance. Finally, religion may modify, sanctify and make for durable performing procedures; may maintain parallel with performance as a becoming and emergent phenomenon, and yoga, in its essence, may obliterate all distinctions between performer, performance and the receiver. In other words, relationship with performance is likely to prove crucial in determining the outcome of discussion on music or any music-related area.

This is the background on which two musicological terms engage our immediate attention: *laya* and *tala*. In my opinion it is advisable *not* to translate these terms in the interests of fidelity to the original vision. Of the two, *laya* enjoys a wider scope. In fact, *tala* is a distinctive manifestation of *laya*. However, the term *laya* has two contradictory usages with reference to *tala*.

Etymologically the term *laya* is traceable to *layate* meaning 'to melt, dissolve'. Another, conceptually closer root meaning is *layati* 'to go, to move'. A seeming contradiction needs to be noted. While *laya*, as the primary movement results from a regulated interruption of the time-flow, i.e., *kalougha*, *laya* is also mentioned as one of the ten vital characteristics of the *tala*. As one of the *dashaprana*-s, *laya* is defined as 'a rest between two actions of *tala*. The two derivations mentioned earlier, help resolving the contradiction. The first root meaning, 'to melt, to dissolve' is connected with *kala* as a force that annihilates. Significantly, *laya* within the *tala*, represents a phase in which *kala* is manipulated, controlled, explored and exploited as the per the creators (i.e., the artist's) wishes. In other words, the arbitrary act of measuring musical time is *also* an act of annihilating the annihilator. The trinity of *kala-laya*, *laya-tala* and *tala-laya* thus indicates combined operations of larger cultural forces, musicological formulations and musico-aesthetic responses to Time, as a dimension of existence, parameter of experience and matrices of creation.

The musical-musicological manipulation of temporality in Indian music is better understood when a cognate creation, namely prosody—and to be precise metric—is taken into account. Tracing back the logical steps, it is easy to see that the fundamental and manifest sound enjoys options: to emerge as language and/or music. Both expressions indicate, in addition to many other features, an act of shaping of sound and/or sense through shortening and/or lengthening. In metrics, the three possibilities of short, long and sustained sounds are respectively known as *hrasva, deergha* and *pluta.* Similar exercises in music yield distinctions identified as *laghu, guru* and *pluta* respectively. The two procedures have coalesced, through interaction and evolution, to culminate into giving a firm, aesthetic basis for creative temporality in Indian music. The two fulfilments of the aesthetic impulse have succeeded in ranging beyond demands of the rational, objective and the exact or precise and enabled Indian musico-literary urges reaching a phase of unprecedented quality, ambiguity and individuality in music. This is the reason why Indian music could produce temporal moulds to function as generative rhythmic patterns. At the same time Indian metrics has evolved temporal patterns which are also melodic moulds.

When we reach the main battleground, i.e., music, it becomes relevant to ask how *tala* is made concrete or embodied in Indian music. The vital procedure of *kriya* provides the answer. The following diagram would clarify:

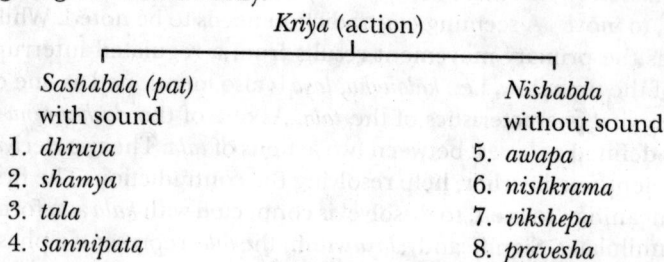

Kriya (action)

Sashabda (pat) with sound	Nishabda without sound
1. *dhruva*	5. *awapa*
2. *shamya*	6. *nishkrama*
3. *tala*	7. *vikshepa*
4. *sannipata*	8. *pravesha*

Action indicated by each term is as given below:
1. Hand to move downwards while fingers are being snapped
2. Right palm strikes on the left
3. Left palm strikes on the right
4. Hands to clap
5. Open palm faces the sky while fingers being closed
6. Closed palm opened downwards
7. Right palm and fingers are open and face the sky, are thrown to the right
8. Palm faces downwards and fingers close.

However, it would be clear that *kriya,* the act of keeping time, is merely one application of a particular technique based on the entity of *tala* which is already been conceptualized. Hence, search for the definition of *tala* would have to continue. This is to be expected because all ten vital features, the famed *dashaprana* of *tala* defined/described in musicology, are in reality, *post facto* consolidations of a performing tradition. They can tell us how *tala* is performed, but they cannot be expected to answer the question why *tala* comes into being or what is its nature. It is the domain of musical aesthetics to answer to these questions. The logical coincidence of musical aesthetics and performance is in stark contrast to the consequential nature of musicology. Hence, an attempt is necessary to outline the conceptual process leading to *tala* as an aesthetically satisfying seed-form. The steps can be described thus:

- Time-flow is divided to make time comprehensible.
- Dividers are transformed into sonar points, i.e., beats, to bring to end sonar continuities. Optionally, dividers are accepted as divisions but are deliberately kept silent. Both these alternatives are deemed equally conducive to music-making.
- Beats make available processes of forming different patterns. Larger patterns may be further segmented to create sub-patterns and to allow centres to generate rhythmic pulses.
- A very significant feature of *tala* is the alternate use it makes of succession and circularity as basic strategies of organizing temporal divisions (sounded or silent). The importance of circularity can hardly be overestimated because it is directly related to production of varied, multiple and enriched time-patterns.

It would easily be seen that all steps described so far succeed in creating a map of *tala*, the existence of which can be called merely *notional*. At this stage, imagined sounds as well as silences, can become accessible only to the initiator—and may remain incommunicable in normal circumstances (i.e., unless one concedes more frequent acts of mind-reading than ordinarily accepted.) Further, on account of its notional status, *tala*-map lacks in the most distinctive aspect which endows music with quality, the reference being to the sensuous presence of sound. Sensation of sound, *per se*, has its own, tangible and significant contribution to the life of music. However, the sensuousness mentioned here, goes far beyond merely being a sensation. Sensation and tonal quality combine to create sensuousness. It is only when tonal quality operates that temporal divisions get *distinguished*, as opposed to merely being *differentiated*. Diverse beats acquire personalities of their own, chiefly because of two factors: the particular configuration of sounds peopling a definite beat-space and the specific instrumental timbre which taps its own resources of evocative powers for arousing aural imagery—the ultimate key to aesthetic experience in music (—in the present instance this is confined to the temporal dimension). Timbre replaces an emotionally neutral and mechanically divided time-flow with musically meaningful units capable of reaching deeper levels of appeal and cultural consciousness. Both basic components of musical patterns (i.e., sounds and silences) acquire quality *because* of associated timbres. Once the mysteries of attack and decay, are somewhat unravelled, 'timbres of silences' would also be better appreciated. Musical time is annihilation of Time and 'timbred' temporal pattern is fertilization of the musical time. Whatever music one is listening to, it is timbre (as distinct from pitch and volume) which convinces as a major factor bestowing value and indestructibility on music.

How does timbre achieve this feat? It is able to accomplish the feat *because* it works through memory, association and collective unconscious to create a spatial experiencing of length, breadth and depth. Therefore, Indian tradition underscores significance of individual instruments even though they may render the same *tala*. Onomatopoeic letters employed to indicate sounds made by different instruments are known as *patakshara*-s. I submit that, in all value-experience a critical phase is reached when reference to the *other* dimension, i.e., the one not directly explored, becomes inevitable to complete experience. However, a direct and obvious switch-over the *other* dimension leaves the story of the former dimension incomplete. In an inspired aesthetic leap, human mind transcends the difficult moment by creating mutual dependencies or correlates in the dimension under direct exploration. This is why we *can*, and *do*, talk about expansive melodies, visual rhythms, tonal colours, intervallic distances, etc. I may venture to add, that timbre has a corresponding entity in shade. Through timbre, music inevitably partakes of selected spatial qualities to complete the experience and yet manage to remain temporal because music has chosen to *move* (*li-layati*) and not *melt* (*lay-layate*). In such phases, space becomes 'space in time.' They, i.e., the two dimensions, are *not* one but mirror each other and, in the present case, the temporal aspect of musicality provides the 'initial' mirroring act. The order would be reversed in spatial arts, i.e., painting or drawing and sculpture or architecture, etc.

So far, the discussion of *tala*, and related issues has chiefly been musicological and aesthetical. It is time to turn to contributions of cultural musicology. The contribution is likely to be connected with performance in varying degrees—as is to be expected of cultural matters. Philosophy, religion, mythology, yoga and literature may claim attention in a major way. My limited expertise, as well as the present narrowed focus, would allow some brief statements:

1. It is to be noted that Indian music does *not* accept concepts of absolute time and pitch. As a corollary, the three basic tempi, namely slow, medium and fast are defined with reference to one another. It is true that repeated and numerous attempts are made to name and define objective measuring units of musical time. For example, time taken to bat an eyelid, or duration of pulse beat, etc. have been mentioned in this regard. However, performing tradition hardly takes notice of these attempts at standardization. It is content to accept the gray areas of arbitrary choices made by musicians about tempo, etc.

2. The act of music-making maintains a tenderly poised relationship with chronological time. Indian norms of *raga*-time relationship would come to mind. In view of the pervasive importance given to the day-night cycle in philosophical deliberations and mythological traditions, musical recognition to it should not surprise. Equally noteworthy is the fact that *tala,* the most temporal of all musical features, is *not* related to day-night and seasonal cycles.

3. Music accepts possibility of shortening and lengthening temporal units. Obviously, these processes become possible because musical time is experienced irrespective of clock-time. However, it is better to describe existence of musical time as contemplative rather than notional. Mythological associations of *tala,* the abstraction necessary to bring it into being, the general tendency of *tala*—and its elaborations—to act irrespective of referential meaning and content—are adequate grounds to describe the nature of *tala* as contemplative. Severing of connections (associations) with mundane life and its concerns, concentration required to study *tala* and sophisticated, subtle ways of its application are also features put forward to complete its characterization as contemplative. To this extent *tala* is placed close to Yogashastra.

4. At the same time, *tala* moves in a direction contrary to the yogic vision. It works on the assumption that temporal units

that succeed each other, in reality, present additions of moments.

5. Finally, it should not be forgotten that *tala* as a concept and practice, is developed mainly in art music, though it finds place in devotional and folk categories of music to some extent. Yet, it would not be far off the mark to say that in non-art varieties of music, *ardha-tala*-s are more in evidence than *tala*-s proper. Categories of music play a decisive role in determining nature, function and importance of *tala*-s. Often they seem to exercise a choice between reliance on *laya* or pressing into service *tala*—a more processed version of *laya*.

18

Colour and Hindustani Music

Frankly, the present discussion should begin by amending the title itself. It should read 'Colour and Music in Hindustan'. The chief reason is that the term 'Hindustani Music' is ordinarily equated with art music, popularly called 'classical'. However, there is no justification to assume that non-art musics in India have no relationship with colour. There is sufficient data to suggest that each of categorial pentad in Indian music (namely, primitive, folk, devotional, art and popular) carries a distinguished record of relationship with colour. These categories respond to the phenomenon of colour in consonance with their respective aims and identities. Hence, I propose to inquire into musics and colour interrelationship obtained in Hindustan, as the term is understood in cultural and specially non-political contexts.

And yet, the ground is not clear, because southern and northeastern musical traditions may need separate discussions. Plurality of musical systems and categories in the land cautions against dangers of assuming pan-Indian stances too easily and too soon. In the present age of information-explosion, one dictum of cultural musicology appears to be more and more relevant: 'musical mapping of the region does not usually follow contours of its politico-administrative cartography.' Inquiries into matters of cultural import have also to guard against another academic risk. An intrinsically felt necessity of cohesive formulation of scholastic continuity should not be mistaken for performing homogeneity. One primary feature of Indian culture is that it continuously comes out with diverse forms of manifestations while the other, equally strong, tendency has been towards scholastic crystallization drawing attention to a common, larger and fairly well-defined pattern. Modern scholarship often offends because it tries to impose over-systematic and inflexible theoretical frameworks inspired by earlier, equally rigid prescriptive expositions. Medieval and post-medieval cultural scene proves remarkably exciting because, during this period, an extremely lively scholastic tradition was trying to catch up with regional, diverse and non-art musical contributions in order to make sense of totality of the musical reality. It was, as if thinkers were in hot pursuit of the ever-receding dream of laying down all-embracing, unifying and generative theoretical structure in art and aesthetics. I submit that to comprehend Indian culture, it is essential to closely monitor rhythms created by 'away and towards' movements between scholastic and performing traditions. A complete agreement of the two was never intended. In fact, new divergencies were welcome as revitalizing forces. In sum, to concentrate on analyzing performing traditions is likely to be the most beneficial strategy of damage-control.

Colour-music: A Partnership of Unequals

One more turn before the first note is heard. Irrespective of cultures involved, colour-music relationship poses a conceptual problem because the two cannot be placed on the same plane. While the phenomenon of colour is at the basic level of perception, music is a highly processed aesthetic manifestation. It is as if examining a relationship between pitch and the art of painting. In other words, while music is a complete coding system, colour represents merely an element of another system. Under such circumstances the discussion would naturally be music-oriented. To overlook this aspect of the situation may lead to invention of unreal correspondences and postulation of untenable cultural and aesthetic positions. Awareness of conceptual differences between colour and music would make it easier to understand the role of colour when it is *with* music in contrast to functions of colour *in* music. In other words, it is necessary to distinguish between interrelationship proper and a mere being together of the two. Everything has some connection with everything else in durable cultural traditions such as the Indian, and yet this is not to be construed as everything being everything else. Performing traditions, on the other hand, demand to be treated as 'hypotheses in action'. Whatever happens in performance—the conduct of which has a long line of antecedents—cannot be mere coincidental. It is better to begin by accepting total meaningfulness of a performing tradition till it is proved to be otherwise. This is the background on which music-colour relationship is to be examined, with the contemporary context as the guiding principle. Music in

Hindustan combines with colour at six different levels identifiable as: vocabulary and terminology; phonetics and literature; pictorial presentation; perceptual acts; aesthetic activity and meta-aesthetic conceptualization. All these themes, it is obvious, need to be approached independently.

VOCABULARY AND TERMINOLOGY

Vocabulary means a systematized compilation of words as speech-units while terminology would refer to words limited to specific disciplines. The word term itself is derived from 'terminus' meaning 'boundary', 'end' etc. Musical, musicological and music-related words pointing to the world of colour are to be examined so that terminology can be sifted from vocabulary.

I could compile a list of one hundred colour-related words exhibiting partial or full colour-orientation by scanning through Prof. Ramakrishna Kavi's monumental work *Bharatakosa*. Some deductions are possible:

1. A very large number of words were connected with 'colour' but, merely to make the words attractive vocables. Such words do not indicate structurally intrinsic or inevitable correspondences with musical items they refer to. As logicians would put it, they are all proper names and hence have the status of merely arbitrary marks. Some example are:

   Varnalankara-s: Indraneela

   Melaraga-s: Ghanashyama, Dhavalangi, Neelaprabha, Neelambari, Rangakaustubha, Shubhravahini, Shyamakalyani, Shyamala

   Tana: Pundarik

2. Some colour-related words combine indication of structural features of musical items with decorative references to colour. On close reading it becomes apparent that in such cases colour-relations are often analogical. Some instances are: *chaturang, trivarna, chitra,* and *vichitraka.*

3. The number of colours, used in formation of music-related words, is very limited. Following colours are mentioned: *neela* (blue), *shyama* (dark-blue), *shubhra* (snow-white), *suvarna* (golden), *rakta* (red), and *dhavala* (glowing white).

4. Some colour-related visual effects also find mention. Noteworthy among them are: *chitra* (variegated), *deepta* (lumi-

nous), and *kanta* (glowing, dazzling).

5. It could be deduced that colour-related terms can hardly be described 'musicologically technical'. However, terms such as *varna, ranga,* and effects such as *deepta, rakta,* etc. stand for musically critical functions.

6. It is clear that if music-related vocabulary and terminology in Prakrit languages are compiled and scrutinized, the result is bound to be enriching.

PHONETICS AND LITERATURE

It must be clarified that both phonetic and literary aspects are to be examined in connection with musical compositions. From phonetics to literature runs a continuum and a comprehensive oral tradition has brought the phenomena together. According to *sphota*-theory of the famed grammarian-philosopher Bhartrihari, act of utterance is the fundamental as well as the first manifestation of Meaning.

In every utterance, vowels and consonants are the likely, main components. Indian music declares a marked preference for vowels over consonants in general, chiefly, because vowels ensure continuity of projection. Practising musicians also associate vowel-sounds with another highly rated acoustic quality, namely resonance. Roundness of voice, as resonance is normally described, is a much commented quality and it is closely linked to vowels. Consonants, aptly described as 'the alphabetical sounds incapable of independent utterance', contribute mainly on account of variety they bring in. It is significant that musicians discriminate between different consonants on the basis of their innate musicality. For example, nasal consonants are specially valued and, it is not a coincidence that, among words describing the nasals occurs a word *rang*,—one meaning of which is 'colour'. However, at this stage of discussion, it is necessary to point out that vowels, consonants and musical notes are all members of an imposing hierarchy. Further, the hierarchy exemplifies convergence of grammar (a branch of philosophy in Indian tradition), linguistics and musicology as they move in search of first principles. In brief, the hierarchy is as follows:

   shabda = 'that which is experienced by ears and is a property of ether'

   nada = it is of two kinds, namely *ahata* and *anahata*

dhvani = 'that which is produced by instruments'

varna = 'that which becomes *udatta*, etc. in music and *svara*, etc. in language.

I would like to emphasize the significance of the bifurcation taking place at the stage of *varna*. One stream gives us foundation-sounds in music while the other renders similar service in respect of language. The substantial nature of this event would become clear when *svara*, the next item in the hierarchy, is examined in some detail.

Svara, as is known, materializes both in language and music, with appropriate changes in connotation. In language *svara* is a vowel sound. The acoustic richness and other performing qualities of vowel-sounds have already been brought to notice. In music, *svara*, as defined by various authorities, has the following characteristics:

- It is luminous in itself.
- A distinct resonance follows its manifestation.
- It is a sound which arouses listener's emotions and provides basis to organize melodic structures.
- It is pervasive and hence universally perceived.

It should now be easier to see the connection between *varna* and *svara*, as well as specific, respective functions of both. *Varna* is regarded foundational, qualitative and pervasive layer of acoustic manifestation, whether in music or language. *Svara*, the phase that follows *varna*, indicates distinguishable, significant and sustained units of projected sound in both music and language. The conceptual interrelationship of performing phases (well reflected in the terms under scrutiny), is traceable to the quest of first principles in both musicology and linguistics. I want to suggest that *varna*, a colour-term from the field of visual experience, is employed to stand for a critical, as opposed to a technical, phase in music-making—which, in itself, is an audio-temporal activity whatever may be the performing format. At this point *varna* does not evoke colour-code, but functions as a force leading to qualitative, potent, undivided and comprehensive experience. Thus, terms otherwise treated as homonyms alone, assume significance *because* they operate at a critical juncture. When patently spatio-visual terms strike roots in audio-temporal manifestations—and that too at critical points, it is deducible that deeper human urges are thereby fulfilled. When more data, especially from the performing tradition, is interpreted the point can be elaborated. We, therefore, turn to the literary aspect.

LITERATURE IN MUSIC

The reference is obviously to texts of musical compositions. All musical categories contain song-texts, though many of them are not written. However, there is an adequate sampler to allow some interesting deductions. Examination of song-texts reveals that many of them have high literary merit (in spite of the oft-repeated proposition that Indian music does not regard words important.). It is true that very often, composer's identity, his period and such other details are not within reach. The original tunes of the compositions may also be missing in many cases. However, other clues—relevant to our purpose—are available. What does the scrutiny suggest?

1. Very few colours are directly mentioned. In the main they are: red, black, blue, green, yellow (golden), saffron and white.

2. Colours generally find mention via objects. An illustrative list is:

    Kale: badal, kesha, kajal (i.e., black clouds, hair and eye-black or collyrium)

    Gore: mukha, gaal (i.e., fair complexioned face, cheeks)

    Hari: chudiyan, sari, vrikawa (i.e., green bangles, *sari* and trees)

    Neel: badal, Krishna, Rama (i.e., clouds, Krishna and Rama)

    Shubhra: vasan (i.e., white garments)

    Soneki: bindiyan (i.e., golden ornament worn on head by women)

    Peeta/Peeli: sari (i.e., yellow *sari*)

    Also mentioned are *abir, gulal, kumkum* and *kesar* powders which are black, red, vermilion and saffron in colour respectively.

3. There are noticeable differences in roles, the categorial pentad allows to colour. From among the five, art music accords the least importance to colour *as* colour. Compared to art music, folk and devotional musics are more specific. These two categories often reveal a remarkable eye for shades, subtle textures, etc. though the palette is not very extensive.

4. Mostly, colours are mentioned as items used in celebrations— Basantotsava, Holi, Ras, Sawan being the main. Life in India of course displays multiple functions of colour, as also a wide-ranging colour-symbolism. However, music seems to accen-

tuate celebratory services of colour.

5. Very few traditional festivities can be described as *secular*. Therefore, celebratory use of colour is inevitably linked to religious symbolism and hence devotional music, as a category, attracts attention for its characteristic utilization of colour. To put it plainly, use and placement of colour, with and in devotional music, does not have a primarily aesthetic motivation. Major traditions of devotional music in Hindustan, such as Sufi, Haveli, Keertana, (e.g., Varkari, Naradiya, etc.) would come to mind. When religion combines with performing arts, results are not and need not be aesthetic, because the entire *rasion d'être* of the effort is different. This aspect is discussed later at some length.

MUSIC-COLOUR INTERRELATIONSHIP: AN AESTHETIC PROCESS

What justifies describing the interrelationship as an aesthetic process? The answer is that the relationship appears to play a mandatory role in effecting qualitative changes leading towards 'transformation of nature into art'—as Coomaraswamy phrased it. In this connection three items are particularly worth noting: timbre, synesthesia and finally, arousal of imagery.

Timbre or tonal colour is accepted as a property of sound which helps distinguishing between sounds otherwise equal. Sounds may also occur simultaneously. Each sound has individuality, and tonal colour establishes it. A separate existence for multiple sources would have been meaningless without recognition of their respective individualities. Individuality is, in fact, an assertion of freedom in the face of gross standardization. Without individuality one could hardly dream of anything valuable and, aesthetics, in the final analysis is, an inquiry into valuableness or otherwise of art-experience. In music, tone-colour is one of the features which makes experience of music value-laden. Authorities in physics, acoustics and other disciplines, deal with the 'how'—aspect of tonal colour. An aestheticians job is to place the phenomenon properly in the relevant, normative structure and explain the role it plays in the creative/evaluative processes. Music-makers search, develop and practice ways and means of bringing tonal colour, identified as a musically enriching quality. Those, who evaluate music, apply the criterion of presence/absence of tonal colours. What should invite attention is that the important aesthetic achievement of establishing music-makers individuality gets defined, conceptually as well as terminologically, through a movement away from the aural medium towards the visual. Operative sensibility (in the present case aural), is transformed, at a critical juncture, by an act of disengagement from its own customary mode of perception to ensure enrichment of experience. The question is: why?

I submit that, at critical junctures, creativity inevitably entails responsorial transfer of psycho-physical forces from audio-temporal to video-spatial and *vice versa*. In other words, no audio-temporal experience is complete unless correspondence with the video-spatial is established. This is not to deny that manifestations or genres, intent on rigorously exploring only one operative modality (e.g., audio or video), or dimension (temporal or spatial) exist. However, even with them, the modal-dimensional transfer *does* take place. Initially it is analogically expressed, to be followed later by resorting to mutual correlatives. The ever-altering size of the body of genres, notable popularity of multimedia presentations and the long-standing, universal practice of combining arts from different families indicate an aesthetic inevitability.

Colour is therefore, sought to be inducted into music to complete the musical experience. It can be done in many ways and the phenomenon of tonal colour is one of them. In Hindustan, the remarkable abundance of idiophones and membranophones, as also the developed status of their 'languages', have a direct bearing on recognition and importance of tonal colour and its aesthetic contribution to music-making. The aerophones and chordophones relied on their innate closeness to human voice culminating in a near total obsession to emulate the singing voice. To an extent this avowed insistence of following vocal music as a model, prevented fuller development of instrumental languages in the two classes. This is the reason of the admirable detailed reference to *patakshara*-s, (i.e., instrumental syllables), of even idiophonic instruments, displayed early in the Indian scholastic tradition. The overall modern neglect of musical and musicological heritage of rhythm and rhythm-based instruments, has exposed a weakness in our musical behaviour, a matter which should have caused more concern. It has already been pointed out that, vowels and consonants, present two different kinds of pleasurable aural sensations in languages employed in musical compositions. Consonants provide tonal 'colour' and that phonetic marvel, the Sanskrit alphabet—presents an exciting classification of consonants according to the manner of their production. Hindustani music-making stresses contribution of consonants. Elaborational techniques emphasize conducive nature of *bol-alap*-s; metrical moulds of marked flexibility and rhythmic variety abound; liquid and nasal consonants find preference due to their specific facilitating powers—these obviously are some major ways in which tonal colour is created in music. It is significant to note that one meaning of the term *rang*—is nasalization.

A more direct link between music and colour, in the verbalized mode, would appear to be words denoting colour, actions indicating colour-use, or descriptions of coloured objects. However, these can hardly be considered examples of colour *in* music. As stated earlier, these merely point to cases of colour appearing *with* music. There is nothing innate about interrelationship so brought about. The qualitative, innate and aesthetic relationship would mean something more, and this is how the specifically perceptual phenomenon known as synesthesia enters the scene.

Synesthesia

It would not be far wrong to say that serious or academic psychology does *not* take synesthesia very seriously. Some brush it away as 'confusion between the senses'[1] and would like to attribute it as occurring 'presumably through loss of normal inhibitory mechanisms which isolate the central processing of the senses'.[2] Others, less dismissing and perhaps more factual, describe it as 'phenomena in which sensation in one sense department carry with them, as it were, sensory impressions belonging to another sense-department.'[3]

Entries on colour music, in different dictionaries of Western Music are more expansive. Noting, that attempts to set up exact, physical correspondences between colour-spectrum and musical scale, keys and colours, or certain works and colours are futile—the dictionaries provide interesting biographical information on composers/musicians' stated associations between colours and notes, etc. These subjective accounts are followed by references to Oriental wide-ranging symbolization which holds certain colours to be associated with certain sounds, etc. In sum, synesthesia is not considered to be a specific, aesthetic phenomenon with a legitimate place of its own in art-behaviour, performing tradition and its accompanying scholastic continuity. On the other hand, reference-works on literature and literary criticism devote greater space to discuss it, clearly recognizing its creative role. Very logically, literary aesthetics sees links between synesthesia as fundamental perceptive process, symbolization as an equally basic process of organizing, interpreting and expressing perceptions. Finally, in the same chain, analogy and metaphor are identified as specifically literary devices. We are told that correspondence of arts became a literary credo only during the nineteenth century, even though it has been a tenet of literary and aesthetic thinking from early periods. The French symbolist poets, and their aesthetic expositions greatly contributed to strengthen tendencies towards a general blurring of boundaries between art and life on the one hand, and between various expressive modes and genres on the other. On this background, what do the Hindustani musical traditions suggest?

It may be useful to briefly glance at some antecedents. Bharata's correlates are *rasa-bhava-varna-devata*. It is interesting to note that the element of sound does not find a place here. *Naradiya Shiksha* clearly lays down *svara-varna* equivalences. By the time of Sharngadeva's *Sangita Ratnakara*, *swara-varna-devata* and *rasa*, have established correspondences.

We find Kumbharaja's *Sangitaraja* making the first reference to *ragadhyanashloka* in which Tantric symbolization combines musicology with iconic presentation. A little earlier, *Kalpasutra* had taken the crucial step of picturizing highly technical musical elements such as *svara*, *grama*, *tana*, etc. A little later we have Pundarik Vitthal's works with reference to *raga-ragini*-s and the Persian *raga*-s. Ragamala-paintings with their splash of colour and music appear on this background. This tradition relies on a theatre-oriented *nayika-bheda*, Krishna-mythology as elaborated by the Bhakti cult and Shubhankara's *Sangita Damodara* for the technical, musicological data. With these antecedents, it is not exaggerating to say that colour-music association has been with us for a long time. And yet, evidence from performing and scholastic traditions hardly seems to support synesthesia. The reason is not far to seek. With us, colour and music come together as constituents of a composite sensibility. Synesthetic situations imply an initial, separate recognition and a subsequent, simultaneous registration of two sensibilities, while composite sensibility involves simultaneous, all-embracing and yet, a layered presentation as well as reception. In other words, composite sensibility, being a more accommodative 'band', subsumes synesthesia.

In fact, I submit that synesthesia may result from an attenuated composite sensibility. Though synesthetic pairings and neurological back-ups suggest a narrower sensory interrelationship, cultures inevitably try to reach out in their search of a complete experience. Conceptualization, nurturing as well as systematizing of composite sensibility certainly trace one way of achieving the goal.

REFERENCES

1. Richard L. Gregory, ed., *The Oxford Companion to Mind*, p. 765.
2. Ibid.
3. James Drever, *A Dictionary of Psychology*, 1963, p. 286.

19

Ragamala-paintings: A Musicological Perspective

Ragamala-paintings inevitably attract interdisciplinary examination. It would not be far-fetched to suggest that Ragamala-paintings, Chitrakathi-s, Pabuji ka Pad, or Yamapat-s and Pat-s, etc. exemplify Indian attempts to bring visual and aural modes together to evolve art forms combining music, painting, and literature or drama. Three categories of arts—performing, fine and literary—join forces and the situation becomes challengingly complex. Ragamala-paintings display capacity to raise questions germane to many areas of Indian studies such as iconography, literature, prosody, mythology and folklore. The present inquiry, however, draws on three music-related disciplines namely, musicology, musical aesthetics and cultural musicology. I do not claim that the approach registers a radical departure—the available literature on Ragamala-paintings would clearly refute such a claim. For example, Ragamala-paintings have been perceptively analyzed to tackle the musicological problem of *raga*-classification. They have also been repeatedly discussed in the context of the *rasa*-theory *vis-à-vis* music. Finally, relevance and causation of these paintings have interested many students of the broader cultural framework of India. In other words, the aim of my presentation could only be to assert a continued relevance of the audio-visual experience that Ragamala-s impart.

The questions raised by the three disciplines are of a kind that demands renewed attention from each generation. This is unavoidable because the disciplines are directly related to performing tradition in music as contrasted with its scholastic continuity. For example, musicological questions have a direct bearing on technique and grammar of music. On the other hand, musical aesthetics shoulders responsibility of judging quality and value of the experience involved. Cultural musicology regards music and culture to be mutual dependents, and hence, it accepts the necessity of considering all musical events afresh when cultural changes are perceived as such. In sum, the scene is likely to continue to be exciting as far as Ragamala-s are concerned.

Experts agree, that Ragamala-s, though barely four hundred years old, have musicological antecedents. The most notable has been the role allotted to human figure as an icon, as an active agent employed to concertize musical speculations. In this context, the all-pervasive *purusha* concept claims conceptual priority. At its most abstract and metaphysical level, the concept is linked to the act of Creation. As Dr. Kapila Vatsyayana has pointed out, "the Absolute Primordial (*purusha*) gives rise to the individual archetype (*puru-sha*)", which is instrumental in creating all products of the *bhuta*-s, i.e., beings—through the aid of sounds and words. The ancient Samkhya philosophy held that *purusha* witnesses creative activities of *prakriti*. He is *tata-stha,* while the stream of creation flows by and on. A little more direct is the tradition of comparing music to the human body and state equivalences between musical notes and bodily organs, etc. (e.g., *sa* = soul, *re* = head, *ga* = arms, *ma* = chest). At yet another level, music is understood as one limb of the larger conception of arts seen as the Body of Man with many interrelated systems. Finally, musicological texts open their expositions on the science of music by describing physical and biological foundations of human life as a prelude to more technical deliberations.

However, these comparatively abstract formulations are inadequate in the context of the immediately sensed visualization, inherent in the act of painting. It is here that the very early vogue of positing wide-ranging non-musical correlates to musical features, makes its contribution felt. For example, correlates from Bharata's *Natyashastra* can be tabulated as shown (Table 1). The *Naradiya Shiksha* moves a step forward in equating *svara* with *varna* (Table 2).

By the time we move to the musicological landmark, the *Sangita*

Table 1

Rasa	Shringara	Hasya	Karuna	Roudra	Vira	Bhayanaka	Bibhatsa	Adbhuta
Bhava	Rati	Hasya	Shoka	Krodha	Utsaha	Bhaya	Jugupsa	Vismaya
Varna	Shyama (light green)	Sita (white)	Kapota (grey)	Rakta (red)	Gaura (yellow-red)	Krishna (black)	Nila (blue)	Pita (yellow)
Devata	Vishnu	Pramatha	Yama	Rudra	Mahendra	Kala	Mahakala	Brahma

Table 2

Svara	Colour	Varna
Shadja	Padmapatraprabha (lotus-petal-red)	Brahmin
Rishabha	Shukapinjara (reddish yellow)	Kshatriya
Gandhara	Kanakabha (golden red)	Half-Vaishya
Madhyama	Kundasaprabha (white)	Brahmin
Panchama	Krishna (black)	Brahmin
Dhaivata	Pitaka (yellow)	Kshatriya
Nishad	Sarvavarna (multi/all-coloured)	Half-Vaishya

Ratnakara, matters are obviously heading towards firm visualization as well as personification processes (Table 3). However, as Gangoly

Table 3

Svara	Shadja	Rishabha	Gandhara	Madhyama	Panchama	Dhiavata	Nishad
Varna	Rakta	Pinjara	Swarna, Atipita	Shubhra	Krishna	Pita	Vichitra
Devata	Vanhi	Brahma	Chandra	Vishnu	Narada	Tumburu	Tumburu
Rasa	Vira, Adbhuta, Roudra	Vira, Abdhuta, Roudra	Karuna	Hasya, Shringara	Hasya, Shringara	Bibhatsa, Bhayanaka	Karuna

perceptively noted, "even though Ratnakara allots protective deities for melodies as distinct from individual *svara*-s, their pictures or images are not described, in any prayer-formulas in the shape of descriptive verses (*dhyana*-s) such as we find in the later texts."[1] Most authorities seem to agree that *dhyanashloka*-s are not found earlier than in the *Ratnakara*. According to Premlata Sharma, the *Sangitopanishadsara* (1350) of Sudhakara, a Jain musicologist, is the earliest work to have them. (Incidentally, Chaitanya Desai has significantly referred to Sudhakara's use of dance-terms etc. traceable to Rajasthani language.) Gangoly, however, gives credit to the *Panchama Sarasamhita* of Narada, dated *circa* 1440, for the appearance of both *raga*-s-*ragini*-s and *dhyanashloka*-s. More importantly, the text of *dhyanashloka*-s, even in the later *Sangitaraja* of Kumbha (again from Rajasthan), dated 1433–68, is to be marked for resemblance of the *dhyana*-s to Tantric *dhyana*-s. This, ostensibly is the reason why the following, and similar terms occur frequently in the early *dhyanashloka*-s: *pasha* (lass/noose), *phalam* (fruit), *abjam* (thousand-petalled lotus), *ankusha* (goad), *shankha* (conch), *chakram* (wheel), *gada* (mace), *abhayakaram* (a Tantric *mudra*), etc. To anticipate a little, the *dhyana* concept needed to be replaced by the *nayak-nayika bheda* preparatory to the advent of Ragamala-s.

It helps to note that *dhyanashloka-s* are mostly related to Grama *raga-s* as distinct from the Deshi. The former belonged to Margi *sangeet*, i.e., sacred music. On the other hand, Deshi *raga-s* are attributed to Deshi *sangeet* which is succinctly defined in *Ratnakara* as "*sangeet* comprising of *gitam, vadyam* and *nrittam,* that entertains people, according to their tastes, in different regions."

One may wonder about the actual link between *ragadhyana-s* and actual performance. Gangoly, Ebling and others have suggested that they were intended to be used by performers to ensure comprehend and capture divine qualities of music and hence they were described as prayer formulas.

Perhaps, one should ponder a little over the concept of *dhyana*. The term is derived from *dhyai,* to meditate upon, imagine, call to mind. *Dhyana* is a mental representation of personal attributes of an image—traditionally of a deity. The concept has been developed in Vedanta, Samkhya philosophies and by Buddhist and Yogic thinkers in their own ways. *Dhyana* has been inevitably linked to divinity-concept interpreted according to the general thrust of the philosophy concerned. Yogic and, to some extent Buddhist, interpretations are comparatively more spiritual, psychological and philosophical than theological. For example, Patanjali defines *dhyana* as *tatra pratyayaikatanata dhyanam*. Without going into the technical details of the process, it could be described as arresting the march of those, otherwise evanescent, impressions received from everything selected as a stimulus-support and the consequent stabilization of a particular impression. *Dhyana* constitutes one of the eight aspects of Patanjali's yoga. It can essentially be characterized as a victory over time because *dhyana* denies succeeding moments their customary power to destroy preceding moments, an act which brings about a state of continuing instability. One important component of the procedures advocated is *alambanam,* i.e., use of a supportive stimulus. It forms the crux of the mental exercise practised by yogi-s to stabilize in the mind, selected grosser forms of the eternal. Developed over centuries, *dhyana* procedures and techniques chiefly consist of two major types known as *saguna* and *nirguna*. The distinction between the two is that the latter involves concentration on the abstract while the former employs concrete objects, etc. for the same purpose. A later Upanishad, called *Dhyanopanishad,* devoted exclusively to *dhyana*-study, significantly mentions Brahma, Vishnu, Rudra,

Maheshvara and Achyut as the main icons, adding sounds of *veena* and *shankha* as the revelatory timbres. The Buddhists made the concept so accommodative as to include ordinary objects as well as *ashubha*-s (inauspicious items, processes) as supportive stimuli.

I have dwelt on the *dhyana* concept at some length because it is imperative to decode *ragadhyana*-s as cumulative, musicological and multi-channelled efforts to shift music away from the pre-empting power of the sacred in India. The *dhyana* philosophy, psychological procedures involved in it, techniques it perfected towards religio-metaphysical ends—all these were skilfully assimilated and adapted by medieval Indian musicology *because* music, music-makers and music-receivers were undergoing a total mutation during the period. One of the basic principles of cultural musicology holds that music is the most reluctant of cultural factors to accept change. Consequently it is also the last to accept and exhibit change. However, music is also the most symptomatic of deeper cultural transformations. When music changes, everything can be assumed to have undergone change. The ascendancy of the *deshi* element in middle ages thus indicates comprehensive religious, linguistic, demographic, political and aesthetic changes, Indian ethos was keen to assimilate. As an aid to the process, non-representational expression, such as offered by music, would need strategic and representational applications, and *ragadhyana*-s were devised with this end in view. Sharnagadeva spoke perceptively of *poorvaprasiddha* and *adhunaprasiddha raga*-s and thus drew attention to the noticeable changes demanding new systematization. It is interesting to note that though he reorganized the prevailing *raga*—corpus by employing the classification of regional and derived (*janya-janak raga*-s), there is no indication of the *ragini* concept being in vogue. Derivative *raga*-s were not called *ragini*-s.

Thus we reach the crucial span of the sixteenth-seventeenth century, the period which produced two major works directly related to Ragamala-s. The reference is to Kshemakarna/Meshakarna's Ragamala (1509) and Pundarik Vitthal's Ragamala (1576). The works listed *raga-ragini-putra* families, provided descriptive verses and followed up with pictures. Obviously, the *raga*-corpus had grown enormously since the times of *Ratnakara*. The concept of *putra*-s was therefore pressed into service to accommodate the new entrants. Notably, the authors came from the Rajasthan-Malwa region. The accumulated influx of new *raga*-s during the intervening three centuries proved challenging to musicologists and musicians alike. Fortunately, a number of musicians appear to be performers too, and this saved them from being originators of desiccated theoretical formulations. It is significant to note that Pundarik Vitthal, not only included as many as 16 Persian *raga*-s in his family of 66, but also mentioned their nearest Indian equivalents. He does not fail to clarify that the Persian *raga*-s are *parada* (gifted by others), but accepts them without further ado. Pundarik Vitthal was a southerner who came to north in search of patronage. He is reported to have written on Hindustani music and dance at the behest of his patron. The two works, of Kshemakarna and Pundarik Vitthal respectively, are the acknowledged foundations of the Ragamala-s. However, discussion of the established Ragamala convention cannot be taken up unless an intervening phase is taken into account.

It is necessary to refer to the *Kalpasutra* manuscript dated late fifteenth century. Ebeling admits that the *Kalpasutra* Ragamala is the earliest, and yet concludes that it is 'a dead end road in terms of pictorial Ragamala-s'. Even if one accepts this judgement, other illustrations from the same Jain source merit serious notice from every cultural standpoint. The illustrations deal with very fundamental musicological concepts such as *grama, svara, sruti, murchhana* and *tana*. For the present purpose some features of these 107 illustrations (described by the editor alternatively as *Chitravali* and *Sangitarupavali*) deserve attention:

1. All illustrations have only one figure in the picture-space and the title is inscribed at the top.
2. Animals and birds frequently find place, but the common format is a figure with human body and animal head.
3. The highly technical concepts depicted in the series, closely follow stabilized and stated musicological tradition. For instance, *tana*-visualizations include animals/birds because different *tana*-s, successively begin on different notes in sequence, and the notes themselves have been associated with the calls of certain animals or birds according to musicology.
4. It is surprising that even though the *Chitramala* proceeds to include illustrations on dance, the concept of *tala* is ignored.
5. Altogether, the series depicts fifteen musical instruments—none of which sounds an unfamiliar notes.

In my opinion, the undiluted musicological orientation of the series can hardly be over stressed. On the other hand, *Kalpasutra*

Ragamala includes *ayudha* (weapon), *mudra*-s, and other visual forms, echoing the *yaksha-yakshini* or *gandharva-surasundari* figures from temple sculptures.

According to Ragamala experts, the *Kalpasutra* effort can be placed at least a century prior to the really important Ragamala-s. As a musicologist, I feel that it *therefore* represents a major conceptual decision of the concerned artists to reject one-to-one correspondence between musical and visual phenomena. This was an essential precondition to make the later Ragamala-s possible. The *Kalpasutra* indicates a kind of breaking away, a liberation from a convention which was ambitiously comprehensive—attempting as it did to encompass too many technical details, and thus hamper freedom of performance, so essential to music. Leaving aside this larger issue, it might be said that the *Kalpasutra* Ragamala, though nearer to *ragadhyana*-s than to the later pictorial Ragamala-s, represents a necessary and logical step towards the latter.

At this stage, a little diversion needs to be made by going back to the *ragadhyana*-s, and especially to their relation to performing tradition. The question is: Is it sufficient to describe *dhyana*-s as prayer formulae to bring out their link with the performing tradition? Perhaps, it may serve to cast the net a little wider and pay attention to another musical continuity, too easily clubbed with Hindustani music.

I suggest a look at the Vaishnava tradition of music in Assam and adjoining areas. This is logical because the Ragamala traditions and the Vaishnava musicology—both leaned heavily on *Sangita Damodara* (AD 1500) of Shubhankara. Authorities on Assamese and Manipuri music refer to actual singing of *ragadhyana*-s after the initial *alapa* which is not set to rhythm.[2] In fact, it has been argued that *raga*-visualization seems to have prevailed in Assam from medieval times, in a form known as *raga-malita*. The same authorities state that Rama Saraswati, a contemporary of Shankardeva (1459–1598), used the expression *raga-malita* in his *Geeta Govinda* and described it as *ragadhyana* while he took musical compositions from Shubhankara's *Sangita Damodara*. Very often, the *malita*-s do not give personified pictures of *raga*-s but link them with some incident from the lives of Krishna or Vishnu. Both these features suggest an independent, early, popular and secular evolution of the concept of *ragadhyana* as a performance-feature. The similarity between the two terms, Ragamala and *Ragamalita* is striking. The Assamese practice could raise many questions about accepted statements on the origin, period provenance and *rasion d'être* of Ragamala-s as a musical phenomenon.

Yet another instance of a significant regional variation is the Nasik Ragamala brought to notice by M.S. Mate and Usha Ranade in 1982. The series is incomplete and consists of only 44 paintings. The set is based on Kshemakarna's Ragamala and displays interesting similarities and deviations. Dated as in the eighteenth century, the series shows a remarkably local touch in the depiction of human physiognomy, dresses, ornaments, general decor and architectural setting. Even in the incomplete version, the inclusion of Jogi-Asavari in the picturized *raga* corpus, may prove significant in view of the fact that, like the *ragini* Gauri, Jogi-Asavari is common in non-elite musical traditions of Maharashtra.

Maharashtra is also credited to have originated a series pictures on *tala*-s dated the late eighteenth century. Whatever may be the verdict on their pictorial worth, the paintings undoubtedly arouse musicological interest.

In the musicological tradition *tala* has never been regarded less important than *raga*. A pictorial tradition, fully responsive to musicological reality and continuity, would logically be expected to reflect the *tala*-aspect of Indian music. It is interesting to note that to the ancients, *tala* represented a sequence of action-reaction, a veritable dialectic of musical forces, between principles of *Purusha* and *Prakriti,* expectably identified with Shiva and Shakti respectively. One might recall the *tandava* dance of Shiva and the *lasya* expression of Parvati. Against this background, the Deccan attempt, however isolated and weak, needs to be appreciated as a corrective introduced to rectify a musico-pictorial imbalance conventionally detected in Ragamala-s. When one remembers that, even in the pioneering *Kalpasutra* tradition, *tala* was not touched (though the work dealt with dance), contribution of the Deccan *talamala* assumes added value.

Usha Ranade and Kamal Chavan, editors of the monograph on the Nasik *Talamala,* have argued that *tala* is difficult to portray because of its secondary role in generating *rasa*. They have also rightly drawn attention to the fact that *tala* is distinct from *laya,* and that the latter is closely associated with *rasa*. Whether it is the early, and seminal *Vishnudharmottara Purana* or the later *Sangitaraja* of Kumbha, emotive aspect of music is clearly linked with *laya* than with *tala*.

But this merely takes the argument further back. The question which could be raised is: why is a pictorial representation of *laya* is not found in the tradition? Perhaps the answer lies elsewhere, and needs to be sought after some more ground is covered.

Once again, turning ears to the north-eastern music-making may prove rewarding. It has been recorded by students of Manipuri dance and music, as also by those who have studied Vaishnavaite rhythmic expression in Assam, that Pung and Khol are played to realize musical forms known as *raga*-s. In the Manipuri presentation, a specific form with this feature is reportedly known as *ahaubi*. In a similar manner, *raga-diya* (*raga* presentation) in the Assamese tradition, includes *raga-talani* which has no reference to *tala/tala*-s actually used in performance of the *geet* that follows. The *raga-talani*, in fact, consists of playing certain *patakshara*-s in a definite sequence. It is thought-provoking, that the oft repeated definition of *raga*—*ranjayateeti ragah*—hardly makes exclusive use of musical notes inevitable for emergence of *raga*. If one considers the traditional *shabda-nada-dhvani-varna* hierarchy, it is easy to follow the logic of having *raga*-s of *mridanga*, or of any other instrument—with no mandatory role for musical notes.

I submit that, contrary to the generally held view, Ragamala-s did *not* aim at reflecting musicological tradition—at least not after the early *dhyana*-phase was left behind. In fact, it did *not* use music— even as a stimulus. The phenomenon became what it is *because* it functioned within its own pictorial tradition. The tradition is better understood if construed as theatre-oriented than music-oriented. This is the reason why the early and pioneering *Kalpasutra* attempt, with its heavy musicological bias, was not followed up. In fact, two other factors turned out to be the controlling agents. They were the *nayika-bheda* doctrine, and Krishna-*leela* literature. It is instructive to remember that the *nayika-bheda* doctrine, as propounded in Sanskrit tradition, was a part of the larger exposition of *rasa*-theory, in which *shringara* dominated. The Krishna-*leela* concept accepted the *rasa*-system but processed it with allegorical devotion through expositions illuminated by Jayadeva, Vidyapati, Surdas, etc. It is also important to note that Rupa Goswami's *Ujval Chintamani* brought into being a comprehensive *bhakti*-oriented Vaishnava theoretical structure to add an invaluable dimension to literary tradition in Hindi.

I suggest that it is the theatre-oriented *rasa*-system which provided foundation to Ragamala-s, while *nayika-bheda*, as propounded in Hindi literature helped to determine its content. The *avatara* concept has always proved conducive to theatric expression because it creates *roles* and *not* characters alone. In addition, the Krishna-*leela* proved apt formulae to humanize abstractions inherent in conceptual structures of the *rasa*-system, literary sophistications in *nayika-bheda*, or philosophical subtleties in the *avatara*-concept. It is against this background, that we can appreciate many components of Ragamala-s. For instance, love as the *sthayi-bhava*, *nayaka-nayika* as the *alambana-vibhava*-s, friend-messengers and natural surroundings as *uddipana-vibhava*-s, *alankara*-s and *bhava*-s of the personages as *anubhava*-s and finally, expressions and feelings depicted as the *sanchari-bhava*-s. This is the reason why musicological authenticity gets weaker and weaker as we move from one Ragamala to the other. Meshakarna and his followers represent musical impulses transformed into theatric ideas struggling to give vent to artistic interest in the mundane (as distinct from divine and profane); secular (as distinct from sacred); and action-oriented (as distinct from contemplation-oriented) theme and content. In addition, there was an urge to articulate regional instead of pan-Indian features. Thus, while the musical labels continued, the content underwent a radical change. The true significance of the Ragamala phenomenon would evade us if we continue to guided by the label.

CONCLUSION

Ragamala-s pose following questions to a musicologist:

1. Why are there no *talamala*-s?
2. Why the Carnatic system of art music does not enjoy this extra-musical but music-related art expression?
3. Where did the basic loyalty of the Ragamala-s lie—to the performing or the scholastic tradition in music?
4. In view of the categorial pentad of Indian musical expression, is it preferable to examine Ragamala-s with a set of criteria other than the customary, historico-musicological?
5. Indian musical expression has been more composite than usually realized. Is it possible that recognition of the fact may explain the rationale governing origin, nature and function of these paintings?
6. What are the plausible reasons which confined Ragamala-s to certain parts of the country? Were there musical reasons

    in operation?

7. Meshakarna's attempt certainly provides the most complete model of genre. But is it possible to ascribe deviations from his line to differences in regional musical traditions? In other words, pictorial deviations from Meshakarna may prove to be musical-musicological conformities.

Dedication

I would like to dedicate the presentation to the late Ardhendukumar Gangopadhyaya, better known as O.C. Gangoly (1 August 1881– 9 February 1974). Like Pt. V.N. Bhatkhande (whom Gangoly respected), Ardhendukumar left a flourishing legal practice to devote himself to work in music and arts. His insights into visual arts and music made him a major thinker analyzing the composite nature of Indian art theory and practice. His book, *Ragas and Raginis* laid a firm foundation for studies in the musical aspect of Ragamala-paintings. The first limited edition of the work in 1935 consisted of 36 copies. The second saw the light of the day in 1947. Gangoly dedicated this seminal work to Pt. Bhatkhande. Gangoly, writes briefly but movingly about how Bhatkhande, from his sick-bed, shed silent tears when he learned that the work was dedicated to him.

Gangoly is thorough, fundamental, comprehensive and systematic. His work is at once encourages and challenges students of Hindustani music.

References

1. O.C. Gangoly, *Ragas and Raginis*, p. 106.
2. Neog and Changkakoty, 1962; Darshana Jhakeri and Kalavati Devi, 1978.

20

The Indo-Portuguese Performing Experience

A country, such as India, needs to *know* components of its own cultural make-up if it is to maintain the desirable equilibrium between forces of change and constancy—the prime shaping factors of cultural identity. In bringing about change, one of the major agents is cultural confrontation, which may or may not be accompanied by political domination, especially, of non-indigenous powers. The Indo-Portuguese relationship requires to be examined in this context. In any such inquiry performing arts assume special importance because they are channels through which exchanges, assimilations, amalgamations and the like take place, mostly on account of internal compulsions. Performing arts, probably constitute the best example of the 'cultural imperative' in action.

However, analysis of performing situations faces certain characteristic difficulties. Firstly, performing situations explore non-verbal channels of communication in a major way, with the result that their content remains non-verbalized. Secondly, even if, and when, content is verbalized and suitable terminological base is created, use of the latter may be restricted to the oral tradition. In other words, evidence of the verbalized content may not be available in written versions. Finally, performing traditions have a disconcerting tendency to go underground for long periods, only to surface later—often under different names, as also in different or analogous life-areas. Consequently, all statements about borrowings, assimilations, etc. acquire character of a tentative probing—which is also speculative. And yet, the task has its own rewards.

*   *   *

The Portuguese came to India before the Mughals, and it appears that, the then ascendant Afghans and Turks were their chief antagonists. In India, the Portuguese strongholds were located in

Kerala, Maharashtra, Goa, Gujarat and to a certain extent, Bengal. Even though the Portuguese were the last European power to leave Indian shores, its hold on different Indian regions exhibits waxing and waning in expanse and effectiveness. For example, their small Goan kingdom expanded in four stages (in 1510, 1543, 1763, and 1788 respectively) before stabilizing. Assessment of the Portuguese overall contribution to Indian culture thus becomes a little complicated. In addition, possibility of an indirect contribution through footholds in Persia and Sri Lanka is also to be reckoned with. It has been strongly held that the Portuguese influenced India in matters of race, language, religion, flora, fauna, agriculture, crafts and industries. To be added are arts—the performing group being the immediate concern.

MUSIC

Some facts are easily noticeable.

Firstly, it is to be expected that converts to Christianity, became followers of Western music. Churches, and other such agencies, ensured exposure to the tradition of Western classical music. More importantly, harmonization, instrumentation and voice-use of a different kind entered the musical thinking of the groups concerned. It is significant that, even though these West-oriented groups could not create major musical personalities ranking high in the wider Western system of music-making, a majority of instrument-players in the Bombay film-industry were Goanese Christians. They also considerably contributed to band-music. As is known, these are the musics which, even today, attempt to introduce phrasings, idiomatic constructions and stylistic organizations moving closer to harmonization. These attempts are much more than mere polyphonic progressions. Lucio Rodrigues has aptly described the musical product as Euro-Indian. As he pointed out, the Euro-Indian music could become a reality because the Churches shaped music-education. Church-based musical grooming and exposure meant introduction to Western notation, plain chant with its elementary harmony, violin-playing in European style and acceptance of some new occasions and ways of music-making, e.g., funeral brass band.

A notable feature is that the Euro-Indian stream of music flows stronger in the folk category. As expected, the range of this category is very wide. A brief description of some forms should prove instructive.

Ovi: In the genre, two prevailing and major types are religious and secular Ovi. The genre is structurally very similar to the Ovi in Marathi (in Maharashtra and Goa itself)—the distinguishing feature being a stanza of three and half lines. Though the pentatonic melodic character could be anticipated, the reported drum accompaniment comes as a surprise. Two kinds of drums, *madiem* and *gummot,* along with a pair of brass cymbals, complete the accompaniment-unit. Fr. Thomas Stephens [(1549–1619), the well-known emulator of Sant Dhyaneshvara (1275–96) of Maharashtra] employed Ovi to compose Kristapurana. However, the performed Ovi intrigues on account of its musical complexity and elaborateness. Mostly heard from persons of Kharvi (fishermen) and Bhandari (toddy-tappers) communities, the chorus-leader (who also plays the *mediem*), is a product of *guru-chela* tradition. The performance requires ritualistic occasions (from the Catholic liturgical calendar), such as Easter, Christmas, feast of a Patron saint or social events such as marriage, sixth-day wake observed after child-birth, etc.

The singing-drumming session is known as *bonn,* so-called because of the special paste of rice-ash put on one face of the *madiem.* Sessions are held in the evening. Players sit round a fire made of coconut husk and cow-dung. The leader opens by intoning the first verse of the 'Sign of the Cross'. Verses are often intoned, one by one, with drums contributing suitably and prominently.

Not surprisingly, the *ovi*-s are also sung by Christian women at the time of marriage. These women's songs are ritualistic and associated with different occasions. Accordingly they are known as *zoti, vers, chuddo,* etc.

Mando and *Durpod:* The forms need to be discussed together as they form a combined, performing unit. *Durpod* follows *mando.* A tabulated comparison might help in bringing out their diverse, yet complementary features:

Mando	*Durpod*
1. Song of passion and love	Of secular, simpler joys of life
2. Reflects aristocracy	Voice of the middle class
3. Sounds more 'foreign'	More 'Goan' in character
4. Appears sophisticated, arty	Ranges from homespun to vulgar.
5. Tinged with melancholy—	Full of joy, laughter—more of

	more of Romeo in it.	Mercutio in it.
6.	Narrates a story	Glimpses of the multiple facets of life.
7.	Deliberateness (presentation)	Improvised.
8.	Elaborate verses, Maiden's yearning, lover's adoration, mutual surrender and fulfilled love—being the four stages.	Verse form elementary single lines, couplets and triplets added at will
9.	Slow movement. Three stanzas of short four lines each. Each held together by rhyme. Refrain, a rhymed couplet.	Brisk rhythms the dialect used lengthens vowels.
10.	Rhyme and theme binding factors.	Tune, and to a lesser degree rhymes unify.
11.	First person plural/singular. Identification with the lover.	Not averse to dramatic form. Duets dialogues between mother-daughter, man-mistress employed.
12.	Violin important, drums secondary.	Drums important. Melody secondary.
13.	Sung in two voices to the accompaniment of violin, guitar and *gummot.* Second voice harmonizes in thirds and sixths.	Male tenor, bass voices take up the refrain, handclaps, ejaculations, reinforce.
14.	With slow, graceful dance. In the early vogue, ladies opened fans, gentlemen waved handkerchiefs—taking the floor with swaying rhythms.	Singers-dancers compete. Vigorous.
15.	Rhythm 6/8—slow waltz.	Tunes in 6/8 measure. Two-four also used.
16.		*Durpod* means refrain. *Durpod dorunk* is to follow a *mando* with a series of refrains.
17.	*Margao* described as the home of *mando.*	

18. Uses Konkani with a large   Uses Konkani.
    mixture.

One other form, *dekhni* can also be considered for its obvious Western musical flavour. However, what has been discussed is adequate to give an idea of the Portuguese contribution to Indian music.

Thirdly, it is also to be noted that some features of the Goan Hindu music are not ascribable to either of the two major systems of Indian art music, namely Hindustani and Carnatic. For example, a *tala* called *jhula tala* is not covered by the two systems though so well codified. However, it is possible that such features may be traced to other Indian and non-Portuguese influences.

On this background it is possible to draw attention to a very specific and deep musical influence traceable to the Portuguese. I refer to the ubiquitous keyboard instrument, called harmonium, in the contemporary Hindustani art and semi-art categories of music, active especially in the vocal mode. No indigenous musical tradition, of any category, in India, has a keyboard instrument in use. According to the current reported tradition, Portuguese soldiers introduced a kind of pedal harmonium in India during the sixteenth century. By 1880s it has acquired considerable prestige and circulation. For example, it was employed in the Naradiya Keertan, *lavani*-presentations, staged music-dramas as well as by wealthy amateurs for music-making. The pedal harmonium was often fitted with imported reeds to obtain a deeper tone and hence it was often described as organ. The instrument was probably introduced in Bombay.

During the second phase of the vaguely dated history of this instrument, a significant development took place. A *baithak* version, obviously more suited to the Indian manner of presenting music, was developed. In India, music-makers prefer to sit down to perform. The 'horizontal' harmonium, with hand-operated bellows, required as the instrument was to be played in a sitting posture, exemplifies remarkable structural modifications and musical adaptation.

It is difficult to imagine and estimate impact of the keyboard phenomenon on Indian musical *thinking*. In my opinion, it is the keyboard which makes chords and chordal progressions easily conceivable and executable. These precisely are the chief contributors to harmonic, as contrasted with polyphonic approaches to tonal material. It is significant that a major charming form of semi-art music in Hindustani music, namely *thumri*, is reportedly the first genre to resort to modulation in a major way. Further, Ganpatrao Bhaiya (d. 1915) of Gwalior is credited to have given *thumri* a new turn and life, by introducing a skilful modulations. It is worth noting that he was also regarded to be the foremost harmonium-player of his times. With an unlimited capacity to easily generate patterns and create a perceivable tonal colour, harmonization spells far-reaching musical consequences. The role and popularity of harmonium is an Indian proof of this musical facility.

Additionally, whatever is accepted in art tradition usually enters folk and devotional streams, sooner or later. Thus harmonium, and the type of musical thinking or logic it carries with it, assumes great significance. One has only to note the circulation harmonium enjoys to accept the important property it represents—that of contributing a timbre—too distinctive to be ignored. It has also been mentioned that the Portuguese were responsible for introducing tambourine in Kerala. It is probable that, in this instance too, the thin and scattered sound proved an attractive timbre.

Obviously, Euro-Indian music is of great ethnomusicological interest. From instrumental colours to organizational principles, from roles allotted to language to the large-scale resource to stylized dance, and from socially communicative rituals to individual expressions— is certainly a wide span. The span is so well covered by this music that it has succeeded in adding significantly to the indigenous musical corpus. A thorough analysis is bound to reveal interesting ways in which music pursued its own dynamics of change and constancy in the Indo-Portuguese relationship.

THEATRE

At the outset it needs to be noted that Catholic religious expression certainly proves more conducive to theatric quality. In its procedures of worship, penance, celebration and observance, theatre is built-in. Rituals enjoy an overall importance in Catholicism and the consequent picturesque meticulousness, combined with theatric variety is beneficial to performing arts in general.

However, what is discussed here is *not* theatric qualities detected in rituals. Attention is drawn to those presentations normally regarded theatric. The illustrative discussion also overlooks distinctions between primitive, folk, art, popular and devotional categories of cultural manifestation.

Broadly speaking, Portuguese influence could be identified as a part of the third theatric stream flourishing in medieval India. The two other streams were—the *Natyashastra*-governed Sanskrit theatre, and the language-theatre which, the Bhakti-movement promoted so vigorously.

In Kerala, the Portuguese were preceded by Syrian Christians. Through relentless efforts, the Portuguese succeeded in bringing Kerala Christians under Papal sway after 1599, Choomar Choondal has identified at least thirteen dance-music forms prevailing in Indian regions influenced by the early Christians, specially on the West coast.[1] Some display a pronounced theatric quality and give unambiguous signs of Portuguese contribution. The following details are instructive:

CHAVITTUNATAKAM

This form from Kerala is prevalent in Tamil Nadu as Terukuttu and Nadagama in Sri Lanka.

As the name implies, the genre gives importance to *chavittu*, meaning stamping of feet. The form is so closely associated with the Indo-Portuguese families settled in and around coastal towns of Cochin and Quilon, that it is also known as *Parankikalute natakam*, i.e., drama of the Portuguese.

1. These plays are based on Biblical, historical and religious themes and participants have to undergo arduous training in martial exercises after an initiation ceremony which begins with oath-taking in front of a Cross.

2. In the plays, roles of kings and military chieftains are customarily given to persons with fair complexion.

3. Performances take place on occasions such as Christmas and Easter, or during the period after harvesting.

4. Crowns, belts, earrings, full-shirts and coats are major items in the costume design. Symbols of the Cross drawn on the king's forehead, are noteworthy. The obligatory use of stockings, wearing of gloves and veils is also to be marked.

5. During performances, music-making employs choral and orchestral modes.

6. It is interesting to note that performances take place on a

raised platform with spectators on its three sides. It is reported that in the early period, the stage was a two-storied structure.

7. Kattiyan or Katiyakkaaran, the jester—is a far cry from the *vidushaka* of Indian classical drama. However, more analysis is necessary to identify origins of different non-Indian features in his portrayal.

8. Fighting scenes are regarded extremely important. Their elaborate staging, distinctive techniques and king's non-participation—all have a non-Indian character. In this context, it is to be noted that from the four Latin Catholic castes, two (Anjuttukar, i.e., the 500 and the Ezunnuttukar, i.e., 700) are known for special protection they enjoyed from the Dutch and Portuguese rulers. They were also given special military training. It is stated that the Latinites claim to have the true tradition of the *chavittunatakam*.

9. Instruments prominently used include tambore, cymbal and *ravekku*. Dr. Choondal persuasively argues that these find place in the performing set as an effect of the Portuguese contribution.[2]

Bake very perceptively observed in 1932 that the *chavittunatakam* "is a kind of village theatre ... which is a remarkable example of the merging of indigenous traditions and imported ideas, originally very foreign to the people ... it has vitality enough to survive through some centuries and to give the Christian villagers a vigorous outlet for their energies, while, at the same time, imparting a kind of moral instruction, more or less of the same character as what the people had known before.[3]

In a very early paper describing dramatic presentations in south India, K.N. Sitaram had pointed out that their prominent features were:

(i) The late introduction (around 1700), of the court fool
(ii) Symbolism in the scenic design
(iii) A format in which players act to music
(iv) Imitation of battles, fights, etc. confined to plays performed by the Nayars.

Obviously, the *chavittunatakam* was a Portuguese-Christian response to prevailing forms. The Portuguese introduced objects, items and procedures identified with their own culture and accepted the rest in order to arrive at a viable cultural mix. It would appear that larger scope afforded to realism, a desire to open avenues of acceptable recreations for the newly converted classes, and projection of religious symbolism characterize the Indo-Portuguese identity emerging in different historical periods.

GOA

One moves up the coast to Goa, and another theatric form, the *tiatr* attracts notice.

It has been pointed out that Konkani *tiatr* itself began in Bombay around 1892 with the staging of 'Italian Bhurgo'.[4] Interestingly, the comprehensive prohibitions which the Portuguese clamped on the Goans, resulted in new musical balances early in history while theatre lagged behind in this respect.

Of the two prevailing *khel*-s, those performed during the pre-Lent Carnival bear Portuguese impress. These musico-dramatic, improvised performances consist of satire and humour, bordering sometimes on vulgarity. Kale mentions four major episodes of performances, clearly bringing out the theatric quality of the presentations. Yet another form, *contra danca* is a variation on *khel*. Accompanied by one or two violinists, performers satirize pomposity and cupidity of landlords through improvisations, less ribald in tone than in *khel*-s. As both *khel* and *contra danca* take place at the invitation of a patron who pays the performers, Kale regards the presentations as ritualistic precursors of the modern theatre, which, in his opinion, is essentially a commercial transaction.

One could, perhaps, refer to the pre-Lent Carnival in Goa in the context of Indo-Portuguese theatric interaction. The wearing of masks, processions, fancy dress parades, etc. have a theatric quality, and with a little stretching of imagination it could be appreciated as a positive force, at least in absence of theatre proper.

Zagar, a form with elements of theatre, is similar to the *jagar* of the Gowda Hindu community. It consists of a series of presentations of caricatured characters with song and dance mixed profusely. Usually, religious festivals provide occasions for *zagor*-s sponsored by the community as a whole. They are now on the decline.

It may not be an exaggeration to say that the Indo-Portuguese interaction has been more fruitful in music than in theatre. Probably, the representational potential of theatre made theatre more dangerous for the rulers and therefore less scope was allowed it to flower. Or operhaps, classes or social strata open to the Portuguese influence proved less receptive to new theatric ideas. Whatever may be the reason, the musical interchange certainly opened up more possibilities.

REFERENCES

1. Choomar Choondal, *Christian Theatre in India*, p. 30.
2. Ibid., p. 122.
3. *Folklore*, vol. 74, 1963, quoted by Choondal, op. cit., pp. 195–205.
4. Kale, 1986.

21

Organisation of Time: Oral and Written Word

INTRODUCTION

To organise is to combine units systematically for attaining a particular goal which, in the present case, is communication. With communication as the final goal, our chief concern is to examine interrelationships between written and oral words, especially in the dimension of temporality. The theme therefore compels us to leave out many other aspects of communication. For example, its spatial, non-verbal and non-human varieties will have to be kept aside, at least for the time being. This self-imposed and artificial isolation of the act will be difficult to maintain as the discussion proceeds. As a performer-thinker I have become increasingly aware of words as multi-sensory, multi-modal and multimedia power-packages. In addition, the changing nature of communication-technologies cautions against the human weakness of confusing strategies for methods and methods for philosophies. The present Indian situation also warns us against regarding the oral and the written as paired opposites. In India written and oral words have a long tradition of complementary interaction and not of mutual exclusion. As I have elaborated elsewhere the Indian oral tradition has the following main characteristics*:

1. Prestige of words *as* words
2. Equal importance of the oral and aural
3. Coexistence with the written
4. The role of *guru*-s
5. The *sutra*-way
6. Memory and its special functions
7. Rituality

*See "Indian Oral Tradition and Hindustani Music" in *Music and Musicians of Hindoostan*, pp. 23-4.

    8. Importance of Sound as a principle
    9. Multiplicity of communicators
    We may do well to remember the complex nature of the oral tradition in India.

THOUGHT-MOVEMENT AND SYNTAX

I have a mild suspicion that the theme, as expressed in English, appears to be a reversal of the actual thought process. Communication, being the all-embracing goal becomes in reality the first factor to guide our action. The contemplated communicative endeavour then selects words to channelize the further activity. Examination of the two interacting *avatara*-s of words (i.e., written and oral) comes next with a special reference to their systematic exploration of temporality. It is noteworthy that the same effort may be titled in Hindi as, *Sandnyapan ke liye Moukhik aur Likhit Shabdaka-kalik Sanghattan.* In Marathi it may be, *Sandhnyapanasathi Moukhik ani Likhit Shabdanche Kalik Sanghattan.* Is it valid to say that the conceptual sequence of the communicative act, i.e., communication-words-time-organization is better reflected in the inflectional Indian languages than in the colon-bifurcated, preposition-divided and conjunction-linked rendering in English? Communication appears to be the *karya* and words the *karana.* The common Indian usage *karyakarana* therefore seems to reflect the effective priorities—the intended result or purpose being given the honour of the first mention. I would venture to suggest that the issues involved are more cultural than linguistic. The order of psychological events would posit experience or the desire for it as the source of all psycho-physical process.

    In the present case desire for communication initiates all activity and subsequent choices are made accordingly. The decisions to verbalize and explore temporal dimension of the process more efficiently and/or effectively is a consequence of the original resolve. The title in English seems to refract than reflect the flow of the process. It is symptomatic that the way it is written, there may be problems in conveying the total sense if the title in English is spoken (and aloud). Can it be that prefixes, suffixes, infixes as also the compound formations facilitate the linguistic recreation of thought-processes more directly? *Prima facie* and with some anticipation I would like to suggest that these structural features (as also the currently out of favour) rhetorical devices work to bring about a simultaneity of multiple experiences in place of isolated stimuli following in succession. Making an excuse of the title we seem to have sent through an excited tremble through the gossamer-web of many issues touching on many disciplines. Such is the backdrop for examining the nature of intra-verbal (and also intra-modal) communication with special reference to temporality.

COMMUNICATION: THE INITIATING PROCESS

Communication needs to be distinguished from at least two other processes employing verbalization. They are: self-expression and information-transfer. Perhaps because of the basic orientation of a performer-thinker, I feel it necessary to treat the three processes as different though they enjoy inevitable overlaps of all social actions. The triad taps common psycho-physical resources and yet display significant contrasts in their respective objectives, performance-formats, audience-receiver-roles, mediums and distribution of sensory modes. The following illustrative tabulation may clarify:

	Communication	Self-expression	Information Transfer
Objective	Sharing the qualitative aspects of experience	Giving vent to individual urges	Transmission of facts considered impersonal
Performing Format	From ritualistic acts to aesthetic presentations	Live action	Media-mediated processing events
Audience receiver role	Participatory	Minimal	Distanced reception
Medium	Selectively explored though multiple	Instinctively resorted to	Deliberately and highly manipulated
Distribution of sensory modes	Audio/Video at the centre	Blurred and spasmodic	Rigidly patterned and multiple

For the purpose of our study communication can now be defined as "an act of sharing an experiential quality through multimedia, 'live' performances employing centrally audio-video modes to present forms ranging from ritualistic actions to aesthetic events providing for audience-participation which functions as a force shaping the final outcome according to the accepted cultural norms." It should be obvious that the definition deviates from those in semantics, syntactics, pragmatics as also in the wider, 'communication studies'. This is so, firstly, because I have placed more reliance on the performing model; and secondly because the quality of experience is the main concern.

WORDS, WORDS AND WORDS . . .

The next item on the investigatory agenda is the communicative word. Words have posed difficulties of defining even though orthographic, phonological, lexical, syntactic and grammatical clues have been tried and met with some success. Yet, definition of words as communicative packages, especially those engaged in transmission of the quality of experience, is rare.

I submit that three Indian disciplines and three theories therein would prove helpful at this juncture. My obvious reference is to: the *sphota*-theory from the philosophy of *vyakarana*, secondly to the *dhvani*-theory from *kavyashastra* and finally to the *rang*-theory from musical aesthetics. I must hasten to add that the story of communicative words is however incomplete until Bharata's concept of *vachik abhinaya* and the *kalavichara* in Indian Sangeetshastra are also taken into account. Results of the combined and often simultaneous operations of these disciplines are cumulative. It is however possible to discern the special thrusts of the individual disciplines.

From Patanjali (150 BC) onwards a long line of durable works on grammar is traceable. Many of these works are distinguished for their elevated view of language, linguistic communication and functions of grammar itself. The Indian tradition regards *vyakarana* to be a philosophy mainly because it discusses issues of fundamental nature. For example identification of linguistic elements, definition of meaning, location of the seat of significative powers, solution to the problems posed by homophones and homonyms, accommodation of secondary meanings, suggestivity of deviant language-use, generation of syntactic relationships and sentence-formation are some of the problems considered by grammarians as well as by other philosophies conventionally accepted to be so. On the other hand *vyakarana*-s also begin with problems pertaining to the ultimate na-

ture of reality. Whether it is *vyakarana*, Mimamsa (science of interpreting sacred texts), Nirukta (etymology), Nyaya (theory of knowledge) Vedanta (metaphysics) or Bauddha and Jain philosophies—
they have a common core of problems—and language-related problems never fail to find a place. Further, most of these disciplines
had their sights trained on the ultimate liberation of human soul.

Coming back to the grammarians, it has been perceptively pointed
out that (unlike in the West) language-philosophers in India have
dealt with the receiver-listener's view more extensively, a fact noteworthy in every study of communication. In addition, there is a near-
consensus about linguistic communication being one of the most
valued human possessions conducive to comprehension of the ultimate reality as well as for the attainment of final release (in spite of
conflicting views, fierce debates and academic outbursts on every
major issue.). In my opinion the *sphota*-theory as crystallized in
Bhartrihari's *Vakyapadiya* (AD 450) is of indisputable relevance in
our efforts to unravel the mysteries of qualitative linguistic communication. It will be foolhardy on my part to describe the *sphota*-theory
in all its implications. I note below some insights offered by the
theory to language-users keen on communicational quality:

1. The *sphota* is definable in two ways; firstly it is that indivisible,
    universal and inherent absolute from which meaning bursts
    forth. Secondly, it is the entity manifested by letters, or sounds
    when spoken.

2. The primary, i.e., noumenal *sphota* expresses itself in the phe-
    nomenal linguistic diversity because of its inner energy, i.e.,
    kratu which seeks expression and also because of the desire
    of the speaker to communicate.

3. *Sphota* as a process is realized through a series of 'errors'
    committed by the speaker in his movement towards the final
    and clear perception of *sphota*. The 'errors' are progressively
    reduced on account of the clearer, residual impressions
    gathered from the speaker's previous cognitions.

4. From the status of being an undiversified, absolute *shabda-
    brahma* one moves to the stages of *madhyama* and *vaikhari
    vac*. In these stages sequence, causation and diversity con-
    tribute to make the *sphota* perceivable ordinarily. *Prana*
    (breath) is the motive force in these later phases of concreti-
    zation.

5. *Vaikhari* manifests the *sphota* (through *prana*) as produced,

sequential sounds while *madhyama* is inner speech. *Pashyanti* lies beyond both sequence and breath, *pratibha,* i.e., intuitive perception alone operates at this level. Even though *dhvani,* i.e., the physical sound is what is actually perceived it merely invokes *shabda* which is the real conveyor of meaning.

6. *Vyakarana* is *yoga* of the word, i.e., *shabdapurva yoga* to be attained firstly, by experiencing spiritual well-being afforded by the use of grammatically correct words and secondly, by concentrating on powers of the purified word to reflect the absolute.

7. Language is equable with the absolute and *shabdabrahma* is to be accorded its due status. All cognition is due to words and the vital spirit, i.e., *chaitanya* is identical with *vac.*

8. From the essentially 'one', unified *shabdabrahman* it is Time which creates the linguistically expressed 'many'. Time does not exist as knowledge, it is an independent power of the *shabdabrahman.*

9. Bhartrihari emphasizes repeatedly that all of us have *sphota* as an entity within us. We also have the capacity to perceive it instinctively. (However the analogy offered by Mandana, the chief exponent of the *sphota* after Bhartrihari, refers to a jeweller who recognizes the true quality of a gem *because* he has earlier and adequate memory traces of what a good gem is.)

10. Bhartrihari expresses firm belief in 'sentence' as the minimal linguistic unit which manifests the *sphota.* Mutual expectancy (*akanksha*), Consistency of sense (*yogyata*), temporal contiguity (*asatti*) the speaker's intention (*tatparya*) govern the format of a sentence.

11. To Bhartrihari the utterance, the act of speaking out was central in the *sphota*-process. At the *vaikhari* level, each person is therefore able to express himself according to one's own *prayatna* (effort) and the resultant *dhvani* carries an individual stamp.

12. Bhartrihari does not fail to refer to the contextual factors that help to determine the final sense of any sentence. It is easy to see that reference to contextual factors means a natural shift to non-grammatical, linguistic as well as non-linguistic thought-processes and disciplines. A smooth transition is thus made to poetics, and especially to the *dhvani*-theory of

suggestivity propounded by Anandavardhana. The following contextual factors conducing to determination of the meaning in a particular application of language are listed by Bhartrihari. *Vakya,* especially, the action expressed in it; context (*prakarana*), in terms of the general activity in progress at the time of utterance; meaning (*artha*) of co-occurring words, or textual context; propriety or suitability (*auchitya*); spatial framework (*desha*), temporal framework (*kala*); relation (*samsarga* or *samyoga*), accompaniment by an entity that would serve to distinguish; absence of an entity that would serve to distinguish (*viprayoga*); mention of an entity that regularly accompanies (*sahacharya*); opposition (*virodha*); indication (*linga*) available in a connected sentence; presence of a specifying word (*anyashabdasan-nidhi*); probability (*samarthya*); gender (*vyakti*); accent (*svara*).

FROM DHVANI TO DHVANI . . .

Anandavardhana used the term *dhvani* to indicate poetry characterized by the predominance of suggested content as opposed to the reliance on indirect or denotative meanings. He acknowledged his debt to the illustrious grammatical tradition of the preceding ages for the terminology he pressed into service. His purpose was however different. According to the grammatical tradition meaning is inherent to *shabda, dhvani* merely invokes it. *Dhvani,* the utterance is transient, individually realized and it is a specific *avatara* of the permanent, omnipresent and indivisible *sphota.* In other words, utterance functions as an agent suggestive of the meaning. The significative power of words works through *dhvani.*

An analogous process takes place in Anandavardhana's exposition of how poetry attains the high, aesthetic quality of *rasa.* According to him the significative power of words would not suffice to make them artistically satisfying. They need to be suggestive, a function much beyond mere meaningfulness. This power of suggestivity is described by Anandavardhana as *dhvani.* Once again *dhvani* operates as an agent but this time it takes off from where the grammarian's *dhvani* had stopped. One espies in this continued terminological usage a spiral repetition, i.e., a recurrence but on a higher level. It is to be noted that Anandavardhana was the first prominent literary theoretician who placed *rasa*-theory at the centre of poetics, i.e., a discipline basically dealing with problems of literary excellence as contrasted with the performing excellence in dance, drama and music with which Bharata had dealt in his *Natyashastra*. This is the reason why Anandavardhana argued in favour of the concept of *rasadhvani*. The grammarian built a bridge between inner speech and its external manifestation while the aesthetician attempted transition from bare meaningfulness to an aesthetically valid construction. Together they formed, in a way, a continuum well-reflected in Anandavardhana's act of achieving a continuity which included a variation. It is therefore not surprising that many other terms as well as concepts in addition to *dhvani* found in Bhartrihari's elaborate list of contextual factors determining meaning—are also present in Anandavardhana's elaborate structure. It is instructive to juxtapose the chains of concepts-effects in successful grammatical and literary processes.

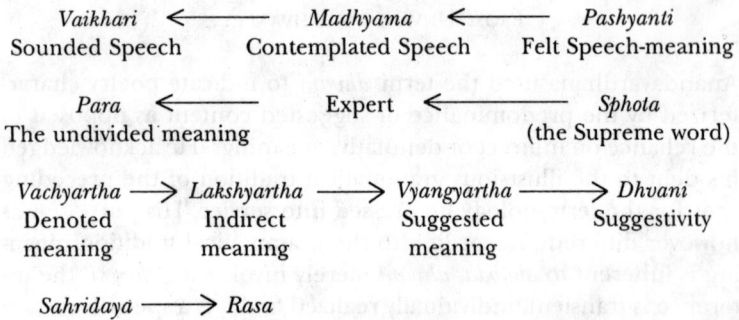

Vaikhari ←	*Madhyama* ←	*Pashyanti*
Sounded Speech	Contemplated Speech	Felt Speech-meaning

Para ←	Expert ←	*Sphota*
The undivided meaning		(the Supreme word)

Vachyartha →	*Lakshyartha* →	*Vyangyartha* →	*Dhvani*
Denoted meaning	Indirect meaning	Suggested meaning	Suggestivity

Sahridaya ——→ *Rasa*

It is of course true that for centuries both traditions developed side by side and what Anandavardhana's exposition brought forth was an accumulated result of the totality. However, the continued use of Bhartrihari's early terminological clusters and conceptual structures merely proves the durability of the original impulse.

It is time to turn to temporality. Bhartrihari's formulations provide a significant lead. Bhartrihari brings in the temporal element at the level of *madhyama vac,* the third level in his language-hierarchy. From *para,* the first level (at which the *sphota* is absolute, undivided, instrinsic and universal), the movement is towards making the *sphota* clear, phenomenal and commonly perceptible. The process of the gradual approximation succeeds chiefly because the principle of time, an independent power of *shabda,* comes into action.

According to Bhartrihari time does not exist as knowledge. As a creation of *shabda,* it makes its first appearance at the level of *madhyama* where Time works to create diversity, succession, causation as also the experience of duration. The operations of the principle continue at the next level, i.e., *vaikhari* where *dhvani* adds to the (already diverse, successive, causal and duration-effective) *shabda* the auditory perceptibility. *Dhvani* evokes meaning as it is understood commonly.

It will be a fascinating study to compare and contrast Bhartrihari's formulations and the insights offered by the modern time-related researches. However this is neither the time nor the place to undertake the venture. What is now pertinent is to connect the positions stated with the written-oral, verbal interface which forms the core of our enquiry. I note below some observations on the contemporary scene to be examined within the framework erected by the master language-philosophers and literary theoreticians.

WRITTEN-ORAL VERBAL INTERFACE: THE CONTEMPORARY SCENE

1. The authentic oral tradition in India included the written word. As persuasively argued by Goody and other scholars, even the Vedic tradition essentially consisted of oral transmission of the written material. It is thus necessary to distinguish between oralities of composition and transmission. Students of Indian culture may have erred in confusing the two and also in overstating the case of the oral tradition. The overstatement can be attributed to a complex which usually plagues those politically conquered.

2. It is undoubtedly true that the advent of the British rule with its characteristic actions on the educational front, recourse to printing press and the pervasive use of English brought about a major change in written-oral verbal interface under discussion.

3. From the array of wide-ranging effects two attract attention: (a) The new and all-embracing vogue of prose as a mode of literary expression, (b) Introduction of a different orthography along with punctuation marks. The former resulted into a highly crafted, 'bookish', unilinear and 'projected' organization of language. In contrast the traditional and overwhelming Indian preference for versification used to yield highly

indirect, oral-aural conditioned, circular and delivered organization of language.

The British-inspired introduction of a new orthography and punctuation marks also led to a linguistic organization marked by: a more visual control of sentence-formation, matter-formulation free of the constraints associated with the actually present hearer-receiver and finally, by features related to linguistic diction (defined as delivery added to style). It is symptomatic that the oft-detected Indian equivalent to *punctuation* has been the term *viram* which indicates rhythms created by the act of breathing while the former refers to the tradition of writing.

4. I submit that the new interface affected the Indian speech-quality in three ways:

   (a) Indians slid into an indifference to the proper values of vowel and consonant sounds. This is observable in all regional languages.

   (b) The expressive use of the varied, rhetorical devices as well as the more rhythmic forms such as proverbs, aphorisms, etc. soon came under a cloud. These and such other language-usages were described rather derisively as 'elocutionary, colourful', etc. The new speech-modes were unconsciously influenced by the ascending star of the prose-mode. The modern prose was accepted as a model of a cool, rational, durable and impersonal expression. Consequently the spoken word became less 'lively' in many ways.

   (c) The pre-British verbal interface relied heavily on operations of memory. It is indeed incorrect and unwarranted to equate the role of memory in oral traditions with the mechanics of mnemonic devices, etc. As Bhartrihari stated, memory-traces are the insights obtained from earlier cognitions and they are a force helping in the emergence of *sphota* leading to a deeper and completed emergence of meaning. In its more qualitative and literary operations, memory retained the self-contained patterns of sounds as well as meanings. These patterns came to life when users of speech quoted from memory or recited aphorisms, couplets, proverbs *nyaya*-s and the like. An act of memory is therefore a speaker's stepping into the past necessarily created by the conscious exploration of *shabda,* especially in its independent power of temporality. Those whose diet was mainly the written word, moved away firstly, from the memorizing procedures and secondly, from the (consequential) dynamic use of the memorized material.

5. It is significant that the act of memorizing which laid a firm-foundation of some speech-enriching procedures (of inserting quotations, etc.) are often described in Indian languages as *pathantara* which, in reality, means 'offering a variant of the written text'. This stands to reason because (as held by Bhartrihari), the *vaikhari vac* endows *madhyama vac* (i.e., inner speech) with *dhvani* and at this level every speaker offers his own version of the inner speech. This is inevitable because individual speakers are bound to differ in their articulatory efforts (*prayatna*) according to their own understanding and ability. The maximum variety attainable by the *vac* at the *vaikhari* stage is attributable to the operations of time and memory.

    What is not realized is that this stamp of individuality, natural to *vaikhari vac,* is not heard in the contemporary speech which has fallen prey to the written stereotypes. The written stereotypes in their turn are a culmination of the progressive drying up of the sources that contributed to the *vaikhari.* It is noteworthy that a great number of creative writers working in Indian languages often refer with recognizable pride to intentional efforts to bring to their respective writings, the character and rhythms of 'live' speech. Critics too have employed the use of speech-patterns as an evaluative criterion.

6. It is at this stage that Anandavardhana's *dhvani*-formulations becomes relevant. In its full power suggestivity of words depends on the quality and proportion of the sensory imagery they are able to arouse. Further, the richness or otherwise of suggestivity is directly related to the number of senses aroused simultaneously. Finally, operation of the synesthetic pairs adds to the fascinating interplay of images resulting into the content as distinguished from the meaning of words employed. It is known that the audio-visual centres form a synesthetic pair—a fact which should explain the loss of power of the printed word, normally suffering from a mechanical uniform-

ity largely unknown in ages more endowed calligraphically. Anandavardhana named his theory after the grammarians but it is also true that aural perceptions and sound-productions are intangible, connotative, suggestive and therefore ambiguous in the best sense of the term. The modern interface suffers as it curbs flights of both written and spoken words.

7. The spoken word, when allowed its natural movement, enjoys three kinds of 'Time'.

Firstly, the duration which can be preferably described as the Activated Time.

Secondly, comes into action the duration which can hold the attention of the listener. It is fitting and proper that this kind is described as Sympathetic time, i.e., the duration livening into action on account of the activated memory traces not directly aimed at.

Finally, we have the Influenced Time, i.e., the duration over which an articulated word exerts a power denying entry to others—not out of considerations of clashing coincidence but for the fear of obstructing the free flow of aural imagery.

The contemporary speech-pattern seems to recreate a temporal pattern which is affected by the same demerits as the spatial pattern produced by the printed word. It would be unfair to lay the sins of the spoken word at the door of the printed word. Both are most probably victims of the all-pervading disregard for a qualitative exploration of time and space.

THE RANG-THEORY

Two more turns and I have stated my case.

Firstly, a brief reference to the *rang*-theory, I have been advocating for some years. It is a formulation that corresponds with the performing reality.

In employing the term *rang* I am obviously alluding to performer's own terminology. They use it with circumspection to describe the desired realization of an aesthetic ideal. A majority of artists in the fields of dance, drama and music in India use the term *rang* to refer to an identifiable, final and positive impact of a performance. As in many other instances, the cryptic quality in a performer's 'language', his references to the *rang*-aspect, necessitate a 'translation'—

to facilitate non-performer's comprehension. In addition, the implied theoretical structure also requires to be verbalized and spelt out in some detail. However, performers are consistent in their terminology and their terminology enjoys advantages of being directly related to the qualitative, experiential aspects.

1. I would like to submit that within its framework, performer's *rang* corresponds to Bhartrihari's indivisible, universal and noumenal *sphota*.

2. An important characteristic of the *rang*-theory is the unclassifiable, emotional/intellectual experience it stands for. Ambiguity of the highest order reigns supreme in the *rang*-state.

3. At a lower level, the *rang* needs to be explained conceptually in terms of the actual making of a performance of dance, drama, music, etc. Performances at this level reflect choices made in terms of sense-modalities (audio, video, tactile, kinetic, etc.), genre-exploration (identification of a suitable performing form, etc.), selection of presentation-techniques and such other matters. One may compare this level with Bhartrihari's *madhyama vac*.

4. The next conceptual level is that of actual performances. Artists translate their performing designs into perceivable entities at this level. Performer's aesthetic intentions get transformed into receiver's experience. A majority of the experiential features are causally traceable to various physical components specific to different arts. Each performer's individual genius may come into effective existence at this level. One may compare actual performances with Bhartrihari's *vaikhari vac*.

5. Bhartrihari's *sphota* becomes manifest through *dhvani* which, as we have seen, invokes meaning. In a corresponding process *rang* seeks manifestation through the agency of *prayoga* (i.e., performance). *Prayoga*, in brief, becomes what it is when a dynamic equilibrium is achieved by the combined action of the trinity: performer-performed-receiver. The phenomenon of *prayoga* can be disassembled into different parts as per the orientations of individual performers and performances as well. It would be seen that what is posited at this juncture is a virtually circular process—that of communication. Even though performers are the agents who set the ball rolling, the moment action commences, each member of the

trinity is dynamically involved. More valuable is their influence on one another. The receiver (i.e., listener, spectator), in other words, ceases to be the end-point because he, in his turn, influences the performer and the performed.

6. The *rang*-theory, its wider ramifications as well as its implications can be stated in greater detail. However the immediate task is to bring out its relationship to the 'verbal interface' problem under discussion. It is in this context that Bharata's formulations, especially those dealing with *vachika abhinaya* assumes significance.

BHARATA AND THE VACHIKA ABHINAYA

Bharata's concept of *abhinaya* in reality signifies communication of the character's true nature through the mediation of an actor's skills in creating a parallel reality. As the term *abhinaya* indicates, actors *take* the reality (on which the character is based) *to* the audience. Hence, *vachika abhinaya* is to be understood as an act of *taking* the true meaning of the *natyashabda* to the audience. *Natyashabda* is a part of the *natyakavya* for Bharata. Bharata defines *natyakavya* as *arthakriyapeksham,* i.e., action-expectant poetry. With his characteristic thoroughness Bharata goes on to deal with merits and demerits of poetry; prosodic moulds and related matters; types of dramatic language; modes of address; and finally merits and demerits of recitation—the last being the corner-stone of the 'performing' edifice, in view of the preponderance of verse as contrasted with prose in Bharata's theatre.

It is obvious that Bharata's exposition is not relevant to us in its entirety, especially because of the narrow span of our inquiry, and yet—it has implications of fundamental importance for the verbal interface debated.

1. The *vachika* is a part of the total *abhinaya* and therefore cannot stand in isolation. In other words the three other varieties namely *angika, aharya* and *sattvika* must, in due proportion accompany the *vachika* to turn mere utterances into *abhinaya* understood as an act of complete communication.

2. The moment the focus shifts to *vachika abhinaya* effectiveness and not correctness becomes the aim. An analogous shift takes place from the poet's *intended* meaning to the *abhineta*'s *interpreted* meaning. I would hold that this is, in

reality, a movement from meaning to content—the latter being the *abhineta's* creation, with suggestivity coming to the force again. It should be borne in mind that the content is *not instead* of the meaning. Therefore the interpreted word does not become a negation of the poet's intended word and meaning. The *abhineta adds* to the given word through the psycho-physical means at his disposal (including the array of the non-verbal).

3. Of special note in this respect are Bharata's pointed directions about the three vocal parameters namely pitch, volume and timbre (though volume and pitch are treated together rather confusingly). Further, a constant awareness of duration is the basis for his prosodic framework. In Bharata's treatment of the *vachika,* the importance of *duration* as opposed to an *instant,* is a recurring theme. This is an outcome of a time-sense in which time is understood as a mental construct. Bharata's description of prose in terms of verse, firm rejection of verse-lines with less than six letters, insistence on a basic verse-unit of four lines, approving nods to pauses of one to four *aksharkala* (letter-times)—all serve as pointers to exploration of a temporal organization towards effective communication, i.e., *abhinaya.*

4. I have already referred to the difficulties in a contemporary application of Bharata's insights in *toto.* With his heavy reliance on verse/poetry it is expected to be so. However, one has to realize that the total linguistic behaviour of any culture with a long history is bound to be a mosaic of widely distributed remnants, echoing the originally close-knit prosodic patterns. Indian languages (and the literary traditions created by them) are comparable to an uncharted ocean with metrical islands of Sanskrit and Prakrit parentage floating freely. The indigenous Indian prose responded to the rhythmic presence of these metrical monads. It therefore always seemed to be an approximation to metricality—even when writing and the written were resorted to. The interface of the oral and written thus meant a continued act of mutual reference.

5. Bharata's concept of *vachika* is, in my opinion, wide enough to accommodate non-dramatic and yet communicative uses of *vac.* It also manages to be specific in matters of methods

and techniques advisable for a communicator. Bharata codifies but never loses sight of the legitimacy that Indian diversity should be accorded. The subtle act of balancing regional and pan-Indian forces comes easily to him. This is borne out the way he describes regional—speech—peculiarities, allocates functions to the Prakrit-s or even in the way he specifies forty odd ways of addressing people. *Vachik abhinaya* is thus established as a well-wrought device of weaving a web of social relationships through language.

CONCLUSION

I am inexorably drawn to the conclusion that the contemporary verbal interface in India suffers from the tyranny of the eye in more than one ways. The spoken word is enjoying an unheard of reach which seems paradoxically to drain off its intrinsic powers. The situation is not desperate because there is a widely shared appreciation of the spoken word as an efficient communicator. It is time the rare unanimity is harnessed for a qualitative improvement in communication so that we have a society instead of isolated groups.

22

Training in Voice and Speech: One Indian Approach

I have been engaged in working on voice and speech for the last twenty and odd years. In general I would have liked to describe my approach as Indian. However, the diversity and multiplicity of training methods adopted and methodologies advocated all over the country drove me to the safety of a title less ambitious in scope. My approach is certainly Indian but I am only *one* of the Indians working in the area. Time has arrived to compare and assess the rationale as well as the efficacy of the current approaches. To facilitate the process it is essential that the individual positions are stated clearly, comprehensively, with a marked performance-orientation and with a due regard for larger cultural perspectives. I hope to do so as far as my viewpoint is concerned. For all intents and purposes the statement is designed to put forward a conceptual framework which controls the emerging theorization, vocal practicals, exercises and finally the coordinating procedures. During the workshop session it should be possible to tackle individual cases and specific issues arising out of the stated framework and the related theatric aspect. In other words the present exercise is pitched at an abstract level, an action inevitable if the desire is to accommodate fundamentals as well as peripherals.

THE TENETS

What are the tenets of my approach? Tenets require to be stated clearly as they are the basic principles or a body of them one believes in.

In this respect I would like to put forward a three-levelled hierarchical conceptual structure.

The first level is occupied by basic concepts, the second by the derived and the third by the applied. Concepts at the three levels are distinct though there are logical overlaps and consequently a mobile class of marginal concepts is also observed. All concepts together make possible theories which are the inevitable concomitants of human actions or facts which they generate. There are no theory-neutral facts in human behaviour. This needs to be stated firmly and pressed home ruthlessly because artists and especially performers are scornful of theories and theorization. Those mournful and frequent references to wide and periodically widening gap between theory and practice, or science and art, or technique and artistry, etc. are inevitable results of lax thinking and crude aestheticizing. Artists and especially performers are engaged in a kind of non-verbal conceptualizing. The ideal position is when performers verbalize these same non-verbalized structures. Alternatively non-performers are expected to translate these structures with reasonable fidelity to the originals. Codification of performing practice (i.e., grammar) is bound to lag behind the performance, but aesthetics does not. Aesthetic thinking, even though not verbalized, keeps abreast with performance. In other words a valid performance is theorizing in action awaiting verbalization.

BASIC, DERIVED AND THE APPLIED

The three concept-types need to be distinguished, I distinguish between them and that is the first tenet of my approach.

The following tabulation indicates the differentiating features:

	Basic	Derived	Applied
1.	Enjoys maximum abstraction	Has a narrower range of abstraction, functions as a meeting ground of abstract and the concrete	Related maximally to a concrete work
2.	Inherently related to multiple life-areas and patterns	Connected directly with specific art-activity	Linked vitally to particular works
3.	Chief feeder disciplines are philosophy, logic and metaphysics	Aesthetics and practical criticism are the mainstays	Craft and technology function as the ruling agencies

4.	Enable establish-ment of, and interconnections between, different world-views	Encourage inter-art relationship in creation and assess-ment	Lead to the mixed-media genre and art forms
5.	Are responsible for offering cultural perspectives	Generate isms and other aesthetic ideologies	Forge methods and techniques
6.	Operate mainly at the ratiocinative level	Reflect the psycho-physical processes that cover the per-forming triad-artists— work-receiver	Exemplify concen-tration on artists as initiators
7.	Indicate dimensions of experience irrespective of quality	Create and move away from notional boun-daries to define art-activity as qualitative experience	Explore specified units according to the current norms of efficiency and artistry

It is my contention that a sound methodology pertaining to crea-tion, training and appreciation can emerge as well as prove work-able only if the three conceptual levels are accommodated well. Omis-sion of concepts at any of the levels is likely to lure one into an undeveloped complex of ideas. An idea proves fruitful if and when it is worked out at all the three levels discussed so far.

THEATRIC UNIVERSALITY, A TENDER MYTH

A tenet which follows from the triad of conceptual levels pertains to the much talked of universality of the theatric impact. Training methods and the underlying philosophy are necessarily conditioned by the theatric content which may be individual, societal, cultural and finally universal. It is to be noticed that the four levels become progressively wider but also more and more abstract. The universal-ity of theatric impact is a myth in the sense that it is an intangible, creative force. It is also tender in the sense that too frequent and gross claims to universality have a withering effect on the original import of the work. Hence my training model has adequate room for exercises designed for communication at the level of individu-als, societal groups, cultural entities, and transcultural societies. It is easy to understand that as one moves from the individual to the transcultural, the training-content becomes less and less dependent on language and more and more voice-oriented. The more abstract the theatric content the more potential it has of transcultural communication. In turn the more transcultural the import the more it depends on non-verbal communication. Voice and vocalization number among the most important of the non-verbal tools an actor has, because apart from gestures the other tools such as make-up, lighting, set-design and costumes are not controlled directly by the actor.

VOICE, LANGUAGE AND GESTURE

The linkage between the three assumes special significance in theatric communication. Firstly, because theatre enjoys/faces linguistic multiplicity even within the country. Secondly, language-based theatre continues to occupy a major place in the theatric world in spite of frequent and varied rebellious stances of the experimentalists. Thirdly, while language is obviously verbal and acquired, vocal and gestural explorations are non-verbal and largely innate. In other words training methods are required to be devised and imparted in such a way as to strike a balance between personal and societal idioms as also between well-defined meanings and suggested contents.

I therefore stress the distinction between voice and speech in my teaching. While improvement in and extension of effective ranges of vocal parameters is taken care of by a set of exercises, another is devised for the language-based units in theatric speech. It is here that training in pitch, volume, timbre on the one hand and vowel-sounds, consonants, nasals, etc. on the other find their respective places and weightages.

A special word is perhaps necessary about the language-gesture relationship, chiefly because it is a relationship that binds verbal activity with gesture which is eminently non-verbal. And yet, a well-written/spoken word provides a matrix for gestures of certain efficacy. A good theatric word is a seed-form and to unravel the mysteries of it is a sure way to unfold an all-embracing *abhinaya*. When I see actors and directors going about clumsily in search of 'business' I do not forget to pray for their continued literacy.

MUSIC-SPEECH, AS A CONTINUUM

Considerations put down so far have influenced me to regard music-speech as a continuum. I take it that to explore the fundamental properties of sound as a phenomenon is a valid quest in case of both the manifestations with the extra emphasis on quality or timbre *a la* music. It is clear that language, though optional in music, is central to speech while a high degree of systematization of acoustic dimensions (obtained in music) is an alternative exploited selectively in speech. Therefore, to trace the music-speech continuum through language is to try to get the best of both the worlds—one dominated by the non-verbal quality and the ambiguous, and the other by narrative powers, multiplicity of meanings and an exclusively human connection. I have often wondered how theatre-thinkers and trainers have failed to profit by the repository of an encompassing knowledge about voice in music. In brief, the lapse could be attributed to ignorance of the wide variety of musical practices as well as to unimaginative adoption of the proscenium-based play during the modern period as the sole legitimate drama of the land. I must add, though as a side-remark, that those who have relied mainly on language to solve the puzzle of the efficacy or otherwise of communicative models have erred because they have ignored communication in music. The non-verbal in gestures has attracted attention—but not the one in music.

It is in this context that I would like to remind ourselves of the mature Indian tradition which places at our disposal an entire hierarchy of sound-connected manifestations. I am obviously referring to *shabda, nada, dhvani, svara,* and *varna* as acoustic manifestations at different, though related levels. While *shabda,* is that property of the ether (*akasha*) which is perceived by the ear (*shravana*), *nada* is that which is produced when something strikes on something else. This *ahata* variety of *nada* is distinguished from *anahata* (the unstruck) which is perceived only by yogin-s. *Dhvani* is that *nada* produced by musical instruments, etc. Finally, *dhvani* when it results into musical notes is called *svara* and the one turning vowels/consonants is known as *varna*.

It should be clear that workers in music and speech would benefit by an awareness of the fourfold Indian mapping of the world of sound. As one moves down the hierarchy, the acoustic expression tends to narrow in application. In a parallel action the criteria becomes finer, and finally the techniques arising out of the operational concept assume a more specific character. The significance of this dynamics can hardly be exaggerated. Whether in creation or reception, preservation or training, structural analysis or constructional sophistication—the fourfold manifestation functions as a guide to a fruitful activity. It is pitifully true and truthfully piteous that the vigour displayed in the traditional formulation is hardly emulated in creative and critical endeavours.

THE IMPORTANCE OF BEING COMPOSITE . . .

Yet another of my tenets concerns the nature of the compositeness theatre proverbially enjoys.

The term composite is from *com* = together + *ponere* = to put. The dictionaries seem content to note that 'composite is one which consists of parts'. Works on critical terminology are however silent. The obvious inference is that the contemporary connotation which refers to composite as 'one, combining many arts' is a case of useful accretion to the original meaning. However, the significance of the concept lies in its perceivable thrust in the direction of inter-arts relationship, an aesthetic issue with a direct bearing on every theatric process, procedure, method and exercise.

WHAT DO WE MEAN BY THE TERM?

The myth of the origin of drama in India speaks of Bharata's selective and sensitive borrowing. The recited, sung and the ritualistic were respectively borrowed from the *Rig, Sama* and *Yajur* Vedas while the *Atharvaveda* was the source of *rasa*, the ultimate impact each drama was to try for. Is it because of the diversity of sources that drama becomes composite?

In my opinion this is not so. The comparatively recent usage of the term composite in aesthetic thinking suggests a phase of reversal after arts have chosen to follow paths of separate and intensive developments for centuries. The reversal of strategies cannot be expected to give the same, early kind of drama because during the intervening ages all theatric arts were busily carving out their own autonomous areas bringing about changes in our aesthetic perceptions. Under the circumstances, a mere coming together of arts cannot bestow a composite character on a product. To earn the rubric 'composite' the arts that come together must owe allegiance to different families. Art-families are formed on varied basis such as the mediums used, explored sensibilities, audience-contribution, scope allowed to artists, etc. The following prominent art-families can be identified to make the point clearer:

Art-family	Member-arts
Literary Arts	Fiction, poetry, drama (read)
Fine Arts	Painting, Sculpture
Performing Arts	Dance, Drama, Music
Combined Arts	Architecture, Calligraphy, etc.
Composite Arts	Films, Drama

Theatre is today composite because of the strategic reversal prompting it to bring together arts that are otherwise fully, independently developed, and performed. The fact is important in the contemporary training which must aim at creating a composite sensibility. My training procedures therefore take into consideration the distances human mind have covered since the time dance, drama and music were *one* expression to reach the present state—when they are *different* entities mingled into *one* expression. This is the reason why I delve deep into poetics, aesthetics, cultural musicology, musicology, musical acoustics, theatric history and other such disciplines to give shape to voice and speech studies in modern times.

These sciences/disciplines enable a willing performer to profit by what other sciences have earned. The insights obtained by musical acoustics into the nature of vowel and consonant sounds thus become available to a speaker. What musical aesthetics has to say about the essential ambiguity of sound liberates a speaker from the shackles of grammatical meanings. Cultural musicology opens new avenues to a performer by stressing the innate relationship between art and the non-art areas of life. Musicology brings home the truth of the unexceptional continuity of the performing tradition as distinct from scholastic formulations. The codifications in their own turn bring to notice the value of firm systematization as an element facilitating deviations. In the ultimate analysis, deviations are royal roads to creativity. The pooled resources of multiple arts and sciences make theatre a composite art without a parallel. If training methodologies do not explore and exploit the body of insights collected by theatric aspects as well as the theatre-related fields of life, it will suffer the fate of an atrophied limb. All multi-pronged attacks on the problem of theatre-training are significant primarily because they move beyond a mere passing on, and acquisition of, particular skills. Training of performers should take care of skills and crafts-manship as well as artistry and creativity.

THREE CHEERS FOR CREATIVITY

It is of course easy of put creativity on a rosary than to put it into practice. One is also aware of the doubtful efficacy of a planned training programme *vis-à-vis* creativity. And yet, on account of my musical training, I believe that it is both possible and desirable to take a trainee up to a take-off point by adopting a training pro-gramme worked out in great detail. My motto is to create an apti-tude and strengthen the attitude. To put it briefly—improvisation, imagery arousal and generation of *ashta sattvika bhava*-s *a la* Bharata (in relation to voice and speech)—constitute my three cheers for creativity. I claim that the three have a valid application in other theatric aspects ranging much beyond voice and speech—though my own efforts have been less ambitious.

IMPROVISATION

The much talked off improvisation comes naturally and easily to musicians. It has been a mystery to me why Indian directors-actors-theatre-pedagogues should look elsewhere to understand and im-bibe the phenomenon.

Improvisation came to the forefront as a reaction against stylized acting. However the conceptual base of the contemporary improvi-sation is absurdly narrow. Most of the improvisatory work limits it-self to movements and gestures. It operates an extremely limited palette of sensory perceptions. I prefer to take my trainees through the paces to profit by the insights offered in the ancient as well as modern readings in perception-psychology. I encourage the use of a wider array of sensibilities. I add to that the acceptance and use of certain mental powers not granted a full legitimacy in the usual theatre-pedagogy.

Finally, I advocate and put into practice the yogic methods of deliberate masking and concentration as tools to psycho-physical coordination aimed at creative expression. My improvisation exer-cises are object-based, music-based and situation-based.

IMAGERY-AROUSAL

A related strategy developed to take trainees towards creativity is, as

I describe it,—'imagery arousal'. In times, when we are (as Coleridge put it) 'suffering from the tyranny of the eye', it is necessary to recall that imagery is not a monopoly of the sense of vision. Imagery is creation of unified responsorial units by each individual sensibility in its own terms. Variety, succession and frequency of imagery leads to richness of experience, and as Henry James suggested, 'to be creative is to experience'. To image is, to some extent, a technique which can be taught. Imaging extends the area of an individual's capacity to feel, sometimes it deepens the existing feelings and in rare cases teaching to image disturbs the trainee into a new consciousness of his own abilities as well as short-comings. Verbalization plays an important part in the teaching of imaging and at certain junctures imaging is coupled with language-learning procedures, though at subtler levels.

ASHTA-SATTVIKA-BHAVA

The eight essential sense-expressions identified by Bharata are: *stambha* (immobility), *sveda* (perspiration), *romanch* (horripilation), *vaisvarya* (voice-breaks), *kampa* (tremor), *vaivarnya* (losing colour), *ashrupata* (shedding tears) and *pralaya* (to merge, to lose consciousness). They are obviously non-verbal. To all purposes the situation is therefore paradoxical.

To solve the problem I accept the paradox, and further, I adopt a procedure which uses words and verbalization, voice and articulation to reach the wordless and the voiceless. In other words the eight essential states are reached after words and vocalizations are fully understood and deeply felt. You then leave them behind to reach the state of *vachik abhinaya*.

CONCLUSION

In my training model a circle is thus completed. I begin by turning every stone to unearth layers of meanings in each and every sound and word. The passionate and an agitated search takes me to many arts and sciences. But finally both voice and word are stilled into a nearly Buddhist silence impregnated with an artistic truth comparable to a pool of crystal-clear, clean and calm water. At the end of the training both voice and speech are at peace with each other as well as with the world without.

23
The Changing Colour of Patronage

A Sanskrit aphorism reads in translation, 'creepers, women and the learned cannot survive without patronage.' The aphorist would not have hesitated to include artists in the galaxy of those needing support. Patronage has always figured in discussions as a factor greatly conducive to art.

Today one witnesses an interesting paradox. There is a general lament about the lack of patronage to art and artists and yet there exists an impressive number and variety of individuals, institutions, autonomous bodies and government agencies extending support to artists and arts. Additionally the international interest in promotion of arts in different regions has also become considerable. It should therefore be instructive to take a closer look at patronage as a phenomenon. Though all arts enjoy patronage the present discussion would concentrate on the performing family of arts. Dance, drama and music create singular situations for patrons because of the essential evanescence of performance. In my opinion the fleeting nature of performance affects the entire act of patronage. Probably a very special kind of pressure builds up on patrons of the performing family.

WHAT IS PATRONAGE?

How could we define patronage? In the present context it obviously reaches beyond suggesting protection or support. Barbara Stoller Miller has rightly pointed out that patronage emerges today as a "multi-dimensional, sometimes loosely codified network of exchanges involving not only the production of art and literature, but also its performance, transmission, interpretation and preservation."[1] Patronage is a kind of protective, fatherly support extended to and by individuals as well as institutions in furtherance of a cause, movement, ideology, tradition or a similar aspect of culture. Patronage connotes a process and not an isolated act. Acts of patronage when viewed in isolation fail to make us aware that they are cumulative results of cultural processes. India has a long history of patronage to arts and other cultural expressions. During the centuries, patronage in the country changed in modality, quality as well as direction. The post-Independence scene deserves scrutiny, firstly, because of the multiplicity of patron-agencies, and secondly, on account of the changed philosophy of philanthropy.

Patronage, it has been suggested, is a process of exchange in which givers and takers change roles in turn. In other words, it is not a tri-terminal process involving giver, taker and the given but a four-phased action. This becomes obvious when Indian terms pertaining to giver, taker and the emergents are examined. An illustrative listing of the Sanskrit/Hindi terms is placed for consideration:

The three lists can be considerably added to, if different regional languages in India are explored, as also by examining a wider range of exchanges in society. However, the lists suffice to bring home the essential circularity of patronage. Features that distinguish the list-categories can be noted:

1. Exchanges in lists A and C are initiated by givers who enjoy *ad hoc* or continued superiority—either due to social or operational status.

2. Activities in list B are initiated by parties in subordinate position—either as a response to a temporary context or because of a stabilized socio-cultural reality.

3. As givers in lists A and B enjoy intangible gains due to patronage, acts in list C are marked off. Exchanges in list C have a character of commodity-transaction.

4. It is necessary to note that gains of the givers in the first list are not only intangible, but also considerably uncertain and distanced, from the actual act of giving.

At this point, it may help to go back a little in the historical past even though no survey of patronage in India is intended. This step is unavoidable because the contemporary patronage is a cumulative outcome of a long process in which many problems related to the activity were faced squarely. Some decisions arrived at during the course of history may appear to be relevant even today.

A specialist such a Vijay Nath has pointed out that "a renewed interest in the institution of *dana* as practised in ancient times may be, in fact, attributed to anthropological field-researches conducted

Giver	What he received	Taker	What he received
		A	
Ashrayadata (One who gives refuge)	Punya (Spiritual Merit)	Ashrita (Dependent refugee)	Ashraya (Refuge)
Data (Giver)	Punya (Spiritual Merit)	Yachak (One who asks for)	Dana (Offering, Charitable gift)
Yajamana (Host)	Punya (Spiritual Merit)	Brahmin (Officiating Priest)	Dakshina (Sacrificial fee)
King, Public	Shreya (Credit)	Kalakar (Artist)	Inam (Money etc. received in appreciation of a performance)
Elder, Superior	Shreya, Santosh (Credit, Satisfaction)	Subordinate, Younger	Bakhshish (One-time reward)
		B	
One seeking favour	Blessings, Assurance	King, Superior	Nazar (Gift)
One seeking favour	Goodwill, Assurance	King, Superior, Equal	Nazarana Ceremonial Gift
Shishya (Disciple)	Blessings	Guru Preceptor	Gurudakshina Offerings
		C	
Employer	Services	Employee	Mehanatana Remuneration
Student	Services	Teacher	Shulka

in the make of Darwin's famous theory of mutual aid."[2] Further, she also noted how Marcel Mauss and other sociologists have concluded *dana* to be an important mode of redistribution and exchange. Most of the religions in India have an extensive literature on *dana*. Kinds of *dana*, possible motivation and the results expected to accrue in each case find a detailed mention. I suggest that changes that have taken place in the *dana*-philosophy need to be linked to the patronage-phenomenon and its role in the modern period of Indian culture.

INDIAN ANTECEDENTS OF THE DANA-PHILOSOPHY

The Vedic vision on *dana* has notably religious as well as mundane orientations. *Rigveda* describes religiously motivated *dana* as *ishta* and the mundane as *poorta*. The religious focus of *dana* became a little diffused in the post-Vedic period. This is borne out, for example, by the multiplicity of terms and meanings of *dana* noted by Panini (500 BC). Distribution of material resources in excess, reallocation of wealth to remedy social-imbalance, *dana* as an expiation of sin or as a ritualistic performance are some of the shades that Panini has brought out with his usual penetration.

The heterodox religious movements, (from the sixth century BC), introduce in *dana* stronger tones of compassion and charity. Giving alms (*bhiksha*) then receives an unambiguous legitimacy. Closer to the Christian era the legal format of *dana*-procedures, and such other matters, get explicit statements. *Dana* is then precisely defined as transference of one's ownership in favour of another. Kautilya is probably to be credited for introducing the concept of *tyaga* indicating thereby a *dana* made to offset concentration of wealth as private property. Religious *dana* made through impressively described rituals also receives a weightage. The Dharmashastra-s are therefore seen to evolve an elaborate conceptual framework to legitimize, sanctify *dana* by making *dana* obligatory or mandatory for a responsible citizen.[3] Thus 'who, when, to whom, how and why should engage in *dana-vyavahara*' is specified. A *dana*-typology of considerable complexity had obviously emerged by the time *Amarakosha* was compiled. In order to bring out the apparent as well as the implied aspects of *dana* the *kosha* lists nine variant meanings. The receiver's formal acceptance of *dana* and the giver's ritualistic declaration of the *dana*-intent (for example with oblation of water, etc.) are laid down. Law-givers in the ancient India obviously wanted to enshrine *dana* as a means of social cohesion. This is the reason why Manu and others connected the concept of *dana* to that of inherent debt (*rna*) (to *pitr, deva* and *rishi*).

It is beyond doubt that in ancient India *dana* developed from an ameliorative idea into a full-scale ideology. The *dana*-process continued to grow with the times reflecting the socio-economic conditions. It responded to the cultural concerns of the society in its evolving, developing or comparatively stabilizing phases. Even a cursory glance at objects considered worthy of the *dana*-process would prove its dynamism. For instance, the Vedic *dana*-objects included cattle, horses, camels as well as cooked food. With the increasing role of agriculture grain, sesamum seeds, garlic, dairy-products, precious metals and forest products acquired importance. Expectably, with greater urbanization, metal ware, stone artefacts, finished goods, coins, luxury items, etc. entered the list of *dana*-objects. Notably, from very early times, the tendency to make secular *dana*, i.e., those of the *poorta*-category appeared and in fact it moved from strength to strength as almost all religious sects and cults approved of it. Hence it is, that digging wells or lakes, maintaining public-gardens, erecting public-halls for distributing alms or supplying drinking water were specifically mentioned as *dana*-s. Of a similar kind was the *dana* made by running hospitals or giving medicines free. Equally important was the *dana* of manuscripts of the epics, Dharmashastra-s and the Purana-s. On such background it is not surprising that even a declared intention to make *dana* by a person breathing his last was considered to be binding on his inheritors.

It is clear that as a consequence of cumulative cultural processes the concept of *dana* became in India a full-fledged policy-instrument employed to bring about socio-cultural changes in operations of the tangible and intangible forces shaping the society. In its evolved form *dana* moved much beyond what patronage suggests. *Dana* could emanate from and end in both individuals and institutions. Kings, chieftains, merchants, *sangha*-s, temples, guilds, farmers, artisans could participate in the *dana*-process the way they chose. (Perhaps beggars would be the only class always expected to receive.) It is on record that performers participated in the *dana*-process both as givers and takers. During the centuries to follow *dana*-modalities or formats did not change radically. There are reasons to believe that different dynasties (and the Islamic ones in particular) chose to continue, or modify slightly, the existing *dana* mechanism. (The recipients changed oftener.) The period of the Islamic dynasties created a situation in which people, with an entirely different cultural background and temperament, came to India not to invade but to settle. They developed increasingly greater stakes in the land and consequently their interest in performing arts became intense as well as more fundamental—in the sense they felt an inner compulsion to introduce substantial changes in them. As has been said drama, on account of its representational capacities, is frequently the first to display deeper cultural changes while music may suggest them earlier (though it is the last to accept them). The medieval period therefore stands for an important phase in the development of patronage in India. In this period (or from this period) patronage moved simultaneously to accentuate the religious as well as the worldly (if not the profane) in art. The royal or the political patronage encouraged the worldly while the temples, etc. placed premium on the religious. It is a known fact that temple-cultures never hesitate to assimilate elements, themes, techniques from the worldly to hold their own against the attractions of the worldly art—but that is a different story. India in the medieval age offered patronage with many faces and bases. Patronage was, for example, offered for the following reasons:

1. Patrons appreciated art/artist.
2. Artists receiving patronage ensured lasting fame of their patrons.
3. Patronage to arts was an integral part of the accepted social behaviour.
4. To support arts was often a revered family-tradition.
5. Conferring patronage was valued as a help in legitimizing patrons political position.
6. Artists, it was realized, rendered important and useful services not obtained through other agencies.
7. Competitively upscaled patronage was directly linked to patrons upward movement in the social hierarchy.
8. Patronage enabled the patron to maintain close links with the traditional society. Thus a clash between the new political loyalties and the inherited cultural identities was avoided. Alternatively the intensity of the friction between the two could be diminished.
9. Art and artists made no demands without, at the same time, bestowing a sense of power on the patron.
10. Art and artists offered unrelieved recreation and relief.

The British Arrival

It is true that the Portuguese, French and the Dutch presence preceded the British in India. However, on account of a better documentation as also because of their more widespread and durable reign the British contribution to Indian culture has become noticeable as well as significant.

As I have pointed out elsewhere, the British were largely and initially responsible for a movement away from the Orientalism of other occidentals during the seventeenth and the succeeding centuries, and for founding the new and necessary discipline of Indology. The early British indologists, however, realized that the discipline (as structured by linguistic, religious, historical and philosophical studies) was inadequate to understand the genius of the Indian people unless performing arts were included in the study-gamut. The result was the welcome British beginning of ethnomusicological pursuits. Their lead was to be followed and, in fact, bettered especially by Germans and Americans in later years.

What is to be marked is the quality of the British patronage as compared with that in vogue.

The British motivation to support performing arts exhibited the following features:

1. British patrons, oblivious to the inevitable time-lag between performing and scholastic traditions, attempted to study and patronize them by keeping 'books' at the centre.

2. There were a few who regarded support to Indian performing arts as a social lubricant. Performances enabled conquerors and the conquered to come together under circumstances of minimal social and political tensions.

3. Expectably, a minority wanted to develop knowledge of Indian performing arts in order to rule the native populace better. Knowledge of the performing arts and their practitioners, was thought to be an efficient device or mechanism to ensure an affective ascendency over the unknown subjects—great in numbers, diverse in the extreme and spread over vast expanses.

4. A few British students of culture were genuinely attracted by the Indian performing *avatara* on account of its inherent richness and aesthetic appeal.

5. The modern period was generally characterized by the interest in sciences of Man. The Comparative method was in full circulation. The issue of 'origins'—of language, religion music, etc. exercised many minds. Music of the non-

occidental world was considered good evidence/data to help solving the 'origin'-problems.

What is of greater relevance is of course the non-British and Indian patronage to performing arts in the British India. The British rule brought about radical changes in many areas of Indian life including patronage to arts. The main features were:

1. The traditional sources such as temples, nobleman's house, wealthy families, etc. continued. However the stratum of the educated upper class emerged as a new source, often because of the changed motivation—if not for their patronage-mode.

2. A very major change was to place performances in a framework designated as art. Traditional contextuality of performances in India kept them close to the day-to-day life. In brief, it was in response to the three cycles (and the phases included therein) namely day-night, birth-death and the seasons, that performing arts sought their validation. Arranging performances as art-activity struck a new note in Indian culture.

3. The Indian patrons came to be polarized between Anglophiles and Indophiles. The first group largely favoured Western orientations in art, while the second was keen on the Indian manifestations. To an extent, entire communities sometimes displayed such preferences (though overlaps were not ruled out).

4. The ebbs and tides of nationalism as an overwhelming general force moulded patronage in a remarkable manner. While language, dress, education, food-habits *et al.* were allowed to undergo sweeping changes, performing arts were rightly viewed as the main, authentic and undiluted expressions of the Indian ethos. To support them was therefore construed as nationalistic. To reaffirm Indianness *through* performing arts became a natural and recognizable political statement.

5. As a corollary to the nationalistic view of performing arts, patronage became participatory. Patrons studied to perform and often became expert performers. The closer identification with the performing reality reduced the distance between performers-patrons.

6. The new patronage, in its zeal to accord a revised and higher status to performing arts, attempted to bracket them with studies in history, social sciences, religion, etc. Introduction

of music-studies on syllabic/curricular lines, acceptance of the proscenium-arch for dramatic performances, arguments put forward against the traditional suppression of dance as an inferior activity—are examples symptomatic of the desire to elevate performing arts *through* patronage. These and similar other attempts finally led to the introduction of performing arts in institutes of higher learning-especially in colleges and universities.

7. The new patronage was often engaged in balancing forces of traditionalism and modernism. On the one hand, the patrons would strive to argue about the uniqueness of Indian arts and hence the impossibility of accepting/applying Western methods, criteria and standards. On the other hand, the new protagonists were equally keen to prove that everything possible to Western artists and in Western art can be shown to have a comparable counterpart or an 'answer' in India. The slogans were 'we already have it' or 'ours is better' or 'we do not need it'. The conceptual tight-rope dancing frequently resulted in contradictory positions. The use of notation and harmony in music, acceptance of realism and the insistence to have essentially symbolic Sanskrit plays performed 'authentically', the traditional low view of dance and the desire to give more freedom to Indian women—are some of the instances of the contradictory stances of the new patrons.

8. Sometimes the Indian patrons seemed to crave pathetically/ ridiculously for recognition from the rulers for the acts of patronage. In other words, patrons wished to be appreciated by 'superior' patrons. They were, as if, proving their 'patron-worthiness' to somebody and an acknowledgement of the success of the effort was deemed necessary. Patronage was thus used for enhancement of social prestige and for recognition from an 'alien' political authority.

9. The new patrons, to their credit, also provided instances of transcultural support, or catholicity of taste, by shifting the boundaries of culture, clime and language. The number of Indians who earned recognizable expertise in Western performing arts was not negligible. A few of them could perhaps be accused of harbouring a slavish mentality or of being 'active sycophants'—but the level of mastery attained by a con-

siderable number in Western performing arts can hardly be brushed aside as insignificant.

It is in this wide perspective that the post-Independence patronage is to be placed. The main features can be summarized:

1. The scene is exciting. Many other autonomous bodies, voluntary agencies, academies, foundations are offering patronage apart from government departments. Temples, religious associations, industrial houses and private trusts continue to function as patrons.

2. Performing arts are today examined from many novel angles as a consequence of tremendous strides made by humanities and social sciences. Interdisciplinary approach has rightfully attracted funding agencies. In practical terms it means considerable increase in the 'sources that provide resources.' It also means that different aspects are explored.

3. To a certain extent, culture in unfortunately equated in many quarters with arts. Thus a number of agencies with intentions to support cultural aims formulated vaguely, focus on 'arts'. In other words, patronage has become generous but disconcertingly generalized or indiscriminate.

4. In keeping with the overall trend, a kind of specialization is taking place in acts of patronage. Performance, preservation, training, documentation, dissemination, appreciation, etc. are recognized as somewhat self-sufficient goals worthy of independent support. Institutes concentrating on a few or many of these functions have been set up.

5. The British, as also the post-Independence patrons, sought to establish governmental agencies, bodies of learning and higher education ('temples of art and education') and industrial houses as seats of continued, directed and diverse patronage. Thus princely courts, temples and community were sought to be replaced. As a consequence, it became necessary to follow different philosophies or guidelines. As explained earlier, the traditional *dana*-philosophy had developed a complete ideology, methodology and system to govern the *dana*-processes. The substitute-patrons have apparently not attempted to consider a continued appropriateness of the *dana*-mechanism (*vis-à-vis* performing arts). Even at the risk of sounding 'sloganish'. I would like to submit that perhaps it is desirable as well as possible to Indianize the

patronage-model by reverting to some features of the *dana*-philosophy.

6. Very early in the discussion, a reference was made to the essential evanescence of performance. These arts are time-bound in a very special sense and they are aptly described as the temporal arts. On account of a view that all arts are similar, and secondly, due to an overweening anxiety to 'preserve', patronage to performing arts is trying to prepare definitive editions of performances as if they are works of literature. Consequently, performers are moving away from individuality, creativity and flexibility.

7. Philosophies, strategies and mechanisms of the modern patronage favours terms such as input-output, accountability, annual reports, monitoring, rationalization of procedures, infrastructure, management of resources. Without in any way questioning the motives of the users, it is submitted that such terms indicate a tendency to ignore the inevitably intangible elements inherent to patronage—at least in performing arts. The market-philosophy of a commodity exchange has apparently 'possessed' patrons who are in quest of certainties of a kind not natural to arts and culture. Patronage must be accepted as a risky activity with no assured returns. We must be realistic enough to realize that patronage has gains which cannot be easily quantified, measured and verbalized. The *dana*-philosophy fully accepted this aspect of the situation and history has proved its creative success.

8. Modern patronage also errs in its heavy reliance on a rather mechanical adherence to procedural validity of the process-irrespective of the support-worthiness of the receiver. Admittedly, even the ancient tradition was intent on procedures. However, realizing the danger of a hollow procedural validity the ancients tried to combine in *dana* religious rituality and legal procedures. Today, patronage seems more concerned about the legality of the procedure than sanctity of the process—a grave error that allows takers empty eligibility to replace *patrata* of the early receivers.

9. It is curious to note that effects of patronage on the receiver's innate capacities are hardly ever discussed. The sad truth is that modern patronage often elicits a self-comforting behaviour from the receiver. Post-patronage work of the re-

ceiver needs to be assessed with stiffer and more refined criteria—which rarely happens as the patronage-mechanism (unlike the traditional *dana*-mechanism) is inflexible. The situation cannot be remedied by framing more detailed rules or regulations as that would probably result in more paper work—given the predominance of the written culture. Paradoxically, the solution may lie in a more conscious acceptance of the principle of mutual trust. Chance, contingency, etc. must be recognized as natural and justified elements of human behaviour.

10. Finally, patronage is obviously a part of a larger phenomenon which has proved to be a poser. The issue is the morality of cultural finance—if one may use such a term. The mechanism of permissible tax-rebates, laundering of funds and in general the habitual mistaking of the explainable for the justifiable has raised an ethical issue: is it desirable to use convicts ill-gotten gains for children's welfare? Admittedly, no truthful reader of history would maintain that kings, zamindars, temples and the like never used tainted money for noble causes. The very fact that *dana* is credited with expiationary powers shows the traditional realistic appraisal of the situation. But the tradition made insistent distinctions between *uttama/vimala* and the *adhama/tamas dana*-s. In other words, the tradition accepted the responsibility to press the society towards the ideal even though social pragmatism never ignored the human fallibilities and moral turpitude. The contemporary social structure, policy-makers and codifications, however, seem to overlook moral imperatives. Philanthropy, altruism, disinterested actions, etc. should not be treated as mere lexical possibilities. Doing so reveals a cynicism demeaning to the human nature.

Patronage should be elevated/sublimated to *dana* instead of being reduced to sponsorship or other 'by courtesy' arrangements. The tradition of giving with the hope of adding to the spiritual merit evinces donors self-respect as well as his trust in the receiver. The way patronage is operated today converts it into a strategy while *dana* is a philosophy. Being a philosophy *dana* does not advocate any *one* model and there lies the secret of a mature and generous view of human predicament. The *dana*-philosophy admits human being to be weak, but it also expresses belief in their strength and a willingness to move towards ideals.

REFERENCES

1. Vijay Nath, *Dana: Gift System in Ancient India, c.* 600 BC–*c.* AD 300. *A Socio-economic Perspective,* New Delhi, 1987, p. 3.
2. Barbara Stoler Miller, ed., *The Powers of Art: Patronage in Indian Culture,* New Delhi, 1992, p. 3.
3. P.V. Kane, *Dharmashastracha Itihas,* abridged by Y.A. Bhat, vols. I, II, Bombay, 1980.

24

Chitra, Pata, and Sangeet in India:
An Aesthetic Appraisal

Indian cinematic music has been criticized by many authorities, nationally and internationally. Even government and semi-government bodies have come down on it heavily. Different objections to it, when brought together, impress one as a veritable charge-sheet. In brief, the objections are:

1. There are too many songs.
2. Any character is seen to sing—*and* at any point of time.
3. The majority of the characters have the same singing voices.
4. Instrumental music, especially the background music, is unrealistic and misdirected.
5. Dances are indiscriminately inserted.
6. Non-Indian music, particularly Western music, is distorted, and suffers the indignity of clumsy use.
7. The present-day cinematic music displays melodic poverty.
8. Most of Indian film music is confusingly similar. The manufacturing formula seems to follow the technique of creating multiple musical images.
9. Musical plagiarism has become the order of the day.
10. All kinds of music from all categories is employed tastelessly, resulting in an overall lowering of standards.
11. Evolution of Indian cinema as an art has been hindered by its music.

Some of the objections listed above, or other similar objections, are tackled elsewhere in this paper. It seems pointless to try to refute the charges till the category of music which cinematic music represents—namely, popular music—is properly understood. It is also fair to say that all cultural efforts are judged best by specimens of their use—and not abuse.

The protagonists of Indian musico-cinematic endeavour do not lag behind. They argue that film music succeeds in creating its own characteristic forms because it satisfies some genuine socio-cultural needs. The following points are often made in defence of film music:

1. It is truly modern and keeps pace with the times.
2. Expression of 'escapist' protest is one of its major functions.
3. No other music can rival it in an alert accommodation of recreational modes coming into vogue at different points of time.
4. It attempts to accord high aesthetic status to the criteria of attractiveness and sweetness.
5. Special mention must be made of its achievement in creating a pan-Indian musical identity by bringing into greater circulation various regional musics through the mass media.
6. It represents an ambitious undertaking to legitimatize a music of descriptive content by a bold recourse to non-Indian systems of music.
7. Cinematic music moves to structure tonal expression in such a way that music gets a scope for parallel and independent operations, though the initial visual modality has impetus as well as overall control.
8. It evokes, however unconsciously, the age-old musico-dramatic stereotypes. For example, the dramatic-song situations allocated to the song category known as Dhruva in Bharata's *Natyashastra* are: (i) entry, (ii) exit, (iii) courting/declaration of amorous intent, (iv) separation, (v) grief, (vi) communal festivities, (vii) singing for the hero, (viii) to conceive together dance, instrument-playing, and singing, (ix) to express sentiments associated with the eight types of heroines.
9. No musical expression, other than film music, goes hand in hand with the verbalized, linguistic formulation/content.

The foregoing discussion clearly suggests that the cinema-music relationship in India has not been examined with adequate intellectual rigour. In particular, the changing compulsions behind the relationship have been largely ignored. As a consequence, it has been uncritically assumed that the coming together of music and cinema has always been prompted by musical and musico-aesthetic considerations. The reality, however, is different. Perhaps a factor that has complicated the situation requires special mention. Indian cinematic culture has undergone many changes, rather rapidly, during a period of about 75 years, and the individual critical phases of the culture have enjoyed shorter life-spans than in other life-areas. On the other hand, the Indian musical tradition goes back to the hoary past and the pace of changes has been less dramatic. The difference in the dynamics of the two arts therefore becomes vital in analyzing the musico-cinematic continuum. Once these complexities are appreciated and the logic is divined, it becomes difficult to accept generalizations such as 'Indian movies always have had an abundance of music' or 'Indian film music means songs that are scattered all over the film'.

What is essential is a minute examination of the critical changes in Indian music to be followed by an exercise undertaken to determine the critical phases in the evolution of cinematic music. A very important principle of cultural musicology requires to be remembered for its illuminating relevance in every study of the performing arts. Music is the last art to accept change. Further, it does so with remarkable reluctance when an alien culture is involved. The following observations are made to highlight this aspect of musico-cultural reasoning:

1. All major film centres in India have also been bastions of art music (e.g., Pune, Bombay, Madras, and Calcutta). The people and institutions operating from these places naturally resorted to art music and mythology when a pan-Indian appeal was their goal. The situation was unambiguously so till Bombay because an assertive metropolitan city around the 1950s.

2. By the time Indian cinema completed the transformation from an overtly artistic medium to a communicative industry, it created four musical landmarks. The emergence of producers, music directors, star artists and playback singers as separate institutions is to be noted in this context. This quartet is indicative of the changing, comprehensive, and cultural response in the audio-visual life-areas.

3. It is an oversimplification to say that Indian cinema has always been full of songs. Four turns had to be completed before the advent of what is today recognized as a film song. The turns are represented by the musico-literary organizations identifiable as rhythmic prose, recitation, *pada,* and a simpler art-composition.

Music touches various spheres of life, assuming in the process of many forms. Problems as to its precise connotation are therefore inevitable. To comprehend music as a phenomenon, it becomes necessary to study and understand a number of arts as well as disciplines. One of the major arts to be studied in this context is that of cinema (etymologically explainable today as the art of graphically noting movement on strips coated with film).

The study of cinema is urgently called for (in contemporary Indian conditions) because all other arts are cinematically influenced in one way or the other. No other medium is so deeply entrenched in the popular psyche. In this sense, the cinema is the dominant medium—a medium in terms of which the greatest number of life-messages are formulated, communicated, and received today. It is also true that Indian cinematic music impresses by its magnitude, variety, and quality. The genre throws an enjoyable challenge to students of Indian music.

To study is necessarily to go beyond personal preferences. Judgements of taste and value are the main aims. The basic concepts acquire a centrality. However, the exercise may prove futile if the abstract and philosophical concepts are not correlated with the actual, living experience. And that is not the full story. All abstract principles along with the related concretizations (or illustrations) get their magnetic power from the cultural context. The framework of the human audio-visual experience, the relevant cultural experience in India, and the specific phenomenon of cinematic music thus provide the basis. Each deserves special and intensive examination. However, even an attempt to establish the linkage is worthwhile.

1. The human visual and auditory organs differ considerably in their respective construction, location, and inherent mobility—with an inevitable influence on their respective perceptions.

2. The audio-visual centres are adjacent to each other in the brain. This is important to note because synesthetic experiences are usually received through operations of the paired.

3. Every culture does not accord equal status to the audio and visual senses. In fact, the same culture may value the audio and the visual differently, in different historical periods.

4. The cinema presents a case of audio-visual communication in which the concerned channels are processed in a particular way. However, the same audio-visual channels are also used profusely in other, non-art segments of life. Factors con-

trolling the ordinary human audio-visual operations will naturally have an effect on the cinema. Those thousands of non-
art audio-visual activities we daily engage in, are bound to
have some effect on our receptivity. This will have to be borne
in mind while examining the relationship between cinema
and music.

5. To discuss cinema and music as art—is to distance ourselves
from all life in the raw. Art, though directly related to life, is
not life. Further, the cinema also passed through a silent
phase before becoming a 'talkie'.

6. Cinematic music belongs to the category of popular music.
It may not be possible to assess the strengths and weaknesses
of cinematic music unless the parent category is considered.
Popular music is a category which renders application of
purely musical criteria, both unnatural and unrealistic.

At this point it will be helpful to gain some terminological insights.
Many Indian languages would accept the explanation of cinematic
music as *chitra* plus *pata* plus *sangeet*. Needless to say, a similar attention to the linguistic and literary aspect would add to the expressive
armoury of the phenomenon. However, the intention here is to
draw attention to the original thrusts of the terms.

The first term is *pata*. It means (as a noun): (1) a tablet, plate, or
a piece of cloth for writing or painting upon; (2) anything well made
or polished. As a verb, it means 'to go or move, to string or weave'.

The second term is *chitra*. It means: (1) a picture, painting, delineation; (2) surprise, wonder.

The third related term encountered frequently in cinematic discussion is 'image', with *pratima* as the Indian equivalent. The meanings are: an image, a likeness, statue, figure, idol.

It may help to note some auxiliary terms:

Pratiman: Resemblance, similitude, often in composition, in the
sense of 'like', 'similar' or 'equal to'.

Image: "An optically formed duplicate, counterpart, or other representative reproduction of an object, esp. an optical reproduction
of an object by a mirror or lens." *(Webster II,* p. 610)

Imagery: 1, A mental picture of images; 2, (i) the use of vivid descriptions or figures of speech in speaking or writing to produce
mental images; (ii) a metaphoric representation, as in music, art or
drama; 3, the art of making such images.

The next term to engage our attention is *sangeet*. It means performance of the sung, the danced and the played.

Terms are indicative of the stabilized concepts based on precepts received and found suitable to the genius of a culture. The purpose of noting down these details of terminological usage is to get a glimpse into the psyche of a culture which has obviously arrived at some decisions and choices. Because of the particular nature of the performing arts, the 'performing' terminology enjoys two possibilities. Firstly, these terms do not lose the capacity to emit the original core meanings even if their current meaning shows changes in semantic thrusts. Secondly, performing terms bring to notice their original meanings while generating terminological clusters of meanings related to them. Therefore, one has to be aware of the total semantic field of the entire terminological cluster to get to the core meaning of a term. Performing terms can in fact be compared to instruments with resonating strings. Their distinctive and total sound is a combined product of the main string (actually plucked/bowed) and those vibrating in sympathy, though unstruck themselves. It is therefore beneficial to grasp the aura of a term suggested by the totality of the term-cluster.

In the present context the terms suggest that *pratima*, the image which is created through a *chitra*, is not visual alone. Consequently, cinema cannot be reduced to a medium explored merely to offer a visual aesthetic experience. The Indian reality consists of a major reliance on the aural in order to create images. This has been one of the reasons for the rise of an all-embracing oral tradition. The terminological cluster clearly testifies to the process initiated to create imagery through audio-visual combinations. It suggests that we have pictures, pictorial series, movement, verbalization (to comment), employment of music to evoke the non-verbal significance— all brought together in various ways to bring into being the *chitrapata*. In respect of *sangeet*, too, the tradition is to conceive together the three separables—namely, the sung, the danced, and the played. Also to be noted is the fact that vocal music enjoys primacy, because of the paramount natural capacity of the human voice to produce a sustained sound. A song, i.e., a *geet*, is essentially a tone that can go on and on.

To think fundamentally about cinema, is to keep *chitra* as distinguished from a picture at the centre. *Chitra*, as noted earlier, is not merely a delineation of lines and/or colours but a completed visual experience able to create effects of surprise and wonder. It is of interest to note that Jean Cocteau used to appeal to any cinematic venture by saying 'Astonish me.', while Eisenstein reportedly exclaimed in a similar vein with the words 'Shock through attraction.' The second step is to appreciate that while pictures are isolated, the *pata* bestows on them quality because the units of a *pata* are not merely brought together. They are woven into a garland. This naturally leads to the seminal aesthetic concepts of sequence, internal dynamics, and movement. Of no less importance is the virtuality of the image. I believe these explanations will be useful to understand not only the cinematic contexts of musical endeavours, but also the cultural framework of Indian cinema as a totality.

To combine picture-play and music, need not be considered an exclusive and sudden accomplishment of the twentieth century. Bringing together different media to impart an arresting, total, and qualitative experience has an aesthetic inevitability about it. All cultures tend to stumble on the aesthetic truth—at one time or the other. In the process, they give rise to many combinations, and sometimes to forms. It is natural that some forms are strong enough to create a tradition while others prove short-lived. India is no exception.

It may be stated that at least five clear phases are discernible as antecedents of the present-day *avatara* of cinematic music. The phases and their Indian manifestations are briefly described:

1. During the first phase, 'still' delineations were so made that viewers got a feel of movement through a series of 'stills'. There was no insistence on an accompanying narration. The combining of the audio and the visual was also optional.

    The first phase is well brought out by the delineations of Shubrai Maharaj (1750-1820). Born in Malur (Madras), he held high posts in Tipu Sultan's court before retiring in 1785 to settle in Solapur. Well versed in music, dance, and literature, Shubhrai was deeply interested in *Adhyatma*. During his Solapur days he prepared picture frames of 6" × 14" (or 18") on paper strips. The way the drawings are made, the successive frames suggest a sequence of movements. In some frames he appears to have moved a step further in creating an illusion. In such frames, human figures, etc. are apparently pasted later against the natural background drawn earlier. The technique results in producing a three-dimensional effect of figures in relief. He tapped the perennial sources of the *Ramayana, Mahabharata, Gita-govinda,* etc. The reds, blues, and yellows he used were herbal dyes.

2. In the second phase still delineations, pictures, or their series were moved mechanically or manually. The presentation includes narration/singing to accompany the visuals.

The second phase reminds one of the Pat traditions current in different parts of the country. Yamapat, Pabuji ka Pad, Jadupat, or the Chitrakathi-s, etc. have a common core. For example, take the Chitrakathi-s of Maharashtra. They find an early mention in the *Manasollasa* of Someshvara (AD 1131). The Chitrakathi-s are professional story-tellers operating with the help of picture-sets. Each Kathi is expected to maintain a set of his own. The pictures are often bound together and depict mythological tales. According to the requirements of the story, a peacock feather is used to direct the attention of the viewers to the relevant picture during the presentation. Two accompanists (on *dholki* and *ektari*) participate in the narration. Versification, recitation, singing, and dialogue are employed in the presentation, which exhibits stylization as well as improvization.

Yet another tradition current in Andhra Pradesh confirms the pattern. The depicted picture scrolls can be vertical or horizontal, even though the former are in greater vogue. The delineations are in a downward sequence. Every frame is separated by a decorative border. The scroll is hung on the wall or from two bamboos. The scroll is rolled downwards and care is taken to ensure that the required frame is in view of the spectators. All the members of the narrator's family are involved in the presentation. Prose, verse, recitation, as well as singing are pressed into service for telling the story. A group of four or five persons provides vocal and instrumental support. Female members, if they participate, sing. Reportedly, the earliest extant *pata* dates back to 1625. In this *pata*, the story is of the sage Markandeya. However, there is a noticeable slant introduced to elevate certain castes and personalities. Some authorities suggest that the right to offer patronage to these shows was confined to certain castes.

3. The third phase was achieved when still pictures were *projected* in sequence and consecutively, though the narration and/or singing remained unaltered.

The third phase of combining image and music was realized through an imaginative use of the once-popular projecting mechanism known as magic lantern. One should remember in this context the attempts of Madhavrao Patwardhan of Kalyan (Bombay). He began making slides around 1890. By 1894 he had perfected a technique for multiple and simultaneous projection of slide strips. Patwardhan employed three projectors: one projected the background scenery while the other two concentrated on the main event. His shows travelled all over Maharashtra and Gujarat, attracting full houses. Patwardhan was the producer as well as the projectionist. He had a number of mythological tales in his repertoire and had prepared about a thousand slides. The presentation also included a running commentary, dialogue, and live music. Describing the apparatus and the programme as *Shambarik Kharolika*, the Patwardhans performed till about 1910.

4. Events were recorded on processed films to be projected later. A controlled manifestation of the sound material was presented through live performers.

The fourth phase consisted of live music supplied by musicians sitting in front of the screen during the silent era. In Bombay, one Mr Seymour conducted an orchestra to carry out the task (1896). In 1920 Debaki Bose conducted music for the silent films of the British Dominion Company.

5. Finally, as today, images, the intra-image movement, and the accompanying acoustic material was pre-recorded separately to be synchronized with the visual material for later projection. The fifth phase began with *Alam Ara* in 1931.

Against this background, some general observations about image-music interrelationships are possible:

(a) The later the phase, the less virtual is the movement of the images. On the other hand, the earlier the phase, the more deliberate is the effort to convey movement through non-visual ways and means.

(b) The 'live' audio was greater in proportion and more meaningful in function, to the extent, the image movement was created through illusion. In other words, the inherent absence of movement in the virtual image was to be offset by the tempo and dynamics of sound. Obviously, an interchange of experience at the sensory level was attempted.

(c) One of the main virtues of any communicative medium is its experiential continuousness. It was to this end that sound was so insistently employed. When other means of introducing movement in the image became available, the qualitative role of sound changed. Then a more purposeful arrangement of the sound of music was expected to reinforce the meaning/significance of images or to put forward alternative interpretations.

(d) Some patterns of combining music with the moving image had been well stabilized during the pre-talkie days. Indian cinematic culture exhibits the far-reaching influence of these 'reverberating' patterns. It is, as if, the patterns were received and respected as *sutra*-s, and commentaries were added later to facilitate further development. What is important to note is that all *sutra*-s, having emerged as responses to the related socio-cultural reality, do not remain constant (at least they ought not.). Consequently, if any of the three basic components— namely, image, movement, and sound—undergoes a qualitative change, the remaining two display corresponding or correlated changes. If this response is not forthcoming, the communicative medium in question fails functionally. Applied specifically to the theme under discussion, this general truth means that the connotation of the term 'music' continued to suggest a sustained tone production while the movement of images remained virtual. However, when the said movement became more real, music began becoming more and more 'musical' (though the fundamental musical characteristic of being a sustained tone retained its place). The promise, music held through the sustained tone, was upgraded when internal tonal dynamics and language joined forces with the fundamental continuity. Thus, the ultimate aim of the cinematic music through the evolutionary process becomes clear: to create parallel, autonomous, and correlated structures in sound, silence, and performance in response to the structures realized through image, movement, and projection.

At this juncture it is perhaps advisable to take a closer look at the elements of music as they are to be the correlates to (the visual fundamentals of) image, movement, and projection. In this context, one must consider sound and silence first. How does Indian musicology understand and value these? The following points are worth noting:

1. Silence is an important musicological entity. It plays an aesthetico-grammatical role which is both positive and significant. For example, the concept of *tala* (fundamental to all categories of Indian music) includes *kriya* as one of the ten important characteristics (*dashaprana*) of *tala.* Significantly, four kinds of silences are brought into operation to execute the *kriya.*

2. And yet it is instructive to note that the *Amarakosha,* the earliest thesaurus in the world, has four stanzas devoted to sound, while silence does not find a place in it. Silence undoubtedly carries out aesthetic functions as important as those of sound, and yet, Indian languages have to depend on a composite word, with a negative prefix, to connote silence. Probably we owe this to our cultural preference for sound over silence.

3. However, Indian culture pays minute attention to the phenomenon of sound. In brief, it can be stated that the fundamental manifestation of sound is indicated by the term *shabda,* defined as 'that which is an experience of the hearing and a property of the *akasha'. Nada,* the first differentiation of *shabda,* has two varieties: *anahata* and *ahata.* Next in line is *dhvani,* defined specifically as being a product of musical instruments. Finally, musical *shabda* is known as *svara* while that employed in language is described as *varna.* It is also significant that an important theory in Sanskrit poetics, based on the suggestivity of the literary word, is described as the *dhvani* theory. Add to that the primacy accorded to vocal expression in India, and the stage is prepared for song—an aesthetic monad. On the other hand, song has also proceeded to include in *sangeet* the sung, the played, as well as the danced. Needless to say, the Indian musicological position, thus stated, seems specially conducive to the abundance of songs or *geets* (a phenomenon commonly noticed with reference to Indian cinema).

4. A factor likely to be overlooked is that, in India, music con-

stitutes only one of the number of oral traditions flowing side by side. These different oral traditions have influenced each other, a fact to be kept in mind.

When two arts come together, two possibilities emerge: both of them hold a balance or one rules over the other. When music is used in cinema, it is the latter which controls the former. So far no cases are reported where cinema is used in music. However, when music is the theme of a cinematic endeavour, music may be identified as the controlling entity. Whenever questions are raised about the cinematic functions of music, this basic premise about the inter-art relationship needs to be taken into consideration.

Music was employed as an agent to mask the unwanted sound of the projector when the chief cinematic function was to create a convincing illusion. It was also employed to convey the temporal aspect, when the silent cinema attempted projection of sequential events, or a narrated story. Yet another function, soon tagged on, was reinforcement of the mood, etc. created through visual means. Music used to create anticipation is also of the same kind. In case an event is intrinsically connected with music, the use of the latter is inevitable (unless one subscribes to different, mainly non-realistic tenets).

Apparently three human cycles are music-related ritualistically. Hence birth-death, day-night, and the seasonal cycle are accompanied by music almost without an exception.

Finally, cinematic music can have an abstract application. There are those non-classifiable emotions or shades of psychological states difficult to express adequately through visual means. Music is harnessed to suggest them. Obviously, experience at this level and of this kind, is ambiguous. Under the circumstances, sound becomes truly symbolic (and this is not merely confined to its musical use). Multiple suggestion, some kind of culture-transcending power, and a unique depth to the experience are the possible symbological strengths of judiciously explored music.

The cinema-maker, it would be seen, is the authority to determine the kind, placement, proportion, and intensity of the musical input admitted. In other words, his first choice determines the aesthetic logic the musical components are to follow. In concrete terms, his initial aesthetic decision affects the cinematic role allowed to silence, sound, melody, and tempo. The quartet explores the temporal dimension in the main. In this context, the chain runs from *shabda* to *svara* through *nada* and *dhvani*. As described earlier, language too is a processed version of sound, but it has its own internal logic. In this case the chain is: *shabda-nada-varna*. Cinematic music becomes specially complex because it is an intricate and tightly knit design of two sound-inspired manifestations further combined with the visual. The marriage of temporality and aurality, with spatiality and movement—presents immense possibilities as well as challenges to creativity. How does a cinema-maker meet the challenge?

On most occasions the problem is posed as: 'What music is to be used for a particular situation?', or 'What should music try to achieve in a particular situation?' Usually the doctrine of realism is invoked. We are all aware of the ingenuities practised to find a realistic justification for music when definite events, localities, characters, etc. are involved. However, a subtle difference in the invocation of the doctrine deserves to be noted. The criteria to select the actual music itself can hardly be described as realistic, though attempts to provide a realistic motivation for the use of music are not lacking.

However, it is common knowledge that there are many who see no reason why a cinema-maker should be bound by the shackles imposed by the philosophy of realism. A strong contention is that the art of cinema creatively aims at moving away from reality in order to transform it into a virtual, 'truer' reality. To those who hold this view, music is expected to carry out an altogether different function. Music, for them, operates to comment on cinematic message or experience.

The third strategy also has an aesthetic orientation, but music is explored in it for taking a close look at structure and construction. The insistence is to identify musical components and organizations responsive to the structural elements of cinema. Frames, the shots constructed within; the seeds of montage as well as their development in the shots; the dynamics, the tempo, and the rhythms realized through editing; the damming and release of the image-flow, and such other structural features are to be matched musically.

The Indian cinematic endeavour *vis-à-vis* music is to be appreciated against the backdrop provided by the foregoing conceptual discussion. This is not to suggest that Indian cinematic music has followed all the contours of the conceptual map. Which cultural force operates without deviations? However, is it not true that all deviations are understood as such *because* of the frameworks erected by theoretical deliberations? Many pleasant or unpleasant features of cinematic music are explained when a reference is made to the relevant theoretical structure. In fact, very often, revolutions are made possible because theories exist. Rebellions can be imagined with ease if grammatical fortifications are visible.

There is an additional factor that makes conceptual discussion and theoretical formulations relevant in any cinematic thinking. Admittedly, conceptualizations and theorizations have exerted the maximum influence on the art of cinema. Firstly, because it is the youngest of the arts. It came of age in a universe people with theories of art. Secondly, those who pioneered in cinematic development have often been keen students of other disciplines (because of the inherent multi-disciplinary nature of the art). The history of cinema has therefore reflected the contemporary literary isms and controversies, features of the antecedent dramatic performing traditions, and the prevailing audience-patron relationship. Against this backdrop is to be appreciated the tripartite nature of Indian cinematic music. The commercial Hindi, regional, and 'new wave' or art cinema are the three traditions. In spite of the usual overlaps, the triad will be seen to generate varied motivation as well as the final cinematic and musical products. The Hindi tradition is usually regarded as the most wide-ranging, accessible, and influential. Yet, it is significant to note that the total Indian cinematic output consists of only 30 per cent of Hindi films. On the other hand, regional cinema has often been adjudged as representative Indian expression at national, as well as, international critical forums. In other words, discussion focused on the Hindi stream may have to be qualified in view of the significant achievements in the two other streams. Musically analyzed, the situation throws up interesting and supporting crystallizations:

(a) Till about 1940 the studios used to appoint 'tune-setters' on the staff. These musicians had strong regional, linguistic, and musical leanings. The early studios were run on a 'proprietor-as-father' principle, and this too contributed to the stabilization of certain musical formulae.

(b) The two pioneering centres of cinematic subculture (namely, Pune and Calcutta) were also major centres of regional cultures. Both Maharashtra and Bengal enjoy rich traditions of art music. Further, they displayed the capacity to explore new avenues of music-making (e.g., stage music in Maharashtra and Rabindrasangeet in Bengal). As a consequence, both the centres created cinematic music with the rich contribution of regional flavours.

(c) Many composers (Vasant Desai, Naushad, S.D. Burman, Salil Chowdhury, *et al.*) produced distinctive music on account of their close acquaintance with regional musics—even after cinema had become a Bombay-based industry. Occasions are not lacking when composers have lifted their own tunes from regional films and transplanted them in Hindi films—and the songs have thrived.

(d) From about 1950 gramophone records of songs began to be brought out before the release of a film. This fact clearly underscores the independent existence of film music irrespective of its filmic framework.

Is the time ripe to pass a judgement on Indian cinematic music? Do we have the sophisticated conceptual framework necessary to place this complex socio-cultural phenomenon in perspective? The advent in recent years of two new combinations of music and image has complicated the situation further. Pending audience research, documentation of regional achievements, and a better understanding of our multiple oral and linguistic traditions, studies in Indian cinematic music are likely to remain attempts to understand Hindi film songs.

25

Cinematic Structure and Music in India

Films are products of the cinematic art. Cinema is a member of the art-family, known as 'composite arts'. The other member of the family is drama. Music, on the other hand, is a member of the performing triumvirate—the other two being dance, and drama. When art-families are discussed, it is usually conceded that, coming together of two or more arts, especially, from different families, yields satisfactory aesthetic results provided operating forces are properly balanced. History tells us that, in order to get the best of more than one art, such attempts are repeatedly made. Indian cinema and its music prove that point. That the combination has aroused the ire of many is known. Many are also intrigued by the hold the combination exercises over vast masses, and that too for long years. It is clear that for many reasons interrelationship of cinema and music is likely to attract critical attention.

However, the debate as well as the interchange of influences between the two, appears to take place under the shadow of circumstances identified normally as 'considerations of the industry'. In other words, cinema and music in India do *not* come together in situations which allow them to clash, combine or coalesce on their own terms. On a number of occasions, they are brought together under duress. On this backdrop, it would be difficult to argue about aesthetic legitimacy or cultural validity of isolated and minority attempts to meaningfully bring together cinema and music. The sampler of such efforts would be inadequate. And yet, the sheer volume, spread and popularity of the phenomenon should compel us to analyze the scene and try to make sense of the powerful musico-cinematic reality. No serious assessment of the Indian mind could ignore this aspect of Indian cultural behaviour. It is too real to be overlooked. As we all are aware, with the cinema joining hands with ubiquitous medium such as television, has only intensified a conflict-situation. We have realized that marriage of image with music can be of unwelcome potency. It is necessary to examine what happens when cinematic and musical structures are brought together.

One more point before we move further. Cinema is a young art (though bringing together image and music is not—it helps to remember). A younger art enjoys advantages of rich inheritance and flexibility. It also becomes complex on that account. On the other hand, older arts have advantages of acquiring variety in idiom and genres. Moreover, they also create wide-ranging associations with non-art areas of life of the people concerned. Therefore, music in India has many things to offer to cinema, while cinema can put music to more numerous and new uses, mostly not foreseen. Hence, it should cause no surprise that Indian cinema is *exploiting*—(and not exploring)—each of the five categories of Indian music and musical experience, irrespective of our preferences. A new medium, as also a younger art is bound to display inner compulsions to employ whatever is existing and available in order to attain ends, it thinks fruitful. Use, abuse and misuse—would all be evident in such a situation. Healthy exchange of views and experiences, free flow of ideas and easy circulation of influences—these alone can help in attaining a cultural equilibrium. New mediums and younger arts may sometimes be cavalier in their attitude to inherited cultural assets, but it would not help older partners to cavil and complain, because this kind of rough use is likely to restrengthen their own resolve as well as reflexes. Thus, it is not necessary to lament the sound-pollution that drowns music in the contemporary Indian cinema. Changing tracks creates noise, but only temporarily.

CINEMATIC STRUCTURES

It is obvious, that in its fast-paced march, Indian cinema has succeeded in throwing up a number of cinematic types, each with its own structure. For example, I can think of the following that have developed to maturity, almost in every major cinematic tradition in the country:

1. Mythological
2. Historical
3. Costume-pageantry
4. Social
5. Hagiographical
6. Biographical

7. Socio-political Satire
8. Folk-tale-based
9. Stunt
10. Art
11. Commercial

Obviously, the cinematic eleven can be added to or subtracted from. It can also be altered, modified or replaced. But, the point is that each genre could be expected to create its own specific structure in order to contain and convey experience particular to it. Only then would it be able to justice to its numerous components, and culminate in something more than a sum of its parts. An ideal study of musico-cinematic structures requires examination of the best specimen in each of the genre—indeed a tall order.

Hence, what I propose to attempt is a different kind of exercise. I intend to put forward and briefly discuss characteristics of musical structures and indicate their inner strengths and weaknesses. In the process, I hope to clarify why and how musico-cinematic *avatara*-s of the Indian genius have come to a critical point in their evolution.

MUSICAL STRUCTURE IN INDIA

Even if it is hard to generalize, musical structures have so emerged in India, that the following rectangularly and vertically presented polarities could be taken to be more or less valid in identifying structural parameters of music, irrespective of musical categories or traditions involved. The bi-polarities involved are: complexity or simplicity, rhythm or melody-orientation, meaningful or sonorous presentation, movement-oriented or place-tied performance, conduciveness or otherwise to role-assumption or characterization.

WHAT DO THESE BI-POLARITIES SUGGEST?

1. No bi-polarity indicates a no-contact position of two opposites. Only degrees of mutual exclusion are suggested.
2. Different bi-polar elements may combine to create one musical structure with certain identifiable qualities. For example, complexity of rhythm, created along with meaningless sound-structures demanding a static presentation of music, and with no place for role-assumption would provide us with *tabla*-solo-s, etc.

3. It is to be noted that combinations of polar elements may, or may not, result in a musical genre—an entity foundational to all music-making. Merely to permutate and combine bipolars, is not adequate to generate a viable musical genre or form. Other aesthetic pre-conditions need to be fulfilled if an acceptable musical form is to emerge. Hence, a mechanical separation or combination of elements is not likely to create acceptable music. It is thus not possible to use the *masala* formula. To add ingredients does not automatically lead to music. It is common knowledge that contemporary Indian films, especially of the commercial category, often appear to believe in the invincibility of the *masala* formula in many aspects of cinema-making.

4. Complexity created by the coming together of one performing, and one composite art, introduces a useful and subtle distinction between music and song. Song is technically a lesser entity than music, but it is also more compact and focused than the former. For example, music identified as 'background' is certainly more accommodative than, and inclusive of, a song. At the same time, the appeal of a song, and its function, is more directed as well as effective. This, perhaps, is the reason why Indian films have relied so heavily and widely on scattering a great number of songs in films. The general abundance of film-songs, as we know, has revolted many minds in India and abroad. Broadly speaking, it is objected that, songs impede flow of the story, distort plot and take spectators away from cohesive and emotional impact sought through other aspects of cinematic structures. Cinematic structural bricks, identified as story-movement, plot-construction, character-building, realistic portrayal, etc. are, it is argued, irreparably (or at least considerably), damaged by 'songs', comparable to parasites. Parasites are, as we know, those organisms which derive sustenance from others without giving anything in return. We are told that even high-flying aeroplanes suffer from the parasite-drag, as their non-lifting parts only weigh them down. Similarly, it is pointed out that the high-flying cinematic imagination suffers on account of 'heavy' song-dance numbers.

5. Keen students of Indian cinema have pointed out that multiplicity of songs has been the consequences of our theatric

hang-over. It is a well-known fact that, many major and modern theatric traditions in the country developed music-drama-s (incorrectly described as operatic efforts). These perfected idioms, in which music and drama (i.e., two arts from the same group) combined, created a unique genre. The genre differed from western opera because music-dramas created musical structures running parallel to the main dramatic theme or stream to exercise influence and achieve effects through a kind of autonomous operation, within the general structure erected by the dramatic intent. In other words, the Indian musico-theatric combine threw up a pattern in which song became an independent entity. This could happen because, even though initially the song was activated by a dramatic impulse, it was not entirely ruled by it in later progressions. This is not the occasion to elaborate on the Indian insistence on rejecting an operatic way of bringing music and theatre together. Suffice it is to say that every culture arrives at a cultural decision in order to strike new equations between music and theatre *because* such ever-changing combinations are, at once, symptomatic and diagnostic of deeper cultural needs. To have more songs, and less music, was a cultural prompting which took care to introduce novelty of expression without sacrificing the nourishment offered by a long-standing, comprehensive and fruitful oral tradition.

6. At this point, it is helpful to note that everything that departs from prose-delivery should *not* to be described as song. To ensure effective, easy and wider communication, oral tradition relies on a continuum from straight, near-monotone delivery of speech to song—the ultimate of music-language relationship. For example, in India, it is possible to trace an unbroken arc from prose-monotone to song through the intervening phases of murmuring-humming-chanting-recitation and metrical rendition. It is only the last phase which is the song proper. Song alone is full of music, others are musical. In this sense, no music-drama in India, nor the early cinematic efforts such as *Indrasabha,* can be accused of being overweighed by songs. Therefore, the alleged sin of devising cinematic formula of having a fixed number of song and dance numbers, at almost regular intervals cannot be laid at

the door of theatric traditions preceding cinema.

7. The ground is now clear to marshall an argument—if not a thesis. Three clear phases are discerned in a musico-cultural movement—away from a monotone speech-delivery. They are: approximations to melody-making, creation of songs and finally movement away from songs to music (as the term was understood, explained and accepted earlier). In the first two stages, musical structures (—because of the parent oral tradition—) do not disrupt the communicative flow, even if the mode of moulding language and sounds in general, has already deviated from 'normal' prose-monotone. When songs proper come on the scene, the communicative channel is not disrupted, but disturbed because of the presence of another, powerful and simultaneous channel which inclined to blur contours of meaningfulness. It is to be marked that except in very rare cases, music, by itself, does not have meaning, though it may have significance. This is the reason why there is no dictionary of musical motifs, phrases, symbols, etc. When composers and others seek to establish relationship of correspondence between words, lines, diagrams, etc. on the one hand, and music on the other, they unfortunately use a language which, to a great extent, creates an impression that they really 'match' music with the non-musical stimuli in action. In actuality, they cannot but make an excuse of the other, non-musical stimulus—to launch into a musical experience distinguished by its non-musical associations. This manoeuvre enables music to reach out of its usual confines. On the other side, non-musical stimuli are able to reach out of themselves and become 'suggestive', a process, expected to make the act more accommodative, but not necessarily clearer in import. Songs thus tend to envelope the entire communicative act in a haze—at once welcome, unsettling and attractive. The power of song to create an ambiguous aura is what makes it so indispensable to artists seeking association with non-musical aspects of expression. Makers of cinema use songs to create a parallel world, a universe of Vishvamitra as one would think in India, to ensure conveying a complex message to receivers whose own desire to interpret and construe is thereby aroused and made more intense. Songs are more autonomous than we usually admit.

They are also more liberating—than is ordinarily imagined. This is the main reason of their popularity and capacity to remain entrenched in memory, even when accompanying and non-musical impetus has ceased to exist.

8. A careful distinction was made earlier between music and song. Time is ripe to elaborate on that a little. The exercise would help in explaining the contemporary craving to 'apply' non-song music in a great measure. Non-song music would largely connote instrumental sounds as also voice *sans* language. Instruments, and their sounds, are carriers of messages which are less culture-bound than voices and languages. To the extent, they can wander easily and transcend more boundaries, effectively, as also with speed. The non-musical structural features of cinematic art in India developed to such a degree by the sixties, that songs became a hindrance to a free-play of the non-musical forces. Instruments are also emotionally more neutral, and it thus became more feasible to grab tonal colour which instruments can bring in without suffering from shackles of language, meaning, voices, etc., inevitably imposed by song. This is how, and why we have today a situation, in which there are *no* songs but more and more music structured 'cinematically'. The recent multiplicity and variety of instrumental sounds, as also of movements and gestures framing them, are products of a kind of sensibility which indicates a cinematic imagination affected, and sometimes afflicted, by a keen desire to speak more through 'eyes' than speak or sing to ears. This change needs to be noted for a special reason.

9. I submit, that on account of many historico-cultural developments, our oral tradition has allowed itself the doubtful luxury of submitting to the tyranny of the eye above all other senses. I hold that this cannot, but lead to a lop-sided imagination as also a fragmented expression of the perceived truth, cinematic as well as musical. Today, we have music clearly moving away from melodic statements and contours. We also have language-sounds employed to dislodge meaning and suggested significance. Visual/kinetic presentations, with no faith in suggestivity, are in command. Direct appeal to eyes, acting as proxy to all senses, is the goal. This is a far cry from the song-dominated films so freely castigated by many. Song-

dominated cinema spoke of indigenous imagination and sensibility, with firm roots in Indian culture. The contemporary musico-cinematic structures are relying on strong rhythms and loud sounds—the two musical components, traditionally and universally pressed into service, to replace individuals with a collective mass, and thinking and questioning minds, with obedient organisms.

Two of Plato's perceptive remarks come easily to mind. He warned, 'Never allow rhythms of your state to change, because that spells anarchy.' Secondly, he observed, 'Rhythms are compulsive and tones are persuasive.'

I think that should be a fitting concluding remark for my plea.

26

The Singing Voice: Some Asian Perspectives

I propose to present an idea-paper. It is an apologetic attempt suggesting how a vital avenue of human expression, namely voice, and one of its fundamental manifestations, i.e., singing, can be fruitfully studied. The presentation assumes perspectives developed in cultural musicology, a discipline known in many quarters as ethnomusicology. The submissions are made with many reservations, qualifications and handicaps. I sincerely hope that they provide hints for an *Asian* methodology to comprehend, appreciate and assess Asian cultural manifestations.

The accent is on the singing voice. There are reasons for this focus:

1. Cultural groups, it is observed, hold fast to their own voice and distinctive techniques of voice-productions, usage, as well as philosophy governing voice-related behaviour. This is irrespective of changes effected, accepted and assimilated in other areas of life and activities therein. Cultural factors of deeper hue are connected more immediately to strategies and patterns of vocalization. As a consequence, the problem of cultural identity can be plainly posed and usefully discussed by concentrating on voice, and its diverse manifestations. Of course, it must be remembered that one use of voice, i.e., speech, brings in more complex considerations, chiefly because it is related to language, as normally understood.

2. A deliberately isolated examination of voice facilitates exploration of intercultural influencing acts and processes *because* voice-study secures a real, firm and an indigenous reference-frame to judge, both depth and quality of foreign and/or alien impact.

3. Voice is given the place of honour also because timbre, i.e., tonal quality—will inevitably prove, in coming years, to be the dominant dimension in all acts of finer and significant

cultural communication. Pitch and volume, the two other parameters of voice, enjoying ascendancy so long, will be compelled to take a back-seat because expression of nuances will become increasingly practicable to communicators and accessible to receivers (due to the ever-improving media-situation). It must be admitted that voice *as* voice 'lives' in timbre—because, in the final analysis, both pitch and volume have less expressive potential.

4. The role of voice, as the most individual and innate aspect of human personality, can hardly be overstated. Observers of the modern human condition have noticed our growing and intensely felt craving to establish, explore and exploit direct as well as effective channels of inter-personal communication. The craving results from a keen desire to avoid social disintegration traceable to the fast-paced and overwhelming globalization. Voice will prove to be the most genuine and 'personal' channel of communication emphasizing the nearly universal human aspirations to reach out.

THE STRATEGY

The general strategy I employ is, to describe singing voice of an Asian culture by using, for reference, those vocal parameters obtained in India. More precisely, I have relied on perceptions clustering around Hindustani musical treatment of voice. It is essential to state that this particular methodological move is made, merely to navigate to positions allowing comprehensible statements—than to make critical and evaluative assertions. Keeping Hindustani voice-uses is *not* to announce them as ideals or standards, but merely to register points—deviations from which are easily, meaningfully and respectfully noted.

Yet another, strategic feature is to alert our ears to capture pervasive similarity of concepts and ideas among Asian cultures which similarity, may, however be accompanied by entirely different and consequent expressions. Obviously, repeated exchanges, migrations, wars, conquests and colonization, etc. have led to a great deal of cultural circulation. Ideas, being both abstract and abstractable—wander freely and permit manifestations that are more in tune with the local conditions—mind, milieu and the moment included. Hence, the interesting phenomenon of a rather disconcerting and real variety based on equally authentic and perceivable similarities. One may deduce that more exhaustive, intense and cultural, interchanges and exchanges, existed in the bygone days than we are ready to imagine. Alternatively, one may believe in multi-genesis of ideas, arguing that given similar, if not identical, inner and outer human circumstances, similar manifestations can take place, independently of one another. Whatever that may be, Asians, while studying Asians, experience a curious and moving feeling of being and not being there, culturally speaking. On this background of a cultural *deja vu*, the strategy is to begin by noting differences, and then proceed to the comforts of perceived similarities between settings which are otherwise new. In other words, Eurocentric attitude (often mistook for objectivity), is to be deliberately replaced by an Asiacentricism.

SONGS FROM MONGOLIA

1. A very striking feature is the unalloyed recourse to high pitch. Entire performance is very often located in the upper reaches. Slight downward shifts or dips come in, but only to be followed by returns to higher pitches, invariably sustained well.
2. The 'overtone singing' is the other arresting peculiarity. It indicates an extremely skilful, and unusual way of vocalization, aptly and alternatively described as 'mouth music', 'mouth-harp' or 'throat music', etc. In this style of vocalization, the singer simultaneously intones a low drone and a series of flute-like, high-pitched and controlled notes or harmonics. Evidently, this is the reason why the mode of music-making is also identified as 'biphonic singing'. Six such styles, under the common name of *khoomil* (which literally means in Mongolian 'pharynx') exist. In these styles, labial, oral, palatal, glottal, nasal and chest cavities are utilized with remarkable application and virtuosity. We are told that people in the Altai Mountains first made melodies in the *khoomil* mode to imitate murmuring streams or echoing caves in the mountains—obviously in recognition of Nature and its beauties. It must be noted that listeners primarily feel, as if simultaneously listening to flute and Jews' harp—and not to singing.
3. Preference for, and prevalence of, high-pitched singing and

the practice of overtone singing considered together—point to absence of one feature of musical progression which is generally assumed: to proceed to musical climaxes by moving from low to high pitches. (This is usually matched by succession of slow and fast tempo. Perhaps more can be said in this respect after additional inputs.)

4. Even though I have not studied samples of Mongolian speech, I surmise that Mongolian singing voice is bound to be different from speaking voice in the culture—so high is the singing.

5. Mongolian singing impresses by quick transitions from high pitch to (—what can be broadly identified as—) falsetto vocalization. Mostly, the changes are not punctuated by unintended register-breaks.

6. The singing is rich in vocal effects. It is difficult to define an 'effect' and distinguish it from its antithesis, i.e., the conventional or customary usage. However, I would like to suggest that effect, as differentiated from consequence, etc., is a result which achieves a considerably greater impact than can be explained or warranted by its cause. The vocalization under study has many unexpected timbre-changes, for example—from normal to nasal. Equally marked, is a sudden narrowing of the vocal stream. Finally, vowel changes are frequent and extensive. Deviations from the normally followed (and defended) vowel-sequences, such as open to close, or from open to round are often noticed. Some amazing and taxing trills and ululations cannot be forgotten even after a single hearing.

7. It becomes clear that in Mongolia vocalization is placed on a continuum. Vocalization is not perceived (and received) as a process broken up by noticeably distanced phases of voice-projection. For instance, I identify muttering-murmuring-chanting-recitation and singing as the most important seats of the Mongol vocal imagery.

8. Yet another, important matter is relationship between instruments and voice. The interrelationship is intense and yet, quite friendly, i.e., not competitive. Instruments often induce and coax voices into singing. They function more as motivating agents than mere supports or musical followers.

9. Numerous duets are sung and participating voices are more

distinguished in breadth, than in pitch-ranges traversed. In a number of cases men and women render the same music. Frequently, a pitch-range of three octaves does not remain a mere idea. A duet may mean singing of male-female voices *together* and not alternatively. Choral expression is explored frequently and audience, crowd, spectators, etc. join in freely and regularly.

10. *Prima facie,* pentatonic melodies are employed. As is granted, the phenomenon of pentatonism is itself sought to be redefined as more and more nuance-studies are undertaken.

11. The repertoire of song-genres consists of: long song, abbreviated long song, extended long song, short song (particularly including lullaby, drinking song, horse-song, work song and songs about animals), game song (for men and women), praise song and folk-song.

12. It must be mentioned that most of the music under discussion, has close connections with poetry of one kind or the other. Both sung poetry, and poetic songs predominate. From epical to a narrative mode, celebratory to a eulogistic one and from a thematic concern for reflections on the day-to-day life to the sacred-magical appeal—is indeed a wide range covered by musico-poetic outpourings of the Mongolian tradition.

13. It becomes obvious that string instruments hold a great sway. The horse-headed lute (*morin-khuur*) is almost omnipresent. (It is characteristic that the instrument is said to be a horse-lover's tribute to his dead horse. Expectably, the instrument discharges both melodic and rhythmic functions in varying degrees. In fact, the ancient Mongol history records employment of string instruments even in martial music, though drums were inevitably put into service.)

WHAT DO THE FEATURES SIGNIFY?

It is perhaps time to hazard a guess as to the cultural significance of the characteristics enumerated so far.

The first is the persistent use of high pitch. I suggest that pitch, being the most easily perceived dimension of sound, importance of music is suggested by placing it in the modality *not* worn thin through mundane applications. Singing is allotted, as it were, a special voice-band. As every person is expected to know singing (as well as, they say, horse-riding), preference for high-pitched singing nearly seems to be a prestigious precondition for earning the Mongolian citizenship. It is obvious that open and vast expenses around also constitute a contributory cause, but no performing feature, however facilitating it may be, is stabilized in a tradition unless it has cultural values attached to it.

The remarkable 'mouth-music', can hardly be left without some discussion. I would like to suggest that the phenomenon might have links with the Chinese tradition of musical whistling as enshrined in the unique work entitled *Hsiao Chih* (*The Principles of Whistling* reportedly written in AD 765). This, extremely rare work, reiterated that every sound in music has its counterpart in Nature. The work defines whistling, lays down methods and study-procedures. It explains different compositions (basic as well as derived) in the genre. When it asserts that 'a good whistler commands attention of the whole world of spirits', the extended appeal, effectiveness and cultural role of music in general and vocal mode in particular becomes obvious.[1] It is of course true that mouth-music and whistling differ, technically speaking. But as far as the wider philosophical context is concerned, both can be considered to be members of the same family. The phenomenon certainly gives a jolt to the usually accepted ideas of vocal music.

Mongolian vocal tradition allows each person, male as well as female, to sing individually to his or her own animals. Five kinds of live-stock are sung to. They are sheep, goat/yak, horse, camel and cow. Songs to soothe animals are an accepted category. If a cow is reluctant to suckle a calf which had lost its mother, a professional *khoomil* would be invited to mediate. To build such relationships between the two 'worlds'—speaks volumes about sensitivity to Life.

SONGS FROM JAPAN

Expectably, Japan is better studied, though I am aware of the lack of Indian interest in musical traditions of this extremely industrious and assimilative culture. At the outset, a few distinctive features of its larger musical tradition can be enumerated.

1. Primacy of vocal music is unmistakable. All instrumental music has developed under the shadow of the human voice.
2. Music in Japan has close relationship with literature. It has

often served as a vehicle for words. In fact, it is not an exaggeration to say that form of music is, itself, determined by the literary expression accompanying the musical impulse.

3. History of Japanese music reveals steady growth of theatre music. The essentially composite character of theatre has inevitably influenced Japanese music, both in form and content. In fact, the myth dealing with origin of music in Japanese tradition, speaks of a dance-laughter-music oriented performance given to propitiate the Sun Goddess.

4. Clan, family and finally teacher-pupil relationship marks the imparting of musical knowledge in Japan. As William Malm, that extraordinarily perceptive ethnomusicologist has remarked, 'The word *sensi* in Japanese has far greater implications than the word teacher in English'.

5. With the country's northward shifts of political power (from Kyushu to Kyoto, to Kamakura to Edo) Japanese musical instruments grew in variety and musical stature. Most of the times the moves originated in Korea.[2]

6. As if in response to its geographical surroundings, Japanese music reveals in developing intricate, delicate and rich effects—all within circumscribed bounds of different musical parameters. In other words, musical expression is couched in nuances.

7. Exposure to Japanese music also brings out the rhythmic discrepancy characterizing melodic and instrumental lines of the musical structure. Techniques which create these time-lags are variously known as *zurasu* (to shift or slide), *merasu* (to slide or lower the pitch), *furuwasu* (to make vibrato), etc.

8. For our purpose, religious music, theatre music and folk music appear to be the relevant categories in the larger tradition.

THE RELIGIOUS STREAM

Shinto and Buddhist traditions intermingle in Japan to such an extent that efforts to separate them, especially while discussing performing contexts, is to deny the fact of their joint and multi-levelled existence.

1. In the Shinto tradition, *kagura*, the music for imperial Shinto functions, and *sato-kagura*, the Shinto folk festival

music—are both dance-oriented. One consequence is that vocalization proceeds under some predictable restrictions. When we notice that *wagone*, a major string instrument, has tones which do not progress in a regular order from low to high but from two separate and broken chords, or when we note that the six-holed bamboo-flute, *yamato-bue* has pitches according to the varying length of the instrument—it should become clear that facilitation of vocalization is not the priority item in the music concerned.

2. Literature, dancing, or ceremonial interests control music and hence, melodic patterns, one observes, tend to be repetitive.

3. The Sato-Kagura festival music emphasizes rhythmic patterns as the main principle of musical organization in Japanese music. This has the inevitable consequence on vocal expression.

THE BUDDHIST TRADITION

1. Derived chiefly through Chinese sources, in Japan, the theory of composing and singing chants, based on the sacred texts became known as *shomyo*. Symptomatically, three languages are used for the chant-music. Songs sung in a presumably ancient Indian dialect are called *bonsan*, those in Chinese are known as *kansan* while those in Japanese are identified as *wasan*. The language-structures/textures would have their respective contributions to vocal patterns affecting at the micro-level. These need to be examined.

2. The Buddhist music flows in two basic melodic moulds called *ryo* and *ritsu* respectively. The essential difference between the two scales, is the placement of note called *kaku* (which is third in the five-note Buddhist scales). It is one-and-a-half step lower in the former, i.e., the *ryo* scale.

3. A prominent feature of the Buddhist vocalization is the ornamentation, called *yuri*, translated as 'swinging', an effect which creates tonal colour as well as a subtle swaying rhythm.

4. Buddhist services are often noticed to have so slow a tempo that it makes rhythmic perception impossible. In addition, each priest is heard to sing in his own pitch, and a score or so priest's simultaneous chanting in as many pitches would ob-

viously create a complex web of voices.

5. Another intricacy is introduced because the chief priest may chant in the ancient Indian dialect, while others carry on in the Chinese dialect. Yet another example of an unusual interrelationship between voice, rhythms and instruments, is provided by religious service of the Judae sect. In it, the priest begins chanting the *wasan* at the end of the service, to the slow beat of a deep-sounding, fish-shaped slit-drum. This is picked up by a chorus of kneeling women, who have small bells in their own hands. Their chant rises in tempo and the whole air is filled by an overpowering but uncoordinated chanting. In Nichiren sect the congregation beats out prayers on the fan-drum while a bigger *o-daiko* drum is also played in syncopation.

In sum, in each case vocalization seems to be overshadowed, either due to accompaniment, or on account of a far from ideal acoustic and performing environment.

In Zen cloisters, twenty-odd instruments are employed to regulate lives of the monks—but occasions which allow music to come to the forefront are almost non-existent. In fact, the overall Zen attitude is to emphasize direct and non-rational instruction than resort to language-based studies of the sacred texts. Strong reaction against Buddhist ritualism and the doctrinaire formalism linked to it, led the Zen to a position which made it rely more and more on annihilation of language. Hence the Zen Master's confident recourse to cries. Called *Katsu* in Japanese, the Zen cries are not carriers of concepts, which are confined to *this* world. Akira Tamba very rightly relates this Zen position and the *Kakegoe* vocal interjections of the Noh drummers.[3]

As Malm has so rightly pointed out, the entire Buddhist use of music 'symbolizes impermanence of life and the inextricable unity of life, death and time.

BUDDHIST FOLK MUSIC AND FESTIVALS

1. Buddhist folk songs often use the chanting style. They are also without accompaniment, though clapping and occasionally drums are added.

2. The *saimon*-hymns, which survive in some dirty ditties used in folk music, were, in their original form, songs sung to lam-

poon and satirize current events etc. Other forms such as
goeika, etc. are pilgrims songs which may be sung in processions today. In festivals, dancers are also entrusted with the
responsibility of singing (for example, the 'o-bon' festival).

In sum, vocalization, being a part of the generally sanctified behaviour is an activity directed to producing mental states, and not
particularly for creating a refined or pleasurable musical effect.

YOKYOKU—THE SINGING IN NOH

1. The highly evolved and aesthetically fine-tuned performance
   of Noh, has actors as well as chorus to sing. The chorus leader
   controls tempo of the chant by sustaining sounds. There is a
   continuous process of mutual adjustment between all music-
   makers.
2. Of the two basic styles, *kotoba* (words) is the heightened
   speech-style and has no definite pitch or melody. The other
   style, called *fushi* (melody), lives up to its name. This also has
   two sub-styles, one softer and the other stronger. The most
   important feature is that these styles may be manifest *within
   a single phrase*—once again drawing attention to the nuance-
   filled aesthetics in the Japanese music-making.
3. The melodic line is entirely controlled by words of the text
   and the overall form of the play. The melodic line is also
   distinguished by a performing formulae, according to which,
   each movement to a lower note takes place only after moving up to a nearby higher tone. Obviously, the texture of the
   melodic line becomes predictable, but the movement is contrary to the usual, low to high progression.
4. The *Kakegoe* cries of the Noh drummers mentioned earlier,
   are guttural cries which are treated as legitimate components
   of the rhythmic cell. This cry, as in the Zen viewpoint, is an
   expression of the internal craving to rouse spiritual essence
   or consciousness within, and the drum-beat which follows, is
   the immediate and inevitable external confirmation. Together, they complete the spiritual function assigned to vocalization as such. As has been pointed out, even the Kabuki
   instrumentalists use the device, and obviously for a similar
   purpose.

The Noh actor-singers also use low, pharyngeal voice with a darker timbre and greater volume. Additionally, vowel-sounds, the main colour-bearers in vocal acts, are produced by taking them further back in the oral cavity, according to the Noh technique. Thus, open vowels are rounded by touching the palate with the middle part of the tongue. It is not difficult to deduce that the technique is performers parallel to a spiritual quest.[4]

Obviously, a more detailed analysis can be taken up, and more attention can be paid to folk-songs as well as musical forms that developed closely with particular melodic instruments. The customary beginning of folk-songs, either below or above the expected note, or the Ainu folk-songs, in which two singers sing into each other's mouth to create strange effects and such other items can also be noted. And yet, this hardly seems to be necessary and some generalizations are possible.

What do the Japanese Vocalizations Signify?

1. The accent on low and lower pitches is noticeable. It has already been suggested that pitch-discrimination is easier for us, than differentiating nuances of volume and timbre—the two other dimensions of sound. Further, lower pitches, though richer in harmonics, are less easy to discriminate when changed. It is instructive to note that while the Mongolian way chose the high pitch, the Japanese preferred the lower reaches. It reminds me of what Eliot said—'the way up and the way down, are one and the same'. Consequently, the Japanese way demands keener attention from the listener-spectator, as well a deliberate acquisition of taste in order to enable receiving the desired impact. It means that the spurs are not easily won.

2. Melody, as such, is not allowed to flower in terms of voice alone. It is destined and designed, to appear in a perspective created by numerous other performing components. In fact, it is possible to say that it is conceived as a package of multi-sensory appeal. As a consequence, its evocation demands to be judged as a totality. The intended multi-sensory manifestations would, however, facilitate communication as each receiver could be expected to have at least one, or a few, (—if not all—) developed sensibilities. The 'message' would get through because multiple alternatives are in-built.

3. Sweetness or pleasantness—(though difficult to define—) are given a short shrift, and effectiveness or the capacity to create an impact is placed at the top. To many ears, the vocal quality would appear to be nurtured according to an aesthetics of rough textures, contrary to many other areas of Japanese life, it I may add. It it of course true that koto, shamisen, shakuhachi, etc. are examples of a kind of plaintive sweetness, but for reasons explained earlier, I am concentrating on what is essentially communicated through voice and vocalization.

4. I do not think that voice-instrument relationship is either competitive or supportive. To me, it gives a feeling of instrumental assertion of a limited freedom to draw a different line of development, which, however, is in consonance with the overall design of the performance. Thus both voice and instruments serve a common master, which is the grand design of the ultimate impact.

5. The role of rhythm *vis-à-vis* voice is intriguing to some extent. While, it is true that the vocal line itself generates rhythmic pulses, rhythmic stresses created by instruments seem to repeatedly break the melodic continuity and generate some fresh tensions, which are not totally resolved. In other words, the totality of music does not soothe or lull the listener into peacefulness. The experience is of an aroused energy, or forces unleashed—so that they are experienced directly.

6. On the contrary, the words, or the poetry (of objects and colours, etc.), which accompany vocalized music seem to be all set to lead the receiver into tranquillity and acceptance. This is a situation which creates an aesthetic ambiguity.

In may opinion, all great art is (at least) ambiguous.

REFERENCES

1. E.D. William, "Principles of Whistling Hsiao Chih", *Bulletin of School of Oriental and African Studies*, vol. 2.20 (1957), pp. 217–29.
2. William P. Malm, *Japanese Music and Musical Instruments*, Tokyo, 1959, pp. 38–9.
3. Tamba Akira, "Confluence of Spiritual and Aesthetic Research in Traditional Japanese Music", in *The World Music*, IICM, vol. XXV, no. 1, 1983, pp. 30–41.
4. Ibid., pp. 38–9.

27

Wilderness, Rama-Ramayana and Music

What is Wilderness?

In most Indian languages the word 'wilderness' would be translated as *vana, aranya* or *atavi,* etc. *Amarakosha* predictably devotes full four verses to describe woods before it comes to trees proper.[1] These words would suggest thickly wooded, natural, and expansive surroundings, allowing sparse or nil human population, nor being open to easy human traffic. These, and similar words, are of course capable of being used as 'terms'—i.e., as those minimal, linguistic and stabilized units employed to technically refer to diverse life-areas, disciplines and interests. For example, *atavi* would indicate forests with possibilities of big game hunting; *aranya* would mean wooded lands where one may retire as hermits used to do; while *kantara* would denote shrubbery.[2] Yet another important word is *vana* which traditionally means a thicket of trees, etc. as also a dwelling in a forest. In the context of our discussion it is important to note that both *aranya*-s or *vana* cannot be equated with jungles, inhabitable as well as inhospitable. They essentially mean wooded lands away from dense human populations and farmlands. But they are habitable. Purana-s mention nine *aranya*-s. They are: Dandaka, Saindhava, Pushkara, Naimisha, Kurujangal, Utpalavartaka, Jambu-marga, Himavat, and Arbuda. Many of them have become well-known on account of various divine and semi-divine events associated with them. The story is the same with *vana*-s. For example, Rama met many sages living and carrying out sacrificial functions in *tapovana*-s. It is symptomatic that paradise is called *nandanvana* in Indian tradition. These and such other terms certainly create nuance-situations which should better be left for experts to handle.

The Positive Face of Wilderness

It is difficult to maintain that wilderness, a state or phenomenon naturally associated with forests, is necessarily to be defined and considered as a negative condition of human life. The way it is placed in the traditional, Indian life-pattern, wilderness impresses as specific kind of isolation to be contrasted with the normally assumed condition of human togetherness, including human contact with non-human beings. Indian ethos has deliberately and assiduously cultivated togetherness and isolation as two conditions fundamental to emergence and development of human qualities inherently beneficial to social (preferably I would call it societal) health, happiness and durability. Moving a level deeper, we see that togetherness results from attachment while isolation is consequent to detachment. I submit that the meaning of wilderness, or at least a significant aspect of it, becomes unmistakably clear if the role and mutual relationship of attachment and detachment, as basic drives, is appreciated.

Wilderness, thus explained, operates in two spheres. The first, of primary importance, is the sphere defined by social groups/societies as collective entities. The second is confined to human beings taken singly, i.e., as persons. It has been often pointed out, that Indian tradition holds human beings as born indebted to three agencies: gods (*deva*), sages (*rishi*), and ancestors (*pitru*). To become an individual is to make a successful transition from 'person hood' (*jana* to being an individual (*vyakti*). A person is a being who exists for himself while an individual is a being who lives usefully for society (of which he or she is a part) by paying off three debts mentioned earlier. (Incidentally, though there were some later changes in interpretations, the three original debts were to be respectively discharged through offering sacrifices, observing certain austerities and ensuring continuation of family lineage.)

It was of course not sufficient to state ideals and ignore the setting up of suitable mechanisms enabling citizens to undertake the responsibility of living up to the ideals. Hence, ancient India evolved a system with two guiding principles of social organization, one of which was aimed at taking care of individuals (as defined earlier), and the other expected to serve the cause of societal groups. Evolution and employment of *varna* and *ashrama*-principles perceptively underscores the importance of human togetherness and isolation as necessary life-conditions. The *varna*-principle was mainly related to careers of groups as society while *ahsrama*-principle led a person to the ultimate realization, i.e., his becoming an individual. In combination, the two formulations strive to balance human life (which is different and higher than mere existence) between two polarities of attachment and detachment. Some more details, obviously called from various sources, would clarify *varna* and *ashrama* as conceptual crystallizations and interplay of attachment-detachment they strongly indicate.

THE VARNA-S

Varna is the first to be considered because, as suggested by the three-debts concept, Indian vision of human existence placed primary value on society and *not* on individual as understood today. The latter was regarded noteworthy, if and when, he or she, fitted well as a component of a larger social whole. In the context of our discussion it is not necessary for us to trace and comprehend the concept historically. Our aim is to identify basic features of the concept in order to appreciate the role it could, and did, play in a feat of impressive social structuring.

THE FOUR VARNA-S

The social institution of *chaturvarna* (lit. four colours) gradually attained its ultimate shape by the time *Bhagavadgita* was composed. In the broadest possible manner, it could be said that the concept, as also the behavioural pattern it represented, passed through at least three chronological and often overlapping phases represented by—Shruti, Smriti and Purana. It was during the last phase that the most complete, rigidly authoritative, frequently contradictory and fascinatingly complex statement of *varna*-principle was to be found.

VARNA AND COLOUR

The initial operations of the principle were recorded during the Vedic times as acts of social differentiation, between conquering Arya-s and the conquered Dasa/Dasyu-s. The word *varna* apparently became inevitable because of real confrontations between diverse races. It is symptomatic that Puranic literature came to describe Brahmins, Kshatriya, Vaishya and Shudra-s respectively as fair, red (ruddy), yellow and dark. According to some authorities, there was an intervening stage when there were only three *varna*-s, —and the

Shudra-s were admitted to the fold last.

Varna and Castes

Gradually, the principle merged with the process of caste-formation. Both *varna* and *jati* were presumably occupation-oriented in many cases. The differentiations thus functioned to stratify a society which was ever-expanding over the centuries.

The Essential Dynamism of the Concept

Socio-cultural privileges granted, and disabilities imposed by the *varna*-principle, predictably varied from time to time as also according to the administrative-legislative authority in power. However, generally speaking, the first three *varna*-s enjoyed more freedom and a 'most-favoured-people' treatment. There is not enough evidence to suggest that the entire *varna*-exposition was a product of Brahmin-craftiness, though Brahmins and Kshatriya-s may have joined-hands to become main architects of the system. They, obviously, were the 'have-class. This is indirectly confirmed by the fact that codes for these two classes are the most elaborate. Further, considerable upward and downward movements took place on the *varna*-scale, and all attempts of forcing hierarchical interpretation of *varna*-s were regularly and successfully challenged. Interesting insights are obtained in this context if 'what is and what is not allowed' to the four *varna*-s in different texts, is comparatively examined. We are told that from the relevant authorities, *Apastambasutra* is the earliest, *Devalsmriti* the latest and Manu is placed in the middle on the chronological axis. It is instructive that *Devalsmriti* specifically refers to proficiency of Shudra-s in arts as well as crafts. Introduction of the concept of *apaddharma,* i.e., (to deviate, etc. from one's own *varna*-code under certain extenuating circumstances) was also designed to meet real and recurring situations.

Differentiation with Sacraments

One of the most important features of *varna*-application was insistence on distinctive sacraments, specific and obligatory to each. While the earlier smriti-s did not specify sacraments for shudra-s, the *Vyasasmriti* removed this disparity, thereby pointing to the greater involvement of Shudra's in social life. As all students of Indian culture are aware, the entire matter of obligatory sacraments is closely connected with the doctrine of inherited qualities and supremacy—an affair which has rightly continued to fuel controversies till today in all walks of life. Close scrutiny also reminds us that arguments in this respect acquire 'aesthetic dimensions' in performing arts and analogous fields.

Varna and Wilderness

In the context of our discussions it is necessary to note that members of the two dominant *varana*-s were prescribed definite life-periods in which they were to detach themselves from worldly affairs. There were thus in-built provisions for members withdrawal from power-struggles and cravings of the quotidian life. These withdrawals, which varied in lengths of time, were also suitably accompanied by rites and rituals to add to their potency. During such periods, members were enjoined to observe austerity—severe in differing degrees. Detachment was thus obligatory, deliberate, purposeful and in most cases, literally connected with forests. However, the literal wilderness was expected and designed to prove conducing to create an 'inner wilderness' with a positive face.

Both Brahmins and Kshatriyas were marked to undergo purifying processes implied by the inner and outer manifestations of wilderness.

As suggested earlier, *ashrama* is the second principle and it brings to notice values placed on detachment in the Indian tradition as a meaningful strategy of meeting social needs.

Ashrama-s

Derived from the Sanskrit root *shram* to work, the term *ashrama* denoted four phases of life, human beings were advised to accept as legitimate 'working' segments naturally associated with fulfilment of four well-known and larger ideals, namely, *dharma, kama* and *moksha*. As argued earlier, each single being is born as a person with three original debts to pay back. How to discharge the obligation properly is what the *ashrama*-concept sought to answer.

The Four Ashrama-s and Wilderness

As in case of *varna*-s, the *ashrama*-s evolved gradually and four *ashrama*-s, namely Brahmacharya, Grihastha, Vanaprastha and Sannyasa stabilized only during the Sutra period, and that too with names, often different than those usually known.

Three of the four *ashrama*-s, namely Brahmacharya, Vanaprastha, and Sannyasa were directly connected with detachment, and symptomatically, with forests. Once again, this was achieved by giving positive connotation to woody surroundings—usually considered hostile or at least anti-social. For example, in the first *ashrama*, persons desirous of acquiring learning of any sort were to live with *guru*-s in forest abodes. They served the *guru,* received education and finally left well-equipped to enter the fray of the world. During the second *ashrama*, i.e., the phase of married life, which came next, detachment was *not* considered relevant. This *ashrama* was very highly regarded and Manu rightly compared it to *prana,* the vital breath which sustained the other three *ashrama*-s. Vanaprastha, the third, obviously entailed living in forest-dwellings, with or without spouse (as per the desire of the spouse concerned). This phase also stands out because it brings together detachment and forests in a very original way. I am referring to Aranyaka-s, which form a part of the Vedic literary corpus. These texts are prescribed to be read and studied by Vanaprasthins. In fact, their teaching to younger students is also to take place in forests or temples. Attached to the Brahmana-s of the first three Vedas, the Aranyaka texts are highly philosophical in content and their affinity with the Upanishadic spirit is easily felt. They also appear to be forerunners of *shikhsa*-s, i.e., manuals which appeared later. One of their principle theme is *pranavidya.* It impresses by discussing the whole universe as permeated with one vital force. The phase stands midway between householders involvement and an ascetic's renunciation. However, as duties, rights, obligations and privileges are clearly laid down, there is no reason to be unduly puzzled by it and consider it as an 'unsatisfactory compromise' as Kathleen M. Erndl appears to do while quoting Wendy O'Flaherty, a keen student of Indian culture.[3] Finally—Sannyasa, the fourth phase, was reportedly included in the tradition only after Buddhism gained support of the populace and succeeded in appealing to social conscience of the meticulous thesmothetes. We are told that there existed a class of wandering monks in the pre-Aryan India, and the early Aryans held it in contempt. But later, the monks' way of life was accepted as a life-phase, beneficial as well as valuable. This change in attitude probably became easier after

Upanishad-s paved the way for high, abstract, metaphysical discussions and the formulation of related philosophies came to be accepted as valued and legitimate socio-cultural contributions. Even though it was common to explain the four *ashrama*-s as phases equally dividing the normal human life-span of hundred years, to jump the *ashrama*-sequence was not prohibited (though reverting to an earlier phase *after* taking to a later, was no normally encouraged). Three viewpoints emerged about this obviously vital matter with Manu, Apastamba (with others), and Gautama as their respective advocates. Manu, the *samuchchayavadin*, insisted that the four had to be lived through in sequence. Apastamba, etc. were the *vikalpavadin*-s, and they opined that one may move directly to Sannyasa from the first or the second. Gautama, the *badhavadin* argued that only the second *ashrama* really mattered.

LEGITIMACY AND EQUAL UTILITY

Expectably, detailed rules were framed to guide behaviour in the four *ashrama*-s. Care was also taken to provide rulers to political administrators with a clear code of conduct to follow in dealing with (the apparently less useful.) social constituents of the third and the fourth *ashrama*-s. This would not have been possible unless there was a general, cultural agreement about their value to society.

It is broadly established that none of the *ashrama*-s was regarded inherently superior to any other. Each had duties, obligations, rights and privileges specific to it and the four-phases were to be taken together—complementary to each other and cumulatively supportive of actions initiated for greater good of the greater of people. And yet, as explained earlier, the four phases marked a possibility/potentiality-curve defined by a single human being considered singly in contrast to their collective *avatara*, namely society.

It can be stated that with human beings at the centre, the Indian way of life advocated exploration of two concentric orbits in order to define fields for human action. The careful definition however, left room from choice and exercise of individual conscience. There were two main strategies laid down to achieve goals set for both individual and collective conscience—they were attachment and detachment.

ATTACHMENT AND DETACHMENT

There is enough evidence in the tradition to suggest that detachment was, and is, presumed to be a mental state more difficult to attain. Secondly, detachment has also been credited with certain corrective qualities and hence, a role is inevitably marked for it even in the day-to-day life of the human players. Why detachment is presumed to be a tougher proposition is easy to understand. Human beings, like members of other species, are biologically programmed—but less rigidly. Their life course is not over-determined. In other words, they have more choice—the only problem is their frequent inability to make proper choices. As human decision-makers are members of a society or a cultural group—sins of their improper choices are likely to visit on others. Therefore, detachment is the *mantra* recommended to help meet the challenge of making correct (it may or any not be the right one though.) choices. This is the reason why detachment came to be institutionalized. Meditation-practices, penance, yogic-procedures, observance of vows, etc. are good instances of institutionalized, voluntary, protective and positive detachment employed as a way of controlling operations of life-forces. All these are obviously cohesive behaviour patterns and they lift the person concerned out of the life-stream, though temporarily, and help him to perceive how and why to act to ensure creation, maintenance or restoration of balance between individual and society.

As a corollary, detachment is also conceived to be a deterrent. Consequently, erring persons, if unable or unwilling to go into isolation on their own, can be compelled to do so. Laws came into being to ensure that. Hence ostracization, banishment, abdication, exile, etc. were allotted a function.

With passage of time, Indian society became more and more complex. Simple or less detailed thought-structures, which allowed more choice, seemed to prove more 'risky' and less relevant (i.e., less efficient in running affairs of the society). The entire social organization, and especially relationships between ruled and rulers, underwent considerable changes. For example, families found that dependence on kinship as a force to hold members together did not suffice, and it became necessary to replace it by kingship as the sole, all-powerful force acting to establish order and integration in social life. (It is not a coincidence that *Mahabharata* chose to declare, 'It is the king who determines the character of the times.') However, being the source as well as the seat of power (combining as it did within one single agency, both legislative and executive functions as it were), a monarch could pose an ever present threat to the organizational equilibrium of society. This is where religion, with its comprehensive connotation in India, intervened and one of its major functions was to limit royal prerogatives through varied means.

PROPHECY AND ITS ROYAL ROLE

One of the means, of immediate interest to us, was the mythopoetic mode working through *prophecy* to 'pattern' monarchical behaviour into submission to ensure that society could achieve what was generally perceived as *shreyas* (i.e., proper and mostly desirable). Prophecy was and is a socio-political device employed hopefully to predetermine, legitimize and apotheosize desirable cultural applications of recognizably powerful and potent human energy which, however, may be inclined to be deviant. In order to curb the Will of the powerful, guide their motivation, and precipitate beneficial changes in structures of authority—prophecy and prophetic tone have been assiduously cultivated and carefully employed in numerous branches of Indian expression. Religion, philosophy, mythology, literature, laws, grammar, and arts would easily come to mind.

What is prophecy? It is an imperious declaration by a being, endowed with culturally recognized uncommon qualities, foretelling a certain course of action or events, considered inevitable and strongly believed to be desirable in the long run for society. It is symptomatic that traditionally a prophet is described as *siddha* and prophecy was *siddha-desha*.

A *siddha* enjoys uncommon perceptions and powers because of purity of mind, body and behaviour. This guarantees that whatever he says would be in tune with the natural course of events, consequently ensuring the inevitable effectiveness of his utterances. There is, as if, a social imperative which compels non-prophets to listen to prophets and finally obey them. It is often said that prophets prove effective because of their ability to see how isolated *incidents* (which are apparent to all men) can lead to their logical culmination, i.e., to *events*. We are also told that prophets prove effective because they merely 'voice' what social psyche is already impregnated with—rightly or wrongly. Prophecies and myths act in combination and their relationship needs to be understood.

MYTHS IN OPERATION

Myths are (in reality.) creative cultural moulds possessing remarkable capacity of prognosis and diagnosis. Human 'products' of culture, as also cultures created by human beings, can be 'read' with the help of associated myths. If a man is known by the company he keeps and the books he reads—cultures are known by the myths they nurture and nourish. Both men and women, as well as cultures, are governed at deeper levels by shared and specific mythologies.

Prophecy provides a tone, a charge investing myths with an immediate power of eliciting action. Myth can become a 'social charter'—an authorization of certain individual and social actions, as Wendy O'Flaherty rightly puts it, because of the prophetic preparatory actions. Prophecy arouses dormant and enveloping mythic energies. Thus activated, myths function effectively when nations march towards their destinies. Prophecies are essentially ambiguous, and *therefore*, more potent. Individuals, who are vehicles of the prophetic tone, usually get a dubious pleasure of knowing 'what is to be done/ who is to be followed' and getting haunted by gnawing inner doubts about the 'correctness' or otherwise of their (.) decisions. In other words, prophets and their prophetic pronouncements stand out as pledges to be fulfilled and questions to be answered *through interpretative acts*. Prophecies are valuable, if and when, somebody acts in accordance with their dictates. They are the reverse of the proverbial zero--the moment prophecies are followed—even by a marginal action—their power increases out of all proportion to the action itself. Ostensibly, prophets are offered choices which, however, have to conform to vaguely pre-etched outlines with seemingly outlandish forms. To this extent their choice is deceptive. The task is certainly difficult. It invariably spells great psychological tension and philosophical anguish to 'the chosen soul'—the prophet. It is obvious that careers of such personalities present various stages. To anticipates a little, the phases are: cultural hero, *avatara* and God.

This is the backdrop on which both Rama and *Ramayana* are to be 'experienced'—*Ramayana* as a creative myth and Rama as a prophesied king. An important part of Rama's prophesied life is related to 'wilderness'—as fact and phenomenon.

RAMAYANA, RAMA AND WILDERNESS

Most evolved cultures appear to be fortunate at least in one respect: they have their own Epic/s. According to many experts, the most common feature of the Epic-genre is inclusiveness. What is said of *Mahabharata*, would easily apply to most of the epics—'what is not here cannot be anywhere. Therefore, it is not surprising that the phenomenon under discussion, namely 'wilderness', finds a significant place in the prototype Indian Epic—*Ramayana*. The work features 'wilderness' of every important and intensity. In this context, one general rule in cultural studies is relevant. If a phenomenon is emphasized in any of the prototype national expressions, a deeper cultural acceptance can safely be deduced thereby. In its turn, no cultural acceptance can become an abiding characteristic of any nation's make-up, unless it answers multiple and collective needs, at one level or the other. In fact, at some point, such cultural acceptances may satisfy urges of mankind in general. This is the reason why epics and epical tone continue to tantalize and attract, provoke and evoke, intrigue and puzzle across ages, boundaries, nations, religions and races.

THE INDIAN EPICAL SCENE

Epics are known to be divided into two broad classes or types—primary, oral or primitive on the one hand and written or literary on the other. (The Indian view is, expectably, different because orality is not equated with primitivity, etc.) The former kind of epic is known in India as *arsha* and the latter, the literary is described as *vidagdha*.

Both *Ramayana* and *Mahabharata* belong to the first variety, at least partially, according to the majority view. As Jawaharlal Nehru once perceptively remarked, the two sage-inspired epics, i.e., the *arsha* epics are the story of India.

Five other works, accepted by the tradition as epics, are placed in the *vidagdha* or literary category. They are *Raghuvamsha*, *Kumarasambhava* (both by Kalidasa), *Kiratarjuniya* (Bharavi), *Shishupalavadha* (Magha), and *Naishadhacharitam* (Shri Harsha). Of course there are many more aspirants to 'epic-dom', if one may use that term—but that only proves the irresistible pull of the genre brought into being in India by *Ramayana* and *Mahabharata*. It is generally agreed that from Magha onwards, epics came to be 'produced'. They were turned out in response to excessively artificial intentions and predominantly literary aspirations. Consequently, they failed to voice the promptings of the nation. This is notwithstanding the eternal question of whether one can so easily talk of India as one nation in the modern sense of the term. There is no dearth of people who maintain that the present India is a cultural federation. Indeed, it has been pointed out that assertion of regional identities has in its wake compelled many to talk of nation as a single entity, homogeneous, monolithic and indifferent to diversity.

Reportedly, there are about 350 epics in Sanskrit alone. Many later epics tend to echo the prototype works. They are often modelled on the early two, even though different heroes are kept at the centre and different themes, subjects, etc. are touched upon. A third wave of epics is of partial or complete 'versions' of the primary epics, restating them with approval and devotion, or distorting and reformulating them seriously, intensely and skilfully. A question to be raised is: are these epics also to be taken as national expression of India? What value are these later versions if we argue on basis of criteria lovingly described as purity, authenticity and originality.

I would like to submit that epics remain meaningful *because* they also continue to be willing receivers of accretions. As a cultural process, accretion has four characteristics: it is natural, it connotes growth, it results into a new, coherent whole and finally, it validates numerous new interpretations in the context of the same, original core. To an extent one may agree with A.K. Ramanuja's statement that 'all later *Ramayana*-s play on the knowledge of the previous tellings: they are meta-*Ramayanas*.[4] As Paula Richman neatly points out we learn more about the diversity of the *Ramayana* tradition when we abandon the notion of Valmiki as the Urtext from which all the other *Ramayana*-s have descended.[5] Even before 500 BC, the period around which Valmiki crystallized the *Ramayana*, the Rama story was in circulation. It is well-known that an inspired Valmiki, newly woken up to his own musico-poetic capabilities, reworked the 'material' into a well-knit oral presentation. What is important to know is what he did with what he found.

While achieving the transformation he ensured an enviable balance between constancy and variability, direct statement or narration of facts, events, etc. on one side and their suggestive depiction on the other. Finally, he exercised a choice between reliance on creative outbursts and recourse to deliberate artistry. (In connection with the last feature, it may be necessary at a later stage to devote some thought to the role of solitude and detachment in Valmiki's creative process.)

This is how, and why, *Ramayana* could become a generative cultural mould to be recited, sung and presented—with music as a major formal element. *Ramayana* continues to be sung with more and more accretions. This typifies the strength of the genre as also of the proto-type work. To talk of *Ramayana* is therefore to think of the cumulative impact registered through its numerous manifestations, roughly divisible in five categories, namely, primitive, folk, devotional, art and popular. It is symptomatic that all five categories flourish in India, and there are deeper reasons for their continued effectiveness. The scene would be all the more complex if we take into consideration the actual multi-genre manifestations of the Epic. For example, the puppet theatre, debates, song-cycle and iconographic traditions, etc. furnish data which is challenging, diverse and effective.

THE EPICAL FUNCTION

Indian ethos, as has been often pointed out, had its initial glimmer of eternal truths in Vedas. There shimmering lights were refined into thought-structures, doctrines and philosophies (*darshana*-s) through Upanishad-s. While these character-forming processes were on, Epics stepped in to carry out the essential task of providing the Upanishadic, minority-perceived, abstract and often other-worldly truths, with perspectives of *desha*, *kala* and *paristhiti* (i.e., local habitation, temporality and circumstances). On this background, Purana-s diligently laboured to dilute, translate and sometimes delightfully distort ideas, philosophies, and principles *because* they preferred the common man or layman as their chosen addressee. The final agency in this elaborate mechanism set up to spread information, propagate didactic ideas, reiterate shared beliefs and respected morals, relate tradition and impart knowledge with sanction of the sacred—was represented by songs, song-cycles, or long-poems, etc. This agency relied on all available material, from every conceivable source and every recognizable format, to respond to needs of the moment, social strata, linguistic or regional traditions or religions concerned. In sum, contemporary Indian minds are to be deciphered as products of the combined action of all these sources and forces. What Thomas Coburn has suggested, while arguing about the relative authority of diverse Shruti and Smriti texts, is valid in the larger contexts provided by different sources mentioned earlier. Coburn says that instead of constituting fixed categories of texts, Shruti and Smriti may refer rather to 'two different kinds of relationships that can be had with verbal material in the Hindu tradition'.[6]

Ramayana lives by virtue of its being the prototype *arsha* epic—in other words it exemplifies an institution which encourages, accommodates and often welcomes forces of change. It also throws up ideas powerful enough to alter or correct the course of personal and (perhaps in the long run) social initiatives.

RAMAYANA

True to its name, *Ramayana* is a story of a person on the move. *Ayana* means movement, usually of impressive magnitude and effect. (For example, no business executive's comfortable drive to his office could be described as *ayana*.) The two other *ayana*-s, known in India are Uttarayana and Dakshinayana, i.e., movements of the sun indicated at the time or period of summer and winter solstices respectively. Further, a considerable part of Rama's movements are related to forests and wilds, expansive rivers and vast sea-shores (it must however be noted that some have argued that Rama never set eyes on the sea, what he encountered were merely expansive waters.) indeed, it may be noted in passing that, even before his epoch-making exile, Rama had moved and lived in forests (e.g., his early training, or his travels with sage Vishvamitra via Siddhashrama). Movement and wilderness are the *shadja* and *panchama*— the fundamental and fifth notes—of his life. And on account of Rama's personal stature, individual role and cultural destiny—these two notes have reverberated through Indian life—at least in the hoary past, ancient age and some historical epochs.

RAMA'S WILDERNESS

What kind of wilderness-conditions did Rama face? Before attempting an answer, some bare, factual and chronological landmarks in

Rama's life can be usefully noted. To begin with, he studied different disciplines (including *gandharvaveda*, i.e., the science of music), as was required of a monarch-to-be. This phase of *brahmacharya* lasted for about fifteen years. Then came on the scene, sage Vishvamitra and took Rama away for protecting seers engaged in offering sacrifices to Gods. They were to be protected from menacing hordes of marauding demons. Having fulfilled the task, Rama proceeded to Mithila, accomplishing more valorous deeds on the way, and subsequently got married. One imagines that these happenings must have consumed at least one year. Rama then lived happily for twelve years enjoying marital bliss—before Dasharatha thought of consecrating him as the future ruler. It is not without reason and authority that the Rasik Sampradaya has 'focused on a single phase of their Lord's story—the idyllic period when the newly married Rama and Sita, having returned from Sita's home city of Mithila, enjoyed each other's company amidst the palatial comforts of Ayodhya.[7] Followed the exile of fourteen years. After coming back, Rama reportedly ruled for 'many' years. He listened to the *Ramayana*-recitation for the first time in the voices of Lava-Kusha during the Ashvamedha-sacrifice.

At least ten to twelve years must have elapsed between his abandonment of Sita, exposure to *Ramayana*-recitation and his final offer to take her back on Valmiki's vouchsafing her unblemished character. In sum, he must have been past his sixtieth year when Sita ultimately disappeared.

The point is that Rama's actual stay in forests and his trials therein, etc. indicate an aspect of wilderness which is too obvious, literal and in the final analysis, less perilous and arduous than imagined, mainly because of his upbringing, education, maturity and his self-conception. (It is also to be remembered that he shared all his forest-stays with those who were dear and near to him.) Thus, the 'physical' aspect of wilderness should not be overemphasized. As pointed out earlier, Rama enjoyed conjugal bliss for nearly twelve years before going into exile. Further, he probably faced merely 'picnic-hardships' till Sita was abducted. (It is interesting that in the Mizo-Rama-*katha* Rama does not suffer the exile at all though otherwise the Rama-*katha* is complete. But then the Mizo *Ramayana*-characters wield guns.) Sita was away for a period of one year before she was brought back to face the fire-ordeal. Rama and Sita were thus reunited following a brief, but an agonizing interval of time. After his home-coming, Rama enjoyed longevity in royal splendour. We are told that Gods finally felt it necessary to remind Rama that his life-work in the human world was already over and it was time he took leave of it. In other words, the kind of wilderness Rama suffered from—and suffer he did—must be located in some other areas of his life. A close textual scrutiny of *Ramayana* and reconstruction of his career-graph, etc. are not likely to help much.

This is the juncture at which all his critical actions and responses draw our attention to something which is intended to be construed in a framework much larger than the trying ups and downs in the life of an extraordinary person ('with a particular flaw in character' as Shakespeare would have preferred to put.) It is clear that the most crucial events in Rama's life are directly traceable to his being a prophesied hero-king who was to rise to the level of an *avatara* and God. It is as a hero-king that Rama began his career and this Rama, i.e., Rama the hero, has spread wide and far. Then came Rama, as an *avatara*. In this version Rama has a narrower field of influence, but there is gain in the emotional intensity he arouses. Finally, we have Rama as God. The narrowest range is enjoyed by this Rama but the influence is deeper. As has been pointed out, Rama's godliness depends to a great measure on the Hinduization of the cultural group concerned.[8] It is still more interesting to note that in none of the versions Rama is depicted with overt and grossly physical signs of superhuman prowess. He does not have, for example, three heads like Datta or four hands like Krishna or three eyes like Shiva. To my mind this is the clearest sign of his larger 'humanity'. A brief look at the machinery which efficaciously executes prophesies would bring the argument in a sharper focus.

DESTINY, FATE AND FORTUNE

The close working together of prophecy and myth have been already mentioned. In addition, curses, boons, destiny, etc. must be taken into account. Allowing for a little simplification, it could be said that according to the Indian world-view, *niyati* (destiny), *bhagya* (fate) and *daiva* (fortune) are three distinguishable, necessary and sufficient conditions which function as non-rational, impersonal and pervasive forces determining course and consequences of human actions. Each of these forces has its own set of active constituents or agents to work towards completion of each 'story'—which, may or may not prove significant in the ultimate analysis. Thus, in order to ensure progression of incidents to their 'natural' conclusions, destiny is equipped with prophecy and myth, fate is armed with curses and boons while fortune of a person depends on his own overt and implied acts including oaths, vows, etc.

PROPHETIC COMPULSIONS AND RAMA

It is the prophetic dimension of life that compels Rama to hark to his destiny, and to ignore or repeatedly fight against promptings of the two other dimensions, namely, fate and fortune. Rama's life thus became a near-continuous exercise in controlled detachment from everyone and everything more personal or individual. In all situations, which would normally acquire group-character, i.e., 'life in a group as a group'. Rama remains a distanced being. He is alone though not lonely. For example, in his long life he became prince, disciple, family-man, leader, warring general and finally, emperor of a vast subcontinent. In all these phases we see a man who participates *because* he was destined to fulfil prophecies made in the interest of social stability, just rule, maintenance of moral (if not necessarily ethical) order and carry out the duty of providing protection to the unprotected. A man of intense energy, indomitable courage and wide-ranging experience of the world, Rama could have opted to renounce the world and complete the well-phased process of detachment in accordance with the *ashrama*-s allowed to persons of his class. And yet, he would not (or could not.) do so because he was preordained to be a vehicle to execute the dictates of destiny as articulated through prophecy. In fact, it could be maintained that Rama's own decisions are clear deviations from the normal interpretations of both *varna* and *ashrama* principles. He chooses to follow the compulsions of his own conscience. It is symptomatic that on various occasions Laxmana, Bharata and Sita argue with Rama on the basis of Varnashramadharma, at various points Rama rejects their arguments by appealing to his own perception of higher truth and *dharma*. As Franck Whaling has pointed out, *Ramayana* is very infrequent in mentioning *moksha* (salvation) which is the stated goal of human life according to Varnashramadharma. This seems logical and inevitable as Rama's main concern is to live righteously according to the higher, self-perceived *dharma on this earth and in this life.* Rama thus remains an archetypal example of controlled detachment. Did he suffer more than Krishna, the other archetypal *avatara* in India? Probably he did.

Is it not significant that Rama is known as *Maryadapurushottama* (while Krishna is known as *Leelapurushottama*)? Is not restraint, self-imposed limits on behaviour, and insistence on living up to public-morality than act in accordance with the dictates of individual ethics—characteristic of Rama's passage through the epical time? (Is this why Rama is so often shown to be a successor to Indra in deeds?) Further, is it not worth-noting that Rama (and not Krishna) came to be associated with the concept of an ideal earthly rule, namely *Rama-rajya*? While we are at it, we may also note that the concept of *Rama-rajya* hardly seems to be dependent on worldly prosperity—descriptions of Ravana's life-style are alluring and they hardly appear to be less prosperous. One may also add that Rama appears to be a hero who leads from the front but does not originate a philosophy (unlike Krishna). One should of course mention the later attempt to compensate for the lack—if it is to be described so. Yogavashistha used the Rama-*katha* to expound a philosophy *a la Shrimadbhagavadgita*. Coming back to Rama as a person, it is seen that on numerous occasions, what Rama felt, thought and desired *as a person*, is unambiguously expressed through Laxmana's words and deeds. It is as if Rama's character is split into two for us by Valmiki and Laxmana is allotted the role to represent Rama's personal unconscious. Rama can and does overrule Laxmana—but only with the help of the prophecies. Rama does so and stoically suffers the consequences. Whaling has emphasized that the personality of Rama develops *through* suffering as did Christ's, and the idea is valuable. Sacrifice and suffering of the hero have always played a significant part in the saga of societies moving through progressive stages of evolution. However, in the process Rama does *cause*—untold hardships to others. Near the end, Rama was in audience with Fate acting as messenger from Yama (the Hindu God of death), and entry was forbidden to anybody on pain of death in the hands of Rama. It is symbolic that (to avoid sage Durvasa's curse) Laxmana is compelled to disturb the proceedings and invite death in the hands of Rama. On the human plane, is this not one of the most cruel of actions demanded of Rama? Perhaps, for the first time Rama decides to follow the decree of his own 'human' self than the prophetic and admits that he cannot kill Laxmana. However, as no prophecy can be falsified Rama seeks refuge in a sym-

bolic action. He decides to renounce Laxmana because renounce-
ment is equivalent to the death of their relationship. This is done.
Laxmana breathes his last through *pranayama*. Now nothing remains for Rama but to undertake the *mahaprasthana*. He has re-
nounced his personal unconscious, he has also outlived his role as
collective consciousness and that is the end of Rama's movement,
the true *Ramayana*. . . .

WILDERNESS AND MUSIC

In what manner has the Indian musical impulse has chosen to respond to the archetype embodied by Rama? If music is as all-pervasive as it is claimed to be, and if Indian culture is essentially as music-oriented as has been often declared—music in India must be
shown to have adequately responded to the commanding cultural
vision Rama and *Ramayana* combine to create.

It is known that Rama-songs continue to fill the air—even today.
And hence, many questions become relevant, at least when they are
posed from the vantage point of the twentieth century. This is a
century poised to obliterate distinctions between past/present/ future tenses and consequently alter the nature of the dimension of
Time itself. The epics achieve a same/similar time-annihilation
through applications of mythopoetic devices and perhaps this accounts for the special affinity between the two. It is not necessary to
remind us that epic or epic tone has recurred in different arts in
the present century.

To what extent, and what manner does Rama-music, taken in its
entirety reflect *Ramayana* as a cultural force? How does it acknowledge themes such as wilderness, which border on philosophy, religion, emotional lives of supernaturally endowed men and women,
loneliness, separation by death or willing termination of mundane
existence through unclassifiable phenomenon such as the *mahaprasthana*? *Ramayana* is nothing, if not a comprehensive reflection
of an entire society in motion. The numerous souls which from a
society follow their respective individual trails as also those of the
body politic—the final goal of both movements being meaningful
existence. And this is accomplished or sought to be achieved by
treading the life-path through moulding the trinity of *achara*, *vichara*
and *uchchara* (behaviour, thought and utterance) in accordance with
norms laid down by religion. Can music do justice to these and simi-

lar weighty aspects? If it can, how is this achieved?

It is at this stage that the categorial pentad, mentioned earlier, needs a recall because each category provides evidence of a selective acknowledgement of the Rama-motif. In order to prepare ourselves for the qualitative and functional differences between kinds of *Ramayana*-s it may be useful to dwell a little on tribal and folk attitudes to Rama-*katha*.

RAMA-KATHA: THE TRIBAL VIEW

From Ms. Singh Datta's fascinating compilation of papers the following observations can be culled:

1. Tribal *Ramakatha*-s often include songs which are older than *Ramayana*-versions the tribes may have. They obviously represent stirring memories from the tribal past. The tribal versions also reflect a sense of awe and respect felt by the tribals for the heroes. Finally, there is a streak of irreverence in these versions.[9] Singh also points out that some tribals identify themselves with anti-heroes of the epic.[10] Rama is shown as a powerful representative of a patriarchal society, seeking to impose the rule of his lineage over new territories and to uphold its honour.[11]

2. In the same publication, N.N. Vyas persuasively argues that Indian tribals have, in general, a similar comprehension of the story of the *Ramayana* because they have a common existential basis—the tribals being found in hills and forests.[12]

3. T.B. Naik, writing on 'Ramakatha among the Tribes of India' points out that there are about 25 million tribals in the country. From among them, the Bhil, Dubla, Agaria, Bhanwar, Gond, Ghogia Pardhan, Bhuiya tribes have *Ramakatha* of one or the other kind.[13]

4. It is also pointed out that many tribes trace their descent from *Ramayana*-characters or families mentioned therein. Many features of tribal life-style are also shown to be linked to events in *Ramayana*. To claim such connection is an attempt to earn racial legitimacy and social prestige.

RAMAYANA: FOLK PERSPECTIVE

Following deductions are worth-mentioning:

1. Folk *Ramayana*-s often exalt local Gods by associating them with Rama.[14]
2. In folk-songs, Rama has been portrayed as ordinary man, a man on the street.[15]
3. Banishment of Sita has been highlighted and many variations on the theme are found.[16] From the classical writers Valmiki, Kalidasa and Bhavabhuti alone have dealt with Sita's second exile, i.e., banishment.
4. The number of folk *Ramayana*-s giving a complete story are less—than episodic songs based on events or songs entirely devoted to Sita.[17]
5. In the Karabi folk *Ramayana*, the heroine is the lead character.[18] Also of interest is the fact that Telugu folk *Ramayana* has songs devoted to Urmila—a much neglected character in the story.[19]
6. On this background the most crucial question can be posed: According to the folk perspective, what is the purpose of *Ramayana*? The answers are revealing. For example, Raju notes that the folk psyche conceived of Rama-hood as the divine aim of devotion.[20] Satyendra Nath Sarma explains how Assamese versions change Valmiki to suit their purpose, depict flora and fauna of Assam and make occasional reference to Assamese beliefs and practices.[21]

This brief discussion of the altered, if not an alternative, view of the Epic is important because this brings into focus the fact that the five categories are complementary—musically as well as experientially. The totality of these responses to Rama-*Ramayana* demands attention if we wish to get a fuller idea of the Rama-*Ramayana*-music relationship. In addition, the categories do not and cannot function as water-tight compartments and they tend to influence each other. However, to examine the entire pentad *vis-à-vis* Rama is a task best left to a team of experts. My observations can claim, at the most, a limited validity.

VALMIKI'S PIONEERING RESPONSE

From the point of view of music what does Valmiki's pioneering response to Rama-*katha*, which he turned into *Ramayana*, indicate? In other words, what were the musical parameters of Valmiki's great composition as presented by Lava-Kusha and how did they function as specific communicative devices?

Perhaps it is necessary to dwell a little on the institution which Lava-Kusha, in their role as reciters came to represent.

THOSE WHO RECITED

In the comprehensive Indian oral tradition there were two kinds of professional musicians who composed stories and praises of brave kings and intrepid warriors to present the same before audiences consisting of different classes of patrons. These were known as Suta and Magadha. In later times the same were described as Charana and Bhat. All these were collectively known as Kushilava. In other words, Kushilava was a class or caste name (just as Bharata was according to some authorities). Incidentally, these professional performers invariably belonged to lower classes and aspersions on their loose morals often find place even in related definitions. It would not be an exaggeration to say that performers were generally considered 'necessary evils' by the ancient Indian society. In my opinion, this is important to note because that brings into relief Valmiki's defiant/courageous attitude in naming Rama's sons as he did. May be Valmiki's own evolution from a robber to a sage made him morally more assertive.

THE BARE STRING ACCOMPANIMENT

Coming back to Valmiki's pioneering performance, one notes that it had two singers with no other accompanists. Is it not interesting that the *Baiga Ramayana* from Central India is customarily recited to the accompaniment of Kingri—a folk fiddle, even today?[22] Or, as Birendranath Datta notes, *Ramayana* presentation is Assam has a form called *bena-gan*, which, as the name indicates, consists of *Ramayana* recitation to the accompaniment of a one-string instrument?[23] Or as Ramanujan points out *tamburi dassayyas*, the traditional bards from the south are also from the category of reciters who choose to have string-accompaniment for their long performances.[24] However, I must admit that there is also a *Ramayana*-presentation which has flute-accompaniment. Mishra tells us that the Gaur-s (milkmen) in Orissa have a form called *bans-geet*, which as the name suggests, employs flute.[25] The use of flute may have something to do with cattle-tending which is the Gaur's occupation. Yet

another interesting instance is, as Mahanta describes, provided by
Bhaona from Assam. This larger presentation is preceded by a form
called *dhemali* which employs drummers, singers as well as dancers.[26] However, dramatic presentations would constitute a different
case and other considerations would prevail.

SEPARATION OF ROLES

It should be noted that the composer, i.e., sage Valmiki himself,
chose not to participate actively in the performance. We are told
that he pondered over the matter and finally decided to place the
responsibility on the young shoulders (or voices) of Lava and Kusha.
This is to be specifically mentioned because separation or otherwise of the functions of composer, poet, and performer is one of
the criteria used to grade or rank music-makers in India. (This is
evident in musicological texts.)

The highest regard is for a composer who is a poet as well as a
performer.

PERFORMANCE AND ITS AUDIENCE

Valmiki's innovative *Ramayana*-performance took place in an arranged situation. Audience, patron and performers were therefore
welded into a performing set according to norms laid down in the
tradition—but the norms do not appear to have made any ritualistic demands. Generally, audiences gathering to witness performance on festive occasions was known as Samaj. The occasion was not
sacred, but it covered a gamut of effects ranging from mere entertainment to a moving gravity of emotions accompanied by arousal
of ethical awareness and social conscience. Satisfaction of fulfilled
duties, participation in a socially valued recreation and communication of a content with a marked utility—were some of the results.

SINGING AND RECITATION

Lava and Kusha 'recited' and did not sing, i.e., there was no elaboration of musical ideas of either melodic, rhythmic or linguistic origin. Lava-Kusha rendered what was essentially pre-composed, methodically arranged and adequately rehearsed. Their act was designed to meet performing exigencies of a specific kind. It would be

instructive to juxtapose, with this pioneering recitation a detail of current folk practice. Describing *Karabi Ramayana*, Terang and others tell us that the Karabi-s have tales in prose called Rama-Lakhan Atomo while songs or lyrics dealing with the Rama story are called 'Sabin Alun'.[27]

By the time *Ramayana* was crystallized, the key-word *sangeet* came to have a wide connotation. Early in its career the word used to suggest *samyak geet* that is, merely a well-executed, complete *geet*. However, in *Ramayana*-times *sangeet* came to include in its operative sphere singing, instrumental presentation as well as dancing. Rama and citizens in Ayodhya, Sugriva and the monkey-people as well as Ravana and his demon-followers are reported to have definite cultural occasions for *sangeet* of this wide scope in their respective lifestyles. (It is amusing to note that Ravana, trying to seduce Sita, mentions good music as one of the tempting items he can make available to her if she yields to him.)

THE VOCAL SPECTRUM

While evaluating the Lava-Kusha performance, it helps to remember that in India, the use of human voice and speech is placed on a continuum. For example, *gunjana* (murmur), *bhashana* (speech), *svarapatha* (chanting), *pathana* (recitation), and *gayana* (singing) are the main identifiable, 'critical' and technically demanding phases or ranges on the continuum. They are intended and structured to satisfy different, though equally legitimate and expressive, requirements. On account of significant functions entrusted to it, the *pathana*-phase is elaborately described and neatly defined in related literature.

Pathya is to have seven notes, three octaves, four *varna*'s, two *kaku*-s, six embellishments; and six aspects. The first two features are self-explanatory. *Varna* in this context means use of *udatta* (emphasized or stressed), *anudatta* (unstressed or tenderly uttered), *svarit* (sustained); and *kampit* (vibrating). These are obviously particular modes of projecting voice and the performer's aim of securing an impact on listeners is unmistakable. *Kaku*, is of two types— *sakanksha* and *nirakanksha*. The former is a modulation of the manner of speaking which raises expectation while the latter gives a sense of completion—both obviously vital in communicating the totality of reciters import. The six embellishments featuring in recitation are: *uchcha, deepta, mandra, neecha, druta,* and *vilambita.* Of these, the first four are phonation—modes and hence refer to areas of vocal mechanism employed in producing voice in the desired manner. Thus head and the *uchcha,* gradual fading—in and the *deepta,* chest and the *mandra,* gradual fading-out and the *neecha* modes are deducible. The last two are obviously instances of what is known as pacing the speech. As all these modes are associated with specific emotions and qualitative effects—their significance can hardly be overestimated. Finally, the six aspects mentioned are also related to speech-projection but in them the organization of word-units comes to the forefront. Thus, *vichchheda* (pause), *arpana* (resonant pronunciation), *visarga* (stressed or unstressed), *anubandha* (joining with preceding or succeeding words), *deepana* (ascending in pitch), and *prashamana* (descending in pitch) distinguish recitation.

On this background it should not surprise us that even today the Ramanami Bhajan tradition, which originated in the 1890s, practices a format which has recitation, singing, as well as conversation as components of the presentation.[28]

The Role of Meter

At this juncture it is useful to remember that meters in Indian poetic traditions are not mere arrangements of word-lengths, durations, stresses or ways of avoiding 'prose'-ness and negative effects associated with it. Indian meters are also tonal moulds. Each meter denotes a definite tune and an approximation to *tala.* It is symptomatic that Valmiki invented Anushtubh meter with specific and marked poetico-performing qualities, recognized even today. Without reading too much into it, the fact that Valmiki's Anushtubh differed from the Vedic needs to be remembered. The meter has been extensively employed in India since. It is instructive to note that regional *Ramayana*-s resorted to meters which are characteristic of the respective regional musico-poetic traditions. For example, Ovi in Maharashtra, Payar in Bengal or Choupai in Avadhi are easy instances one remembers. However, Valmiki's astuteness as a performer is evident in the fact, that though he stuck to one single meter (which he had perfected) throughout the work, he took care to bring in variation by changing the tempo. We are told that the recitation considered of three *pramana*-s, i.e., tempi, namely fast, medium and slow.

Valmiki's Epical Aims

Valmiki's composition was so systematic, the planned presentation was so non-ritualistic and Valmiki's instructions were so clear—that the Lava-Kusha's recitation could be discontinued after presentation of twenty *sarga*-s. Valmiki's intention to *construct* the epic is also evident in his use of literary embellishments, etc. Valmiki was aiming at achieving an effect, a discernible impact on the audience. This was a far cry from his spontaneous and self-sufficient composition of the first-ever *shloka* he aired. Valmiki, the composer of epic, was differently motivated than the person who intensely felt about the separation-pangs of the Krauncha pair. Ramanujan is right in pointing out that the incident at the beginning of *Valmiki Ramayana* gives the work an aesthetic self-awareness.[29]

Lava-Kusha recited to the accompaniment of a string-instrument, i.e., *vina*. As I have often argued, the two primary tempers of Indian culture are well-represented by the *venu-sanskriti* and the *vina-sanskriti*. These culture-phases are of course not successive or sequential and they do not suggest anthropological criteria based on determining and classifying means of production of a certain society. *Venu-sanskriti* stands for manifestations of ambiguous, elemental, pervasive and ecstatic urges of the Indian ethos while *vina-sanskriti* points to more organized, sophisticated, narrower but direct disturbances in the Indian psyche. The twin avenues are explored by energies released by nations as occasions demand. I dare to say that Rama and Krishna stand for these two eternal Indian tempers.

Further, the reciters were not accompanied by drums of any kind. Instead, they used a string-instrument 'rhythmically'. This usage closely parallels performances of folk and devotional kind in India even today. This ability of Lava-Kusha to coordinate string-strokes with recitation is mentioned by the word *tantrilayasamanvitam*—a very clear indication of the conscious rhythmic employment of the strings.

References to music in *Ramayana* clearly indicate that art of music, castes of performers, norms of aesthetic appreciation and protocol of dispensing patronage were features well-defined and generally accepted. However, music actually used by Valmiki for presentation of his work drew sparingly on the available musical resources. Meticulous as he was, Valmiki must have been moved by strong considerations. Is the inclusiveness of his epical vision in con-

tradiction to his musical parsimoniousness? I do not think so. In my
opinion he exemplifies aesthetic astuteness as also a creator's frank
admission of what music can and cannot (or should not) do.

MUSIC—MADE, TRANSMITTED AND RECEIVED

Whenever music is made, actually three musics are in the fray. One
is 'actually' made by a performer, the other is the music as 'transmitted' to receivers and the third is music 'imaginatively recreated'
by audience on the basis of the two previously mentioned. The three
musics, together, constitute a musical entity which we refer to as
one, single act and this serves as a basis for further related behaviours. This active triangular relationship obviously creates fields of
different cultural charge in five categories mentioned. The overrid-
ing aim is to initiate cultural or social behaviour of varied thrusts to
ensure sustained and meaningful existence of society. An integrated
cultural vision apportions communicational roles to all social activities including art, craft, language, religion, science, philosophy,
medicine and other segments of life. Consequently, different categories and genres, instruments, performance-norms, etc. are del-
egated responsibilities corresponding to their inherent and potential powers. They are therefore expected and encouraged to explore areas demarcated for them to the maximum possible extent
and yet not to encroach on other categorial territories to avoid cultural damage.

The kind or category of music Valmiki used and advocated for
the purpose of recitation was known as Marga Sangeet. The category is notionally contrasted with Deshi Sangeet. It is instructive to
note that the former music, used by our seer for recitation does *not*
aim at entertainment or art. We are told that firstly, it is invented or
discovered by Brahma. Secondly, it is performed for Gods and thirdly,
it is expected to help in attaining salvation (*mukti, abhyudaya*).

Perhaps it is pertinent to note the language Valmik chose for
Ramayana-recitation, because that choice also indicates his overall
concern for informing, enlightening, and reaching audiences wider
than those in kingly courts. The tradition was to rely on four kinds
of language for the *pathya* discussed here. They were: *atibhasha,
aryabhasha, jatibhasha* and *yonyantaribhasha*. The first was to be used
in relation to Gods, the second in connection with kings, the third
for different castes and races in the country and finally, the fourth

to refer to animals, birds, etc. Is it not thought-provoking that, in spite of the fact that Valmiki's story is about a God-king, he uses *jatibhasha*? It is one more indication that he took upon himself the role of a teacher, reformer and educator in the larger sense of the term. I would use the term *sanskaraka* to describe him.

We have seen that wilderness has two 'faces'—personal and social. It has two roles to play—private and public. It features two functions—individual and collective. Finally, it has two dimensions—negative and positive. As would have transpired from the earlier discussion, all these are legitimate and in their respective places—relevant. All categories of music cannot deal with all facets of wilderness and they should not try to do so. In fact, the kind of performance Valmiki brought into vogue cannot be interpreted to have, as its aim, assimilation and presentation of wilderness *qua* wilderness. To translate or transmute wilderness into music as a musical idea, would have been tantamount to accepting it as an essential, human condition of 'man in society'. Such an acceptance would of course have allowed elaboration of musical ideas. It would have created great, imaginative music with ample scope for individuals to show (off) their artistry and superiority. This could have created a 'likable' wilderness and perhaps Valmiki was more keen on its instructive depiction.

Was this not the reason why he kept away from the song-cycle format, in which Rama-story was already circulating? It is worth noting that Valmiki also rejected the *akhyana* (story-telling) format that had come on the scene next. It is clear that story as a format contains the primeval appeal, prompting the question: 'What next?', but Valmiki wanted his listeners to raise the nagging and challenging query 'Why thus?' Epic-composers are social activists . . . if one may borrow from contemporary terminology. For Valmiki and his likes, music-orientation is just a way of using communicative powers of a medium to reach information, create attitudes, document history and invoke action. The music which Valmiki created was therefore musically inferior, musicologically justifiable and ethno-musicologically significant. It cannot be a coincidence that Madhava Kandali of Assam, a court-poet to a Kachari king of Jayantpur (*c.* fourteenth century) explicitly stated that he agreed to compose the Assamese *Ramayana* 'for the edification of the uneducated folk'.[30]

THE CONTEMPORARY SCENE

It is instructive that today Valmiki's epic provides a base for many individualistic (and often deviationist) songs and their cycles. In other words, Valmiki's format, which primarily encouraged emergence of a social conscience, has been once again compelled to make room for the Song-genre—because only a song can hope to build a bridge between 'they' and 'I'. The special potency of song as an expressive genre has attracted attention of many. For example, Edwin Ardener has proposed a theory of muted groups, who are silenced by the dominant structures of expression and who therefore resort to songs.[31] In addition there may be sheer musical reasons too.

One can note other instances which prove that inclination towards song instead of a narrative in verse or prose, or drama has a tradition in India. For example, Pravin Chandra Das refers to the sixteenth century *Durgavari Giti Ramayana* in Assam. It consists of songs set in *raga*-s,[32] Basant Goswami points to Bodo Kachari-s in Assam who have episodic Rama-*katha* woven in wedding songs and in songs known as 'bambol pita git'[33] Birendranath Datta provides more instances from the north-east India when he refers to *wariloba* (traditional story-tellers), *pena-skapa* (ballad-singing with single-stringed *pena* to accompany) etc. where songs are preferred to other modes.[34]

As Ravindranath perceptively pointed out, Indian art music cannot sing of individual or personal emotions. Whatever emotion it touches—gets universalized—which is its strength as well as its weakness.

REFERENCES

1. N.G. Sardesai and D.G. Padhye, eds., Amara's *Namalinganushasanam*, Pune, 1969, pp. 33–4.
   The long list includes: *atavi, aranya, vipin, gahan, kanan, vana, maharanya, griharam, upavana, udyana, pramadavana, vithi, ali, varavali, panktishreni*, etc.
2. Jayashankar Joshi, ed., *Halayudhakosha*, Lucknow, 1967. With slight variations. Halayudha confirms the differentiation traditionally made between varieties of wooded surroundings and their respective purposes or functions. For example, it defines *aranya* as that which is frequented by beasts.
3. Paula Richman, 'The Multilation of Surpanakha', in *Many Ramayanas*, ed., Paula Richman, New Delhi, 1991, p. 82.
4. A.K. Ramanujan, 'Three Hundred Ramayanas', in ibid., p. 33.

5. Thomas Coburn, 'The Diversity of a Narrative Tradition in South Asia', in ibid., p. 9.
6. Quoted by Ramdas Lamb, in ibid., p. 236.
7. Philip Lutgendorf, *Many Ramayanas*, ed., Paula Richman, p. 220.
8. 'Ramakatha in Karabi Folk Tradition: Terang, Ohonta, Gohain and Parampanthi' in *Ramakatha in Tribal and Folk Traditions of India*, eds., K.S. Singh and Birendranath Datta, Calcutta, 1993, p. 185.
9. Singh and Datta, 'Introduction' in ibid., p. 3.
10. Ibid., p. 52.
11. Ibid., p. 54.
12. Ibid., pp. 11–12.
13. Ibid., pp. 31–37.
14. N.N. Vyas, in ibid., p. 17.
15. K.D. Upadhyaya, in ibid., p. 68.
16. Ibid., p. 76.
17. Ibid.
18. Terang et al., in ibid., p. 186.
19. D. Rama Raju, in ibid., p. 85.
20. Ibid., p. 80.
21. Ibid., p. 11.
22. Mahendra Kumar Mishra, 'Influence of the Ramayana Tradition on the Folklore of Central India' in ibid., p. 23.
23. Ibid., p. 128.
24. A.K. Ramanujan, 'Three Hundred Ramayanas' in *Many Ramayanas*, p. 35.
25. Ibid., p. 23.
26. Ibid., p. 136.
27. 'Ramakatha in Karabi Folk Tradition' in *Ramakatha in Tribal and Folk Traditions of India*, eds., K.S. Singh and Birendranath Datta, p. 184.
28. Ramdas Lamb, 'Personalizing the Ramayana: Ramanamis and Their Use of the Ramacharitmanasa' in *Many Ramayanas*, pp. 243–45.
29. 'Three Hundred Ramayanas' in ibid., p. 40.
30. Goswami in *Ramakatha in Tribal and Folk Traditions of India*, eds., K.S. Singh and Birendranath Datta, Calcutta, 1993, p. 187.
31. Quoted by V.N. Rao, in 'A Ramayana of Their Own' in *Many Ramayanas*, p. 133.
32. Ibid., p. 139.
33. Ibid., p. 168.
34. Ibid., p. 180.

Index